Timeless Illustrations for Preaching and Teaching

Timeless Illustrations for Preaching and Teaching

Over 500 Stories, Anecdotes & Illustrations

Donald Grey Barnhouse

Hendrickson Publishers, Inc.
P.O. Box 3473
Peabody, Massachusetts 01961-3473

Printed in the United States of America

ISBN 1-56563-3180

First printing Hendrickson Publishers edition — February 2004

Illustrating Great Themes of Scripture © 1969 by Donald Grey Barnhouse
Let Me Illustrate © 1967 by Fleming H. Revell, a division of Baker Book House
Company
Reprinted with permission of Baker Book House Company, Grand Rapids,
Michigan, 49516, U.S.A.

Table of Contents

Dedication to
Let Me Illustrate

The art of illustrating was one of God's great gifts to Dr. Donald Grey Barnhouse. This volume containing many of his finest illustrations is made possible through the dedicated services of Miss Olive DeGolia.

As a member of his church and of the staff of the Evangelical Foundation, she has meticulously catalogued, classified, correlated and indexed his messages and illustrations covering a period of more than thirty years of his remarkable ministry.

Her devotion through many years as a staff member has been an inspiration to us. Her disciplined services and unique contribution to the extension of the ministry of Dr. Barnhouse will be appreciated by all who are helped to know the Lord and His Word better through these illustrations. It is therefore most fitting that we dedicate this volume to Miss Olive DeGolia.

Russell T. Hitt, EXECUTIVE DIRECTOR
EVANGELICAL FOUNDATION, INC.

Foreword to
Let Me Illustrate

One of the books I intend to write is a book on the whole art and procedure of illustrating the sermon. As an introduction let me tell the story of the time I meditated on the fact that we were chosen in Christ before the foundation of the world. Suddenly I realized that in the plan and thought of God, I was older than the sun, the moon, the stars, the earth, the trees, the garden, and everything else.

"Since God planned me before He planned trees and lakes and mountains, and storms and sunsets," I said, "everything that there is was created in order to illustrate spiritual truth. Everything. I don't care what it is—the way the echo sounds if you clap your hands, the way light gleams off metal, the way paper tears, you name it—you can find a sermon illustration in it. A sermon illustration is in the things right around you."

A tape recorder turning is a wonderful illustation of the fact that all of our thoughts are being recorded, and that some day we shall give an account of every idle word. I was driving with three of my small children. I told them this, and my six-year-old said, "Well, how is the white line down the road an illustration?"

"Oh," I said, "That's easy, 'There is a way that seemeth right unto a man, but the ends thereof are the ways of death.' If I felt that I had a right to go over in the left lane and just stay there, ultimately a truck would come and slam me, and I'd be dead. God says, 'You keep in my path, and my path is properly marked.'"

Another child said, "What about the telegraph poles? How are they an illustration?"

I replied, "Well, there's that pole, and somebody in the next town back of us and somebody in the next town in front of us are talking over the wires. Their words are going over the wires in both directions right now. Suppose one of those poles got knocked down, what would happen?"

The child said, "The wires would break, and they couldn't talk."

I said, "Exactly, and exactly the same way we must keep our communication with God because we're talking with God. We say, 'Lord, Lord,' and the whole of our conversation is carried on by the principles that God puts forth in His Word, and we must not allow sin to destroy any of the points of communication, because if sin comes in, then the communication can be destroyed."

Again, one of the children asked, "That bird sitting up on the wire, what can that illustrate?"

I said, "Do you see his little claws holding tight on the wire?"

All three children chorused, "Yes."

I said, "In that wire somebody is talking. Although the words are going right under its feet the bird doesn't know anyting about it. Maybe somebody's saying, 'Grandpa died,' or 'Oh, there's been an accident,' or just chatting. Those words go through the little bird's feet, but he doesn't know anyting about them. In exactly the same way I'm resting in God; it doesn't make any difference what things whirl about me, what messages are bad or evil, I can trust the Lord and know that because I am resting in the Lord, nothing can touch me. None of the bad news that passes through the bird's feet can hurt it. Thus, 'we know that all things work together for good to them that love God.'"

One night a short time later, a friend took us out to get some ice cream. We were talking about the illustrations I had used that evening, and he said, "How on earth do you get such illustrations?"

I told him what I had said about illustrations being everywhere. One of the young women pointed to the sugar bowl and said, "Give us an illustration about this sugar bowl."

I said, "This sugar bowl looks as though it costs at least a dollar or two. If, instead of sitting in this modern, good class restaurant, we were in a cheap, dirty restaurant over on the avenue, the sugar would be in a rough, ten-cent mug. This one costs a dollar. If we went over to the Waldorf, we'd probably find fine bone china. Whether you get a crockery mug, or an ordinary one like this, or a very fine one in the Waldorf depends upon how long it has been put in the fire. The Bible says that we are vessels of honor, fit for the Master's use. You must be purged and burned in the fire to take on the proper work. Whether you are going to be an ornament cheap and dirty, or whether you will be a vessel fit for the Master's use depends on how you yield to the Lord for His work in your life."

Donald Grey Barnhouse

Preface to *Illustrating Great Themes of Scripture*

Unquestionably, Donald Grey Barnhouse was one of the twentieth-century giants of the evangelical Christian world. Many thousands came under the influence of his strongly Bible-oriented ministry as he served for thirty-three years as pastor of the historic Tenth Avenue Presbyterian Church of Philadelphia, but this was only a part of the outreach of this gifted Bible expositor. For many years, before his death in 1960, Dr. Barnhouse carried on a fruitful radio teaching ministry through the 140 stations carrying the Bible Study Hour. Each summer, he appeared as speaker on Bible conference grounds all over the continent.

As editor of *Revelation*, and later, of *Eternity* magazine, he found still another means of communicating rich scriptural truths to countless numbers of readers of his editorials and Bible lessons.

Most of the brief essays comprising *Illustrating Great Themes of Scripture* first appeared in the pages of *Eternity*, and are brought together here with topical organization for the blessing and instruction of a new audience, as well as for the delight of Dr. Barnhouse's longtime admirers, who will be grateful to have available in one volume so many gems of teaching from this master expositor.

Let Me Illustrate

Access to God

The French Priest

During my student days in France, I was pastor of a little Evangelical Reformed Church in the French Alps. Once a week I went to a neighboring village for an instruction class. Each time I made the trip I passed the local priest, going on a similar errand in the opposite direction. We became good friends and often chatted together for ten minutes or so before we went our separate ways. On one occasion, he asked me why we did not pray to the saints. "Why should we?" I asked. He launched an illustration of the way one might get an interview with the president of the French Republic. One could go to the Ministry of Agriculture, or to the Department of the Interior, etc.; any one of the cabinet members might succeed in opening the door of the president's office so that I might see him. His triumphant smile implied that the simplicity and clarity of the argument were such as to preclude any reply. At that time Raymond Poincaré was President of the Republic; he lived in the Palace of the Elyseé in Paris—the equivalent of the White House. I said to my friend, "But Monsieur le Curé, suppose that I were the son of Monsieur Poincaré? I am living in the Elyseé with him. I get up from the breakfast table and kiss him good-bye as he goes off to his office. Then I go down to the Ministry of the Interior and ask the fourth secretary of the second assistant if it is possible for me to see the minister of the Interior. If I succeed in reaching his office, my request is for an interview with my papa."

My friend was thunderstruck as I added that I was a child of God, heir of God and joint-heir with Christ, and that I had been saved through the death of the Saviour and thus had become a son with immediate access to the Father.

The Front-Door Key

A son, who had gone to military service, wrote to his father: "I am sending you all my keys except the front-door key; some day when I get leave, I may walk in unexpectedly and give you a surprise." When the parents read the letter, they thought, "This is a good son. He has no secrets from us, nothing to hide, no bluebeard chamber that must not be entered, no forgotten corner where old shameful things lie. He knows himself and he trusts us. He gives us the run of all his affairs. He sends us all his keys. He knows us, too. He knows he will always be welcome; that he can always walk in without waiting; that he has full right of entry into his father's house. Our house is open to him, and his heart is open to us."

Give God all your keys, and He will always give you access to Himself and all blessing.

The Guilty Clothes

An analysis of the dust from the trousers of suspected counterfeiters disclosed that clothes can betray guilt. Particles of certain metals and chemicals used in this irregular way of making money convicted them.

It makes no difference how you are dressed as you approach the Lord God of judgment. Your clothes will betray you; you will be cast forth as was the wedding guest who appeared without the proper wedding garment. The only way to approach the God of all holiness is to be clothed in the righteousness of the Lord Jesus Christ. That will stand the analysis of the light of God. Those thus clad will be seen as "faultless to stand before the throne."

Oil Reservoirs

Geologists knew that there were great reservoirs of oil deep down under the ground of west Texas. The ranchers lived in their modest homes and had large flocks of sheep that grazed the vast reaches of the semi-desert plain on the surface. The oil was underneath, but there was no access to it. Then great wells were sunk, and the oil gushed forth and out flowed the black gold. The wealth transformed the lives of those who had entered into its possession. The oil had been there all the time, but access to it determined possession more than a title deed; it made it a present reality.

The believer who is justified through the atoning work of the Saviour, has direct access to the grace of God. We may think of grace as a bountiful store, hidden in the being of our God and Father, but the Lord Jesus Christ has opened up a way—a new and living way—by which we come boldly to the very presence of God (HEBREWS 10:19,20), who is the source of all grace. There we find that with Christ He has given us all things (ROMANS 8:32).

Tribal Warfare

The famous missionary, David Livingstone, spent a year or two with a certain tribe in South Africa. Then, urged on by his desire to spread the name of Christ, he went far into the interior with his wife and child. When he returned to the first tribe he discovered that they were in sore straits. Another tribe had killed many of their soldiers and had taken the chief's own son as a captive. An ambassador in from the victorious tribe asked for friendship and peace. The victors were motivated by the fact that Zulus were about to attack *them;* they wished to protect their rear. The village chief was a good man who desired nothing better than to live at peace with his neighbors. He said to Livingstone, "How can I be at peace with them when they still hold my son a prisoner?"

If this attitude is true in the heart of a savage chief, how much more is it true of God the Father toward those who trample under foot His Son, and who count the blood of the covenant wherewith they were set apart as an unholy thing, and who continue to despise the Spirit of grace (HEBREWS 10:28,29). Access to God must begin with Jesus Christ. Christ set it forth in unchallengeable terms: "I am the way, the truth, and the life; no man cometh unto the Father but by me" (JOHN 14:6).

Adoption

Adoption of Marcellus

At one time in the Roman Empire it was the custom for men to have a ceremony in which they acknowledged their sons publicly. On the opening pages of *The Robe,* by Lloyd Douglas, Lucia described the ceremony held for her older brother. Her father had bought Demetrius [the Corinthian slave] six years ago and had presented him to Marcellus on his seventeenth birthday. All of their good friends assembled in the forum to see Marcellus—clean shaven for the first time in his life—step forward to receive his white toga. Cornelius Capito and the father made speeches. Then they put the white toga on Marcellus. Lucia had been so proud and happy that her heart pounded and her throat hurt. She was only nine then, but she knew that Marcellus was expected to act like a man now. Marcellus himself described the ceremony in later pages. His induction into manhood was one of the high moments of his life. His father made an address, welcoming him into Roman citizenship. The boy's eyes swam with tears. Then good old Cornelius Capito made a speech, about Rome's right to Marcellus's loyalty, courage and strength. Tough old Capito had a right to talk of such matters, and the boy was proud that he was there. The two beckoned to Marcellus; and he stepped forward. Capito and his father put the white toga on him and life had begun.

Adoption is not just adopting a child into another family; it is the welcoming, as a grown-up man, the child that long since has been born again. We have not received the spirit of bondage to fear, but we have received the spirit of a son come of age, publicly acknowledged by his father in the forum.

Adversity

The Moth and the Lion

There is a beautiful picture in one of the Old Testament prophets that shows how God is for us, even in the hard things which He must bring upon us. After speaking of the sin of Israel that took that nation away from Him, God says, "Therefore, will I be unto Ephraim as a moth . . ." (HOSEA 5:12). Some little insect comes into life and nests among the things we value. Suddenly we realize that corruption is there. God means this for a sign that will cause us to turn to Him immediately. If we accept the work of the moth and return to God, He will restore to us all that He has taken away.

But suppose men do not turn to God when He sends His insect-troubles? Two verses later He gives another word which is more terrible: "I will be unto Ephraim as a lion . . ." (5:14). This is the progress of God's love. He will not let us lose ourselves without exhausting all of the resources of His love. The moth may have eaten valuable possessions, but we can turn the rug around, we can put the couch against a wall where the ravages cannot be seen, we can move a lamp so that the light will not shine upon the destruction. Then He is forced to send the lion. With no warning at all, great trouble springs upon us like a beast of prey. Fear grips us. Our blood runs cold. Happy are we, if we realize that this is the Lord of love, who calls us to turn from the path where lions lurk and to run to the path of His will where no enemy can assail us.

Thousands of people, however, have had the moth and the lion and have not been moved by them. God is forced to hide His face from them. They are left, perhaps in unconcern, perhaps in restless and uneasy worry, but in it all, God is being good to them, showing Himself for them by holding the door of salvation open, and calling them to Himself.

No Pain

Little Beverly Smith, born in Akron, Ohio, almost never cried. She never cried when she fell down; she never cried when she bumped her head; she didn't even cry when she burned her hand on a hot stove. She cried only when she was hungry or angry.

The doctors soon discovered that she had a defect in the central nervous system for which no cure is known. She could not feel pain. The doctors told the mother she must watch Beverly constantly: the baby might break a bone and continue using it until it could not be set properly; she might develop appendicitis without nature's usual warning of pain. Spanking her to make her more careful about hot stoves and knives would do no good; she wouldn't feel it. Life without pain would be perpetually dangerous.

The spiritual application is simple. The Lord sends troubles into our lives for a purpose. "For whom the Lord loveth he chasteneth and scourgeth every son whom he receiveth. . . . if ye be without chastisement, whereof all are partakers, then are ye bastards, and not sons" (HEBREWS 12:6,8). If we accept the warnings of the little chastisements, we will be kept from the bigger hurts, just as the warnings given us by our nervous systems keep us away from fires and other hurts.

Let every Christian examine himself to see whether he has become insensible to the presence of sin.

Tangled Threads

A textile factory with complicated machinery posted instructions: "If your threads get tangled, call the foreman." One of the workers, a diligent and busy woman, got her threads tangled; she tried to disentangle them, but only made them worse; finally she sent for the foreman. He glanced at the threads and said, "You have been trying to do this yourself." She answered, "Yes." "Why did you not send for me, according to instructions?" he asked. Rather sullenly, she said, "I did my best." He replied, "Remember this: that doing your best is sending for me."

Andrew did. Though he was a sinner like the rest of the twelve disciples, he has no recorded failure. No such failure was recorded because he brought every difficulty to Christ. Our best is to bring our difficulties to Christ.

Through Tomorrow

The night before they were to attack the German lines, a hundred men wrote letters home. The chaplain, whose duty it was to censor the letters, put them in a mail pouch until after the battle. When the battle was over, the men again wrote home, telling of their ordeal. The over-burdened chaplain had both sets of letters to censor.

Here is a sample of what he read before the battle: "Dear Mother, we're going to attack in the morning and I've been thinking of home and you, and I vowed to God that if I come through tomorrow, I am going to be a better man." Some even said, "I believe I'm going into the ministry."

But after the battle, in the same handwriting, three days later, to a friend in another regiment: "Dear Joe: Can you get leave? The last time we were in Paris, we had a hot time, didn't we? I've just come through a scorcher up front, and we were near death at every moment. If you can get leave and meet me in Paris, boy, we'll go out on the town!" Before the battle: "Oh, God, if I get through tomorrow!" After the battle: "Well, I got through, God, so I don't need you any more."

For many people God is a very present help in time of trouble; but let the trouble pass, and God moves out of the picture. And there are many people who, when they are sick, cry out, "Oh, God!" but when they get well, "Oh, me!"

Assurance

I Know!

I was planning to spend the entire day reading and typing in our motel in Hot Springs, Arkansas. We told the cleaning woman to make the beds but not to touch the books that were spread around. My Bible was by the typewriter, and I said, "Just leave my Bible there." Immediately she seemed interested so I said to her, "Do you know the Lord Jesus Christ?"

"Oh, yes, I know Him. I couldn't have lived without him. My mother died when I was a little girl, and He has been my help through all my life."

"And are you sure that you are trusting Him as your own personal Saviour?"

"Oh, Mister. I don' have t' reckon. I know."

The conversation that followed revealed her clear knowledge of the Saviour, clear insight into spiritual life and clear certainty of full assurance of eternal life.

Tramps Vs. Multimillionaires

Come with me to an underpass outside of the freight yards of one of our great railroad centers. Here are two or three men—hoboes, vagabonds, tramps. One says, "I hope that I will have a million dollars." Another says, "I hope that I will have two million dollars." A third says, "I hope that I will have ten million dollars." The total assets of the three amount to forty-three cents!

Now go to the paneled board room of one of New York's great banks. Here are several captains of industry. One explains that the expansion of our economy calls for the expenditure of sixty millions of dollars to build a new chemical plant. A Du Pont says that he will put up fifteen million dollars; a Rockefeller agrees to duplicate this sum; a Ford and a Mellon nod their agreement and the matter is settled. But you ask, "Gentlemen! Do you really have money like that?" They nod with assurance and say, "We know that we have it." "You mean that you hope that you will have it?" we question. "No," they reply, "we know that we have it."

The difference between a tramp and a multimillionaire is the difference between a professing Christian who hopes that he will have eternal life and a possessing Christian who knows that he has eternal life.

The Bible

The Bible

About a hundred years ago, the King of Prussia had a discussion with his chaplain on the veracity of the Bible. The king said to the chaplain, "Tell me in a word the proof that the Bible is the inspired

Word of God." The chaplain replied, "Your Majesty, I can prove to you in one single word that the Bible is the Word of God."

The king looked at him in amazement and said, "What is this magic word that would carry such weight of proof with it?" The chaplain replied, "Your Majesty, that word is *Israel*."

And, of course, he was right. There are other single words that also prove the Bible—sin, salvation, Christ—but the history of the people of Israel is sufficient to show that a divine breath came down upon the men who held the pens that wrote down the Word of God.

The Carpenter's Square

A dozen carpenters sawed boards to make flooring. The foreman measured every board with a carpenter's square, an L-shaped rule that forms an exact right angle. If a man cuts a board at other than a right angle, the fit will be crooked, and the board must be recut to conform to the carpenter's square.

For the Christian, the Bible is the instrument by which every spiritual thought is to be squared. Every idea is to be accepted or rejected according to whether or not it meets the standard of the Word of God as illuminated by the Holy Spirit.

Level Ground

In certain spots the contour of hills gives a tremendous illusion that the law of gravity is askew. Near Los Angeles is a hill where thousands of motorists stop their cars, shut off the engines, release the brakes and seemingly roll up hill. But a plumb level placed on the ground where the cars "roll up hill," will be shown immediately that the cars are actually rolling down hill. The eye can be deceived; the level cannot.

God has given us a similar apparatus—the Bible. When my situation in life is placed next to the Word of God, the Holy Spirit immediately establishes the true aspects of the situation and reveals whatever unevenness or distortion there is. It is not safe to form judgments on the basis of our senses or our emotions—we must prove all things, test all things (I THESSALONIANS 5:21).

The Match and the Powder

Let us suppose that there are ten thousand barrels in a field. I am told that dry powder is in some of them; I do not know how many barrels contain the dry powder, and I do not know which ones contain the powder. I am told that it is desirable to light the powder wherever it is found, and I am given an unlimited quantity of matches. These can be struck only upon a certain prepared surface. What shall I do? If I toss unlit matches into barrels, nothing will happen. If I strike the match on the wrong surface and toss it in, it will still be unlighted and ineffective. But if I strike the match on the proper surface and toss it into the right barrel, it will light the powder, if the powder is there, and it will burn out if there is no powder there.

So I am told to take the Word of God with the light of the Holy Spirit and throw it into every life that I see. That Word will fall into lives illuminated by the Spirit; it will set them alight if it falls into the midst of effective, personal faith. "For as the rain cometh down, and the snow from heaven, and returneth not thither, but watereth the earth, and maketh it bring forth and bud, that it may give seed to the sower, and bread to the eater: So shall my word be that goeth forth out of my mouth: it shall not return unto me void, but it shall accomplish that which I please, and it shall prosper in the thing whereto I sent it" (ISAIAH 55:10,11).

The Platinum Bar

In Washington, in the Bureau of Standards, there is a platinum bar that is used as the standard meter for all measurements in the United States. It is approximately 39.37 inches long. This bar is kept in a high vacuum at a constant temperature. An argument about the measurement of any object must be settled, ultimately, by comparison with the standard meter in Washington. If your bar differs from the one in Washington, it is in error. If your bar is exactly the same as that in Washington, you can say that your bar is without error. But it would be wrong to say that the measure in Washington is without error, for that would mean that you are constituting yourself the judge—

measuring the Washington meter by some other standard that is above it. We must come to the conclusion simply that the Washington meter *is* and that it cannot be judged.

God has given us His Word; it stands as the only infallible rule of faith and practice. Our lives are tested by its truth. All of our thoughts and philosophies are tested by the Word of God. If we find a human thought that is opposed to what is set forth in the Bible, we say that the human thought is in error. If we find that the human thought is in agreement with what is set forth in the Bible, we say that the human thought is truth. Every little particle of human thought must be judged by the entire revelation of God's truth. But the Bible stands alone as the final court of appeal.

The Study of the Ocean

Some time ago we went to Atlantic City to preach in one of the churches there. One of the great hotels had given the church a lovely suite and we enjoyed looking out across the Atlantic in its everchanging moods and enjoyed its beauty to the full.

Let us suppose that a young Iowa friend, who had never had the privilege of journeying to the coast, asked us to write him about the ocean. What would you think if we wrote as follows: "We have a beautiful room and a picture window gives us a sweeping view of the ocean. The window is twelve feet two inches long and four feet eight inches high. It is divided into three sections. We have had a scraping of the glass analyzed and can tell you the chemical formula of the glass. We have had an expert from one of the great glass companies tell us all about the glass; we are giving you herewith a history of the invention and development of glass. The glass is set in steel frames that are painted black; we have had the steel analyzed and the paint analyzed; you can read the analysis in our second and third studies affixed to this letter. We have discovered that the panes of glass are kept in the frames by a putty composition, and we have scraped down some of this putty and are giving you a long addenda on the chemical composition of the putty. Finally, we have inquired and learned from the hotel management their method of keeping the windows clean; you will be delighted to learn from the subjoined study the whole process of window-cleaning and the formulas of the special detergents needed to cope with the salt spray from the ocean. In closing, let us say that we hope you have enjoyed our study of the ocean."

We smile at such a farcical parable, but we must admit that there are people who seem to forget that the Bible exists only to bring us to the Lord Jesus Christ. He is the ocean beyond the window. The young man might decide that seeing the ocean was not worth a trip to the Atlantic Coast; if it were no more than a study of the window through which the ocean might be seen, surely he would be right. Many spend so much time on the Bible itself, that they fail to look through the Bible to see the Lord Jesus Christ.

Trembling on the Rock

The old Scotch lady was right when she said, "I often tremble on the Rock, but the Rock never trembles under me."

The Word of God is the guarantee of our salvation and the ground of our assurance. There is nothing evasive about the message; it is direct and sure. This is one reason why so many people find comfort in the Word of God.

Work Calories

According to findings of two German physiologists who studied the relation of food to output in the Ruhr coal mines during the war, it takes three slices of bread for every ton of coal cut by a miner. Each man, they found, required between 155 and 200 calories per ton of coal produced. These represent "work calories," which are required in addition to the 1600 to 1800 calories needed every twenty-four hours just to keep alive. When the proper "work calories" were not supplied, the study revealed that any increased output—stimulated by bonuses and cigarettes—came from the "very substance of the body"; this showed up in the weight lost by the miners. Another study showed that in peacetime work lack of sufficient "work calories" resulted in only about half the performance, so that the job of one man had to be done by two or three.

There are some very important spiritual analogies to be drawn from this. The Word of God is the food of the Christian; every Christian needs a certain minimum of food from the Word of God to live his life day by day. If, in addition, he has special work to do for the Lord, he needs special feeding from the Word. The more his output, the more he must feed upon the Word. The greater his service for the Lord, the greater his need to consume at the table which God has laid. The Word is milk by which we grow (I PETER 2:2). The Word is strong meat (HEBREWS 5:12,14). The Word is honey (PSALMS 119:103). Those who would advance in God, must, like the prophet, say, "Thy words were found, and I did eat them . . ." (JEREMIAH 15:16a).

Bible Reading

Tripper

Edward Hutton, English author of the finest travel books on Italy, was awarded the highest civilian honor of the Italian government—Commendatore of the Order of Merit of the Republic. In an interview, he described the difference between the Italy of his first studies and the Italy of the present time. Italy then, he said was the land of the traveler. Today it is the land of the tripper, the tourist: "They don't understand what they see." It is so possible for a person with no classical background to look upon the amazing relics of the past and be unaware of their meaning.

Hutton's remark is a perfect illustration of the way in which many Christians read their Bibles. Instead of being travelers, who journey slowly, absorbing the spiritual blessings and plunging into the spiritual depths, they are tourists who rush by at high speed, not knowing what to read. One girl who "traveled" in Italy said she remembered Rome as the place where the shoe polish spilled on her best dress, and Venice as the place where the hairdresser burned her hair with curling irons. Have you really spent time with the Word of God, or are you a tripper?

Body, Soul and Spirit

The Three Story Building

We all have seen pictures of the World War II bombings of London, in which the explosion caused the third story of a three-story building to collapse onto the second story. The pictures show large holes gaping in the second-floor walls; we can see the debris of the third floor strewn on the floor below. The first story has withstood some of the shock—it still stands—though there are cracks in the walls and it is ultimately doomed to crash.

Thus it was with Adam. His body was the repository of his soul, and above that was his spirit. When sin came into his life, the spirit fell down into the soul; the debris of the two became hopelessly confused so that, as we consider fallen man today, it is impossible to distinguish between the soul and the spirit.

Call of God

The Uneducated Miner

An uneducated miner in Scotland began to preach among his fellow workmen with great power. Soon his witness took him far beyond the confines of the mining towns. Someone asked him how he had received his call to preach. He replied, "Oh, I had such a burden on my soul for those who did not know the gospel, I argued with the Lord that I had no education and no gift. But He said to me, 'Jamie, you know what the sickness is, don't you?' I answered, 'Yes, Lord, the sickness is sin.' 'And you know what the remedy is, don't you, Jamie?' I answered, 'Yes, Lord, the remedy is the Lord Jesus Christ.' And He said to me, 'Jamie, just take the remedy to those who are sick.' That is my call to preach."

This is God's call to every believer.

Chosen by God

Dearest

George Beatty of Cleveland, Ohio, had a wonderful jewelry store, remarkable for its window displays. Over the years, Mr. Beatty had bought a stock of small precious stones that he kept in pint cups. He had a cup of small rubies, a cup of topazes and a cup of diamonds—all sparkling brilliance. Some of them were small stones and chips that were worth very little. Early in the morning, before the customers came, he made pictures by placing the stones on black velvet squares; a magnificent peacock with its tail spread out was on one. He put these portraits in stones in the window, and many people stopped to look.

After one of my meetings, Beatty invited me to come to his basement workshop. Here he worked in wax and made settings for rings and pendants. Into the wax molds, he poured the liquid platinum; after the platinum was molded with an artistic and beautiful scroll design, he set the jewels in it.

A wealthy customer wrote Mr. Beatty that his dearest granddaughter was going to have a birthday; he wanted something distinctive of real beauty. Five times in the letter, the customer spoke of the granddaughter as "dearest." The old man looked at me and said, "I prayed and asked the Lord to give me an idea. I noticed how many times 'dearest' appeared, so I underlined it. When I sent my customer the sketch and told him what I proposed to do, he was greatly pleased and thought my idea was wonderful."

Mr. Beatty sent him a ring with baguettes so beautifully cut that the light scintillated from them. Across the top of the ring, the first stone was a diamond; the next, an emerald, then an amethyst, a ruby, a second emerald, a sapphire, and then a topaz. I looked at it and asked, "But why do you have two emeralds?" He smiled and said, "Because there are two e's in 'dearest. If you take the initials of those stones, it spells the word 'dearest.' "

Before the Lord God Almighty created the sun, the moon and the stars, He chose us, and—as it were—He put us in a ring to be worn as a signet upon His hand. Spelled out in the heart of God, we are his dearest.

Christian Growth

The Artist

An artist, visiting a museum where one of his masterpieces was on exhibition, saw one of his early paintings. He turned away from the comparison with sadness. A friend told him he should be pleased because of the progress he had made. The artist smiled sadly and replied that he was grieved because he had realized so little of the promise he had shown in his youth.

Let us, who are Christians, be delighted with the progress that we see in the revelation of the Son of God in others; but let us be grieved that we see so little development in ourselves as we realize how far we fall short of showing a perfect portrait of our Lord Jesus to a world which so sorely needs a sight of Him.

The Bride's First Kiss

In Africa we stopped overnight at the mission house of a young American bride and her Australian husband. The subject of their wedding came up, and they brought out some pictures a friend had taken of the affair. There was some good-natured chaffing on our part, and the young husband said, "I had always said that the last thing I would do is marry an American." We laughed, and he continued, "You know, she never let me kiss her even once until the wedding ceremony." We all laughed again; she blushed and started for the kitchen. He called after her, "But after I got the first one, the rest came easy."

The young bride turned as she went through the door and cast her husband a blushing look; it did not take much perspicacity to know that he had found the way to her heart and that he might come instantly. It may have taken him a year to find the way, but once it was found, it was forever open.

And this is our Lord's way with us. We do not have to repeat the slow processes of Christian growth. The steps, once taken, are taken forever.

Building Factories

An engineer, who was responsible for building great factories, said that all such construction is now planned with the machines that are to be housed in the factory in mind. The walls and floors of the buildings are constructed so that a machine can be built into the very foundation and structure of the building, rather than set in as an afterthought.

This is the way the Lord builds believers into Christ. We are built upon the foundation of the apostles and prophets, Jesus Christ himself being the chief cornerstone, and in Him all the building is fitly framed together, so that it groweth unto an holy temple in the Lord (EPHESIANS 2:20,21). That is surpassing even the modern engineers. They can frame their building and foundation and machines together "fitly," but they cannot make the building "grow." The true believers are fused in Christ and grow in Him together with Him and together with one another.

Learning to Fly

When an eagle wants to teach its little ones to fly from the nest high upon a cliff, hundreds of feet up in the air, it prods one of the little eaglets and with its beak, noses it out of the nest. The eaglet starts to fall, and the great eagle flies underneath, puts its wing out, catches the little one on its back and flies a mile into the air. When you can hardly see the eagle as a point in the sky, it turns sideways, and down falls the little eaglet, goes fluttering maybe a thousand feet. Meanwhile, the eagle circles around the eaglet and underneath it; the eagle catches the eaglet on its wings and carries the eaglet up in the air again. After dishing the eaglet out again and letting it go, the eaglet comes down farther and farther—sometimes within a hundred feet of the ground. Again the great eagle catches the little one on its back and up they go another mile. The little eagle is at perfect rest and learning to fly. Way up there in the sky, the great eagle will bow over again and little by little the eaglet will learn to fly. The eagle knows when the eaglet is tired; it spoons the eaglet into the nest, noses out the next one and starts off again.

God says, "That's the way I take care of you." But you may say, "I don't like to have my nest stirred up. I like everything cozy and tidy, and I just like to stay in my baby ways where I am." But God loves you. That's why He won't let you stay as a baby; He wants you to learn to fly. Sometimes you have to be carried aloft, and you may have a horror of having to go by yourself, but it must come if you are to grow.

Christian Liberty

The Argentinian Speed Racer

For a time, an Argentinian was the world's champion automobile speed racer. He could drive a car at 150 miles an hour, and he had won all the great road races of Europe. On the public highway he was the most careful and conscientious of drivers; young men drove alongside, gunned their motors, and grinned at him. He could have left them as though they were standing still, but he never used his ability for his own ends. If he saw that someone wanted to pass him so they could brag about it, he would drive under the speed limit. He sacrificed his pride for the sake of his example. If he sought to exercise his ability according to his liberty, he might say, "You slow-pokes! You cannot react as quickly as I can. I can change direction in a tenth of a second, without harm. If you can't do it, crash into that tree and kill yourself!"

If he took this attitude, even though driving at a "safe and reasonable" speed, he would be defying the law of humanity.

Each believer stands before God in perfect liberty, but each is bound before God as to how he uses his liberty. And if a believer in Christ uses his liberty for himself alone, he defies not only the law of humanity but the greater law of love.

Hindu Vegetarianism

One of the principal tenets of the Hindu religion is that the cow is a sacred animal; its flesh must not be eaten. This belief has led to complete vegetarianism. Suppose we Christians move into an Indian town; whether we are professional missionaries or employees of the United States government, we are ambassadors for Christ. Now, there is no butcher shop, since nobody in town eats meat; but, animated by the love of Christ, the believer will not make an issue out of it. He will abstain for the sake of the weak ones who watch him. If people in the town become Christians, they must be taught the heart of the Christian doctrine of grace; they must learn that vegetarianism is not a requirement of Christianity. The American Christian may travel away from the town and eat meat freely in the hotels and restaurants of the large cities of India, but he will not flaunt his liberty before these babes in Christ. Instead, for the love of Christ, he abstains from eating meat while living among them.

On the other hand, if I were living under such conditions and had been the means of bringing some Hindus to a saving knowledge of Jesus Christ, I would seek to teach them the liberty that is in Christ. When traveling with them to a large city, I would teach them the necessity of eating meat at least once to prove their liberty in Christ, and to aid their spiritual growth. When they returned to their hometown, they would resume the practice of vegetarianism before the weaker brethren and the unconverted; but they would never make it a matter of legalism within the framework of Christianity. In time, all the believers might grow strong enough to include meat in their meals. On a large scale, this would not only bring spiritual liberty to the believers, but would certainly improve economic conditions in India.

Walking Freely

In America we are at liberty to walk around as we please; at night we can go out in the garden and enjoy the stars or the cool air of the evening. On the missionary field, no one may walk freely at night; no one can spend too much time looking at the stars. One must keep one's eyes on the ground and a flashlight on the path ahead for the cobras that come out of their hiding places at night and slip among the paths. It would be as much as one's life is worth to plant a foot on the body of a cobra.

Someone might say, "Do I not have the right to walk freely, without carrying a light at night? May I not exercise my right to keep my eyes on the stars?" And the answer is that you really do not have the right to your own way in this matter. To insist on your rights would mean death.

Thus it is in the Christian life. There are many restrictions that we voluntarily place upon ourselves; not because we are not free to do something, but because it is not expedient to do so. The believer who has understood the Christian way will gladly carry the light in his hand; he will gladly accept this limitation of his freedom so that he may see the path that the Lord wishes him to follow, and avoid the cobras the enemy may seek to put in his way.

Christian Life

A Clean Kitchen

After an evening meeting that followed a dinner in the home of a young minister, a group returned to that home for a time of fellowship. The young wife began to work hard in the kitchen cleaning up after the dinner. She said, "I hate to come down to a dirty kitchen in the morning, so I always clean it up at night before I sleep."

At the end of every day, we must come to the Lord and let Him clean up absolutely everything in our whole life. "If we confess our sins, he is faithful and just to forgive us our sins, and to cleanse us from all unrighteousness" (I JOHN 1:9). This cleans up the kitchen; this cleans up the bedroom; this cleans up the living room; everything is ready for the next day. We open our eyes in fellowship with Him and smile. There are no hangovers from a previous day to mar the beginning. All is in fellowship, all is clean; God has done it, and the new day lies before us.

The Congo

I first saw Africa's great Congo from a plane, flying from Libreville in French Equatorial Africa to Leopoldville (now Kinshara) in the Congo. We swooped down out of the clouds to fly two or three hundred feet above some of the greatest rapids on earth. It was a marvelous sight from the air, and a few days later we set out to see the Congo at closer range.

At and above the city of Leopoldville, the Congo River is as calm and placid as a mill pond. The Stanley pool swells out until it is almost forty miles across. We crossed the river to Brazzaville, on the lower edge of that pool, and could hardly see a ripple. We had to look closely in order to see the direction of the river's flow. Then we took a car and drove ten miles down the river; we walked a mile or so under the tropical sun, crossed a small swinging bridge high above a tributary, and came, at last, to the rocks on the edge of the rapids. The vast flood of the Stanley pool and the waters of half a continent push down through a narrow place between the rocks, scarcely half a mile wide. The roar of the water is like thunder. The pressure is so tremendous that at times, waves fifty feet high are tossed into the air. The river is chocolate brown from the erosion of more than a million square miles; it flows in a still basin forty miles across, and churns through rapids that are tearing in their torment. Up the river, calm and peace; down the river, rapids.

So is the life of the Christian as it is revealed to us in the Word of God. In the highest heavens, seated with our Lord in the throne of His

Father, we have a peace that passeth all understanding. In the lower heavens and on the earth we have a turbulent roaring conflict. Yes, the Christian life is a downright wrestling match, not with human beings our own size and weight, flesh and blood which we might compass, but we wrestle against principalities and powers, against the world rulers of the darkness, against spiritual hosts of wickedness in the Heavens (EPHESIANS 6:12).

The Cormorants

While we were in Japan we went to Cifu. Just after dark, fishing boats sweep down the broad river; fires burn in the cages that hang from the prow of each boat. These fires attract the fish to the surface. Each master-fisherman manages a dozen large birds—cormorants; each bird is tethered by a cord ending in a metal ring, fitted around the neck of the bird. The cormorant thrusts his bill into the water and scoops up a large fish which will go down his long throat only as far as the ring. The master-fisherman then draws the bird back into the boat. The bird disgorges the fish and is fed a smaller one that slips down his throat past the ring. He then dives into the water again to catch another fish. It is amazing to watch the master-fisherman hold the cords of a dozen birds and keep them from tangling. The birds dart about after their fish; sometimes two will struggle for the same fish, but the master-fisherman keeps them all in order, without fouling the lines.

I applied this illustration to myself and the management of my life. I thought of how I have allowed lines to get tangled, and how difficult it is for any of us to keep all our lines of communication from tangling. When we understand that God is running the world, we stop threshing around and become quiet in Him. How wonderful to know that He has all things under control, and that He is working all things after the counsel of His will!

Dikes

Every child learns easily the geography lesson of Holland because of the fact that most of the land lies below the level of the sea and that the power of the water is restrained by great dikes. The Hollanders know from experience what their sea walls have done for their nation in rolling back the encroaching ocean, hungry to swallow up their low-lying land. Any breach in the dike would be repaired immediately. Any attack upon it from men or nature would be ruthlessly resisted.

The Christian should be just as sensitive to any encroachment on the barriers God has put up for our protection. The first day of the week is for our rest, worship and feeding in the Word of God—"Not forsaking the assembling of ourselves together as the fashion of some is . . ." (HEBREWS 10:25). This is one of God's dikes. Time spent every day in the study of the supernatural Book, time spent in prayer, these are God's dikes. The power of the enemy is ceaselessly helpless against them. The Christian must be most energetic in watching unto their preservation.

The Discordant Chime

An old clock that stands in a corner once had a beautiful chime; now it has a harsh metallic sound. A bit of broken spring fell against the chime while it was being repaired, and this little piece of metal is causing all the discord. As soon as this bit is removed, the hour will strike again in a rich, full tone.

Is there discord in your life? It takes but a bit of anything to deaden the note of joy. Whatever it is, great or small, it may be re-moved by yieldedness to our Lord Jesus Christ. David knew where to go when he cried, "Restore unto me the joy of thy salvation . . ." (PSALMS 51:12).

The Empty Gas Tank

A garage man in Mangum, Oklahoma, answered the distress call of a woman motorist, whose car had stalled. He examined the car and informed her that it was out of gas. "Will it hurt," she asked, "if I drive it home with the gas tank empty?" It would be cheaper to drive cars without gas, and quite pleasant, but anyone who has ever tried it has found out that it just does not work.

The same is true in the Christian life. Those who attempt to go on without power divinely provided by God may find that they are able to coast down hill for awhile—even roll up a little grade for a moment—but soon a time will come when the road will not permit further coasting; then life is stalled. Fortunately, God provides the power for us any time we are willing to have it, if we keep the funnel unclogged with sin and turned toward the supply that comes from His grace.

The Flower Show

I turned on the television in our motel room, as the presentation of a great flower show was beginning. Our TV was in black and white. The camera peered around various exhibits, each darker and gloomier than the one before. It was a colossal waste of time. Anyone who had never seen a flower show would get a wrong idea; anyone who had seen a flower show would be disgusted. There was neither color nor perfume, and, in fact, little form.

Thus it is when people try to have religion without Christ. You cannot capture the fragrance of Christ and the unfolding beauties of His presence in test tube or logical argument. He is received by faith, manifested in love, and awaited in hope. We should so live that everyone can see Him in us.

Forests

A *New York Times* editorial, "Fingers of the Forest," points out that once there were forests over much of the northeastern part of our country, and that most of our civilization has been planted on clearings in that once great forest. It then points out that wherever man has left a hedgerow between fields, the forest extends its fingers. "A hedgerow is a germ of a woodland. It has all the elements of a great forest and is a unit in itself. Young trees form the frame of the loom; the pattern is woven of alder and sumac, osage, high-bush cranberries, poison ivy and bittersweet. . . . Over the Northeast man has pushed the forest back, but the power of the woodland waits, keeping its fingers extended over man-made clearings."

This is a great illustration of the life of the believer in Christ. Our dwelling place is carved out of territory that was once occupied by the forest of our Adamic nature. We have made clearings, and with the help of the Lord, we keep the fields plowed and planted and cultivated and bearing a good harvest.

The Garden

I saw a garden overrun with weeds. Then cover plants were set at intervals among the weeds. After a year one could see that a battle was going on between the weeds and the cover crop. As time went on, the cover crop outgrew the weeds and, in a few years, it completely crowded the weeds out.

The Christian life somewhat resembles this process. The Christian starts out by being a part of this world and by becoming alive through the new birth. Henceforth, though he is in the world, his roots have been cut and a new planting has taken place. Christ must dominate every part of our lives. This is God's purpose for us and in us.

The Helmsman of the Leading Yacht

When the jumble around the starting line of a certain yacht race cleared, the helmsman of the leading yacht remarked rather uneasily, "I never expected to find myself in the lead." He made the same remark several times, but his crew told him it was nothing to complain about. As they rounded the first mark, well ahead, he said, "I think we'll have to let this boat pass us." "No we'll not," said the crew, "we're doing fine." "The trouble is," said the helmsman, "that I don't know where to go next. I was so sure there would be other boats in front that I didn't take the trouble to study the course."

There are too many Christians who will have a poor place in heaven because they are living their Christian lives like this helmsman. They were meant to be conquerors, but the last shall be first and the first last because they did not study to show themselves approved unto God—workmen that need not be ashamed.

In Daddy's Footsteps

The story is told of a man who had to be very careful of his life because he realized that he was the ideal and example for his son. One Christmas afternoon the father made the rounds of several houses and partook of various brands of cheer; he made a crooked path as he weaved his way across a field on the way home. Finally, he heard the voice of his five-year-old calling out behind him. He turned and faced the lad coming by a very crooked path. The father was sober enough to realize the boy was not walking straight; he realized, as he saw the lad taking giant steps in the snow, that the boy was following his father's trail. With a smile the boy said, "See Daddy, I'm walking right in your footsteps." The father resolved that he would have to mend his ways; he would have to be more careful of the way he walked, if his son were to walk after him.

But when we walk after the steps of our Lord, we need have no fear, for He has furnished the perfect example for the Christian. Only the believer can look to the Lord's life as the example of his walk.

Killing the Sound Waves

A gadget has been invented that reaches out to kill sound waves before they hit the ear. Electronically they are able to reduce the air pressure in the vicinity of certain apparatus just enough to cancel out sound waves. The result is a small "quiet zone." For a distance of two feet, it reduces to one-quarter the loudness of deep-toned noise. The effect is like shutting a door against the noise. They expect to build a gadget run on one watt of current that can be hung over the head of a sleeper to protect him from sleep-destroying noises. The gadget will be used in airplanes so the deep roar of the engines will be reduced, while the higher tones of the human voice will not be affected as much.

A spiritual gadget like this has existed for thousands of years. God speaks, and men have accustomed themselves to making a "quiet zone" around their ears for all sounds coming from Him. Any voice that is from the world, the flesh or the devil can get through, but Christ was forced to say, "He that hath ears to hear, let him hear" (MATTHEW 11:15).

The Locked Gate

While taking a walk at sunset in a north India hill station, our host led us on a path that followed the flank of the mountain. Here and there private paths led from the main one to the homes that dotted the hillside. At one of these junctions the owner had planted a post on either side of his private path, and between these posts he had placed a gate. The posts were strong, the gate was heavy, a chain held it shut, and a padlock secured the chain. But the posts were not connected to any fence. Within a step of one of these was a well-worn path that led around the gate, and anyone who wished could walk on the path and go his way as readily as if the postholes had never been dug or the gate planted across the path.

Is this not a picture of much of Christian effort toward a life of victory? The forms of religion are well planted; ideas of sanctification may be securely locked into the framework of proper doctrine. But it is not joined up to life and living. Provision has been made for the flesh in direct disobedience to God's command.

Noise

Scientists report that noise has a definite effect on our working efficiency. Noise increases the pulse, quickens the blood pressure, and upsets the normal rhythm of the heart.

Spiritual noise has just as bad an effect on spiritual life. The man who is occupied with the things that keep him from hearing the voice of God in his heart is spiritually frustrated. It is impossible for those who are spiritually noisy to have true peace of mind, peace of heart, and peace of soul! This is why God has said, "Be still, and know that I am God . . ." (PSALMS 46:10).

Olympic Games Contestants

Before the last Olympic games the contestants who represented our country were chosen according to certain rules. Anyone in the whole nation could have run up and down in the vicinity of the stadium.

Before entering the stadium, many visitors might have confused such a person with the real members of the team. But none of these imitators would have been allowed by the judges to compete in the events; and therefore, none of them would have been eligible for the prizes.

It is precisely the same with the race of Christian life. Many people are running around in Christian uniform, drawing the gaze of the casual onlooker who does not know the marks of a true Christian and who does not realize that not all Gentiles are Christians, and that many thousands of church members do not possess the supernatural life of Christ.

The Olympic Teams

Every four years great contests are held in the world of athletics; they are known as the Olympic games. It is considered a great honor to be on the team that represents our country at these events. Not everyone who desires can compete. There are elimination contests and finally the team is chosen. Then the team crosses the ocean and the various contests are held. Our athletes compete against men of other nations and some will be fortunate enough to be prize winners. After the teams have been chosen and the boat has sailed, the status of the athletes is fixed. If, after being chosen, one man does not seem to show the form that had been promised by earlier tests, he is, nevertheless, accepted; he is not dropped from the competition, though he may not be a prize-winner. Another man, who passed the tests with the thought that he might be a mere pacemaker may turn out to be the world's champion when the moment of the test comes. But their eligibility to compete depends entirely upon the fact that they have passed the elimination tests and have become members of the national team.

So it is in the Christian life and judgment. God tells us that the Christian life is a race. All who desire may enroll for the race. That is equivalent to becoming a Christian. The only way to become a Christian is by accepting God's verdict about the sinfulness of your own heart outside of Christ and by accepting God's verdict about the eternal satisfaction of all of His demands since Christ has perfectly satisfied them by His death upon the cross.

A Piece Out of the Cake

The little girl watched her mother put the finishing touches on a newly baked cake. "Mother," she said, "your cake would look like the pictures in the magazines if you would cut a piece out of it."

Your Christian life would look more like that pictured in the Bible, if you would start giving yourself away. What you keep grows stale. What you give becomes nourishment for the whole of the true church. We feed on what the Lord multiplies of Himself through us.

The Poor Millionaire

Several years ago, I preached in a church in the southwestern United States. When I went into the pulpit on Sunday morning, the pastor whispered to me, "Notice that woman on the front row who is badly dressed and who wears a broken shoe." I saw a miserable, pitiful figure of a woman, probably in her late sixties; one foot stretched out to reveal a large hole in the sole of the shoe, the edge of which was so worn that the leather stood away from the sole. Her dress was patched and dowdy, and her old hat looked like something out of a rag barrel. A wave of pity came over me, and my first thought was to give her a few dollars to help her in her misery.

Later, the pastor told me that this woman and her husband had been sheep ranchers, pasturing a large herd on ground that was almost desert. Their miserable cabin's toilet facilities were fifty yards away in one direction, a hand-pumped well fifty yards in the other. They drove a jalopy of ancient vintage and lived most simply. Then oil was discovered on their property, and they became very rich. After a time, the husband died, leaving everything to the wife. She was extremely frightened and refused to sign the papers the lawyers brought her. Her royalties began to pile up. Drilling continued until there were a hundred wells on her ranch. Within a few years she was worth several million dollars, but she spent hardly a cent. She still lived in the old cabin, used outdoor facilities, and pumped water by hand. She still drove the old jalopy. Possessing enormous wealth, she lived in abject misery.

I pointed out to my preacher friend that her manner of life exemplified the spiritual life of multitudes of believers. We have been told that we are heirs and joint heirs with Christ, that all things are ours, that we have been blessed with all spiritual blessings in the heavenly places in Christ, and that God has given us all things richly to enjoy. God tells us that we have not because we ask not, and that we ask and do not receive because we ask in a wrong spirit. The riches are there; the supply is unlimited, but many simply do not avail themselves of all that God has promised, or of even a small fraction.

The Red Rose

Some years ago, a friend of mine moved into a new home. The house had been unoccupied for a long time; the garden was untended and high with weeds. The first morning my friend looked from an upstairs window into the garden, and among the weeds he saw a beautiful red rose. He went to pick it, but the weeds were so high he could not find it. Returning to his upstairs window he located the rose, noted landmarks near it, and on his second trip to the garden, succeeded in finding it. As he pulled it from the weeds, he discovered that the stem ran nine feet to its root in his neighbor's well-cultivated garden!

That is the Christian life. Rooted in Heaven, it blooms among the weeds of earth.

Seeing the Gospel

A man came to a mission station in Central China and asked to become a Christian. When he was questioned, he replied that he had never heard the gospel preached. He also said that he could not read. When he was asked how he knew about the gospel, he said that he had seen it. Although his village was far removed from any preaching center, he explained, there lived a man who had long been known as a worthless opium addict and a lazy, good-for-nothing. The man had journeyed to a faraway town and had returned absolutely transformed; he uprooted the poppies in his garden, repaired his house, planted and tended his crops, and provided for his family as a decent man should.

The former good-for-nothing said that the gospel of Christ had changed his life; his neighbor, hearing about it, came all the way to the mission station to become a Christian.

The gestures of the Christian life explained more simply and more potently than any arguments could have done. May we define our Christian life in this way.

The Snow Tracks

Five boys, playing in the woods one winter day, decided to see who could make the straightest set of tracks in the snow. They were very careful to put one foot directly in front of the other, but when they had crossed the clearing, one track was curved, one was crooked, and two were almost zig-zag. Only one boy had a straight track. When they asked him how he did it, he replied that he had not looked at his feet; he had picked out a tree across the clearing and had walked straight toward it.

If we are to leave a straight track in our daily walk, we must not have our minds centered on ourselves. We must fix our gaze upon the Lord Jesus Christ. We are to "run with patience the race that is set before us, looking unto Jesus . . ." (HEBREWS 12:1,2).

Spending

A wife can never be satisfied merely because her husband is a good provider. If he laid everything at her feet that money could buy, there would still be a lack of just exactly everything because he had delved into his purse instead of his heart. But many a happy woman gladly does without the fripperies of luxurious living, if she has not only the large bills, but the small change from the heart of the man she loves.

The analogy may be carried into all the relationships of our life. Never spend money from your purse for that which should be purchased with your very self. The Christian knows that this spending of the heart is the natural—or should we say, the supernatural?—pouring out of the life that is released through the indwelling presence of the Lord Jesus Christ. He Himself said, "He that believeth on me, as the scripture hath said, out of his belly shall flow rivers of living water. But this spake he of the Spirit, which they that believe on him should receive . . ." (JOHN 7:38,39). Even the money that comes from the purse will have the effect of self that pours from the heart, if it is spent in the light and life of the Lordship of Christ.

Still or Moving Pictures

We went to the steamship office at Kobe to get baggage that had been checked through from Yokohama. An English-speaking Japanese was detailed to take us to the custom house. As soon as we were in the taxi, we began to talk with him about Christ. He had been in contact with Christianity and was under deep conviction. What were his objections to Christianity, I asked him. Many Christians did not live up to their profession, he replied. It was easy to say, "I am a Christian, I am a Christian," but especially for the poor man, it was not so easy to be a Christian. Japanese employers, especially those in the hotel business in which he had spent many years, wanted their employees ready to lie; they did not wish to employ men who might develop a conscience. These are not his exact words, but the thought is conveyed. Then he gave us a real message. He said, "A true Christian should be a moving picture, but many of them are only still pictures, and there is all the difference in the world between the dull flat photograph and the depth and animation of the highly developed cinema."

We are, all of us who name the name of Christ, living epistles, known and read of all men. In modern days, the world has learned to illustrate everything; twentieth-century Christians are living epistles—illustrated editions. The non-Christian is finding that many who call themselves Christians present still pictures to the world—often under-exposed, out of focus. The result is a caricature instead of a reflection of Christ.

Sure-Footed

As a young man in Europe, I did considerable mountain climbing in the Swiss Alps and in the more dangerous and difficult French

Alps. Roped together with other young men, I scaled many a peak; my snapshot book records moments of difficulty and peril that make me wish to restrain others who might venture into similar places. The first time I went out with a young Frenchman, son of a pastor, and a young Swiss bank clerk; they gave me sound advice, "You have two hands and two feet," they said, "and that makes four. Always be sure that three out of the four are firmly on the rock. It is the only rule of safety."

This advice is also the rule of spiritual safety in our Christian life. In one of the Psalms, David told of slipping feet. He had been looking at men and their circumstances. He saw the righteous suffering and the wicked flourishing, and he could not understand; he was, in fact, dismayed. He had looked at men and their doings instead of looking at God. It is as dangerous to take your eyes from the Lord in spiritual things as it is to take your feet from the rock in mountain climbing.

The Three Pillows

An old lady was very calm as she approached death. Her minister said, "I have noticed your calmness in so many things." She said, "When I was just a girl, an old preacher told me that each night he slept well because he rested his head upon three pillows—God's grace, God's power, and God's wisdom."

There is no doubt that if you have those three pillows, it is going to make easy sleeping, easy dying and easy living day by day; your attitude toward the Lord will be such that prayer changed the whole attitude in life, because prayer is the linking of your soul to the Lord in absolute trust.

Two Rulers

Mr. Six-Year-Old came into the study in tears. In his hand were the two pieces of a broken ruler. Mr. Nine-Year-Old had done it, he affirmed. The investigation, however, showed that the older brother had merely set an example by putting his ruler in the inkwell hole and bending it. When the small brother followed the example the ruler snapped because there was a knot in the wood. Actually, the smaller brother had done the breaking, but we took the good ruler and gave it to the younger child while the older brother had to be content with a nicked and stained substitute of inferior quality before it was finally replaced at the end of a month. Another punishment was given to the boy who had done the actual breaking.

There had to be some explanations. The older boy was not quite sure of the justice of the punishment, but ultimately it led to the explanation of the responsibility of the stronger for the weaker. It is a distinct Christian principle that the strong must help to bear the infirmities of the weak. The life of Christ within our hearts makes any small privation pleasure. He never allows Himself to be in debt to us, and when an honest heart has given up something that might cause no harm to self, the Lord has a way of filling up the emptiness with "solid joys and lasting pleasures."

Walking on Ice

Walking on an icy street in Haddonfield, New Jersey, a little boy reached up, caught hold of his father's finger, and slipped. As he slipped, he let go of his father and went down. The father helped the whimpering boy up and they walked on. The father tried to take hold of the boy's hand, but the boy slapped at his father's hand and finally caught hold of the finger by himself. Once more he slipped; the automatic reflexes opened his hand and down he went. He whimpered again, and this time the father just reached down and caught the little fellow by his fist. The boy still wanted to do the whole thing, but the father wouldn't let him and so they went along. All of a sudden, the boy's feet slipped and the telegraph reflexes from the boy's fist ran through the father's arm to the father's head; before the boy's feet could fly out from under him again, the father lifted him up. The boy kicked in the air for a moment; the father set him down, and they walked on together again.

There are two ways of trying to live the Christian life. If you try to hold on to God's finger, something is going to happen, and you are going to try to let go. But if you say, "Lord God, I can't stay on my own feet, hold me," He'll do it. When you slip, you may kick around in the air for a minute, but He is strong enough to let you kick and then to put you down again very quietly and let you get your footing and start on again. He will keep you this way.

Walking with Father

Many of us can remember, perhaps, incidents of our own childhood when we walked before our own parents. I can recall our Sunday morning walks to Sunday school—skipping along the sidewalk, stopping to examine a place in the cement where a group of children had left the prints of their hands and bare feet and another spot where a horseshoe had been imbedded in the walk. At a certain place I used to run far ahead, then wait at the curb for my father so that I might cross with him. There was one yard before which I paused, waiting for my father to come up close, that I might have him near at hand before passing a huge barking dog. Walking before my father was a place of absolute safety. His eye was ever upon me, and his voice could call out, if I strayed from the way he wanted me to go.

Certainly it is so with our Heavenly Father. He has us walk before Him in the path of great security. "He knoweth the way that I take. . . ." (JOB 23:10). We need never fear when our Father, our Heavenly Father, is behind us. He started us on this walk, and put us there in His sight, and He expects to bring us home.

Walking with the Children

Each day I watched a father and his children taking their walk, in the midst of the big city. Perils of traffic, and other city dangers were on every hand. Their training went on, day by day: the children walked ahead of their father; they were permitted to run ahead to a certain tree, some fifty yards away. If they ran beyond it, they had to walk just five steps ahead of their father for many sedate minutes while they fretted for their liberty. If they promised that they would observe his limits, they were freed again. I can see them running up to the fixed goal, standing with their toes to a line—little soldiers obeying with absolute precision. When once they learned to stay within their prescribed limit, the distance was lengthened to one hundred yards, and more. Finally, they were released at a certain point and given permission to disappear around the corner, if they stopped at a certain known goal. When that lesson had been learned, they were allowed to cross a quiet street where there was little danger of traffic. Once such a crossing had been successfully negotiated on many successive days, the children were permitted to cross at a busier corner. Time was passing. Where three-year-old steps had been halted at fifty yards, and four-year-old steps had been permitted to go around a corner and out of sight, five-year-old steps were crossing streets.

One day the father sent the boys a block ahead, where they had to cross two streets, gave them money to go into a familiar store, make a purchase, and wait there for him. The distances were lengthened, the sums of money entrusted to them were increased, the importance of the errands grew. Finally, there came a day when a ten dollar bill was given to them and they were told to go to a bank three or four blocks away, get change and bring it home. Faithful in few things, they were made faithful over many.

This is the desire of the father-heart. This is why the heavenly Father tells His children to walk before Him. He desires their growth, their discipline, their training, that they may be strong in the powers He has given them.

The Well-Dressed Christian

In a certain city in the western part of the United States, lives a woman who has become famous in Christian circles because of her great testimony for Christ. She has transformed the life of one of the greatest churches in the land, and has led dozens of young people into full-time Christian service. This woman dresses in stylish clothes; her grooming is equal to that of the most worldly people with whom she associates. In a nearby town lives a godly shoemaker who makes good money and lives on the slenderest budget; he supports much Christian work with his gifts. One day, the shoemaker attended a banquet at his church; the city woman was the special speaker—splendidly coiffed, gowned and well-manicured. When the service was over, he asked her why she dressed the way she did. "Why are you wearing a necktie?" she asked. He was taken aback and finally stammered that it was the custom; that if he did not wear a necktie, people would think that he was queer. She then answered that she lived and moved among multitudes of people who dressed well and for whom the custom was to appear much as she appeared at that moment. If she did not dress somewhat as they dressed, she would be conspicuous and they would think her queer; they would not be willing to listen to her presentation of the gospel. He nodded and turned away without further argument.

How important it is for Christians not to judge one another in trivial things. Each one of us must answer to God for the way we dress, the way we walk, the way we talk, the way we act, the way we live, the way we think, the way we manifest the love of the Lord Jesus Christ to those who are around us, dead in trespasses and sins.

We've Won

As Canon Guy King stood waiting for a train to London, a train discharged a football team returning home after a game in another city. It was before the days of radio and telephone, so nobody knew the result of the game. A small boy pushed through the crowd and asked one of the players. Leaping joyfully, he ran outside shouting to the others, "We've won, we've won." He was not a member of the team, nor of the school represented by the team. But he was filled with joy over a victory with which he associated himself.

Thus it is, that we face our daily life. We can live in joy and in triumph. We can shout, "We've won!" over the victory that was accomplished by our Lord Jesus Christ on Calvary nineteen hundred years ago. If we are in the midst of some defeat in our lives, we have the right to know what our Lord won for us, and to enter into the triumph of it.

Wilted Roses

Back in the days of the depression, a Philadelphia woman of Scotch ancestry, who also had a Scotch name, was called Mrs. Mac. She and her husband had a lovely home, chauffeur, gardener, hot house and all the rest. Mrs. Mac taught a Sunday-school class of high-school girls. One day her car drove up before the house of one of the girls in her class. The chauffeur hopped out, and gave the girl a big box of roses. When the girl opened the box, she saw that the roses were wilted and faded and that the petals were beginning to fall and turn brown. Why on earth would Mrs. Mac do a thing like that? Had the chauffeur been given them two or three days ago, and forgot to deliver the package?

When she met Mrs. Mac on the street later that day, the girl said, "I want to thank you for the roses you sent me this morning."

Mrs. Mac said, "Oh yes, they were so beautiful, I cut them last Monday, I have had them in my bedroom, and I have been enjoying them to the full. This morning I noticed that some of the petals were dropping and they were beginning to get old and faded, so I thought about you, and I decided to send them to you.

She said, "But Mrs. Mac, I don't understand."

Mrs. Mac said, "Just the other evening Mr. Mac and I stopped in front of the drug store. While Mr. Mac went inside on an errand, I sat in the car in the dark. Some girls came down the street. I heard one of them say about the meetings that we were having over at the church, 'Well of course, I mean to be a Christian sometime, but now while I'm young, I want to have a good time.' "

The girl's head dropped. She said, "I remember I did say that, but I didn't know you were in the car listening."

Mrs. Mac replied, "Don't you see what you're really saying is 'Lord, here's my life. I'm young, I have youth and charm and beauty, and I want to enjoy myself, I want to live for myself. When I begin to get wrinkles and I'm not as popular as I was, when I'm beginning to fade, why Lord, you can have what's left. I'll give you the rest, but while it's young I want it for myself.' "

There are people who, when they were young, lived utterly for themselves. And only when they began to be wrinkled and weren't as popular as they were at eighteen, twenty or twenty-five, they began to turn to the faith and come back toward the Lord.

Christians

A Good Automobile Driver

A good automobile driver never thinks about his driving, he merely reacts. If it were necessary to think about putting on the brake, the delay of a fraction of a second could cause many accidents. When someone else is driving, a good driver may frequently "put on the brake," automatically reacting and stamping on the floor boards. His mind is so conditioned by thousands of miles of driving that certain motions become natural in certain situations.

The Christian, through thousands of hours of fellowship with the Lord in prayer and Bible study, over the years acquires a conditioned pattern of thinking that becomes more glorious as time passes. The burden of sin is gone; he knows that he is saved; sensitive to His presence and His holy hatred of sin, he learns to glance at Him when danger threatens; by reason of use he has his senses exercised to discern (HEBREWS 5:14). His thought of death is one of glory, not of fear; life is filled with praise.

The Aspic Salad

A lady makes tomato aspic for a luncheon party. She pours the aspic into individual molds and sets them in the refrigerator. When her guests arrive, she takes the molds out of the refrigerator and turns the aspic out onto salad plates. The firm shape of each aspic bears the imprint of the mold.

We are in the mold of the world, but God Almighty puts us into fire until we melt, then he pours us into the mold of Christ. We meet the temptations of the world by refusing to be conformed to it; we yield ourselves to God so that He may make us like Christ.

The Battleship, Missouri

A few years ago, the great battleship Missouri was stuck on a sand bar in the harbor of Hampton Roads. *Time,* reporting the incident, said that the Navy's face was red. And well it should have been, for some navigator had defied the evidence of charts of the harbor and had run the ship onto a sand bar.

Many Christians know what it is to be perched on a reef while the tides of life pass them by. They wonder how they got there and how they can get back into the channel. God is willing to refloat any man's life if the man will confess his own inability and ask for the leading of the Lord.

The Bavarian Wood-Carver

A Bavarian wood-carver found a piece of wood in the mouth of a sack of grain. The wood was exactly the same color as the grain. The man carved imitation grains of wheat on the wood until he had a small handful of them. He mixed them with real grain and defied his friends to tell them apart. The wood-carver had performed his work so well that he, himself, was not able to tell the natural from the artificial. Ultimately, the only way to tell the two apart was to put them in water for a day or two. The natural grains sprouted. The carved ones remained exactly what they were—dead imitations.

God has created life within the hearts of those who have been born again. It may be possible for men to imitate the life of the Christian by copying some of his ways and echoing some of his words, but in the long run, the difference between the two shall be made manifest by the gaze of God who can tell the difference between the real and the false. In the meantime, we who are Christians must be "careful to maintain good works" (TITUS 3:8).

The Broken Toy

One rainy day, two small children whiled away the hours by playing with a Noah's Ark. They pleaded to float their ark in the bathtub, and permission was reluctantly given. From the next room the mother could hear the conversation of the children; as they decided to pull the plug and let the waters abate on the face of the earth while the ark came to rest upon the Mt. Ararat of a sponge.

"What did they do after that?" asked small sister.

"They offered a sacrifice," replied the brother who knew his Bible stories.

"Well, what shall we sacrifice?" asked the little girl.

There was silence for a moment as the children poured the little wooden animals out on the rug, and then the boy answered, "Here is a camel with a broken leg. We can offer this up in sacrifice."

Thousands of Christians give offerings of the same nature as the children's broken toy. If it be applied to the unsaved, the analogy lies in the fact that the Lord cannot receive the offering of their "good works" which are not good in His sight. If it be applied to believers, the Lord will judge them for their lives after they are saved. "I beseech you therefore, brethren, by the mercies of God, that ye present your bodies a living sacrifice, holy, acceptable unto God, which is your reasonable service" (ROMANS 12:1).

The Burma Soldier

During the Burma campaign a soldier was forced to live month after month in the rotting jungles. He went from fox-hole to foxhole, underwent the torments of the tropics, was blinded by the sweat of his labor. As he slogged his way forward, he dreamed of a white cottage with a garden path running through the flowers and his love standing at the door. When the turn of the battle called forth supreme effort, the etching of his dream was more sharply drawn, and from this source of his life he drew the morale for his daily fight. "If ye then be risen with Christ, seek those things which are above, where Christ sitteth on the right hand of God. Set your affection on things above, not on things on the earth. For ye are dead, and your life is hid with Christ in God" (COLOSSIANS 3:1–3).

Dr. Alexis Carrel

When he was only a boy, French physician Alexis Carrel, Nobel Prize winner and one-time head of the Rockefeller Institute in New York, determined that he was going to be a surgeon. At a very early age he began to prepare his hands for the flexibility and suppleness necessary to perform delicate operations. One means was to secure the cover of a matchbox, place it over the two smallest fingers of either hand, and with a needle and suture, to stitch the edges of cigarette paper together. Then he tied a fine knot in the suture to finish off the "operation"—all this in the narrow confines of that box top. As a surgeon he later amazed the medical world with his manipulative skill in the narrow recesses of the human body. Dr. Carrel's head was in complete mastery of his fingers.

In the domain of the spiritual life we are frequently awkward because we have not allowed the Head, the Lord Jesus, to control our coordination and to teach us the possibilities of complete domination by our Lord. In the Word He has set before us the possibility of bringing into capitivity every thought to the obedience of Christ. The world will never look at clumsy handlers of the problems of life, but will stop in some awe before the life that has trained itself to a skillful proficiency in the craft of Christian living. Men did not admire Carrel's fingers, they admired his head; men will not admire the man, but the Lord Jesus when they see your good works. Our Lord Himself has said that such living would cause men to glorify the Father which is in Heaven.

The Electric Light Bulb

An electric light bulb may be screwed into the socket and the current turned on, but if there is no filament in the bulb, there will be no light.

A human being may have the outward form of a Christian, a professing Christian, but only by the miracle of the new birth, the creation within of the new man by the touch of God, can the light of Christ shine in any life. Some obstruction may cause the current to be cut so that there is but a tiny glow on the filament, but it is still capable of lighting up with full power. The presence of the Lord Jesus Christ is what makes a Christian.

Falling Out of Bed

A little boy constantly fell out of bed. No matter what his parents did, the boy could not sleep without rolling out of bed. An uncle came to visit, and in the middle of the night the usual thump and cry was heard. In the morning, the uncle teased the boy and asked him why he fell out so frequently. The little boy thought a moment and then replied, "I don't know, Uncle, unless it is that I stay too close to the place where I get in."

Certainly, this is the valid explanation of the fall of many Christians. They have come to the place where they have believed in all sincerity that they are lost sinners and that Jesus Christ took their place on the cross to bear the weight of the wrath that was due on account of their sin. They have been seen of God as being in Christ and so have passed out of death into life. The tragedy is that they seem to remain in that same spiritual condition so that no one can really know whether they have been born again or not.

In His First Uniform

The first time a recruit of the United States Marines walks out in his uniform, he pulls himself a little taller. From the Halls of Montezuma to the shores of Tripoli the cloud of witnesses moves before him. The splendor of names fill his memory—Guadalcanal, Saipan, Okinawa; he knows he belongs to a proud first-rate outfit.

When God tells us we are compassed about with a great cloud of witnesses (HEBREWS 12:1), we must not think that our departed loved ones are watching us—conscious of our secrets and our failures—for the next logical idea would be to pray to them. The cloud of witnesses is real, yet invisible. The Christian may be sneered at by little minds and sinful hearts, but he holds himself straight. Abel is whispering in his ear; Enoch is walking before him; his Father Abraham is setting an example of faith; he knows he marches to join that host.

Irrigation

Irrigation is necessary in many parts of our country, because ordinary rainfall is either seasonal or insufficient for the needs of the land. If the channels are not kept open the land will revert to its arid condition and the crops will fail. From those great valleys, teeming populations of the past drew their life from the rich soil, but today, the valley, like the Euphrates and the Tigris, are half desert, half lands of low yield. Archaeologists can trace for you the system of canals that carried water to the far fields in ancient times. The dams were allowed to fall into disrepair; the channels became filled with silt; dryness and the death followed the breaking down of the flooding system.

The situation is similar in the hearts of believers. They must lay bare their hearts before the examining gaze of the Holy Spirit, so that He may flush out the debris that has clogged the channels of living and bring the smooth flow of love to its highest level.

The King's Shilling

For generations recruiters for the armed forces of Great Britain have handed a shilling to the man who joined up. Once he has accepted the King's shilling, the recruit is considered "in": he is subject to military or naval discipline; he is dependent upon the government for support. He has accepted the King's image on the shilling, and he is, henceforth, the king's man. The nation will not hold him guiltless if he takes the king's shilling in vain.

So it is with those who receive the Lord Jesus Christ as their Saviour. They are "renewed in knowledge after the image of him that created [them]" (COLOSSIANS 3:10). Having taken the Lord and been given His invisible image, they belong to the Lord. They may expect Him to care for them in all things and may expect to be subject to His discipline. ". . . the Lord will not hold him guiltless that taketh his name in vain" (EXODUS 20:7).

The Mexican Spider

A certain kind of Mexican spider does not spin a web to catch insects as our spiders do, it lives on tiny edibles that grow on the bottom of shallow streams. The spider blows a bubble of air around itself, then goes down under the water and feeds at the bottom of the stream. When he has exhausted the oxygen in his bubble, he lets go of the pebbles, and the air carries him to the surface where the bubble breaks. Another bubble forms, and down he goes once more.

Since he has been born again, the Christian's very breath of life is of an atmosphere that is not of this world. He must indeed work and live and find his pleasure in the midst of a deep flowing stream that is at odds with the very life principle that is within him. But God has viewed him as being in Christ, and as we move out into the world system that knows not God this is our protection. We are here in the world system because we have been sent here by Christ. This is the sphere of our present activity. This is where He has placed us.

Noise

Records, kept for a year before and a year after the installation of sound-absorbent walls in the offices of a large insurance company, showed that the decrease in noise resulted in a decrease in errors that amounted to 29 per cent by typists and 52 per cent in the work of calculating machine operators.

Many verses in the Bible call the Christian to quietness and stillness with God. The frenzied rush of life must be stilled if we are to get what God wants us to have. The percentage of errors in life will decrease if we learn to "be still, and know" our God (PSALMS 46:10). ". . . in quietness and in confidence shall be your strength . . ." (ISAIAH 30:15).

The Orchestra Conductor

It was long past midnight; my elder son and I had talked for hours. The conversation turned to music, to the Boston Symphony Orchestra, to the role of the artist as distinguished from the role of the composer. I wrote down one paragraph from our conversation, for I saw its immediate importance as a parallel for every Christian life.

My son said, "A man like Koussevitsky must be the servant of his art. He must be nothing but the medium between the composer and the people. He himself must be completely subjected to what the composer wrote into the score of his composition. Any deviation or shortcoming from this subjection is adulteration of the music. The conductor is nothing but a channel."

Apply this to yourself as a professing Christian in any walk of life—minister, banker, lawyer, nurse, soldier, sailor, student, homemaker, whatever you may be. Then say of yourself, "A man like myself must be the servant of my faith. I must be nothing but the medium between the Lord and the people I meet in Christian witness. I must be completely subjected to what the Lord wrote into His revelation; any deviation or shortcoming from this subjection to His Lordship is an adulteration of the Christian life. The Christian is nothing but a channel."

Reminders

No matter where he traveled, a sailor from Colorado kept his watch on mountain standard time in order to remember home. When the watch said five A.M. he knew his father was milking the cows; in the evening at seven-thirty he knew the family sat around the table, thanking God for what was on it and asking Him to watch over the absent son.

"It's thinkin' about those things that makes me want to fight when the goin' gets tough. I can find out what time it is where I am easy enough; what I want to know is what time it is in Colorado."

So the Lord, our Father, has surrounded us with innumerable reminders of what is going on in heaven. It's easy enough to see what is going on on earth. A flower can remind us of God's power—a baby of God's holiness, some great need of Christ's intercession for us. Set your affection on things above.

The Scotch Shepherd Dog

If a Scotch shepherd dog is left to guard his master's coat, he will not leave it until the master returns. Nothing can draw him from the task to which he was appointed. If a rabbit runs by, almost under his nose, he will not move. A deer may break from a copse and cross the glen, so close that the dog could easily bring him down as prey; the dog will not move. If the dog had the mind of some Christians, he might reason, "Oh, my master was unaware that a rabbit would pass or a very valuable deer. Surely, he expects me to use my intelligence and leave my appointed job to run after the game."

Many Christians run away from the thing to which they have been appointed. The lure of the great and the showy draws them away from the steady devotion to their humble appointed task.

The Stolen Money

Henry Trotter, a railway worker of Marshalltown, Iowa, reported to police that his life's savings of $14,000 had been stolen. The money, which he had been accumulating for many years had been kept locked in a bureau drawer in an unused bedroom. Imagine the consternation of this worker when he discovered that all the penny-pinching and years of labor had resulted in absolutely nothing.

So it will be with many Christians who build upon one foundation of wood, hay and stubble. Their works shall be burned away and they will be saved so as by fire (I CORINTHIANS 3:11–15). It behooves us to lay up our treasures in heaven.

Toppled Trees

One autumn, a great hurricane ripped across the middle Atlantic states and left a swath of toppled trees. A great pine tree, almost a hundred feet tall, blew over on the roof of my kitchen, ripped a hole four by five feet in the roof and brought a stream of water into the house. When the storm subsided, I went out and examined the root structure of the great pine and was amazed to see how shallow it was. Although it had spread out in a large circumference, seeking its food from far surfaces, it had no taproot to anchor it; the storm had bent it over with ease. As I drove through the countryside during the days after the storm, studying the effects of the wind, I saw hundreds of such trees, similarly uprooted. I decided to replace the fallen monarch, not with another pine, but with a tree that would develop a strong taproot. Although I would not live to see it, the years would strengthen and beautify the tree so it would stand and withstand the gales of the future.

People are like trees in many ways. Some are brittle and snap with easy pressure; some bow before the winds of adversity; some stand the severest tempest and live through the ages, like the cedars of Lebanon and the oaks of Mamre. So should the Christian be able to stand. If the dry rot of sin is not infecting the heart, the Christian should be able to withstand any pressures that life may bring.

Two Russian Fortunes

During the Russian Revolution, a certain nobleman had all of his goods seized by the Bolsheviks. An Englishman living in Russia be-friended him, took him and his family to his own home, provided all expenses and gave him the necessary money to leave the country. Some time later the Englishman returned to London and found himself a wealthy man. The Russian friend had not only accounted for every penny, he had also invested so wisely that a fortune had amassed in the Englishman's account.

At the same time, another Englishman in Russia refused to deprive himself; he helped no one, but worked hard to gather a fortune in rubles—only to see it valueless as straw. Forced to flee, he arrived in London penniless and so he remained. Both of these men had been diligent: the latter in a selfish cause, the former in an unselfish one.

The Christian must exercise his zeal to provide himself with a fortune in Heaven that cannot be corrupted; he must give of himself instead of acquiring an earthly currency that has no exchange value at heaven's frontier.

Christians, Carnal

The Perfume Bottle

A man, visiting Paris, bought a bottle of perfume and brought it into the United States under his customs deduction. The perfume was very expensive and in a beautiful bottle. His wife was delighted and used it freely. Even after the perfume was used up she kept the bottle on her boudoir table to impress friends. They came into her room and exclaimed, "Oh, how wonderful—such-and-such a perfume." A function turned up and the woman longed for some of the expensive scent, but the bottle was empty, so she put a handkerchief into the bottle and closed it. Enough of the perfume was left to give a faint fragrance to the handkerchief but after that it was done. Enough odor remained around the bottle however to elicit, "Oh, that was such-and-such," from friends.

Many people in our churches are like that. As far as they are concerned, their bottle is empty. They have no life and fragrance of Christ.

I told the story that way once, and at the close of the meeting, as I walked down the street to my hotel, I overtook three people who had attended the church service. One of them was saying, "I liked the story he told about the perfume bottle because it reminded me of a very expensive perfume that Frank brought me from Paris. It is a beautiful bottle. But I have never broken the seal. It sits right there on my dresser and the light shines through it. It is a beautiful amber."

When I broke into the conversation, they recognized me and laughed that I had overheard them. I said, "Don't you see that the perfume was given to you for use? And what an illustration that is. Too many Christians have been given so much, yet they keep it tightly sealed in themselves. No one passing near would know for a moment that they have the life of God in them, for not the tiniest particle of the essence is allowed to come forth. The wonderful thing about God's perfume is that as fast as we waft it forth He keeps filling the bottle; its fragrance may change and grow, but it is more glorious every time we send it forth. That is God's way." "Now thanks be unto God, which always causeth us to triumph in Christ, and maketh manifest the savour of his knowledge by us in every place" (II CORINTHIANS 2:14).

Worldliness

A young minister, starting off in his first parish, had an elderly woman warn him against a woman in the congregation. He was not to entrust this woman with any spiritual task because according to the gossip, she was "worldly." The pastor had already been apprised of the true situation and defended the accused woman. His informant persisted: the woman in question danced, drank cocktails, smoked and used too much makeup. The pastor knew his Scripture; he answered, "On the contrary, you have not told me one item that would make me think she is worldly. She is what the Scripture calls 'carnal'; you are the one who is worldly." The aghast woman protested that she did not do this, she did not do that; she abstained from this, she avoided that. The minister replied, "Nevertheless, you are the worldly one. All the things you mentioned against her are in the realm of the flesh. You are worldly because you are the one who wishes power and who loves display. You want to be the head of organizations. You delight in show and position. When the various circles met in different homes, the other women finally returned to the church for the meetings because none of them could keep up with you. When the women went to your house, you made an ostentatious show of your linen, your china, your crystal. As you have no children, you have more income to spend on other things. Your conversation concerned the cloth and napkins you bought in the Azores, the ornaments from Dresden, the antiques from a little shop in England. Your supposed coat of arms is framed in a prominent place on your wall; every time anyone remarked on any of your heirlooms you explained from which ancestor it had come and described, without understatement, his particular honors in life."

For the average Christian there is widespread confusion as to what constitutes worldliness and what constitutes carnality.

World Maps

You can't put a round world on a flat map. Mercator's projection distorts the polar regions in order to get more accuracy near the equator. Other projections have other distortions; all are faulty in some manner. Most important in modern warfare is the azimuthal projection that shows the shortest lines between two points, it shows the shortest way from New York to China as directly over the North Pole. On all such maps the distortion increases geometrically away from the point of projection (center) until the geographical shapes near the edge of the map become almost unrecognizable.

In spiritual matters the map of life for the unsaved man or the carnal Christian is projected on the center of self; everything away from self is distorted. Only when the constraining love of Christ (II CORINTHIANS 5:14) moves us from the center of self to the new sphere of Christ can we bring all things into relationship with reality. The Greek word of separate in I ROMANS 1 is *aphorizo;* note that our word "horizon" is kin to it. When we are separated unto God, we are moved from the distorted horizon around the center of self to the perfect horizon center of Christ.

Christian Service

The Fellow Whom a Job Has

Charles F. Kettering of General Motors once said that he didn't want any fellow "who has a job working for me." Kettering wanted a fellow whom a job has. The job must get the fellow, not the fellow get the job. That job should get hold of this young man so hard that no matter where he is the job has got him for keeps. That job should have him in its clutches when he goes to bed at night. In the morning, that same job should be sitting on the foot of his bed telling him it's time to get up and go to work. When a job gets a fellow that way, he'll amount to something.

If the world's industrial leaders desire this kind of service from those who are their lieutenants, what kind of service does our Lord have the right to demand of us? We are to be "instant in season, out of season . . ." (II TIMOTHY 4:2); we are to be "in diligence not slothful, fervent in spirit, serving the Lord" (ROMANS 12:11, RV). When we have done all those things that are commanded, we must say, "We are unprofitable servants: we have done that which was our duty to do"

(LUKE 17:10). But we serve the best Master man ever had; living with Him will make our work for Him live.

Citizenship

The Drunken Driver

Many years ago, parked on the street of a large city on the West Coast, I witnessed an accident just a few yards away. A car wove crazily through traffic and collided head-on with another car. The driver, obviously drunk, was pushed from his seat by a companion who took the wheel, and awaited the arrival of a policeman. The pseudo-driver complained bitterly to the policeman that the driver of the wrecked car was at fault. I spoke up immediately, showed where I had been seated, and told how the exchange of drivers was effected. I identified the drunken man as the actual driver at the time of the accident. There was a growl from the crowd that had gathered: Why should I interfere, they wanted to know. I answered, "There is a matter of right and wrong here. This good driver is being accused of bad driving; actually, the fault is this drunk's. I was not twenty feet away when the other man took his place and removed him from behind the wheel. If this man perjures himself in court, by swearing that he was driving, I will come from Philadelphia to testify against him, and I will identify this drunken driver by the scar on his cheek." The policeman took my card; I gave my name and address to the innocent victim. As I returned to my own car, bystanders cursed me. I don't know why they were against the law. Perhaps they figured that the penalty would be less for the innocent driver than for the drunk; perhaps they knew the latter personally. Whatever caused their attitude, they were violating every principle of righteousness—human or divine—they were failing to hold fast to that which is good. They were willing to be party to perjury, the friend of wrong, willing to see an innocent man condemned. They were not willing to stand for truth, honesty and right.

A Christian must stand up and be counted wherever there is a moral issue. If it is necessary, a Christian must be willing to lose two or three days' pay to go to court to testify on the side of truth. A Christian must be willing to take the sneers of the world of evil, which hates those who stand for righteousness without regard for cost.

Compassion

The Drab Typist

One evening in New York, I said to a group, "You who have any place of leadership, turn your smile on the little underlings who will never have a place of leadership." A few weeks later I was reminded of my words by a young woman who was private secretary to the president of a large commercial firm. A brilliant personality, she had risen to her privileged and highly-paid place by her rare gifts. The day after she heard me speak, she walked through her outer offices and saw a typist, whose sallowness of personality was due to a certain loneliness. The secretary invited her to lunch. The two girls lunched together, and the drab girl thanked the brilliant one at least a score of times for her kindness. During the next few weeks the private secretary greeted the typist, smiled at her, occasionally lunched with her.

The brilliant one said to me, "It is a trifle embarrassing. She looks at me like a dog at his master, and some of the other girls can't understand my interest in her." After a few weeks the drab girl came to the knowledge of Jesus Christ and the secretary said to me, "I don't think I have ever been happier than when she prayed with me and thanked the Lord Jesus for bringing me into her life, and for the salvation of her soul. "And now," she continued, "I try to smile at all the file clerks, and the lesser assistants, and say a cheery word to the porters and elevator operators. Some day I shall be able to follow up my gestures with a word for Christ."

We underestimate the number of lonely hearts that are in every neighborhood. If we have been blessed with robust vigor, we should turn our strength toward the feeble and the weak.

Conscience

The Sundial

The conscience may be likened to a sundial that is made for the sun, even as the conscience, rightly directed, reflects God's will. Suppose a sundial is consulted by moonlight—the dial may read ten o'clock, but it may be only two. By a candle or some other light, the dial may be made to tell any hour, at the whim of the one who holds the light.

Conscience, which man took from Satan, can be a safe guide only if it is turned toward God for His illumination. Once a man turns away his conscience from God and lets some other light shine upon it, his conscience is no longer reliable.

Contentment

The African Porters

A missionary told about getting a company of bearers to carry his goods through an African trail. They went along day after day, the missionary forcing them, because he was anxious to get to his destination. They were all at full stop one morning; the missionary impatiently said, "Why don't they get up and start?" The headman replied, "No, massa, they're not moving today. They all say they have to wait a day for their souls to catch up with their bodies."

A great many people in our country need to wait a while to let their souls catch up with their bodies. So many people are in movement, and too often the movement is that of a merry-go-round. It has jingle; it has noise; it has movement, but it never gets anywhere. Now they need to come and rest in the Lord and to know how the Lord is taking care of us.

Being the Joneses

I saw a cartoon recently that illustrates American suburbia—perhaps all of America. The cartoon showed one of those household tragedies where one mate was screaming at the other; the caption read, in effect, "You are not content with trying to keep up with the Joneses. You want to be the Joneses with whom everyone else is trying to keep up."

To such attitudes comes the Christian command: ". . . be content with such things as ye have . . ." (HEBREWS 13:5)

Five Pounds

Lord Congleton overheard one of his servants say, "Oh! if I only had five pounds, I would be perfectly content." He thought the matter over and decided that he would like to see someone "perfectly content," so he walked into the kitchen, and handed the woman a five-pound note (then about $25.00). She thanked him profusely. He left the kitchen, but paused outside the door for a moment. As soon as she thought he was out of earshot, the woman complained bitterly, "Why on earth didn't I say ten pounds?"

The human heart can never find contentment in the things of this earth. We are told by God to be content if we have the necessities of life, and to be content with such things as we have. Paul learned to be content, regardless of the state he was in. It is still true that "godliness with contentment is great gain" (I TIMOTHY 6:6).

No Two Things Alike

No two blades of grass are alike. No two grains of sand are alike. The invention of the microscope was able to confirm a fact that had been known in the sphere of the great to be true also in the sphere of the small. God never repeated Himself in his work. A photographer, who succeeded in photographing more than ten thousand snowflakes, found each one of different design and all were mathematically perfect.

God never made any two people alike. Although we have our varying personalities and diverse needs, complete satisfaction in all things is to be found in the heavenly Father. For our infinite needs we have an infinite Lord. Come just as you are; you will find that the One who made the blades of grass and the grains of sand will take you to Himself in a newness of reality that will give you perfect peace and satisfaction.

Sheep

A shepherd, who had spent many years with flocks on the hills of Scotland, asked me if I had ever seen a sheep eat while lying down. When I confessed that I had not, he told me that no one had ever seen a sheep eat in that position. "If a sheep is lying down," he continued, "there may be a lovely tuft of grass within an inch of her nose, but she will not eat it. She will scramble to her feet, lean over and eat the grass that was in easier reach before."

When the Lord, our Shepherd, makes us lie down in green pastures, we have so much, we just can't take any more; we are beside the still waters, we have slaked our thirst with the contentment that comes alone from Him.

Convictions

Eric Liddell

In the summer of 1924 the young Scot, Eric Liddell, faced two great moments of his life: As a student of the ministry he was soon to be ordained; as an aspiring sprinter he was favored to bring glory to England by winning the 100-meter dash at the Olympic games in Paris.

When Liddell discovered that this event was scheduled for a Sunday afternoon, it was a crucial moment for him; he believed that it was not to the glory of God for him to compete on Sunday.

The young Scot made one major change in his daily round of study and athletic practice; he dropped his customary nightly discussion with his classmates. After the evening meal he left the dining hall, disappeared, and returned to his room hours later, tired and spent. His friends were perplexed, but he never told them where he went.

The whole world learned his secret, at the Olympics. Eric Liddell, received the Gold Medal as 400-meter champion.

Eric Liddell not only made a record for speed in the 400-meter class; he made a record of God's work in a man's heart, and a testimony to faithfulness. Eric Liddell was faithful in one thing, and the Lord honored him in another.

God needs men and women who are willing thus to be made strong for Him—to go forward without compromise. Even if you do not become a champion and receive the plaudits of the world, the day will come when you may stand on God's winners' platform and hear Him say: ". . . Well done, thou good and faithful servant: thou hast been faithful over a few things, I will make thee ruler over many things: enter thou into the joy of thy lord" (MATTHEW 25:21).

Cults

The Practical Joke

Many years ago, when I was just in my teens, a group of friends and I decided to play a practical joke on some unthinking passersby. We went to a busy intersection and stared intently up in the air. One of us pointed, another said, loudly enough to be overheard by the passersby, "It is not." A third member argued, "It is so." One or two people stopped and began to look in the same direction we were looking and pointing. As our argument grew more heated, others stopped to gaze fixedly at the point our group discussed. One by one we slipped out of the crowd; we regathered a few yards down the street to watch the result of our strategem. By this time about fifteen people were looking and talking. One man who had left the group said to another, "I think it is a balloon." (Remember this was about 1915 or 1916). The crowd continued to change; as new passersby came along they joined the group, and those who had been staring longest left. Twenty minutes later several people were still looking upward; several had drawn off to the side and were leaning against a building, looking upward for something that was not there and never had been there.

That little incident is a good illustration of all the earth-born religions. People talk about having faith; they tell you to look in a direction where there is absolutely nothing. Some people are so desperately in need of seeing something that they will look till they are almost blind, yet they never catch a glimpse of anything real. Their persistence in looking for something that does not exist reduces their vision to see the truth, which they really do not want to find.

Death

The Dying Shepherd

A Scottish story tells of a fearful old man who lay dying. The minister, an understanding man, asked him if he had not been a shepherd. The old man replied that he had watched the sheep many a day. "And," asked the minister, "did you never stand on the hillside and watch the wind drive a cloud across the valley?" "Many a time," said the old man. "And when the shadow of that cloud came racing along the heather, coming toward you and your flock, were you afraid?" The old man drew himself up on his elbow and cried, "Afraid of a shadow? Jamie has covenanter's blood in his veins, and he has never been afraid of anything." And then the wonder of the passage broke upon him as the minister read, "Yea, though I walk through the valley of the *shadow* of death, I will fear no evil."

It is only the shadow of death that can touch the believer. The grim reality of death laid hold upon our Shepherd, as it must one day lay hold upon those who are not His sheep, but the shadow of death is all that can ever touch the one to whom He has given life eternal.

Home from the Armed Forces

An aged mother talks constantly about the return of her son who is in the armed forces. "When John comes, he will take me riding." "When John comes, he will dig the garden." "When John comes, he will fix that shelf." "When John comes, he. . . ." "When John comes, he . . ." One day there is a step on the stair; the door opens and the delighted mother cries out, "John, you. . . ." Why does she change the pronoun? The answer, of course, is that John has come in; and she is no longer speaking of an absent one; he is one who is there in her presence.

With this in mind let us read the twenty-third Psalm. "The Lord is my shepherd, I shall not want; He maketh me to lie down in green pastures: he leadeth me beside the still waters. He restored my soul: he leadeth me in the paths of righteousness for his name's sake." *"He . . . he . . . he. . . ."*

But let death approach us and see the marvelous change. "Yea, though I walk through the valley of the shadow of death, I will fear no evil: for thou art with me; thy rod and thy staff they comfort me." *"Thou . . . thy . . . thy. . . ."*

It is not alone that He is with me, or that His rod and staff shall comfort me in that hour. That would indeed be comfort, but the comfort of an absent Lord is somewhat like the comfort given by the photograph of a loved one in comparison with the warm embrace of one that is loved. So it is when death comes, there shall be no more parting. Then shall we speak no more of the Lord as distant on the throne of Heaven. Then the door of Heaven has swung open. Then He has moved to the bedside of the dying one.

The Murals of Puvis de Chavannes

In Boston for a few hours, I went to the public library to look once again at the wonderful mural paintings there. Some of Puvis de Chavannes' most wonderful work is there. One of his paintings typifies modern invention and intercommunication; wires are stretched through his picture, indicating the telegraph; two beautiful figures painted with the thrill of speed vivifying them, hasten with their messages. One is all in white, bearing an olive branch—message of good tidings. The other is in black; the hand that is not guided by the wire covers the face of the angel messenger of death.

Unhappy the home this Resurrection Day that does not have the Lord Jesus there to take the hand away from the face of death and let us see that it is no longer a grim and dread messenger. He has destroyed its power forever. He lives who once was dead.

Discipline of Children

The Hole in the Fence

A father told his son the story of the lost sheep: it found the hole in the fence and crawled through—how glad it was to get away—it wandered so far it couldn't find its way back. Then he told the boy about the wolf that chased the sheep, and of the shepherd who came and found the sheep and carried it back home. The little boy had only one question: "Did they fix the hole in the fence?"

Preventive care for a child is far more important than work among juvenile delinquents. The only proper way to fix the hole in the fence is to lead the child to a knowledge of his own sinfulness and his need of the Lord Jesus Christ.

The Missing Penny

One day we took a street car out to the Cleveland, Ohio, airport. Two girls, of four and five, got on at a kindergarten and got off again near their home. The fare for school children was a penny. One little girl put her penny in the conductor's box; the other, standing on tiptoe, made a movement as though she were putting the penny in. The fingers opened, but there was no rattle. The hand was empty. The conductor asked her where her penny was. First she said that she lost it; then that her mother had not given her one. He scolded her severely, and, of course, let her off; she ran away with a gesture of contempt. When the car had started once more, the conductor said, "Some mothers are terrible. Every day we have children who are taught to lie, and mothers are surprised that they grow up wrong."

We agree that too much attention cannot be paid to little things, but Christian parents should certainly be meticulous in teaching their children what we might call the pagan virtues—virtues which even the unsaved expect to have.

Obeying a Five-Year-Old

In a large hotel, I heard a mother ask her five-year-old child if she might leave the table in order to go and see someone across the room. She explained that she would be back in a moment. The child answered with a blatant, "No." The mother asked pleadingly two or three times more, and the child said, "No, if you go, I'll not eat my meal at all today." The mother sat there helpless; by her own lack of discipline she had created a monster who now ruled her.

Prayerful discipline of children in a biblically stern fashion is one of the most important Christian doctrines. It is included in the commandment, "Honor thy father and thy mother." Any parent who fails to enforce this commandment by disciplining his children is guilty of definite sin against God. Christian parents should see to it that the wills of their children are brought into subjection to the parents' will on all matters where it is right to have such discipline. The wills should be guided to self-choice of the right wherever possible, but if the child will not accept the right with his own will, he should be forced to accept it prayerfully, and if necessary with the utmost chastisement. "He that spareth his rod, hateth his son . . ." (PROVERBS 13:24). This is the definite Word of God, and its application by parents is an act of believing faith.

The Screaming Child

An item in the *New York Times* reported a court case of a mother who brought a nine-year-old son into Juvenile Court; the boy screamed, stamped on the floor and pounded with his fists. The court psychiatrist said, "It is sheer blackmail. He screams to blackmail his mother. When he gets his own way, he stops screaming. He has been heard to tell his younger brother to scream for what he wants. Now the younger boy has become a kind of deputy screamer." The boy was perfectly normal at school and only screamed for his mother. The psychiatrist said, "This is an extreme case of individualism, and the symptoms are a pathological manifestation."

These are long words for what the Bible would call an outburst of the "old Adam." If the child had been spanked when he was a baby and refused his own way, he would not have grown up to blackmail his mother. If the first time the child had ever screamed, he had had a sound application of the "board of education to the seat of knowledge" the screaming would not have been repeated. The Bible says, "Train up a child in the way he should go: and when he is old, he will not depart from it" (PROVERBS 22:6).

Discipline of God

The Arm Amputation

One of my dearest friends, a man of my own age, lost his left arm at the shoulder when he was only seven years old. Until he was twelve, he cried himself to sleep every night. It was hard to regard this amputation as the good, well-pleasing and perfect will of God. Then he began to conquer his handicap. By tucking a longhandled hoe under his armpit, he learned to hoe as many rows as his brothers; and he didn't get as tired as they did hoeing, for in using two arms they overworked their wrists. Later, he sold life insurance and was a success. He learned to play handball, soon beat all comers, and held the national championship for many years. One day he learned that a thirteen-year-old boy had just gone through the same amputation. The boy had no will to live, and his condition was rapidly worsening. My friend took his scrapbook and went to the hospital to see the boy. Nothing was said about the arm, but the boy looked at the various newspaper clippings that recounted the one-armed champion's prowess at golf, hunting and fishing. Finally, he asked if it were really true. My friend removed his shirt and showed his armless shoulder. The boy sighed deeply and soon fell asleep. Three days later he was on the mend, and soon after left the hospital. My friend has spent his life with insurance, athletics and Christian work among young people, in that ascending order of importance; he has testified many times to his satisfaction with life and with the will of God for him. It was not well-pleasing at first, to be the town cripple, but the compensations were so great that he soon learned that God's way was the best way for him, and he would not have it any other way.

Whenever we recognize the rights of God and trust in the Lord Jesus Christ as Saviour, He takes up this work of discipline in order to give us His best.

Discrimination Between Good and Evil

Poison and Clear Water

There are poisons that look like crystal spring water. A glass of such poison, placed next to a glass of clear water will fool the eye; the two look exactly alike. But one has death in it, the other life. You have to discover by other means than drinking the true nature of the two liquids.

In the same way there are many things in life that are deadly, but have the seeming appearance of goodness. This is why, when you must make a choice about some pleasure, amusement, or action, you must not come to your decision on the basis of appearances.

Pouting Baby

In a hotel, I watched a mother tell her child to come inside. The child, about two or three years old, rebelled with no uncertain terms and gestures. The mother said nothing and started toward the stairs. The child came inside and stamped her feet. The mother continued on upstairs and out of sight. The crying child went to the foot of the stairs, and started slowly up, stopping occasionally to stamp and cry louder. The mother was nowhere to be seen. I followed the child; eventually she reached the top of the stairs, turned down the hall and entered a room.

The scene comes back to me again and again as an illustration of how so many of God's children act with Him. He gives His commands, and the Holy Spirit has told us that they are not grievous. Yet we stamp our petulant way, step by step, drawing back from what is certainly better than our own choice, and ultimately we make a little progress.

Reading the Newspaper

I know a man who spends considerable time each day reading the newspaper. He can tell you the doings of all the comic-strip characters and the standing of all the great baseball teams. Ask him about the tension between China and Russia, or what is being done to help the emerging peoples of Africa, and you will draw an absolute blank. He is simply not interested. He is wise to that which is ephemeral, but ignorant of any of the great issues that will affect his life and the life of his children.

It is the desire of God that we grow in our knowledge of all that is good, and that we remain naïve concerning that which is evil. We must develop a Christian life that excludes the worthless and builds the worthwhile.

Eternal Life

Dead Leaves

Shortly after the Armistice of World War I, I visited the battlefields of Belgium. In the first year of the war the area around the city of

Mons was the scene of the great British retreat; in the last year of the war it was the scene of the greater German retreat. For miles to the west of the city the roads were lined with artillery, tanks, trucks and other material of war which the Germans had abandoned in their hasty flight.

It was a lovely day in spring; the sun was shining; not a breath of wind was blowing. As I walked along examining the German war material, I noticed that leaves were falling from the great trees that arched above the road. I brushed at a leaf that had blown against my breast; it became caught in the belt of my uniform. As I picked it out I pressed it in my fingers, and it disintegrated. I looked up curiously and saw several other leaves falling from the trees. It was not autumn. There was no wind to blow them off. These were the leaves that had outlived the winds of autumn and the frosts of winter.

Now they were falling, seemingly without cause. Then I realized that the most potent force of all was causing them to fall. It was spring; the sap was beginning to run; the buds were beginning to push from within. From down beneath the dark earth, the roots were taking life and sending it along trunk, branch and twig, until that life expelled every bit of deadness that remained from the previous year. It was, as a great Scottish preacher termed it, "the expulsive power of a new affection."

In the measure that we allow the new life of God to fill our being, that life will naturally care for the question of what we do and how we act as Christians.

The Insurance Salesman

An insurance salesman once told me that he had schooled himself to think constantly in terms of selling life insurance. When he met a man for the first time, he was alert for an opportunity to sell insurance. Even at a social function, a church service, a funeral or a wedding, he sought to form acquaintances in order to get new customers. He joined a lodge and took up golf, in order to meet men and approach them about life insurance. He spoke to the attendant at the gas station, to the clerk in the grocery store, to shoe salesmen, and to the tailor who made his suits. Consequently, he sold a lot of life insurance.

Paul had this same type of mind, but he pleaded with the lost to take eternal life insurance; and for those who knew Christ, his desire was that they might grow.

Live Soldiers

Imagine a battlefield with troops advancing under heavy fire. They flatten themselves to the ground and hold their prone position until the enemy artillery is silenced. Imagine further that all of the soldiers are either dead, or alive and unwounded. He that gets up and walks has life. Does that mean that life is given to the soldiers who get up and walk or that the soldiers who possess life manifest it by getting up and walking? It is obvious that the latter can be the only meaning.

This meaning is illustrated in the passage in the fourth gospel: "He that heareth my word, and believeth on him that sent me, hath everlasting life . . ." (JOHN 5:24). The hearing and believing are the marks of the existence of the new life of God implanted within the individual.

The Lovers

Think of a couple in love; it is autumn and they know they cannot be married until the end of the school year. Before long the young man says, "Darling, think! we will be married in just two hundred and fifty days!" The two delight in counting off the days: the two hundred and thirties, the two hundred and twenties; one hundred and ninety-nine days is a landmark. The numbers decrease, but slowly, oh! so slowly; it is the one hundred day mark. Ninety days, sixty days, thirty days, ten days, tomorrow! All true lovers know this loving groaning toward their day of hope, the consummation of their joy. This was the purpose of their falling in love, that they might be together, that they might be one.

When God planted eternal life within us, it was nothing less than the life of eternity that is to be lived in time, and we groan while we wait for its fulfillment.

Eternal Security

Belongingness

A young pastor attending summer sessions at a State University heard a visiting lecturer of psychology speak of the importance of security in the normal development of a child. The professor said, "Security is that feeling of 'belongingness' which is based not on what one is, but on who one is." The child may be naughty, yet still enjoy the security of the parental home simply because he is a child of the parents.

How well that sentence illustrates our security in the heavenly family! We are saved because of what Jesus Christ is; we know it because of what He says. The fact that we feel secure is, of course, based not on what we are, but on who we are. The whole denial of the security of the believer by those who teach that a person may be lost after he is truly born again is based on self-works. Those who believe in the security of the believer are giving glory to the Lord. We are saved, and boasting is excluded. Is it not wonderful to know that "the peace that passeth all understanding" is based not on what we are, but on who we are? "We are the sons of God, therefore the world knoweth us not," but we can say, "Behold, what manner of love the Father hath bestowed upon us . . ." because He has made us the children of God (I JOHN 3:1).

Duplicate Bills

A cleaner and dyer had to take his accounts home one night because his bookkeeper was ill. By mistake he sent out several hundred statements to people who had already received similar statements some weeks before. Some of his customers wrote or called, questioning their bills; they showed receipts that proved them paid. The cleaner apologized and explained his error. But to his amazement about one-third of the accounts were paid a second time. People were careless about their own bookkeeping and relied upon his honesty; they sent in their check a second time. The cleaner set up a system: he sent bills promptly on the first of each month, but the bills overlapped—each included work done over a period of about thirty-five days. If anyone complained his name was removed from the special list and correct bills were sent thereafter. But his list of those who paid double was a profitable one for him.

One day, however, four men came into the clubhouse after playing golf. One of them pulled an envelope out of his pocket and said, "I think so-and-so has a very poor bookkeeper. I think I paid that cleaning bill last month." Another man said, "I had exactly the same experience with him." A third man said, "So did I." The fourth man said, "I have been paying my bills as they came in, but I thought them rather steep." They all agreed that it looked rather crooked, and when more men came into the locker room and joined the conversation, they decided to turn the matter over to the Better Business Bureau. It was not long before an investigation brought up the indisputable evidence of the systematic practice of collecting accounts twice, and the man was sent to prison.

The man who holds that a believer may get out of the body of Christ, may undo the baptism of the Holy Spirit, and leave the identification with Christ on the cross, is, in reality, making out that God is a chiseler. Having collected the account in full from the Saviour, God now seeks to collect a second time on an account that He Himself once receipted in full by the resurrection of His Son from the dead. What God does is well done, and eternally done. The Christian has been identified with the death of Christ in the complete removal of his guilt and his consequent justification in the sight of God.

Giving Away a Soul

Martin Luther had a servant named Elizabeth, who, in a fit of displeasure, left without giving any notice. She subsequently became dangerously ill and asked Luther to visit her. He said, "Well, Elizabeth, what is the matter?" "I have given away my soul to Satan," she replied. "Elizabeth, listen to me," rejoined the man of God. "Suppose, while you lived in my house, you had sold and transferred all my children to a stranger. Would the sale and transfer have been lawful and binding?" "Oh, no, for I had no right to do that." "Very well, you had still less right to give your soul to the archenemy; it no more belongs to you than my children do. It is the exclusive property of the Lord Jesus Christ; He made it, and when lost, He redeemed it; it is His."

Anyone who believes that one who has been truly born of God can get out of relationship with God and be finally lost is blind to great sections of truth in the Word of God. They look at some experiences in life instead of at the Word of God; they judge the Word by what they see in life, rather than judging life by what they see in the Word.

Seals

In modern times the use of the official seal is diminishing, but official documents are still marked with a seal. On a United States passport, the seal of the nation is crushed into the fabric of the paper so that it would be impossible to eradicate or alter it. Corporations still have seals, and these are affixed to legal documents. A notary has a seal that confirms the oath of an affidavit with that seal. In ancient times each man had his own seal and carried it with him at all times. Most people could not write, so the seal was affixed as a mark of the individual's responsibility. Today we know that the signature of an individual cannot be duplicated without chancing detection as forgery. The signature takes the place of the seal. If you add together everything that is confirmed by an official seal and a personal signature, you get the idea of the biblical meaning of the seal. ". . . grieve not the Holy Spirit of God, whereby ye are sealed unto the day of redemption" (EPHESIANS 4:30).

Salvation is not dependent upon the whim of an individual Christian, but upon the justifying work of God. The Holy Spirit is implanted once and for all; when the believer is placed in Christ by the Holy Spirit, the same lord—the blessed third person of the Godhead—puts the seal of certainty upon us and shuts us into Christ. We are not only saved, we are safe.

The Spring Freshet

During the spring freshet an express train rode confidently through a flooded area even though the tracks were covered with water. The steel rails underneath accounted for the confidence of the engineer and the safety of the train.

No matter what flood covers the path of the believer, he can go forward with true courage. God has traced his way for him.

Eternity

Memory

As we grow older the years seem to pass much more quickly than in the days of our youth. A chemist offers an interesting formula to explain this. A child of eight remembers about four years back—one year, or 25 percent of the total. By the time the child is twelve he remembers eight years, and one year is only 12 $^1/_2$ percent of the total. All through life the ratio continues to dwindle, in old age a single year represents only a small fraction of man's remembered time—it vanishes into the past at a rapid speed.

But with the child of God, who has entered the path of the justified ones, which shineth more and more unto the perfect day (PROVERBS 4:18), there is a reversal of the process. God has put eternity into the heart of the believer (ECCLESIASTES 3:11, RSV); time becomes relatively unimportant, its passage leaves no regrets, brings delight that the fullness of eternity approaches at such a rapid pace. But that swiftly passing time is to be redeemed (EPHESIANS 5:16), for the days are evil, and the Lord has entrusted us with time for His purposes.

Faith

The Broken Bridge

Faith is worthless in itself. If faith is not properly founded, it can lead to nothing other than disaster. One night cars sped along the main highway between Jackson and Vicksburg, Mississippi. The drivers had faith in their cars and in the bridges over the streams. They passed over some bridges at fifty or sixty miles per hour. Everything was lovely, the concrete spans stood firm over the rivers and bayous, and the cars went on their way. Suddenly, the twin taillights in front of a truck melted into the road and disappeared. The driver of the truck caught only a glimpse of a black gap in the concrete before he too plunged into the stream below. Breaking glass, he succeeded in freeing himself. He swam ashore, but before he could reach the highway, other cars zoomed smoothly up to the gap and vanished. Frantically, he tried to flag three others. Their drivers ignored the dripping, scarecrow figure and sped on into the void. Each time there was a single booming splash, sometimes followed by a few hoarse shouts and screams.

All the drivers had faith in a bridge that was out. There is only one bridge across the gulf of death. Christ has said, "No man cometh unto the Father, but by me" (JOHN 14:6). Woe to the man who attempts any other highway. His faith will carry him to a Christian eternity and not to heaven. Faith must have a proper foundation— Christ.

Captain of the Guards

It is said that Napoleon, while looking at some papers, let slip the bridle of his horse, which reared so that the Emperor was in danger. A corporal of the grenadiers leaped forward and caught the bridle, bringing the horse under control. Napoleon saluted the corporal and said, "Thank you, Captain." "Of what company, Sire?" asked the corporal. "Of my guards," replied Napoleon. The young corporal picked up his musket, hurled it aside and walked across the field toward the Emperor's staff, tearing off his corporal's stripes as he went. When he took his place among the officers, they asked him what he was doing. He replied that he was a captain of the guards. "By whose order?" queried one of them. "The Emperor's order," he replied.

The incident may never have taken place, but the truth involved is supreme. God is ready to do a great deal for you, if you are ready to take Him at His word. A man of less faith might have picked up his musket, stepped back into the ranks and boasted for the rest of his life that Napoleon had called him captain. This describes the difference between the Christian of little faith who has a head knowledge of the position and titles which the Lord Jehovah has given each believer in Christ, and the Christian of applied faith, who takes God at His word and enters into the blessing.

Hyssop

Botanists have not been able to agree on the identification of the plant, hyssop, that is mentioned in the Scriptures. It certainly has no relationship to the plant of the same name that has been domesticated in parts of our country. But a verse in Kings speaks of the wisdom of Solomon, who studied many things: "the hyssop that springeth out of the wall" (I KINGS 4:33). I saw a plant that fulfills this description in Palestine, under interesting conditions. The first time I was in Jerusalem I was taken into the palace of the Grand Mufti and then into the Hall of the Sanhedrin, where few tourists ever penetrate. In this room is a window that looks down upon the wailing wall. At the foot of the wall, beating their heads slowly against it, were groups of Jewish rabbis, mostly from central Europe, and as they bowed forward they wailed—reciting the book of Lamentations over and over again.

Above their heads was the high expanse of wall, and from it grew the long trailing plant that was identified as the hyssop of the Bible. The remarkable thing about this particular plant is that it has a very short root—sometimes not over half an inch long. It can cling to the surface of the rock, drawing its sustenance from the air, from the wind, from the rain when there is any, from bits of dirt that fall from above or are borne on the wind to the meager roots, or from particles of nourishment in the rock itself. From that tiny root the plant flourishes, sometimes twelve to fourteen feet long. What a great plant to grow from such a slender root. Is it any wonder the plant can be such a symbol of faith?

Faith, in itself, is worthless, just as a root is worthless if it is unattached. If one grasps the branch and pulls the root away from the rock, the branch will soon die. Faith to be of any value, must cling to the rock. Faith, nothing in itself, becomes everything when it clings to the Lord Jesus Christ, the Rock of Ages.

"If"

We constantly use the word "if" to express disbelief and to express belief. A young man might tell his parents that he was leaving the house to go to the drugstore, and his sister might look after him and say, "If you're going to the drugstore, I'm Joan of Arc." Later the mother of the household might start to leave the house, saying that she was going to the drug store, and the daughter might say, "Oh, if you're going to the drug store, bring me some tooth paste." In the one sentence she expresses doubt and disbelief; in the other sentence she expresses confidence and trust. The "if" in the text, "Now if we be dead with Christ, we believe that we shall also live with him" (ROMANS 6:8) is of the latter variety. Because we died with Christ, we believe that we shall also live with Him.

We possess that life, that new man, in and around and overshadowing all of our thoughts and actions and being. That new man not only resembles Christ, but that new man within us is Christ Himself; for we are made partakers of the divine nature, and it is Christ in us which is our hope of glory.

Plowing the Field

When I first learned to plow, I got on the seat of the tractor, pulled the lever that dropped the plow into the ground, and started across the center of the field. After I had gone a few feet, I turned around to look at the furrow and was entranced by the rushing flow of topsoil along the plowshare—rich and black, the soil turned over. Then I turned back to look where I was going. When I had turned around the first time, I had unconsciously carried the wheel of the tractor with my movement and gotten away from the straight line. I pulled the tractor back into line and looked back at the furrow once more. Behind me, wavering across the field, the undulating line of my furrow revealed, as though etched in the earth, the wandering vision that I had had.

I soon learned that there was only one way to plow a straight furrow. When you are about to accelerate the tractor and pull the lever that sinks the plow into the ground, you must sight across the field at a distant point and keep the nose of the tractor squarely on the sighting point. You must not turn around to see how the furrow is coming; if you do, give only a hasty glance to see that all is well. Make certain that the fixed point is straight ahead, and bring the eye back to it. Now I can plow across a field and leave a furrow black and straight a quarter of a mile long; because I have learned that when the guide furrow is being laid in the field, the plowman must keep his eye on a fixed point, be it a tree, a barn, a distant hill, or some other point. Woe unto the man who plows his furrow looking aside, or looking behind, or looking at a crow that may fly across his line of vision.

If we are not to waver, we must have our eyes fixed steadfastly upon the Lord Jesus Christ.

"Sukiyaki"

We received a telephone call from a Japanese girl, who had promised to cook up her native *sukiyaki*. One member of the household copied down a list of things to be bought—beef cut in a certain way, rice of a certain grade, and special vegetables—and told someone else to buy them. The Japanese girl would bring other ingredients which we could not purchase. Now this incident was an exercise in faith. The person who answered the phone believed the Japanese girl, and the other person believed her report of the conversation, so they acted on the information received. They spent money and brought home provisions, all on the basis of a few sentences in a telephone conversation.

This is exactly how we must believe God. He has given us promises, and how many and how wonderful they are! He tells us to commit ourselves to Him and believe Him, and He will work in our behalf. If you can believe what a voice says to you on the telephone, you can believe the Holy Spirit's pleading for control of your heart, where He wishes to spread a feast for you.

Through the Wall

True faith does not look at the obstacles, but rather at God. A dear old woman had a very beautiful faith; she was obedient, and obedience is the only beauty of faith. Some one said to her, "I believe that if you thought the Lord told you to jump through a stone wall, you would jump."

The old lady replied, "If the Lord told me to jump through a wall, it would be my business to jump, an it would be His business to make the hole."

It would be impossible to define more simply the exact relationship between obedience and faith. Here is the essence of true faith. Although we do not understand every step of the way by which we must walk, we are fully persuaded that whatsoever God has promised, He is able to perform (ROMANS 4:21), and we leave all of the matters that are not comprehended to the mind and heart of the God whom we know to be the loving heavenly Father, through Jesus Christ, our Lord.

Trading Stamps

One member of our household was collecting trading stamps. For months we gave her all we got in trade, and various friends saved stamps for her. One day she exclaimed that she had 8,400 stamps, sufficient to get an electric blanket. She believed the announcement and the promise made in the premium book. She telephoned the trading-stamp company and was told that the redemption store was twenty miles from our house. She believed them, got into her car and drove the twenty miles, taking the stamps with her. Two hours later she returned, proudly bearing a large package; she opened it with great glee and triumphantly displayed the electric blanket. At every step of the transaction, she exercised faith.

The faith exercised in these household transactions is exactly the same kind of faith that we need to exercise in the Christian life. If you can believe what you read in a book of instructions about trading stamps, you can believe what you read in the Bible. If we take the trading stamps of faith to the place of redemption, we shall enter into the joy of the daily premium of full contentment.

Faith and Works

Fire and Smoke

On an early May morning a man walked down the street. He was about two blocks from his house when he saw a large puff of smoke arise from his chimney. As well as though he had been standing in his living room he knew what had happened: the furnace had been allowed to die down several days before, and now a chilly spell had caused someone to light a fire in the fireplace. He was in a position to get a good view of both scenes; his physical eyes saw the smoke, his imagination saw the scene in the living room.

This is the exact difference between the epistles of Paul and James. In Paul's epistles, God tells how He looks upon the heart and justifies men by the true faith in Christ. James tells how an outward observer can see the effect of the inward faith. With Paul it is justification by faith; in James it is works by the justified which demonstrate faith. The one is a divine view, the other is human.

Rowing

You cannot row a boat properly without two oars. If you use only one, the boat will turn around and around and make no progress forward.

We must have both faith and works in the Christian life. Belief alone is not sufficient, for faith without works is dead. Works without faith will disturb the surface of the pond, but will not take the boat forward. The two must go together. Paul emphasizes faith in Romans for he is describing salvation from God's viewpoint. James emphasizes works in his epistle for he is describing salvation as men see it.

The Fall

A Sliding Scale of Penalties

We have adopted a sliding scale of penalties for what we consider a sliding scale of aggravation. We send a man to prison for ten days for stealing a dollar. He will get a sentence of ninety days for stealing ten dollars, a sentence of two years if he enters an open house and steals a moderate amount of jewelry. He will get five years if he pries open a window or a door, ten to twenty years if he steals ten thousand dollars worth of loot; if he has a blackjack or a revolver on his person at the time he commits his burglary, he may get a fifty-year sentence. No human court in the world would consider the death penalty against a man who stole some fruit from an orchard, not even if he had come with a truck and stolen all the fruit from all the trees in the orchard.

After one single act of disobedience on the part of Adam, God passed the death penalty against him, and against all of Adam's posterity to the remotest generation; not only was the sentence of condemnation passed, it was executed against every member of the human race.

Running Away

The pathetic little figure carrying the valise down the front steps of his home could not have been more than five. Around the block he trudged, and around again. He kept going around and round until it got dark. A policeman stopped him. "What's the idea?" the officer asked. "Runnin' away," explained the boy, sadly. "Look," said the officer, "I've had my eye on you and you've been doing nothing but walk around the block. Do you call that running away?" "Well, what do you want me to do?" cried the boy tearfully, "I ain't allowed to cross the street alone."

Ever since Adam fell, mankind has been running away—but God has arranged it so that man cannot run away from his fears; man cannot run away from his frustrations; man cannot run away from sin and its fruits; man cannot run away from death; man cannot run away from himself. There is only one refuge—go back into the house to God, who awaits on the other side of the cross. That is the way in and the way to peace.

False Motives

The Office Bet on the Baby

A young fellow who works in an investment house was impressed and very appreciative at the interest his business associates took in the news that his wife was going to have a baby. Every day one or more of them would drop around to his desk to inquire: "How's the wife doing?" "What does the doc say?" "Any news, old man?" "Many more days?" He did not know that every man in the office had a bet upon when the baby would arrive. The interest in his affairs really concerned a greedy desire to win the office bet.

It is possible for Christians to have false motives. This is why the Holy Spirit says, "Let love be without dissimulation" (ROMANS 12:9). The Greek says, "Let love be nonhypocritical."

Fatherhood of God

"Junior" The Impostor

Police court annals tell the story of a young man who registered at one of the leading hotels in New York shortly after the turn of the century. He wrote down one of the most famous names in the United States, and the hotel clerk was very deferential to him. He had an air of being to the manner born. When packages began to arrive from several large furnishing houses and a jewelry store, the hotel received them and paid the accounts. After a few days the time for settling came; the young man brushed them off with excuses, which aroused the suspicion of the hotel management. They notified the police and a quiet investigation revealed the startling fact that the famous man whose name the young man had written on the register with "Junior" after it, did not have a son. The young man, confronted by the authorities, put on an air of bravado; he blustered that there was some mistake. Finally, it became necessary to take him down to Wall Street, to the office of a well-known millionaire. The latter walked into the room and looked at the culprit. He said simply, "I never laid eyes on this young man before in all my life." That sealed the doom of the impostor.

Multitudes of people who claim that God is their Father are just as guilty as was this young man. In order to address the Creator of the universe as Father, an individual must have accepted the truths which make this relationship possible.

Fear

The Boatman and the Rapids

Back in the middle thirties, before the railroad was finished between Changsha and Canton, in the south of China, I went overland through hundreds of miles of the most primitive country imaginable. At one place we had to take a boat in order to travel down a river treacherous with boiling rapids. Although I had been told that the passage would be dangerous, I also knew that Chinese traders went down river in their own boats, so I assumed that the stories were exaggerated. My doubts started as we neared the rapids. Two or three miles before we plunged into the swift current, the boatman took a chicken, a knife and a bowl to the prow of the boat. He placed the bowl beneath the prow, and we moved over to the shore to a place where stairs were built into the stones of a high cliff. We made fast and followed the boatman and his helpers; they climbed several hundred steps to an altar where they placed the sacrifice and burned joss sticks on the altar. From the little temple, we could look down the gorge at the turbulent waters, and I could understand the fear of the boatmen. Only after such preparation, would they commit themselves to the swirling waters below. We, of course, were trusting in the living God who had made the waters and who controls all things. Although it was impossible for me to communicate with these men, I was able to read, written large, their sense of the supernatural—their belief in powers outside themselves and greater than themselves; it was evident that they had great fear of death and of that which might follow death.

Even paganism is shot through with the sense of sin, and the consequent sense of the fear of death and the necessity of going out to face God.

The Bride's First Meal

Several years ago I married a young couple who were, and still are, very much in love with one another. They had met when they were thirteen and fourteen, had never looked at anyone else, and wouldn't today after all these years. They went away on their honeymoon and after a few weeks came home again. I saw them in church the next Sunday and greeted them with a little pleasantry. I asked the groom if his bride had burned the roast for the first dinner. They laughed, and she said, "Oh, I was afraid that I was going to. I had read so much about the bride being unable to cook that I decided that John was going to have the very best meal a bride could prepare for her husband. So I began about three o'clock. I got everything out and started to work. When I finally put things on to cook, I wanted everything to turn out well, and I was afraid they wouldn't, and, of course, he had to be a little late, and I was so afraid things would be spoiled." I interrupted her and said, "You have said three times that you were afraid. Did you think that he was going to beat you?" She pouted and said, "Of course not." She looked at him with all the love of her heart in her eyes. "But," I persisted, "you said that you were afraid." She broke in, "You know what I mean." And of course I knew what she meant. Her fear was not fright; her fear was a great desire to serve the one to whom she had given herself entirely. In this case the fear of John was the beginning of good cooking.

Perhaps that will enable you to understand how the fear of the Lord is the beginning of wisdom. Some Christians do not understand the difference between fear of the Lord and fright of the Lord. If you have bowed before God and accepted the gift of His love and mercy through the Lord Jesus Christ, you need have no fright. Fear in the Bible sense is a godly thing, a wonderful thing, a lovely thing.

Fellowship in Christ

Broken Fellowship

One evening I was the dinner guest of a young Canadian minister in Toronto, Ontario. Seldom have I seen a child brighter or better disciplined than his beautiful little daughter, Jean, aged three, who sat at the table in her high chair. During the meal, she did some childish thing that caused her father to admonish her. "Jean," he began in a firm tone. The child looked up and raised her hand, just as a policeman might lift a hand to halt traffic. "Don't speak, Daddy," the child said, as though she were in command of the situation, and then repeated it, "Don't speak." Thus quickly had her sense of guilt been aroused. Thus quickly she felt that she had offended against love. Thus quickly did her hand arise to ward off the separation of fellowship that might come even for a moment.

The child of God who has his sense of guilt aroused, who knows that he has offended against a holy God and a loving Father, who feels the chill that comes from broken fellowship, is in a situation quite different. We need not raise our hand to say to God, "Do not speak." For God has spoken and God has acted. His words of grace and His act are the act of the cross. If for a moment I am tempted to lift my hand as though to ward off some blow from Him, I hear Him say, "Put down your hand, child. Fear not. I did not spare My Son: I delivered Him up for you. You have all things in Him."

The Fall on the Deck

A man, walking along the deck of a ship, might fall. His fall might hurt him, but it would not be the same as falling off the ship.

The believer, when he sins, has "fallen on the deck," but he certainly has not gone overboard. When a man is born again, he cannot be unborn. He may get out of fellowship, but he cannot get out of relationship. God has made provision for restoring him to fellowship. Christ will see to it that no wave—death, life, angels, principalities, powers, things present, things to come, height, depth—shall ever sweep us off the deck.

The Lost Watch

A man who operated an icehouse lost a good watch in the saw-dust. He offered a reward, and men went through the saw-dust with rakes, but they were not able to find the watch. When the searchers left the building for lunch, a small boy went into the icehouse; a few minutes later he came out with the watch. They asked him how he had found it, and he replied, "I just lay down in the sawdust and listened. Finally I heard the watch ticking."

Some of you have lost more than a watch. If you will be very still and listen quietly, the Lord will speak to you and show you just where you lost the power and the victory which you so sorely miss. Then you will find it again—through the Lord Jesus Christ—as He shows you how sin came and interfered, and how you can get back into fellowship and peace.

The Wayward Sheep

A Scotch shepherd had a sheep that ate from his hand and followed him everywhere. When he was asked to explain the close relationship, the shepherd smiled and said that the sheep had been the most wayward in the flock. In its first year of life, the sheep had wandered away many a time; it had cost the shepherd many dreary hours of search. Finally, the shepherd took the sheep and broke its leg. He then bound the leg in a splint and carried the sheep with him to the hills; he fed it by hand and brought it water for its needs. Day by day he took care of it, and when the sheep was fully healed, it never went astray again; it followed the shepherd more closely than a dog would follow his master.

The shepherd leads us to the still waters from the eternal springs. Then the wandering sheep feels the need of restoration, for we have within us the seeds of sin, and they send forth a tangled growth that must be cut back day by day. But when we have wandered away, "He restoreth my soul."

Forgiveness

Forgiveness

An elderly woman, Mrs. X, has a daughter whose close friend is Miss Y; Miss X and Miss Y are mature Christian women. Many years ago, in a letter to Miss X, Miss Y made an indiscreet statement concerning the mother; the letter was read by Mrs. X, and from that time, she has never permitted Miss Y to enter her home. Miss X, is the major support of that home, she respected her mother's wish, and the two Christian friends, met outside the home.

Only a few days ago we pointed out to Mrs. X, the necessity of Christian forgiveness; we suggested that she show the Christian spirit and invite Miss Y to her home for dinner. We were horrified to hear her reply, "Oh, I forgave her long ago but she can stay in her own place."

Forgiveness without forgetting is like vultures feeding on a dead carcass—even the breath of prayer smells of the putrid thing. You will find that a double blessing of God comes to you when you ask that He bless those who may truly have offended you.

Fruitfulness

The Banyan

The banyan is one of the most beautiful trees of the tropics. Its height and spread and the thickness of its trunk make it a glory of shade and beauty. Its branches reach out and down to the ground. Wherever the tip of a branch touches earth, it takes root and a new tree springs up. This is one of the reasons why tropical forests are so impenetrable.

The Christian, if he is living up to the last command of his Lord, is putting out branches that bear "fruit," "more fruit," "much fruit" (JOHN 15). This is because of the power given by Christ through the Holy Spirit (ACTS 1:8). But the quality most needed on the part of

Christians today is that spiritual virility which will enable them to beget a spiritual posterity that in turn will produce fruit unto eternal life. It is what Christ speaks of "your fruit that should remain" (JOHN 15:16). It is by this fruit ye shall know believers.

The Wired Plant

Once I had a small flowering tree in my garden. A wooden tag was attached to one of its branches by a tiny wire. As the branch grew, the wire began to cut into it. I saw that the leaves were not flourishing like those on other branches, so I removed the wire. In a few days life was flowing to such an extent that the branch began flowering. Soon the marks of the wire disappeared.

Some of you may be in danger of withering because of the constrictions of sin. If you will return to the abiding place which is Christ, you will discover that He will begin to work through you; once more you will demonstrate that abiding in Christ is the sure condition of fruitfulness.

Fullness of God

A Pint of Seawater

Preaching on the Pacific Coast gives one an opportunity to look out over the broad expanse of the largest ocean on this planet. The glorious stretches of shore, sky, and sea are wonderful. Imagination quickens and thrills as our littleness is placed alongside that of the unending expanse. Suppose I were to take a pint jar to the edge of the water, lean down and allow the ocean to run into the jar? It will take just one gesture to fill that jar with the Pacific Ocean. But how could I fill that jar unto all the fullness of the Pacific Ocean? If I carry my bottle back to Kansas, to someone who has never looked upon the ocean, and tell him that he can now understand the ocean because I have it in my bottle, he will not see what the ocean really is. All he will see is a pint of seawater. There will be none of the mighty sweep of distance, none of the power of the waves, none of the swelling of the ocean surfaces, and none of the wonders of its depths. I cannot put into a bottle the combing breakers or the vast reaches of the sea.

Such a sampling might be the comprehension of the verse, "filled *with* all the fullness of God" if it were to be rendered, merely, that God proposes to fill us with His fullness. But if it were possible for me to put the whole of the ocean into the bottle, then we could understand what God proposes to do with those He has redeemed.

He does not purpose to make us little samples of the Deity. He does not look upon us as little beings who shall display pints of His power. He purposes to increase and enlarge our capacities forever and ever. We are to be filled *unto* all the fullness of God.

Queen Mary

In 1935, I reached Jerusalem from India just as the time of the jubilee celebrating the twenty-fifth anniversary of the coronation of George V. There was celebration in all of the British Empire. On the actual day of thanksgiving, an announcer, broadcasting from the steps of the National Gallery in Trafalgar Square, told us that he could see the royal carriage emerging from Whitehall. The roar of the crowd grew greater as the carriage approached. The announcer described King George and Queen Mary as they answered the plaudits of the multitude. He then turned us over to another announcer in Charing Cross and the progress of the carriage moved from announcer to announcer as the cavalcade accompanying the royal carriage swept on into Fleet Street. Finally, from St. Paul's Cathedral, we heard the great organ sweep into the "Te Deum" of praise to God for His grace. All of the announcers had described Queen Mary, fully. Yet who was she? Was she of queenly birth? Was she a queen by inheritance? She was not. She had been Princess Mary of Teck. There were a hundred princesses of equal rank among the noble families of Germany. But he who was to become a king set his love upon her, and immediately she became the fulness of him that filleth all in all in the British Commonwealth. Without his love she would have been unknown. With his love she became queen. There she sat in regal splendor, her every action casting praise and glory upon her husband-king.

If we can understand this on the level of the throne of the British Commonwealth, we may be able to catch a faint glimpse of what it will be for us, who have been chosen to be the bride of Christ, the fullness of Him that filleth all in all in God's universe.

Generosity

The Brazilian Taxi Driver

One morning in Brazil, I stepped into a rather rickety taxi; the driver was very poorly dressed. I gave him a certain number on Buenos Aires Street, and he responded, "That is the Bible House! Are you an evangelical?" I answered that I had come to preach on the occasion of the one-hundredth anniversary of Protestantism in Brazil. When I asked if he were truly saved, he gave a heartwarming testimony. I asked about his family; he said that he had never married because he had taken in first one, then two, then three small street orphans; he fed and clothed them and took them every morning to school; on Sundays he took them to Sunday school and church. At the Bible House I asked the driver to wait while I went to the fifth floor to meet a friend. The friend said he would drive me back to the hotel, so I went down to pay the taxi driver. In American money, the fare would have been under two dollars; in *cruzieros* it was twice that amount, but the driver would not accept my money. He said it was such a joy to drive the North American pastor that he wanted to do it free, in the name of the Lord Jesus. He had never had an opportunity to exercise hospitality as the New Testament said believers should do, and he wanted to do this for the Lord.

How wonderful to look into the eyes of a simple man, to see the love that Christ has planted within, and to realize that he is seeking to live for Christ and to do everything in His name.

Christian Lepers

In Formosa two Christian lepers took a third leper into their hut at the government leprosarium, because there was no official opening for him. Although the two were already existing on little more than starvation rations, they willingly stretched the rice they received for two, and made it do for three.

They knew the Lord Jesus Christ, and in receiving Him, they received the gift of giving liberally. They were giving their very life. This is the exercise of a divine gift.

Presents for Mother

After the first world war, I traveled extensively in Europe, and I often sent gifts to my mother—a bit of lace from Brussels, a marble vase from Rome, and so on. Suppose I had written to her, "I am sending you these gifts so that you will love me." My Irish mother would have answered sharply that she loved me before I was born, that her love for me did not increase or diminish by the gifts I sent. But I did tell her that I sent her the gifts because I loved her. This heightened her joy and increased my own.

This is true Christian giving. We give because we have received all things from Christ, and we are moved by the love of Christ to do for others as He has done for us.

The Victoria Cross Hoax

In London, the Queen gave a garden party for some 300 holders of the Victoria Cross-Britain's highest award for bravery. A parking lot attendant crashed the gate by wearing an imitation ribbon and pretending to limp. He was placed in a wheelchair and greeted by the Queen. Authorities fumed when they learned of the hoax. The Queen had spoken to him very kindly and sympathetically.

There need be no regrets in such a case. It is better to do good to ten impostors, than to abstain from helping the truly needy because some fakes might benefit. We work in the name of the Lord Jesus

Christ, and He will find His purposes fulfilled by our loving in His name, ". . . let us be not weary in well doing: for in due season we shall reap, if we faint not (GALATIANS 6:9).

The Would-Be Suicide

In England I knew an officer in the Cold Stream Guards. When he came to this country for a visit, I met him at the New York airport. For a couple of hours I showed him New York City. Down on Wall Street the traffic was congested, and we had to wait for a place to park. Ultimately, we drove into a service station, and I asked, "Can I have the car greased and the oil changed?" As we got out of the car, one of the most miserable human beings that I have ever seen came up to us. The man looked as though he had slept in a coal bin for weeks. Filth, dirt, and coal grime were in the pores of his skin; his hair was matted. He was one of the most formidable looking creatures of despair. He put out his hand and said, "Will you help me?" The Englishman had no American money, but he put his hand in his pocket and said, "Oh, I don't have anything." I drew some money from my own pocket, and said, "We give you this in the name of the Lord Jesus Christ." The man began to cry; the tears ran down his face. He said, "I know, I was brought up in this." I spoke to him about his soul, and he replied, "You know, I have gone down to the docks at least ten times and said, 'O God, I'm going to throw myself in and drown myself,' but always there's something that keeps me." We talked for probably fifteen or twenty minutes; and after telling him not to use the money for drink, we gave him the name of a mission where he could be taken care of. The man said, "Oh, thank you, thank you." We said, "You know we give you this in Jesus' name." And he replied, "God bless you."

Now, I don't know that man, but when I think of Christ on the earth, I think of that man. For Christ said, ". . . Inasmuch as you have done it unto one of the least of these my brethren, ye have done it unto me" (MATTHEW 25:40). "He that hath pity upon the poor, lendeth unto the Lord . . ." (PROVERBS 19:17).

Gifts

Capacities

Let us think of each man in terms of capacity. The great and gifted leaders who may be described in terms of thousand-gallon capacity are few and far between. There are more who have hundred-gallon capacity; still more with ten-and five-gallon capacity; multitudes with the one-gallon capacity, and vast multitudes that must be measured in terms of quart, pint, even gill-capacity. Judged by worldly standards, those with great capacities seem to have all the breaks. Honor comes their way. They are seen, known, praised, and rewarded. They own the larger portion of this world's goods. A thousand-gallon tank that is half-full appears infinitely superior to the half-pint jar that is overflowing.

But, as God sees them, they may have great lacks. If the Bible teaches anything, it is that God is more delighted by the overflowing half-pint than He is by the thousand-gallon tank, half-full of its own doings. When any person becomes enamored of his own capacity, he becomes useless to God. He forgets the foundation principle of our gifts differing according to the grace that is given to us.

The Chinese Laundryman

When Charles Evans Hughes was appointed Chief Justice of the Supreme Court of the United States, he moved to Washington and transferred his letter to a Baptist church there. His father had been a Baptist minister, and Hughes had been a lifelong witness to his faith in Christ. It was the custom in that Baptist church to have all new members come forward during the morning service and be introduced to the congregation. On this particular day, the first to be called was a Chinese laundryman, who had moved to Washington from San Francisco. Ah Sing, who kept a laundry near the church, stood at the far side of the pulpit. As others were called they took positions at the opposite side. After a dozen people had been called, Ah Sing still stood alone. Chief Justice Hughes was called; he took his place beside the laundryman. When the minister had welcomed the group into the church fellowship, he said, "I do not want this congregation to miss the remarkable illustration of the fact that at the cross of Jesus Christ the ground is level." Mr. Hughes behaved like a true Christian. He took his place beside the laundryman, and by his act he prevented embarrassment to the humble Chinese; he showed, too, the love of Christ—he had this gift of standing by.

So often people hate Christianity because they do not want to stand on a level with others. Spiritual pride takes a terrible toll among those who are vindictive in their hatred of true Christianity; it is because they have no respect of persons, race, family, wealth, culture, social position, character or morals. Men stand level in their lost condition before God, and God stands ready to meet the universal need. Let everyone of us who has named the name of Jesus Christ understand that we are to take our places quietly beside those in need.

The Cube and the Sphere

One day I went into the nursery and watched our two-and-a-half-year-old son; he was occupied with a lesson from his mother. A blindfold was placed over his eyes; I placed little wooden objects in his hands and asked him to identify them by their shapes. He answered correctly as his little fingers felt the cube, the sphere, the cylinder. In order to make it one step more difficult, I placed in his hand the cube and the sphere and asked him to hand me the cube. I would not have confused the little mind by asking him to give me something that he did not have in his hand. First I gave to him, then I asked him to give back to me.

This is precisely God's way of dealing with His children. The Word of God establishes the principle that God never asks anything of his child that He has not already provided as a gift. He asks us for perfection, but only because His grace has provided it for us freely at Calvary. After we are born again He asks many things of us, but only because He has already provided these things for us in Christ.

Different Army Duties

In an army, many men perform many different duties. The man who carries the rifle must be backed by the interworking of the whole army. In order for one GI to land on the Normandy beachhead in World War II, he had to be supported by artillery, naval and air units. These, in turn, were supported by those who supplied food, ammunition and fuel. The man below decks in the engine room of the tanker knew that he was helping to keep the tanker moving so that the oil and gasoline on board might be delivered ashore. There the truckers would deliver it to a forward position; and there, the planes that landed on the first airstrips could be fueled and go up to blaze the path for the infantry.

We forget, at times, that this is how the church of Jesus Christ interlocks. Each believer is given some gift by God; each is put into a particular place to perform a particular task for Christ; each is empowered by the Holy Spirit.

"Herrps"

We were sitting in the study, talking to Leland Wang, the Chinese evangelist. Wang thanked us for the help our office had provided in arranging meetings, forwarding correspondence, writing scores of letters introducing him, smoothing out schedules for him, and doing other odd jobs that are difficult for a stranger in a strange land.

We said that one of our chief delights was playing office boy for those who were in the work of the Lord. He looked out of his Oriental eyes and said, "Herrps." We did not understand, and knew that somewhere there was an English word corresponding to that sound, but we had not yet arrived at the meaning.

"Herrps," he repeated, and then continued, "It is in I Corinthians 12:28. The Lord speaks of the gift of "herrps."

We had to look it up before we compassed the Chinese difficulty in pronouncing the letter "l"; we found that which we had often read and never taken in fully: the Lord has given to some the gift of "helps." And how needed this gift is.

The Skater

One winter day, passing through Rockefeller Center in New York, I watched the skaters whirling about on the ice. A girl in her teens was getting instruction from a brilliant skater. She moved around the large orbit of the rink; the man skated in a smaller orbit, nearer the center, but close to her. One could see that she was not sure of herself; once her hands went up, and it was evident that she was going to fall. Swiftly her teacher came to her side and steadied her with a touch. She went on a little more surely; he executed classical figures, but kept his eye on her every moment. Again she became unsteady; in a flash he was by her side, his hand on her elbow helping her to maintain her balance.

It was a perfect picture of the life to which the Lord Jesus has called us. God has given to many of us the gift of helping those who are younger in the Christian life or those who are in need. We live our own life, but our eyes must always be open to the needs of those around us. We must be ready with the helping hand, but we must extend that hand without show. The unsteady one will know that he has been helped, and that the touch at the right moment kept him from falling. The world will not notice that we have helped him, but he will know and the Lord will know. This gift each of us may have.

God

Beautiful Flowers

I have a friend who is a great florist; sometimes I have seen thousands of plants at his hothouses. He never had time—no one ever could have time—to go all through those great greenhouses and say, "Oh, look how beautiful this flower is. Now look how beautiful this flower is!" You cannot, when there are a hundred thousand of them.

But God saw every one of them. He saw every petal. If you should take a magnifying glass and put it to one of those petals, you would say, "Oh, how exquisitely beautiful!" Well, God does not need a magnifying glass. The invisible things are clearly seen by the things that are made. So the creation is God's poem.

The "Big-Godder"

I learned the idea of a great God and a little god from my old professor of Hebrew, Robert Dick Wilson. Wilson was one of the intellectual glories of Princeton Theological Seminary in the days of Warfield, Davis, Machen, and others. After I had been away from the Seminary for about twelve years, I was invited back to preach to the students. Old Dr. Wilson came into Miller Chapel and sat down near the front, while I set forth the Word of God. At the close of the meeting, the old gentleman came up to me, cocked his head on one side in his characteristic way, extended his hand, and said, "If you come back again, I will not come to hear you preach. I only come once. I am glad that you are a big-godder. When my boys come back, I come to see if they are big-godders or little-godders, and then I know what their ministry will be." I asked him to explain, and he replied, "Well, some men have a little god and they are always in trouble with him. He can't do any miracles. He can't take care of the inspiration and transmission of the Scripture to us. He doesn't intervene on behalf of His people. They have a little god and I call them little-godders. Then there are those who have a great God. He speaks and it is done. He commands and it stands fast. He know how to show Himself strong on behalf of them that fear Him. You have a great God; and He will bless your ministry. He paused a moment, smiled, said, "God bless you," and walked out.

Men are always in difficulty with their faith because their God is too small. If they once see the true God, and get the perspective that sees Him as filling all in all, then the difficulties of life will rapidly diminish to their proper proportions. God knows all, is all-powerful, unchanging, eternal, never-failing. He has never made a mistake; He has never been surprised by anything that happened, for He has always known and decreed all things.

Father and Son

If a man begets a son, in consequence of that act, he is always, the father of that son. There have been men who have been fathers of sons who have never been fathers *to* their sons. But many a man who begets a child, gives himself to that child. He is with the mother in the training of the child. The boy is with the father in his free moments. The father enters into the boy's studies; he participates in the boy's games. He makes the boy's hobbies his own hobbies. No question of the boy is beyond the patience of the father. He explains things to the child in great detail whenever the child shows interest in an answer. He trains the boy, leads him on, truly educates him. It can be said in the highest degree that this man is not only father *of* the boy, he is father *to* the boy.

This is the picture that our God wants us to have of Him. More than any earthly father could be a father to his son, so God is a God to us.

Glass

Here is a simple illustration that expresses a great spiritual truth: If we look through a piece of red glass, everything is red; through blue glass, everything is blue; through yellow glass, everything is yellow, and so on.

The glorious truth is that when we believe in the Lord Jesus Christ as our Saviour, God looks at us through the Lord Jesus Christ. He sees us in all the white holiness of His Son. That is the great New Testament doctrine of the imputation of our sin to the account of Christ and His righteousness to our account.

The Hand Loom

The first time I saw a hand loom was in a little village in Belgium. It stood in a corner of the large kitchen; an unfinished white bedspread upon it. I was very eager to see how this weaving was done, so my host showed me how the threads were placed, first on the frame and then in the shuttle. He operated the loom to show me how the shuttle moved back and forth over the threads, creating the even, firm texture of the material and developing the pattern that existed in the mind of the weaver. Little by little, the small threads that fell from the busily moving shuttle became the tissue and pattern of the material.

The principle which I saw demonstrated in that loom was in the mind of the Holy Spirit, when He inspired some of the sacred writers to express the idea of thoughts. "For my thoughts are not your thoughts, neither are your ways my ways, saith the Lord" (ISAIAH 55:8). The word which is here translated "thoughts," means literally "weavings." "My weavings are not your weavings," we might paraphrase it. Everywhere in Scripture we are face to face with the absolute difference between God and man in all of God's ways of thinking and doing.

Oriental Silversmiths

In the great bazaars of Istanbul, Damascus, or Cairo, you will see men sitting at their places in the section of the silversmiths. Beside them you will generally find piles of United States twenty-five, fifty, and ten-cent pieces. Thousands of travelers give American coins as tips, and all of those monies are melted back into silver and poured into little silver charms that are sold back to the tourists. This is done in the most old-fashioned way. I have watched a silversmith drop a coin into the molten silver; in a little while the coin is melted down under the hot fire. Every once in a while the man gets up, lifts himself over the little bowl of silver, and goes back to sawing on some little pin that he is making, a silver clasp or ornament. Again he will get up and look in the bowl; he will take a sieve and scrape off the scoria that is on the top. He takes away the dross, and if you should ask him, "What are you waiting to see," he would say, "I keep it on the fire until there is no more scum; when I lean over it, I can see myself reflected there as in the best mirror."

That is what it means in Malachi when it says that God shall sit as a refiner of silver. God says, "I am going to keep you in the fire until I see My face in you; this is what I'm working for. I want to purge away the dross. I want to make you like the Lord Jesus Christ. I want you to understand the particularity of love that I've bestowed upon you, that I have called you my sons; and whom I love, I chasten and scourge every son whom I receive."

The Pet Dog

A small boy has a pet dog which he loves very dearly. He plays with that dog every day, and the dog sleeps beside him at night. One day the boy opens the door of the family garage just in time to see his father killing the dog. The fatal shot rings out; the boy screams and rushes toward the dog. The father catches the boy who kicks at him and screams: "You killed my dog. You killed my dog. I hate you. I hate you." The father carries the boy into the house and says, "My son, I will tell you why I had to kill him." But the boy runs from his father, screaming, "I hate you. I hate you. You killed my dog."

In order to make our parable fit the spiritual facts we are trying to explain, we will continue in a somewhat absurd way. For men who act in an absurd way toward God may not see their own absurdity in the parallel. This boy, we will say, continues to live in his father's house, eating the meals that are provided by his father, wearing the clothes that are provided by his father, yet constantly saying that he hates his father because his father killed his dog. The boy grows up and begins to have some understanding of disease and pathology; he is given clippings that tell of an epidemic of rabies in his neighborhood, and that a mad dog had bitten several children—some of them had died. He even finds a clipping that states that the mad dog bit several other dogs in the neighborhood and that it was necessary for the owners to destroy those pets. From his maturity the boy can look back on his own childhood and see how warped were his opinions of his own father. He had carried hatred of his father through the years because his father had crossed his childish will. Now he sees evidence that his father was acting in wisdom and love, that his pet dog might have bitten him and caused his own death.

We should understand that God has reasons which are unknown to us. It should be sufficient that we have God's Word for it.

The Potter

Years ago, when I was living in France, I knew a potter who made various types of vessels for all sorts of uses. Often I went in to watch him turning the wheel and molding the various vessels according to his desire. At times he let me work a lump of clay, although I worked awkwardly at the craft that he did so beautifully. I had been reading the great passages in Isaiah and Jeremiah that have to do with the prophet's visit to the house of a potter, and the illustrations that grew out of that craft. One day I asked the potter what determined his choice as to what he should make. I saw him make tableware, then kitchenware, even spittoons. He said that he got the feel of it as he began to work. When he was rested he made beautiful things; when he was tired, he would slap the clay on the wheel and turn out ordinary vessels that sold in the market for menial uses. He put clay on his wheel; I asked him to make a menial vessel, and he tossed one off in a moment. I then asked him to make a vase, and with great care and love he made a vessel of beauty. I asked him if he ever switched from one object to another while he was in the midst of the work. He began again and speedily there arose before my eyes a vase. While the clay was still wet and whirling, he struck it from above with a heavy sweep of his hand and crushed it to a lump and speedily ran up the form of another vessel. Moment after moment I watched various forms succeed each other, all according to his desire, and all from the same lump of clay. A deft touch and a bowl appeared—a plate, a cup, a dish. He was absolute master of his clay.

God sets before us that He is the absolute Master of His creation. He does not work by whim, nor is He ever so tired that He should shift to another pattern. He has His purposes that are right according to all that He is in His inward nature, and it is this that He wants us to recognize, that our hope and trust may be in Him alone.

The Zeiss Collection

When the United States Army took all of the material in the optical museum of the Zeiss optical plant in Germany, it secured the greatest collection of its kind in the world and gained possession of samples of every lens known to German scientists. One lens was so powerful that pictures could be taken of buildings twenty-five miles away; fortifications across the English Channel, for example, showed as plainly as an ordinary photograph. Most extraordinary was a lens that had a 210-degree angle, that could take a picture even of a portion of the scene behind the camera.

Hagar learned to call the Lord "Thou God seest me" (GENESIS 16:13). And we can be sure that our Lord looks upon us at all times, and that nothing is hid from his sight. His look can be a look of conviction as when the Lord looked on Peter (LUKE 22:61); His look can be a look of compassion as when He gazed upon the rich young ruler (MARK 10:21), but above all His is a gaze which sees to the very heart: ". . . for the Lord seeth not as man seeth; for man looketh on the outward appearance, but the Lord looketh on the heart" (I SAMUEL 16:7).

God's Power

Breeder Reactor

In announcing the success of the breeder reactor at Arco, Idaho, Atomic Energy Commission Chairman, Gordon Dean asked his audience to imagine that the world has only one hundred gallons of gasoline; when the gasoline is burned in the presence of water it turns some of the water into new gasoline. If the amount produced is less than the original stock, the world would soon run out of gasoline. If the amount is greater, the gasoline stock could grow bigger and bigger until all the world's water had been turned into fuel.

Breeding atomic fuel works in somewhat the same way. Natural uranium contains only .7% of fissionable U-235. Nearly all the rest of it is nonfissionable U-238. But when U-235 fissions (splits in two) and produces heat, it also yields free neutrons. Some of these are needed to keep the reaction going; they make other U-235 atoms split. Some neutrons escape or are absorbed by structural materials in the reactor. The rest of the neutrons enter the nuclei of U-238 atoms and make them turn into plutonium, which is just as fissionable as U-235 and can be used as atomic fuel.

The importance of this development can only be realized if we consider that one pound of uranium has been the equivalent of about 18,200 lbs. of coal; under the new process the same pound of uranium would be equivalent to 2,600,000 lbs. of coal.

Believers should understand that here, indeed, is a great illustration of the principle of the increase of power from God. The Lord has organized the Christian life on the principle of the breeder reactor. He gives us the knowledge of His power in our lives in a small way and puts before us a small test. As soon as we use His power to overcome the difficulty that is involved in that test, we discover that we have a larger knowledge of His power. With that knowledge comes a larger test, then a larger deliverance and still larger knowledge. As the spiral goes upward, it is expanding at all times. Thus God will never give us a test beyond our present knowledge of power, and we will ever grow into His infinite self.

The River Basin

If we look at a map of the central United States, we can see the courses of rivers from many sources, all debouching into the Gulf of Mexico. Waters from Pennsylvania flow into the Ohio River; from Montana and Wyoming they flow into the Missouri River; from Tennessee and Alabama they flow into the Tennessee. All these join the Mississippi, which rises far to the north in Minnesota. If we read this map in reverse and follow the mighty rivers back to creeks, from creeks to brooks, from brooks to rivulets, we have the picture of the source and flow of power. From one spring, all power flows.

All power comes from God, and the powers that be are ordained by God. Power exercised by any creature, even the power of a cat to kill a mouse, or of one insect to kill another, derives originally from God. How much more is this true of human affairs, where God is working out His great plan!

Splitting the Tomb

A "believe-it-or-not" picture showed a tomb with a fig tree growing out of the middle of it; the tree split the great slab of stone that formed the top of the sarcophagus into three great pieces, and pushed out the side walls with the force of its growth. The tomb, it is said, is in the grounds of the parish church of Watford, England, and is that of a naval officer, Ben Wangford, whose dying request was that he might be buried with a fig in his hand. The life of that fig took hold of the death of that hand and the power of the life split the tomb.

If physical life is a powerful thing, eternal life is even more powerful. It is rooted in the wounded hand of the Lord Jesus Christ and out of that hand grows the life of the resurrection which God communicates unto us. Here is a power that enables us to be delivered from sin.

The Unseen Kite

A boy, flying a kite, was so successful that the kite went out of sight. He stood on the green with a cord in his hand that bent upwards into the sky and was lost. Someone asked him how he knew the kite was there, and he let them put their hand on the string; they could feel the pull of the unseen kite.

The world may not recognize the existence of God, but those who know Him in Christ can feel the drawing of the invisible power that they recognize in every phase of spiritual life. And the unbelieving bystander will be forced to recognize that the true believer possesses "something" which he does not have.

Gospels

Works on Napoleon

The great libraries of France house thousands of volumes printed about the life and work of Napoleon. A quarterly review devoted to studies of the Corsican has been published for over fifty years. If a scholar wants to work on some phase of Napoleon's life it is not necessary for him to include these mountains of accumulated material. He need not even be chronological. If he is writing on Napoleon, the man, the codes or Austerlitz may not be mentioned, but Josephine certainly will. If he writes on Napoleon the strategist, he may never mention Marengo, Iena, Waterloo, and Moscow. Remember, however that he may, for his purpose, mention Waterloo before Austerlitz and may weave events of various epochs of the life of his hero into the same paragraph. I have read a volume on Napoleon that mentioned none of his battles, except incidentally, and never spoke of Josephine or of the empress. It was a book on Napoleon as a codifier of laws.

In the same way the Holy Spirit has used Matthew, Mark, Luke and John to present four different phases of the person and work of the Lord Jesus Christ. Matthew writes to the Jews. His purpose is to show that Jesus was the Jewish Messiah. Mark presents Jesus as a servant. There is no genealogy at all. Mark is writing about a servant, and a servant works from beginning to end. Luke, however, presents Jesus Christ as a man. John presents Jesus Christ as the Eternal God incarnate.

Grace of God

Bataan and Guadalcanal

When the Japanese launched their attack against the Philippines, several thousand United States' troops were on those islands, totally unprepared. How bravely they fought on Bataan, slowing down the enemy and making him pay heavy losses for each foot of gain! The men fought on, hoping against hope that reinforcements would soon be available. But our fleet had been severely wounded and there were no reinforcements available. A year or so later, however, we were ready to launch the great offensive in the Solomon Islands. The papers that bore the news of the great battles raging on Guadalcanal, also published an assurance from our Secretary of War. He said, "There is twice as much food as the soldiers can eat; there is twice as much ammunition as the soldiers can fire; there are twice as many nurses and doctors as would ordinarily be needed in any military engagement; there are twice as many medical supplies as could be needed. There are twice as many airplanes as are possessed by the enemy. We are prepared for every contingency."

Most certainly we can say that the method in which the Lord provides for all our needs is like Guadalcanal. God never had a Bataan in all of His dealing with the sons of men. All of God's gifts to us are in abundance.

A Better Pitcher

Years ago a minister named Harry Morehouse was walking in a poorer section of the city, and he watched as a boy of five or six came out of a store carrying a pitcher of milk. The little fellow made his way carefully along the street; he slipped and fell; the pitcher broke, and the milk ran all over the sidewalk. The boy let out a wail, and Morehouse rushed to see if he was hurt. There was no physical damage, but the youngster would not be consoled; he kept crying over and over, "My mama'll whip me! My mama'll whip me!"

Mr. Morehouse said to him, "Maybe the pitcher is not broken in too many pieces; let us see if we can put it together again." The boy stopped crying at once; he watched Mr. Morehouse place the base of the pitcher on the sidewalk and start building up the pieces. There were one or two failures and each time the boy started crying again but was silenced by the big preacher. Finally the whole pitcher was complete except for the handle. Mr. Morehouse handed the piece to the little fellow; he poked it toward the place it belonged, and knocked the whole thing apart once more. This time there was no stopping his tears, so Mr. Morehouse gathered the boy in his arms and walked down the street to a nearby crockery store. He bought a new pitcher; then he and the boy returned to the milk store and had the pitcher washed and filled with milk. He carried the boy on one arm and balanced the pitcher of milk in the other hand until they arrived at the boy's home. Very gently he deposited the lad on his front steps, put the pitcher carefully into his hands and asked, "Now will your mama whip you?" A smile broke on the streaked face. "Aw, no sir! 'cause it's a lot better pitcher 'an we had before."

Whether you accept the fact or not, the pitcher of your life and its milk were once spilled beyond regathering. You may have spent much time trying to patch the pieces together again, but God assured you that you were broken beyond repair. When we were thus, broken and hopeless, in the despair of our lost soul and our crashed hopes the Lord Jesus intervened to save us. He may have watched our efforts at patching for a while, until we came to the place where we believed beyond question that it was impossible for us to repair our lives in a way that would ever satisfy the holiness of the Heavenly Father. It was then that He carried us in His arms and purchased for us an entirely new nature, a new life, which He imparted to us on the basis of His loving kindness and tender mercies. It was not because there was good in us, but because there was grace in Him.

Chemistry Examples

We have many examples in chemistry that show how the introduction of a second element will completely debase or transform a product. If you put a dime in a bottle of hydrogen peroxide, the silver will react so rapidly that a moment later nothing will be left in the bottle but liquid. If you put even the smallest spark of fire into a barrel of gunpowder, you will explode the whole barrel. Terrible oil refinery fires have been caused by a single drop of perchloric acid coming in contact with some heated organic liquid—gasoline, kerosene, or aniline.

If salvation is by grace then it is not of works, for as soon as there is a mixture of even the smallest percentage of works, grace is debased and is transformed into something that is horrible to consider. The whole idea of works is that man can provide a basis that will force God to give him some blessing as a just reward for the works. The whole idea of grace is that God acts toward man according to that which is to be found within His own divine nature of love. The two ideas are mutually exclusive and destroy each other when placed together.

Facing the Wall

Sir Edward C. Burne-Jones, the prominent nineteenth-century English artist, went to tea at the home of his daughter. As a special treat his little granddaughter was allowed to come to the table; she misbehaved, and her mother made her stand in the corner with her face to the wall. Sir Edward, a well-trained grandfather, did not interfere with his grandchild's training, but next morning he arrived at his daughter's home with paints and palette. He went to the wall where the little girl had been forced to stand, and there he painted pictures— a kitten chasing its tail; lambs in a field; goldfish swimming. He decorated the wall on both sides of that corner with paintings for his granddaughter's delight. If she had to stand in the corner again, at least she would have something to look at.

When a Christian commits sin and is put into a corner, God does not send him to hell. When a child of God sins, he does not fall from grace. Wonderful though it is, instead he falls into grace. If your particular sin has been confessed, God has restored you; when God put you into the corner, He went to you there and painted a picture of His forgiveness and love.

The Reservoir

If you poured a single test tube of disease germs into a reservoir of pure water—the entire water supply—even that for an entire city— would be contaminated.

This illustration cannot speak strongly enough to show forth the degree of contamination that is to be found where God's free grace is diluted by even a small part of human works.

The Texas Oil Owner

Suppose that a great depression brings many men to the point of bankruptcy. They wish, of course, to keep themselves above the flood and to bring themselves out by their own efforts. Their natural pride wishes to keep them from confessing their failure and acknowledging the desperation of their circumstances. For the sake of our illustration, let us imagine a small town in Texas that is dominated by a man fortunate enough to have discovered oil on his property; he has also bought all the oil leases in his neighborhood so his fortune runs into scores of millions of dollars. He announces that he will bring all of the business men of that small town out of bankruptcy, if they will write a letter acknowledging the certainty of their failure. He will then pay their debts and supply them with a new capital to start their business afresh. If there are men in the town who are proud to the point of insanity, they may refuse to bow before this offer from a kind benefactor. In that case, they remain insolvent and are forced to pay the penalty of their pride. But there are others who recognize that the man who makes the offer is a man who has known them for years, and that he recognizes that his success is a matter that involves certain obligations and responsibilities; they realize that he holds certain values in trust. He wishes to help them because of the generosity of his nature. They, therefore, determine to write to him and set before him the true nature of their plight and avail themselves of the offer made them in free grace. Immediately, the local bank is instructed to take care of their needs, to pay off their debts, and to grant them the credit they need for the maintenance of their affairs. Someone might say to them, "And because this friend has come to your aid, in spite of the fact that you are absolutely bankrupt, your situation is one of brilliant hope because of the grace that pays your debt and provides the capital which you need."

We are brought day by day to acknowledge freely before God our utter bankruptcy. We can do nothing for ourselves. If then, we are to have any blessing, it must come to us moment by moment from the flowing stream of grace which begins at Calvary and comes to us because of the love of God, and in the power of the Holy Spirit.

Gratitude

Thanking God

A minister who was visiting an insane asylum, was accosted by one of the inmates, "Sir," asked the patient, "have you ever thanked God for your reason?" The preacher had never done so, but he vowed that he would be unthankful no longer.

There are thousands of things besides your reason for which you might well bow your head right now and give a heartfelt prayer of thanksgiving to the Father.

The Hope College Janitor

While I was preaching at Hope College in Holland, Michigan, the janitor, who was an elder in the church, came up to me and said, "I would like to ask you a question. I can understand 'God bless me,' but how can I bless God? 'Bless the Lord, O my soul.' How can I bless Him?"

I said, "Do you have any children?"

He replied, "Yes, I do."

"How old are they?"

"Well," he said, "I have a child who is five and one who is seven."

"At Christmastime do they ever give you a Christmas present?" I asked.

"Yes, they do."

"Do you know what they are going to give you?"

"No, I don't."

"Who picks it out?"

"They do, with their mother."

"Who pays for it?"

"I do."

"That's exactly it," I said, "You pay for the Christmas presents which your babies give you. You're so glad that they talk about it and have secrets with mother. I can remember when my own children were growing up, how wonderfully excited they were that they were going to surprise Daddy. They came and said, 'Daddy, here is a blessing for you.' It came from me, but it was a blessing because it had come as the boomerang of love."

So it is when we cry blessing and glory and wisdom and thanksgiving. We bless Thee, O Lord. What with? With the blessing that He puts in our lives. Everything that we have and are comes from Him. How delighted we are to offer it back to Him and to acknowledge before all the world that there is nothing that we have or could be that does not come from Him.

The Yellow Cur

One Saturday evening several years ago, on my way to Pensacola, Florida, I had a flat tire and had to pull over to the side of the road. I was tired; I had driven over three hundred miles that day and preached twelve times that week. As I eyed the tire, a jeep came down the road. I flagged it and a young man got out; I told him I would give him a dollar to do the work for me. He agreed with alacrity and came over to my car, followed by a little yellow cur. In order to get to the spare tire, we had to unload about two hundred books piled in the trunk of the car. The young man opened one of the books, and, seeing that the matter concerned salvation, said that his wife would be interested in something like that because she was active in the little Baptist church down the road. When I asked him about his own faith, he expressed total indifference.

As he worked his dog stayed close beside him, nuzzling him when he stooped, putting his head between the man and his task, coming back when he was pushed aside. I remarked that he and the dog seemed to be very fond of each other. He stopped, looked at me with a level gaze, and said earnestly, "That dog saved my life once." I asked him to tell me about it and the story came quickly. The reason he was not in the army—it was at the height of the war against Germany and Japan—was that he had more than a dozen broken bones. He was a rodeo rider and had often been thrown by bulls and horses. He worked as a cowboy, he told me, and once had nearly been trapped in quicksand. He had jumped from tuft to tuft of the marshy ground and had suddenly lost his footing. He threw himself on his back at once, to spread his weight, but he was caught almost to his knees, and he knew that there was no deliverance from any quarter. There was not a human being within a couple of miles. Out of nowhere, the dog had appeared. He came to the man, allowed him to put his arms around his haunches. The man was able to straighten himself, and with the dog pulling, he released first one leg, and then the other and finally reached safety.

The young man said, with a wry smile, "That dog is always with me. He can have anything I have. He eats with me, and though my wife doesn't like it, he sleeps with us." I said to him. "What would you do if, down there at the store where you are going, one of the men deliberately kicked that dog hard?" With a look of unabashed ferocity, the young man said, "Mister, I believe I'd kill him." I put my hand out and touched him on the arm, saying, "Isn't it strange that you take such good care of a dog who saved your life at no cost to himself, yet you treat so indifferently the Saviour, the Lord Jesus, who saved you at such great cost to Himself? For Christ didn't pull you out of the quicksand of sin by a mere effort of strength on your behalf! He actually died for you to save you from hell."

A look of wonderment came into the man's face and he said, "You know, Mister, that's right. We don't take much account of Him. And I reckon it's because we can't see Him, and we can't feel hell like I sometimes feel that quicksand on my legs."

When he finished changing the tire, he rather shyly asked if he could have one of my books instead of the dollar. I gave him both and he shook my hand earnestly. He said, "You know my wife is going to be surprised and glad when I tell her I am going to church with her tomorrow, and when I start reading the Bible. But you know, Mister, that really got me—to think that I could treat a cur better than Jesus Christ who died for me."

Is it not strange that there are men who would treat a yellow cur better than they would treat the Lord Jesus from Heaven? But it is true, and the reason can be found in the depths of sin within our Adamic nature. Mass indifference characterizes the nation and the race of mankind. What David said of the unregenerate can be said even of a man who frequently sits in a church pew: "God is not in all his thoughts" (Psalm 10:4).

Guidance

Baby's First Steps

In the evening, the young father came home from work. His wife greeted him with the excited announcement that she was sure the baby was about to take his first step. The baby was all clean and dressed in his best. The father got the motion-picture camera and pointed it toward the child. The mother held the baby by his armpits, his little feet on the ground. She began relaxing her grip so that the child carried all his weight on his own two feet. He sensed the excitement that was in the air. He balanced precariously as he stood all by himself. He lifted one foot, took a tiny step, and held his balance while the camera whirred. There were exclamations of delight from his parents. Did the thought occur to the baby: "Evidently that is just what I was supposed to do—lift up my right foot and and put it forward"? So he lifts the same right foot and puts it forward, loses his balance, and down he goes. Does the father rush at him to spank him? Nonsense. Does the mother scold him? Ridiculous. The mother picks him up with shining eyes, and says, "There's my little man. He took a step. He'll soon take two." And he will, too!

The Heavenly Father is far more eager to lead us out into a developed Christian life than any young father and mother were to see their child take his first step. When we fall, God does not strike us down. He is leading us as one leads a child of tender age.

The Feather Fan

On a country road in Formosa, we saw a farmer driving a large flock of ducks. There must have been a hundred of them, so tightly packed together that some of their heads could not be seen. The only guidance they had came from the breeze of a large feather fan waved behind them by the driver. If a duck strayed from the group, a breeze was fanned at it, and it returned to the body of the flock.

Thus the Lord leads believers. If they will be led by the wind of the Spirit, He will blow His steady guidance. He never takes stern measures to the believer who accepts the soft caress of His breeze.

Flathead Lake

One summer we had a cabin on the edge of Flathead Lake in Montana. Every day we went into the lake. Father took his small boy just turning five, out beyond his depth. The boy cried and cried, even though he was just as safe as if he had been on shore. Only when he was convinced of that fact could he rest quietly on the water, supported by father's arm.

Oh, Christian! Realize that the Father wants to teach you—He is leading you out beyond your depth with full purpose in His heart and mind. It is the power of the risen Lord Jesus Christ, personally appropriated moment by moment, that gives us our victory and our peace that passeth all understanding.

Training Soldiers

We commit the young men of our nation to the authority of our armed forces, and these men surrender themselves to the orders of their superiors in perfect confidence. They do not argue, although they may complain among themselves. They must do what they are told to do. It is galling to the flesh to go through strenuous drill routine; muscles that are unaccustomed to certain exercises cry out on long route marches with sixty pounds of gear on the back. But the soldiers who do any thinking soon realize that they are being turned from boys into men. They must become aware that their flabbiness is giving way to hardness, that they will face their foes in the hour of danger as conditioned warriors and not as awkward fledglings.

If we would only learn from the leadings of our God that He is preparing us for Himself in much the same way that a soldier must be conditioned by all his training.

Heaven

Going Home

A refugee from Hitler says that so many tales were told about America that his whole family felt they knew this country well. So settled was this knowledge and love of the land he had not yet seen, that as he departed for America his mother said to him, "You are going home, and I am staying in a foreign land."

The Christian who realizes the tyranny of life in this world is glad to escape to the land that is fairer than day. When our loved ones go before us, we are forced to say, with tears for ourselves, "You are going Home and I am staying in a foreign land."

Holiness

The Blind Officer

A young officer who was blinded during the war, met and later married one of the nurses who took care of him in an army hospital. One day he overheard someone speaking about himself and his wife; and they said, "It was lucky for her that he was blind since he never would have married such a homely woman if he had had eyes."

He rose to his feet and walked toward the voices, saying, "I overheard what you said, and I thank God from the depths of my heart for blindness of eyes that might have kept me from seeing the marvelous worth of the soul of this woman who is my wife. She is the most noble character I have ever known; if the conformation of her features is such that it might have masked her inward beauty to my soul then I am the great gainer by having lost my sight."

The Bible says that God seeth not as man seeth "for man looketh on the outward appearance, but the Lord looketh on the heart" (I SAMUEL 16:7b). The Bible also says that God prefers holiness to glamor (I PETER 3:4). If a man or woman possesses physical beauty, they may be thankful for it, but they should realize what a temptation it can be to them and must ever surrender it to the Lord.

Genius

If we should give you a copy of Shakespeare's dramas, and ask you to produce an equal, you would be forced to reply that you could not do it; you lack the genius. If we should place before you paintings of Velasquez, or Rembrandt, or of any of the other great masters and ask you to create new masterpieces, again you would be forced to reply that you could not do it; you lack the genius. Your answer would be the same, if we offered you great works of music, architecture, or the arts or sciences. Genius must be innate in the true master of an art.

The same is true of the life of Christ. Myriads have looked at Jesus Christ and have known that they were sinners, but no man in this world has ever become holy by looking at the example of Jesus Christ. A Christian is a man or woman in whom God has worked a miracle by planting a new life within. This is the genius of holiness, and it becomes possible for a man to let this indwelling life of Christ be manifested to those about him.

Holy Spirit

The African Breeze

On landing in Africa, one of the first lessons we learned was to find out on which side of the house the wind was blowing. Coming out the front door to sit on a porch, we walked first to one end, and then to the other. Generally, a breeze would be in one place or the other, and there we placed our chairs. When there was a calm, we stifled; when the breeze blew fresh and strong, we sighed with joy. The movement of air made life livable.

Thus we must seek the motions of the Spirit. When we realize that the Holy Spirit moves as He desires, then we know a revival cannot be pumped up by human effort, but must come from God. At times the wind blows a tempest, at times there is a gentle breeze, at times there is a dead calm of the doldrums. At times He has been pleased to blow us a Luther, a Calvin or a Wesley, great tempests of spiritual movements; at times the church has been in a hot suffocating calm, where the true believers almost gasped for life.

Initiation

When I was a boy, a group of fellows who lived in our part of town formed the Pastime Athletic Club. It was a big name but it did not mean much. The four or five who started the Club decided to initiate other fellows who were going to join. The boys wanted the initiation to be held in our house because we had plenty of room. The initiation rites were such that my parents would not let me remain a member of the club, but I learned something about initiations that night. An initiation is a work or rite performed by a person who is already a member of a society, upon someone who is becoming a member.

All this will help us to understand the baptism of the Holy Spirit, for it is the baptism of the Holy Spirit that is the initiation of an individual into the greatest of all societies, the church which is the

Body of Christ. No one can become a member of the Body of Christ without being baptized by the Holy Spirit, and everyone who is baptized by the Spirit so becomes a member of the body of Christ. This is an invisible society seen by God alone, so this work of the spirit is also invisible.

The Isolated Colonists

During the latter part of the eighteenth century many colonists left Virginia and started through the mountains to settle the valleys that lay far to the West. Fear of Indians, the death of a horse or the breaking down of a wagon forced many to stay in the mountains. For over twenty years, these settlers saw no white men at all, until a group of travelers straggled into the neighborhood. Naturally, there was much conversation about the outside world. The travelers asked the mountaineers what they thought of the republic and the policies of the Continental Congress. The isolated ones answered, "We have not so much as heard of a Continental Congress or a republic." They thought of themselves as loyal subjects of the British King, and had not even heard of George Washington or the Revolutionary War. It took them awhile to comprehend their new status, but once they did they became American citizens by knowledge and volition, just as they had been for some time by fact.

In the same manner, many of the children of Israel had traveled down to Jerusalem in the days of John the Baptist; they had heard him, followed him and been baptized by him. Then they returned to their remote homes; since they were isolated they knew nothing of the happenings of the intervening years—that Jesus Christ had been manifested, had died and been raised from the dead, had ascended into Heaven and sent forth the Holy Spirit. But as soon as they were told by Paul, they realized their new status, and they identified with the infant Church and became members of that body by the work of the Holy Spirit.

Orson Welles' Picture

One day, when Orson Welles was making a picture a cameraman said to him, "You had better wipe that sweat off." Welles replied, "Horses sweat; men perspire, and (looking at the actress who was working with him) she glows." He meant that she had a glowing personality and great physical attractiveness.

Less known, because it's more rare, is the personality that is so filled with the Holy Spirit that it radiates the presence of Jesus Christ. The man or woman who is filled with the Holy Spirit is aglow with His presence; and, like the rulers of Israel, people will recognize "that they had been with Jesus" (ACTS 4:13). The glow of the Spirit is the warmth of the soul touched by the love of Christ.

Painting the Bird

Several centuries ago, the Emperor of Japan comissioned a Japanese artist to paint a bird. Months passed, then years. Finally, the Emperor went to the artist's studio to ask for an explanation. The artist set a blank canvas on the easel and in fifteen minutes completed the painting of a bird that became a masterpiece. The Emperor asked why there had been such a long delay. The artist then went from cabinet to cabinet; he produced armloads of drawings of feathers, tendons, wings, feet, claws, eyes and beaks of birds; these he placed one by one before the Emperor.

The Holy Spirit operates in the life of the believer, so that we may be conformed to the image of God's Son (ROMANS 8:29). This is not done in the moment of our new birth. That moment is no more than the declaration of the divine purpose; It is just the beginning of the long work. The whole process is a detailed and painstaking progress "until Christ be formed in you" (GALATIANS 4:19). Then the day shall come when the Emperor of emperors will come for us, and the completed work will flash forth in a moment. "It does not yet appear what we shall be, but we know that when he appears we shall be like him, for we shall see him as he is" (I JOHN 3:2).

The Truck and the Puddle

One rainy day as we drove at more than sixty miles an hour on a highway in the southwest, a great truck approached us; it hit a puddle and flung gallons of muddy water in front of us. As I cautiously applied the brakes, the wiper and the fresh rain worked together to clear the windshield and to restore visibility. At no moment were we endangered by the muddy bath.

Spiritual onslaughts are wiped away by the power of the Holy Spirit who maintains us in the heavenly places in Christ. I have learned to enter into the secret place where "no weapon that is fashioned against you shall prosper, and you shall confute every tongue that rises against you in judgment. This is the heritage of the servants of the Lord and their vindication from me, says the Lord." (ISAIAH 54:17).

Honesty

Weighing his Thumb

A butcher, asked what difference it made to him when Christ entered his life, replied, "I stopped weighing my thumb." He then told that before becoming a Christian, he put the meat on the scales in such a way that his thumb trailed down, affecting the weight by as much as an ounce. He had included that thumb in the weight of beef, pork lard, and every other item of his merchandise. But after Christ came into his heart, he stood away from the scales and gave a full sixteen ounces of meat. And when he served customers whom he had formerly cheated, he added an ounce to make up for past peculations.

Christians, especially those who believe in the doctrine of the security of the believer, must be eternally vigilant, yielding to the presence of the Holy Spirit to warn them from deviating from high standards of honesty and integrity. Too many Christians weigh their thumbs when they deal with others. Thus through all the gamut of sins, Christians will permit themselves a thumb's weight on their account.

Hope, Rejoicing In

The African Twins

When I was in of Africa, I took a picture of two young women; smiling and beautiful they wore flowers in their hair. They were brought before me for special attention because they were twins—the first twins ever permitted to grow up in that part of Africa. To Africans the idea of twins was horrible. Even today in many of Africa's tribes, twins are killed at birth. Their superstitious religion had a great fear connected with the birth of twins, but in this instance the gospel of Jesus Christ had come to the tribe some thirty years earlier. Shortly after the parents were saved, the Lord gave them these twin daughters. Their newfound faith was strong enough to resist the public outcry against the children, and they were allowed to live. When they reached womanhood, they married two fine young men of the tribe, also Christians. The twins stood before me, living proof of the hope that is in Christ, and I rejoiced in this hope that so transforms individuals and even tribes and nations.

The Japanese Buddhist

In the lobby of the Imperial Hotel in Tokyo, Japan, the girl at one of the airline desks spoke Chinese, Japanese and English; she was obviously from a cultured background. I asked her if she was a Christian. She replied that she was a Buddhist. Further questions elicited the information that she had heard of Christ and knew that there was a sacred book, the Bible; but she had never read it and knew nothing of Christian truth. I then asked her, "Do you love Buddha?" She was startled and said, "Love? I never thought about love in connection with religion." I said to her, "Do you know that in the whole world no God is truly loved except the Lord Jesus Christ? Other gods are hated and feared. You have statues of fierce monsters to guard the gates of your temples, and the people stand at a distance and try to awaken their gods by clapping their hands. They burn incense and offer sacrifices to them as though they were gods who had to be appeased. But Jesus Christ loves us; He came to die for us, and those of us who truly know Him have learned to love Him in return. 'We love him because he first loved us' (I JOHN 4:19). Mohammedans do not love Allah; Hindus do not love their gods, and neither do you love Buddha. But we love the Lord Jesus because He died for us." Before leaving Japan, I arranged for a missionary to take a Bible to this girl and to show her how she might know the Christ of God and enter into His love.

When you meet the sadness of a pagan Japanese who fears her god, you enter into the meaning of the text, "Rejoice in your hope."

The Nigerian Pastor

At a mission station in Nigeria, I met a pastor who was faithfully ministering to his flock. His skin was very black, his features were sharp-cut and there was nobility about his head. His eyes—those windows of the soul—impressed me especially by their gentleness. He accompanied the missionary and me on a visit to his brother, chief of the tribe. When we arrived at the compound he explained the layout to me. The houses for the various wives of the chief were grouped about the threshing floor; the storehouses for grain were in another part of the compound. Finally we were taken to the large area where the chief lived. Like his brother he had a commanding physique. I asked them to stand together while I took motion pictures. I have looked at those pictures many times since that day, and they speak to me of the darkness of Africa without Christ, and the light and joy of the heart that knows Christ. The difference between these brothers lies not in the gaily colored garments of the chief, and the white robe of the pastor, but in their faces, especially in their eyes. For the eyes of the chief show great cruelty; his features are hard and pitiless. One would never seek mercy from a man with such a formidable look of wanton savagery. The face of the pagan chief was even more revealing as he stood next to his pastor brother, whose face showed calm nobility and gentle goodness. The faces of those two men revealed their inner natures.

The life of Christ made the difference. Once the child of cruelty, the pastor had become a child of hope.

The Skidding Car

One year shortly after Christmas, my wife and I drove from Philadelphia to San Francisco. We encountered about one hundred miles of ice from western Pennsylvania to the Ohio line, another one hundred miles of icy roads in central Colorado, and a similar stretch in central Nevada. Once we passed the scene of an accident and shortly afterward heard on the car radio the statistics of road deaths over the New Year weekend. We had a heavy car, good tires and were experienced at driving on snow and ice. We had committed ourselves to the Lord and were driving below the legal speed because of road conditions. Suddenly, we felt the car skid. A truck, going much too fast, passed us just as we skidded and covered the windshield with spray. A moment later the car righted itself and we were safe, our vision once more clear. One of us chuckled, and the other said, "I had the same thought." Then we laughed, for we had both been thinking, "Lord, if you want to take us to heaven from the wreck of a car on a highway across the Rockies, that is all right with us." We were sure the Lord had led us by this route. We were in His will and on His business, and we had not a trace of fear. No wonder we laughed! We continued in prayer, often interlarded with general conversation—prayer—bits of humor—prayer—comments on scenery—prayer—discussion—prayer—driving directions. In our car, we were not two but three, for we knew that He was with us so there was constant rejoicing.

We have been delivered from the fear of death and consequently are delivered from the bondage which chains those who do not have our hope. We rejoice in hope.

Human Heart

General Liu

A news magazine described the Chinese Communist General Liu as taciturn, cold, uncommunicative; a mechanical man who came close to fulfilling his own dictum: "A party member is required to sacrifice his interests to the party unconditionally." General Liu revealed so little about himself that newsmen could get almost no personal data; but, when he spoke, he revealed the true state of his heart. A small child cut its hands tending potato vines in a commune, and the General said, "Don't be scared by a little blood." An educated man remarked to Liu that it was living hell to work in a boiler room, and the Communist leader replied, "We need more such hells."

Here is an illustration of the truth of the Bible—out of the abundance of the heart the mouth speaks. By contrast, out of the abundance of His heart God has spoken for our blessing. In Jesus Christ He has revealed that He is love and holiness, goodness and kindness; that He hates sin and desire men to be saved, that He longs for their highest good.

The Ice and the Clay

When we were living in the suburbs of Philadelphia in a twin-house, the people who lived in the other half of the house went to the seashore one day and forgot to tell the iceman not to bring ice. He put a great chunk of ice on the back porch in the warm sun. About the same time our little girl went out onto our back porch with a lump of modeling clay in her hands. Another little girl called her to play, and the clay was laid down on our porch, just a few feet away from the ice. What happened, as both lay there in the sun? Did the ice get hard and did the clay melt? Why, of course not. The ice melted and the clay got hard. What was the matter with the old sun? There was nothing the matter with the sun; the matter was with the ice and the clay. It is the nature of ice to melt in the sun and it is the nature of clay to harden.

People's hearts are like that. Some will not receive the gospel, and some will. It shines on all. There is nothing the matter with the gospel;

the matter is with the hearts of men which are evil, full of guile and deceit.

Soil Maps

One of the most humiliating failures in a government project in modern times is that of the British groundnut (peanut) adventure in Africa. Launched with great expectations, millions of acres of wild land were to be converted to peanut growing in order to produce edible oils for Britain's fat-hungry citizens. But the land turned out to be so full of quartz sand that plows and other implements rapidly wore out. The soil's consistency was like cement; unless ample rains softened it at just the right time, the ground became so hard that the sprouts couldn't push though it. Four years after the project was launched, $100,000,000 had been spent; not enough peanuts had been produced to equal the amount used for seed, and the project had to be abandoned. Lack of good soil maps had doomed the project.

There is no lack of good soil maps for the human heart. The Lord tells us that we must receive the seed into good ground not rocky, shallow, or thorny ground. Then we will have a harvest that is thirty, sixty, or a hundredfold. It is all charted for us in the Word of God.

Human Race

Weighted Dolls

Some dolls have a half-sphere of lead in their base so that they will always swing upright, no matter how they are placed. Stand them on their head, and they will almost leap to turn over; lay them down flat, and they will come upright immediately. One of these dolls, fashioned like a clown, has a large head filled with lead; the clown always winds up standing on his head. Place him upright on his pointed feet, and he will immediately turn over and stand on his head.

This is the true picture of the human race since sin entered the heart of mankind. Man looks at everything in his universe from a distorted position. Man's whole world is upside down. When a man is born again, transformed by the power and grace of God through the Lord Jesus Christ, a change takes place in him. It is as definite as removing the lead from the head of the clown and putting it in his feet so that he can stand upright.

Incarnation

The Judge's Son

Several years ago, while crossing the Atlantic Ocean, I preached at the Sunday service. After the service a group of college students came to tea; they gathered around me for a discussion of faith and the atonement. One girl became so eager that she sat on the table in front of me, surrounded by her friends. I used the illustration of a judge who saw his son come before him, accused of reckless driving. The charge was abundantly proven, and the judge fined the young man the full amount permitted under the law. Then the judge adjourned court, stepped down from the bench, and paid his son's fine. The girl, who was spokesman for the group, interjected, "But God cannot get down off the bench." I replied, "You have given me one of the best illustrations of the incarnation that I will ever have. For Jesus Christ was no more or less than God, come down off the bench to pay the fine which He had imposed upon us."

Influence

The Finger and the Molten Metal

The brother of a friend of mine worked in the steel mills of Gary, Indiana. He was a reckless fellow and a gambler. One day as molten iron was being poured from a furnace, he gathered a group of men and bet each one of them five dollars that he could take his naked finger and whip it rapidly through the inch-thick stream of fiery iron. They all covered his bet. He stooped to the floor, took up a handful of the powdery dust all around the furnace and used it to dry all the body oil from his finger. Coating his finger with this hot, dry dust, he thrust it at the liquid iron and caused the sparks to fly in many directions. Another workman watched the incident, went down to another place in the mill where a similar stream of iron was flowing and bet a group of men that he could whip his finger through the molten metal. They, likewise, covered his bet, and he whipped his finger through the stream of metal. But he did not know the secret of wiping the body oil from the finger with the parched dust. They took him to the first-aid station where a surgeon removed his entire finger. This man's ignorance caused the loss of his finger.

The man who knew the secret might be jocular about it and say that he could keep on at the practice any time that he found anyone foolish enough to wager him on the matter. But the man who has even a semblance of common decency and regard to the weakness of others would say, "I will never use my position of knowledge in a way that would cause another man to lose his finger."

There are some things which the believer will abandon because they might have a bad influence upon others. The believer must consider every act of his life in light of how it affects his life and his testimony.

Inheritance, Our

The Down Payment

After World War I, I lived in a home in the Quartier Louise in Brussels, Belgium. Each day I spent eighty minutes on the streetcar going to and from my office. There were some nice residential streets near my office so one day I rang the bell at a house that exhibited a room-for-rent sign. It was just what I wanted—size, location and price. I told the landlady that I would take the room and asked if I might move in in about ten days, as my rent was already paid in the house where I was then living. She consented and then asked me a question hesitantly. The conversation was all in French, and there was one word she used that I did not understand. She said, *"Est-ce que Monsieur voudrait verser des arrhes?"* I showed my incomprehension and repeated the line questioningly, *"Verser des arrhes?"* She replied, in French, that she was sure that I was honest and that I intended to return in ten days, but that if she took the sign out of the window and I did not return after the ten days she would lose ten days of advertising. But if I would be willing to pay something down on account.... I comprehended immediately and gave her enough francs to satisfy her. I went back to my office and said to one of my fellow-workers, "What does it mean . . . *verser des arrhes?*" He replied, "It is in the first chapter of Ephesians."

I looked it up and discovered that God tells us that when He saved us, He gave us the Holy Spirit, sealing us into Christ by Him, as the earnest, the pledge, the down payment of our inheritance.

The Inheritance

Suppose that you are sitting in your home some night and the door bell rings. A man is there, and he says, "I'm an attorney with such and such a firm, and we're trying to find a relative of a missing person. Your name is so and so. Did your mother come to this country from Scotland fifty years ago, and did she have a brother who went to Australia? You say, "We have the family Bible here. It's all written down. There's my mother. She was born in Edinburgh on such a date. She had a brother and he went to Australia, and we never heard from him since. "Well," says the lawyer, "This is wonderful for this is the last link in the evidence. He went to Australia and had a son to whom he left his fortune; that son died and left no heir. The lawyers in Australia have traced it back to Scotland; the Scotch people traced it over here, and we have come to you for we believe that you are next of kin." You say, "Yes, undoubtedly." "Well," says the lawyer, "I'm very happy to inform you that you have a very large inheritance." You say, "I can get that new Chevy I've been looking for." He says, "It's a very large inheritance." You say,

"Buick." "In fact, your uncle had coal mines." You say, "Cadillac convertible." The lawyer says, "Now, of course, it's in the courts and you can't get anything very soon except the down payment. Your uncle owned hundreds of thousands of acres of sheep ranches; oil and gold have been discovered there. It's going to be three or four years before you can get it all, but they have a little down payment that's ready for you now." "Well, what is this little down payment?" "This little down payment is only fourteen million dollars." "If that's the little down payment, what's the whole thing going to be?"

Not all the certified public accountants in the world could ever add up the glories of the inheritance reserved for us. It would be impossible for a team of bankers, accountants and lawyers to get together and tell us what the total is. All they can do is to tell us a little bit about the interest on the interest. That is about as close as anyone can get to understanding our inheritance, because the down payment is God the Holy Spirit. This inheritance is nothing short of the fact that we inherit God Himself.

Jesus Christ

The American Citizen

Years ago, in the midst of a Latin American revolution, an American citizen was sentenced to death by the authorities who had seized power. As the victim was about to face the firing squad, an American officer took a large American flag and draped it around his compatriot. "If you shoot this man," he cried out, "you will fire through the American flag and incur the wrath of a whole nation." In those days America "spoke softly, but carried a big stick," and the revolutionary in charge knew the force with which he had collided. The prisoner was released and went on his way with the officer who had come to his rescue.

If we are surrounded with the Lord Jesus Christ, then nothing can touch us unless it passes through Him. If Satan is to reach us with one of his fiery darts, he must first of all pierce the Lord Jesus Christ who protects us. Nothing in the world can ever touch us until it has passed through our Lord. As we reckon ourselves to be in Christ, and therefore immune from defeat as long as we have hold of Him, joined to Him in His death, so do we learn to reckon ourselves to be alive unto God.

Caught in the Clothes Closet

When his bed caught fire, Edward Sweeny, of New York City, awakened, ran to the door, opened it, went through it, and slammed it behind him only to discover that he was in a clothes closet and could not get out. Meanwhile other tenants smelled smoke and sounded the alarm. The firemen extinguished the blaze and released Mr. Sweeney from the closet when they heard him pounding on the door.

How like human beings! Caught in the sleep of death, they race to any door and rush through only to be trapped in their false hope. Is it any wonder that the Lord cries through the prophet, "Turn you to the strong hold, ye prisoners of hope . . ." (ZECHARIAH 9:12). Christ is the stronghold and the only door. Any man who attempts to find safety by any other door will find himself trapped forever.

The Damaged Oak

Of several oak trees I planted near my house, all but one grew more than twenty feet high. That one was damaged; it died at the soil line, but the root system remained intact and a shoot came forth— spindly and weak. I was about to tear it out to make room for a new tree, when a horticulturist told me that this shoot would catch up with the other trees. Although I could hardly believe it, I let it alone; after two years it was six feet high; after four years, more than twelve feet. It had a fine branch system, all fed from a root system equal to that of the other trees.

God slices through the gentle forest like a hurricane, lopping boughs with terrifying power, hewing down the tallest trees with His axe of judgment. Then, from the most unlikely stump, comes forth a new tree. Jesse, the father of King David, was in the royal line from

Abraham to the Messiah. Who would expect that a ruler of little Israel would surpass the Caesars? God's forestry is not like man's. When He speaks, a dead stump brings forth life: Christ comes to deliver His people.

Elder Kim

Several years before the second world war, I spent a month in Korea ministering to groups of missionaries. At Sorai Beach, scores of missionary families were spending the summer, and there were many opportunities for social fellowship. One evening a group of us were seated on the sand under a magnificient moon. I said to them, "Now I have been teaching you twice a day for several days, and I want my pay. Tell me your best missionary stories." After a moment of silence, one man said to another, "Tell him about Elder Kim." Here is the story:

Kim, a Korean layman of wealth and prominence, was elected elder of one of the Presbyterian churches in Pyongyang, the chief city of northern Korea. Because of his outstanding character and reputation, he was asked to address the annual meeting of the General Assembly of the church. He began modestly, reminding his hearers that he was a simple layman, not trained in a seminary or Bible institute. He was not going to preach or attempt to teach, but he wished to put before them a great problem and to ask their advice for its solution.

"A year or two ago," he began, "I received a letter from a friend of mine in Seoul. A young dentist, he wanted to establish himself in Pyongyang, and he asked me to find a place that would be suitable for his home and office combined. Although there is a great housing shortage, I did all I could to help him. I seached the town for three days, found a place and wrote to him about it. I told him that the house was in bad condition: the wall surrounding the property was in disrepair; there was a hole in the house wall; the roof leaked very badly; the house was in a very bad neighborhood; next door was a house inhabited by 'singing girls.' Furthermore, the price was exorbitant. In spite of this adverse report, my friend telegraphed me to buy the house. A day or so later I received a check for several thousand yen for the down payment, so I signed the papers to purchase the house. The down payment was made, and the final payments were to be made in three days, at which time the owner agreed to vacate the house. The payments were made, but the owner asked for a day or two more in order to find another house. I granted him this period of grace, but after a week he was still there. Two weeks, three weeks, a month, three months, six months have passed. The man who sold the house has bought new clothing for his family, and they are eating polished rice instead of the cheaper grains. He knows that I am a Christian and that in Korea we Christians never go to court against other Christians, and we try not to go to court against unbelievers. He laughs at me when I come.

"Now, Fathers and Brethren," Elder Kim continued, "my friend is greatly embarrassed because his capital is tied up in this house, and he is in a very difficult position. What am I to do?"

Several of the members of the General Assembly responded. One pointed out that Elder Kim was not acting in his own behalf, but as an agent. Another pointed out that he was evidently dealing with a man who was a thief at heart. All agreed that Kim had the right to go to the authorities and ask for an eviction order. Kim asked for a show of hands, and all voted that he had the right to proceed legally.

Elder Kim concluded: "Thank you, Fathers and Brethren, for the way you have considered my problem. Before I sit down I wish to draw one conclusion. Nineteen hundred years ago the Lord Jesus Christ came down from Heaven to purchase for Himself a dwelling place." Then striking his hand upon his breast, he continued, "He bought this old shack rundown, in a bad neighborhood. He bought me because He wanted to take possession and dwell in my heart. He gave Himself for me, and He gave me the Holy Spirit as a down payment on my inheritance, bringing me innumerable blessings with His redemption. But I cling to my tenement and leave Him outside. Now if you say that I have the right to seek the help of the authorities to evict the man who is occupying my friend's house, what shall you and I say of ourselves when we deny the Lord Jesus the full possession of that for which He gave His own life?"

Christ died and rose again that He might be our Lord. Let us, then, recognize Him as Lord and commit ourselves to Him in obedience. He wants to rule our lives. The Lordship of Christ in our lives is to be evidenced by our recognition of the fact that since He is Lord of all who trust in Him, no believer can judge another. He is to draw us to Himself. He is to be Lord over all the life of each believer.

The Home

When I first met the man I knew little about him. Then I met his wife; she was cultured, charming and spiritual, and my opinion of the man went up, for I saw that he had chosen his wife with the highest part of his nature and had not been looking for the standard equipment of the glamor-girl type. He had chosen character and Christian life, with all the component gifts and graces that go with them. After I had talked to this couple for a while, their charming sixteen-year-old daughter entered the room. The girl had intelligence, charm and manners; she was looking forward to giving her life to the Lord's service. Meeting her made me know her parents better. A few minutes later two boys came into the room, one about fourteen, the other about twelve. Their deportment, bearing and manner gave me further insight into the character and attributes of the father. I could see a home, well-run, well-managed, and with a proper system of priorities— putting the Lord first, and developing all the gifts and graces with which He had endowed the children.

If it is possible to know a man better because I have seen his wife and watched his children through the course of an evening's meal and a social hour of family conversation, how much more will it be possible to exhibit the wonder of His being and the marvels of His grace through all of the infinite company of the saints who have been redeemed by His blood and saved through His grace!

The Irish King

There is a legend of an Irish king who disguised himself and went into the banquet hall of one of his barons. He was escorted to a lowly place among the throng who sat at the feast. The brilliance of his conversation and the nobility of his manner soon attracted the attention of someone with sufficient authority to escort him to a higher table. The same thing occurred once more, and soon he was seated among the nobles of the realm. After a display of great wisdom, one of the lords spoke out and said, "In truth, Sir, you speak like a king. If you are not a king, you deserve to be." Then the king removed his disguise and took his rightful place among his subjects.

When our Lord Jesus came from heaven's glory, His subjects were so blinded by their own darkness of heart that they were not willing to stoop before Him. The King of Kings and Lord of Lords was there, but they received Him not, even though He stated over and over again that He was the eternal God come down to redeem them.

Korean Prisoners of War

Almost a quarter of a century ago, the Reverend Harold Voekel went to Korea as a missionary. When the Korean war began, he entered the United States Army as a chaplain, and was assigned to prisoner of war camps. Tens of thousands of North Koreans were imprisoned in great compounds. The Communists had infiltrated the camps with their agents, and there were riots and rebellion. Chaplain Voekel came with the truth of God. He entered the first pen of several hundred men and began to talk to them in their own tongue; their resistance faded, and they crowded around him and waited for his message. He told them he wanted to teach them a song. It was a rude Korean translation of the child's hymn, "Jesus loves me, this I know." He kept them about an hour and told them he would be back the next day. He then went into the next pen and began all over again. Day after day he entered a dozen or more pens, teaching them to sing "Jesus loves me." Weeks passed and then months. By this time several thousand North Koreans were professing their faith in Christ as their personal Saviour. The discipline became easier in the camps. The Communists could not find easy followers as they had at first. When the question of repatriation came up, these men insisted that they did not want to go home. They wanted to live in the free world. The commanding officer, General Harrison, testified of the wonderful results that came from the preaching of the love of Christ to these men. When the time came for these prisoners of war to vote for their future, they turned their backs on communism by the thousands and gave the whole world a great example of the desire of men to remain free from red slavery. The message of the love of Jesus Christ transformed these men; it gave them vision not only of the world to come, but of free life here on earth.

The message that was preached to these prisoners was the same simple message that has challenged the hearts of millions through the ages; it is just as effective today as it was when the disciple John leaned on the bosom of Christ.

Old Photographs

I once spent some time in a hotel in Florida that was patronized almost entirely by older people taking the winter sun. One day, in the lobby, a group began talking about their grandchildren. Some carried portfolios of photographs while others had snapshots of their loved ones. "Look at that boy," said one old man. "He is the spit and image of me. When I was that age, they took an old tintype of me, and it is just like that." The man's eyes were alight, his face radiant. Other men and women were likewise filled with loving pride at the thought of their children's children.

I can draw no conclusion other than that Christ had a similar joy and a proper pride in all of His redeemed when He ascended into Heaven. He had gone to the cross and died in order to buy you and me. He was proud of us—sinners though we are. For God the Father, Son and Holy Spirit does not see as we see—in the sight of the Godhead we were not only redeemed, but we were already glorified.

Street-Sweepers' Wages

We might think it strange if the President of the United States met with the Prime Minister of Britain and the heads of other states and spent a good deal of time discussing a common standard of wage payment for street-sweepers in the various capitols of the world. There would be many who would think that these men in positions of great power should spend their time on more important things—things that affect the peace of the world and the flow of history.

In like manner, it might be thought strange that the Lord Jesus Christ should be on the throne of heaven considering the matters that are now before Him. Yet the Bible shows us that He is not now concerning Himself with the great plans of governments and the movements of nations. These things have been planned before the foundation of the world and written down in their permanent form. Nothing can change the course of events that God has determined for this earth. Christ has all the time in the world and in heaven to be occupied with the flood of His love toward those whom He redeemed with the price of His blood. He is seated upon the throne of God, occupied with nothing other than your best interests.

Visiting the Mint

Years ago when I visited the Philadelphia mint with my children, gold pieces were still being manufactured. We watched men take sheets of gold and sheets of silver—roughly 16 x 20 inches—and feed them into a great hydraulic press. The machine caught the edges of these flat pieces of metal and took them into the middle of the press. Then we heard "clump," and fifty or a hundred coins came out into a basket on the side. The man who was showing us around said to the children, "Pick some up"; the children picked them up, but dropped them very fast, because the tremendous pressure of two hundred tons hitting, knocking a coin out and making it hard, left a great frictional heat. We watched as they poured out twenty-five cent pieces to be weighed, and again the man picked one up. In one place coins were examined through magnifying glasses; a man could tell by looking at a coin what was happening to the die inside the press. By magnifying it tremendously, he could tell from which die a coin came; as soon as any particular die showed any type of wearing, it was taken out and another die put in its place. We could not see the dies inside the machine, we saw only the twenty-five cent pieces but each coin was the express image of the invisible die.

God says that the Lord Jesus Christ was the Lord God Almighty, the express image of His invisible person. God the father is invisible, Jesus was visible.

Joy

The Atlantic Storm

There has never been a storm on the Atlantic, whose roots went deeper than the surface, even if the waves were so great that they combed over the bridge of a battleship. A submarine always finds the water fifty feet down as calm as a pond on a clear June day.

If a believer is not joyful, it is almost certain that he does not possess the peace of God; one may even doubt whether he has righteousness. Joy must not be confused with mirth; the latter is effervescent, but joy is the steady tenor of our being. When all is chaos on the surface, deep down there is joy.

Crackers-and-Cheese Christians

Years ago, a Scotchman arrived in Liverpool where he was to embark for his journey to America. He fingered the few shillings that made up his total earthly capital, and decided that he would economize on food during the trip in order to have more money on hand when he reached New York. He went to a small store and laid in a supply of crackers and cheese to get him through the days at sea. But as the voyage progressed the sea air made him very hungry. To make matters worse the dampness in the air made his crackers soft and his cheese hard. He was almost desperate with hunger. To cap the climax he caught the fragrant whiff of food on a tray a steward was carrying to another passenger. The hungry man made up his mind that he would have one good, square meal, even though it might take several of his shillings. He awaited the return of the steward and asked him how much it would cost to go to the dining room and get a dinner. The steward asked the Scotchman if he had a ticket for the steamship passage. The man showed his ticket, and the steward told him that all meals were included in the price of the ticket. The poor man could have saved the money he spent on crackers and cheese; he could have gone to the dining room and eaten as much as he liked every meal time.

This is a humble picture of the position of many people who have believed in Christ as Saviour. Because of that faith, they are saved, but they go on their miserable way without appropriating any of the blessings that God has for them in Christ. How terrible is the responsibility of these crackers-and-cheese Christians, who show no joy to those who are looking for the reality of joy in life! Such Christians cannot show it because they do not have it. Yet it was all provided for them in Christ. "He that spared not his own Son, but delivered him up for us all, how shall he not with him also freely give us all things?" (ROMANS 8:32).

The Fractured Leg

Imagine a man who has been in an automobile accident. His leg is twisted out of its socket, and the bone is broken. He tells the doctor, "Give me a sedative quickly so that I can be at peace and rest. I want to sleep. Just give me a drug and go away and leave me." What a fool he would be! No man in his right mind would say such a thing, and yet millions are seeking for some opiate of peace without righteousness. The doctor must set the fracture and put the leg back in its socket. Then nature will take its course, and he will know healing and peace.

It is certainly thus in the sequence of God's dealing with man. God simply will not allow any man to know true peace until that man first possesses divine righteousness. One reason for the terrible frustration of mankind is that peace and joy are sought without righteousness.

But without the righteousness of God there can be no peace, and without the peace of God there can be no joy.

The Royal Standard

In London, Buckingham Palace flies the royal standard to show that the sovereign is in residence. Day or night the flag can be seen, and the people know that their queen is not away, but at home.

Thus joy flies as the flag over our lives to show that Christ our king is in residence.

Troubles of my Own

A layman wished to perform some kind of Christian service, so his pastor suggested that he go to a rescue mission and help. The man duly presented himself to the superintendent of the mission shortly before a service for the down-and-outers who walked along Skid Row. The superintendent told the man to stand out on the sidewalk and invite passing men to come into the meeting. The man accosted the passersby and, in a mournful tone, asked them to enter the mission. Each man to whom he spoke glanced at him and went on. He learned his lesson, however, when one man responded to his doleful invitation, "Brother, wouldn't you like to come in to the meeting?" Cynically, the man looked at his solemn face and said, "No, thanks; I've troubles enough of my own."

We are certainly not good recommendations for the Lord Jesus Christ if we have not learned the great truth that joy is one of the prime requisites of the Christian life.

Judgment of God

An Ancient Palimpsest

Exhibited in one of the cases in the library of the Vatican is an ancient palimpsest. Centuries ago, men had written line after line on sheets of papyrus until their work filled an entire volume. Many years later, when paper was difficult to secure, someone found the old volume and wrote a new work across the original manuscript, in lines perpendicular to the first. Today the blacker ink of the second writing is more legible, but the text underneath is still clear enough to read with ease; scholars frequently take more delight in reading the older than they do the more recent writing.

Such is the heart and conscience of man. Across the fresh page in the youth of the race, God wrote the eternal truths of His being, His holiness, His justice, and the certainty of His wrath against sin. Men turned the page sidewise and wrote with blacker ink the history of their doings until, in some places, the earlier writing is almost effaced. But the day will come when the acid of God's judgment will eat away the writings of man, and the strong X ray of the light of God will bring to the surface the original writing by which man will be judged.

The Coat Button

"Button, button, who's got the button?" may be more than child's play. A woman bought a coat in a shop in Brooklyn for ninety dollars and soon lost a button from it. The shop did not have an extra button, so the woman wrote to the factory. The factory recognized the button as one that matched that from a stolen coat. The woman led detectives to the shop, and the owner was jailed as a fence for receiving stolen goods from shoplifters. From button to coat, from theft to thief—the chain led to judgment.

With man it takes detective work, but to God all things are naked and open. All missing buttons will be located in that day—every wrong will be brought home to the doer unless he has let the Saviour settle out of court for him.

Church Barriers

Listen to people crossing from Canada to the United States, talking about how to cheat the customs: "Oh, just say you have been in Canada more than forty-eight hours," one woman may tell another. "You can bring in up to a hundred dollars' worth if you have been here forty-eight hours." "But I only came yesterday," the other answers. "Oh, they will never check up on you." A dozen similar conversations go on.

One day we must all pass the customs barriers at the bar of God. No good works may be imported by the one who has not received Christ as Saviour. Such souls will be naked and speechless before the great Searcher of hearts (ROMANS 3:19). Even those who are believers may enter nothing that has not been done for the glory of the Lord. There can be no deception. "Neither is there any creature that is not manifest in his sight: but all things are naked and opened unto the eyes of him with whom we have to do" (HEBREW 4:13).

The Fallen Plane

We have all read about expeditions to the antarctic and of the possible establishment of an airbase in the south polar region. Let us suppose that a plane comes down in these waters, south of New Zealand. The pilots know that there is no other plane, no ship and no land within a thousand miles of them. Three men are cast into the water: One is able to swim only a few hundred feet; the second can manage to stay afloat an hour or two; the third is the world champion long-distance swimmer. Is it sensible for the champion to show the first man his best swimming strokes? Will the champion say, "Take me as an example?" These men do not need an example, they need a saviour. One will drown in twenty minutes, a second will drown in two hours, and the third will drown in fifteen hours.

Thus it is with men; they do not need an example, they need a Saviour. The convict is like the man who can swim only a few strokes, the average man is like the man who can swim for a while; the very, very good man is like the man who can swim for fifteen hours. But all three are doomed to die under the circumstances I have set forth.

So it is with men before the judgment of God. The very best that a man can do in deeds of kindness and charity does not change the unalterable fact that his character and his works are cursed by God. The only thing that will satisfy a holy God is that man shall take sides with Him, accept the shedding of His blood for the remission of sins, cross the chasm through Christ and stand with God in all His estimates, judgments and verdict.

The Hunting Accident

A hunter experiences a terrible accident. His gun goes off as he climbs over a fence; the bullet enters the back of his friend, killing him instantly. There are some doubts that the death was accidental because the survivor stands to gain financially by the death of his friend, and a coroner's inquest is held. The district attorney wishes to intervene. He thinks the hunter should be brought to trial so that all evidence may be brought forth in court. The lawyers argue over the wording of the indictment. If the district attorney brings in an indictment of murder in the first degree, a conviction will carry a mandatory death sentence. If the indictment is for manslaughter, the accused will be tried, but the penalty will not be death. Or the bill may charge him only with criminal negligence: he may be sued for damages that may take away his property. The wording of the indictment will make all the difference in the outcome of his trial, and in the sentence that will be imposed if he is found guilty.

The sinner is guilty before God. Christ Jesus has carried the penalty of the sinner's guilt. The one who believes in Christ can never, therefore, appear in a judgment where he could be condemned to the second death. That judgment has been removed from him forever. It would be as impossible for God to bring me to a judgment that might end in sending me to hell as it would be for God to send Christ to earth to die again.

Murder or Manslaughter

The cases of two men awaiting trial have been bound over by the grand jury. One of them, the evidence shows, has planned and plotted the death of a friend. He schemed for months, bought his instrument, planned the time and committed the murder. There is every evidence of the sanity of the killer, and there is every evidence of premeditation. The charge against him is murder in the first degree. The second man is also on trial because a man lies dead, but the evidence is quite different. He was driving his automobile on slippery pavement. Evidence shows that he leaned out of the car window and waved to a friend, calling out a message. He had carelessly taken one hand off the wheel and was going faster than the conditions warranted. Suddenly the car skidded and ran up on the sidewalk and killed a man. There is every evidence of carelessness and negligence, so he is bound over for trial; the charge is manslaughter. What will be the difference in attitude as the two men go to trial? The first man has every right to be apprehensive that he will go to the electric chair. Will the second man fear the death penalty? Certainly not. He knows that the extreme penalty for such a charge is but twenty years in prison; he has hope that his known character and ability to pay all the damage claims arising from the accident will probably cause the jury to recommend leniency, and that a suspended sentence may be his lot.

In precisely the same manner we may interpret the question of future judgments. The unbeliever has every reason to fear. The penalty that lies before him is that of the eternal separation from God. But that penalty has been removed forever from the believer.

Unpolished Shoes

A soldier found it difficult to get out of bed one morning; he appeared on parade with shoes that were far from polished. The inspecting officer barked at him and asked why the shoes were in that state. Without blinking an eye the soldier replied, "I tried two kinds of shoe polish, sir, and they neutralized one another." The nonplussed officer passed on down the line.

Multitudes of Christians will appear at the judgment seat of Christ with no luster in their life because they have been double-minded in all their ways (JAMES 1:8)—unstable, neutralizing the power of the Spirit by the drag of the flesh.

Unprepared

The Pearl Harbor Report demonstrated that not only were an admiral and a general unprepared, the authorities were unprepared and the whole nation was in a lethargy of self-satisfaction. In spite of all the evidence that an attack would come, people were amazed when it did.

Thus is the approaching judgment of God going to come upon the world; the Bible informs us that judgment is coming. Men are warned to flee from the wrath of God. They are warned that sudden destruction will come upon them, that it will come suddenly as a stroke of lightning from the east and the west and as unexpectedly as a thief in the night. In spite of all these warnings the world sinks in its lethargy of self-satisfaction. It will be awakened by a blow far more rude than Pearl Harbor, for just as the gifts and calling of God are without repentance, so are His judgments.

Justice of God

Sculptured Justice

One evening a friend introduced me to a lawyer who practices in Philadelphia. We discussed certain questions connected with the crime situation and the dispensing of justice. I contended that there should be a much more drastic use of the law, and pointed to the traditional conception of justice. When an architect gives a contract to a sculptor for a decorative piece for a courthouse, the result has usually been the figure of a woman—to represent chastity, she is blindfolded, to indicate that justice is no respecter of persons; she holds a balance in which evidence is to be weighed minutely, and a sword without a scabbard, ready to strike wherever there is guilt. The lawyer listened to my description and then added with a smile, "And is to be found only in statuary."

As far as earthly justice is concerned this is probably true. In meting out justice perfection is not to be found in earthly courts. Fearing a mistake and knowing that we are all guilty in a certain measure, we are not perfect in knowledge or in holiness and therefore we are slow to act.

When we face the justice of God, however, we are dealing with One who is absolutely perfect in knowledge, who is absolutely holy, and who is perfect in His justice.

Justification

The Hymnbook in the Hand

When I was about fifteen years old, I heard a man give a vivid testimony for Christ. I spoke to him about his experience because I was not very settled in mine, and I knew that he had something that I did not have.

He took my left hand and drew it out, palm upward, all the while fixing me with an intense gaze. "This hand represents you," he said. On that hand he placed a large hymnbook. He then said, "This book represents your sin. The weight of it is upon you. God hates sin, and His wrath must bear down against sin. His wrath is bearing down upon you, and you have no peace in your heart and life."

He drew my other hand forward, palm upward, and said, "This hand represents the Lord Jesus Christ, the Saviour. There is no sin upon Him, and the Father must love Him, because He is without spot and blemish. He is the beloved Son in whom the Father is well pleased." I saw my two hands before me: one covered with the large book, the other empty; I realized that I had the sin, and the Lord Jesus Christ had none.

Then this man put his hand under my left hand, the hand that represented me, the hand upon which the Book was lying; with a sweeping gesture he turned my hand over so that the Book came down upon the palm of my right hand—the one that represented Christ. My left hand he put back as it had been; I could see that the burden was gone from it entirely. He then said to me, "This is what happened when the Lord Jesus Christ took your place upon the cross. He was the lamb of God, who was bearing away the sin of the world.

This is the justification that acts upon our sins to take them away from us and to place them upon the Saviour.

Paying Bills

Every one of us at some time or other has walked into an office to pay a bill—for telephone service, electricity, or some other obligation we have incurred. We hand the money to the teller who counts our money, takes the bill we owe, and presses a rubber stamp upon an ink pad, stamps our bill and hands us a receipt. The company could never collect that bill from us again, for if they tried to do so, we could produce the receipt and they would know that the matter had been cleared, and that we were free from the obligation forever.

The Lord Jesus Christ walked up to Calvary, which was God's desk for the payment of the bill of our sins. The account was heavy against us, and the Lord Jesus Christ could settle the account by shedding His blood in dying for us.

The Rented Field

Suppose that one man rented a field from another and promised to pay a hundred dollars for the rental. The agreement is signed; the day of payment comes. If the harvest has been poor because of drought, pest, unseasonable storms, or poor fertilizing, the man who rented the field may wish that he had not signed the agreement. He may wish that the owner would take half of the harvest instead of demanding cash, but the agreement has been signed; there is nothing to do but abide by it. If, however, the owner should say that he would accept fifty bushels of corn instead of money, there is an end to the argument. If the owner should say that he would accept twenty bushels of grain instead of the money, there is an end to the matter. If the owner should say that he would free the man from his debt provided that the debtor sing for him, then that would be the end to the matter. It is the owner who must be satisfied.

God must be satisfied in the matter of our sin. Justification is expression of the fact that God declares Himself fully satisfied by virtue of what the Lord Jesus Christ has done for us.

The Wrong Criminal

Bertram Campbell spent three years and four months in Sing Sing prison for a forgery he did not commit. The real criminal finally confessed and cleared him. The innocent man was taken to Albany and the Governor of New York, who had been the prosecuting attorney who convicted him, signed a pardon that was not really a pardon at all. The traditional wording of the pardon had been changed from "fit object of our mercy" to "innocent of the crime for which he was convicted." In other words, Campbell was not pardoned; he was justified.

The Lord Jesus Christ does exactly this for the one who puts his trust in the work of Calvary. The blood cleanses us from all sin so that in the sight of God we are justified. Justification puts new Paul alongside of old Saul, glorification takes old Paul out of the picture, and new Paul is forever absolutely justified in Christ.

Law

Catheterizing the Heart

Several years ago I learned from an outstanding medical professor, who is a member of my church that a new process had been devised to study the heart. A slender, hollow plastic tube can be introduced into the antecubital vein at the elbow, and skillfully worked up the vein until it passes over the shoulder and down into the heart. A cloudy chemical can be released which shows the fluoroscopist the nature of the flow of blood within the heart; by maneuvering the catheter through the ventricles, a blood sample can be secured from within the lungs. This work preceded the operations which have cured so many "blue babies."

It interested me greatly that the Scripture verses that speak of the Lord as "trying the heart" are rendered in the great French translations as "catheterizing the heart." ". . . by the law is the knowledge of sin" (ROMANS 3:20). Paul is really telling us that the instrument the Lord used for this delicate work was the law He gave through Moses. The law is a probe that enters into the inner recesses to reveal the true nature of Adam's being which is in us.

Hydrogen Bomb Explosion

Suppose a great hydrogen bomb exploded over Washington, D. C. at a moment when every member of the executive, legislative and judicial branches of our government was present in the capital. Not one high official would escape. Since it would be necessary for some authority to take control, let us further suppose that a strong man arose to lead the nation. He might govern by a benevolent dictatorship, issuing decrees that would establish some sort of working order, but his decrees would also become the working law of the land, and he would not act according to the provisions of the federal constitution. Such a change in government would obviously do away with our constitution.

The coming of the Lord Jesus Christ worked a far greater change than that from a constitutional republic to a one-man dictatorship. The coming of Christ established Him as the Lord God Almighty stepping into his own visible universe to do what He pleased. His coming did away with the law and established the rule of the Holy Spirit. Henceforth, the Holy Spirit is the *only*—it is important to repeat it—the *only* representative, the *only* vicar of Christ on earth. Christ is the end of the law for righteousness, but love is the fulfilling of the law, and believers are to receive each other in love.

The Mirror

If a man observes himself in a mirror and sees that his face is dirty, he does not take the mirror down from the wall and start rubbing it upon his face. The mirror shows him that his face is dirty, but the mirror cannot wash his face. The purpose of the mirror is to drive him to water. Any other use of the mirror is plain folly.

Anyone who tries to be saved by keeping the Ten Commandments or by living by the Sermon on the Mount resembles those who would seek to wash with mirrors. It cannot be done. All he will do is to smear himself yet more.

The Nick in the Cup

Many years ago, in London, I bought a set of china at wholesale prices. In the providence of God, we still have it in our home and there has never been a nick in any piece. I bought only demitasses because I did not have enough money to buy cups and saucers. Over the years we enjoyed our plates and other dishes, but we needed larger cups.

Once while I was preaching in Cleveland, Ohio, I came to an antique store that displayed a Wedgewood cup and saucer. I had read enough about china to know they were real Wedgewood—possibly part of a set. I bought them for a modest price, and as I traveled over the years I picked up a cup and saucer here and another there. I always set a price, in advance, for I would not pay more than a certain amount for it.

One day, in Vancouver, British Columbia, I passed an antique store that had a beautiful cup and saucer finished in a green tint that I knew was powdered jade. "How much is this?" I asked. He gave me a price that was beneath my set price. I said, "There is a little nick in it," and he replied, "If that little nick wasn't there, that cup and saucer I am offering you for a few dollars, would be worth a hundred." I bought the cup and saucer because the little nick didn't mean that much to me. It was only about as big as a pinhead, but from his point of view, that nick prevented the cup and saucer from being a perfect one.

God says that the little nick is JAMES 2:10: "For whosoever shall keep the whole law, and yet offend in one point, he is guilty of all." If you had committed only one sin—a little pink-white lie—God says that you are also guilty of murder; you are guilty of adultery; you are guilty of thievery; you are guilty of pride and arrogance. But you say, "Lord, I only did this." God says, "The law is one. You have broken it, and it doesn't make any difference whether you break it here or there. If you've broken it, you've broken it, and that is it."

No Speed Laws

Fifty years ago no road signs set up fifty-mile-an-hour zones. Why not? Because no one had ever gone fifty miles an hour. Then men began to drive recklessly. Cars buzzed through villages and towns, causing chickens to scatter, horses to run away and wagons to be turned over. Men looked darkly after the speeding cars and said, "There ought to be a law." Before long there was a law, and the highway department sent employees out along the roads to put up signs: slow, curve—35 miles; school zone—15 miles; and so on.

Thus it was before the time of Moses. God had called Abraham and had saved him by grace alone. There was nothing but the covenant of grace—promises that were absolutely without condition. Abraham and his descendants transgressed. It was though an angel might have said, "There ought to be a law." And so God called Moses and gave him the law, Moses came along, somewhat like a highway employee, and put up the signs of the commandments: "Thou shalt not. . . ." "Thou shalt not. . . ." "Thou shalt not. . . ."

Probably no automobile driver in this whole country has ever obeyed all of the traffic laws.

Unfortunately there are those who have a similar attitude toward the laws of God. They think that if they go along approximately in the general direction they think the laws indicate, God will not be too hard on them. They think of being brought before the judgment bar of God somewhat in terms of a traffic violation. They do not realize that the slightest infraction of the law of God is spiritual death—with a penalty that can be removed only by the shedding of the blood of the Son of God.

The Parking Meter

An item in the *New York Times* told about Louis Booth from Poughkeepsie, N. Y. A policeman put a summons on Booth's windshield for failing to put a coin in the parking meter on Church Street. City Judge Charles Corbally dismissed the case when it was brought out that the meter had been set up after Mr. Booth had parked his car. The policeman had not seen the workman who did the job.

If we grant that parking the car in the spot indicated, was in itself harmful to general traffic, this incident becomes a perfect illustration for a spiritual truth. Something was added to the wrong that gave it the character of a transgression. Before the parking meter had been put up, the man could not be fined. After the parking meter was put up, he could be.

In the Epistle to the Galatians the Holy Spirit, after showing us that salvation is by grace, gives the reason why law has added, four hundred and thirty years after God had given the promise of salvation by grace. He asks the question and answers it: "Wherefore then serveth the law? It was added because of transgressions, till the seed should come . . ." (GALATIANS 3:19). Put in modern language it would mean that it was added in order to give to sin the character of transgression. Also, we read, "For until the law sin was in the world: but sin is not imputed when there is no law" (ROMANS 5:13).

Russian Versus British Jurisdiction

British authorities arrested a man on the German frontier, at a point that lay just between Russian jurisdiction and British jurisdiction. The Reds asked for the man; they claimed he was an escaped murderer; they wished to try him for his crime. The British knew that surrender of the man would be his death warrant, so they refused to give him up. Finally, he was set free; and defected to the West. All the while he was free from the sentence of death that had been passed upon him in the Russian jurisdiction.

Thus we were once under the jurisdiction of the law of sin and death. But when the Lord Jesus Christ was placed on the cross by the Father and put to death in accordance with the divine plan, God so joined us to our Lord in the death and in the resurrection that followed that He could righteously place us under the jurisdiction of the law of the spirit of life in Christ Jesus. It is this which forever frees us from the jurisdiction of the law of sin and death. God himself cannot hold anything against the believer whom He has joined to the Lord Jesus Christ.

The Ten Link Chain

A small boat in a stream of swiftly rushing water is secured to shore by a chain of only ten links. How many links must be cut to set boat adrift? A lady, wearing white gloves and wielding fine steel shears, may open one link—there goes the boat. Just one little link, but the boat is gone. A man may come down with a blow torch. He burns out all ten links—there goes the boat.

The man who commits one delicate little sin is the same in God's sight as the man who breaks all the commandments. If a man is less perfect than God, he is seen to be a sinner. Whether one link is broken or all the links are broken, the boat is adrift.

Law and Grace

The Truck Collision

Driving along a highway, you are stopped by an accident. A truck driver lies in the wreckage. Half a dozen men from passing cars place themselves shoulder to shoulder and try to lift the bumper. They tug and they pull until you see the veins standing out in their necks, but they cannot free the man. Still they keep straining at the impossible task. Finally, a wrecker drives up and is placed in position to hoist the weight of the disabled truck. But the only available spot for the wrecker to attach its hoist is that bumper at which the men are tugging. If the wrecker is to do its work, *the men must get out of the way.* If they persist in monopolizing that place, the wrecker cannot get in to do its work. There is no moral charge against these men; their strength is simply insufficient for the task.

The law must be abolished in order to let grace do the job the law cannot do.

The Undertow

I was born within a few miles of the Pacific Ocean, near Monterey Bay. The beach near our home had a very swift undertow and we all were aware that fatal accidents had occurred there more than once. The sandy beach that ran out level for a few yards, dropped suddenly and caught the unwary. One day when I was just learning to swim, I walked into the surf and was pretending to swim. One foot was balanced on the sand every other moment, while my arms thrashed the surface of the water; I looked as though I were swimming. I bounced along in this way for some time until—the bottom was not there. I had stepped off the ledge of sand and into deep water. In the Providence of God, I was buffeted by the waves and caught on a strong incoming roller and pitched up into the shallow water. I scrambled to my feet, retching from the water I had swallowed, and fought my way to the dry sand. I can still remember the terrifying panic at being out of my depth—nothing under me, strong currents pulling at me, the waves tossing me. I was at the mercy of the gray-green flood, not knowing in which direction it might take me.

Many Christians are brought to the place where they must step out of the sphere of doing something for themselves and into the place where they are to be borne along on the will of God without any possibility of doing anything about it. The transition from law to grace is so great and overwhelming that a vast number of believers in Christ never reach the place in their Christian experience where they know the freedom from law and the irresistibleness of grace.

The Widower's Housekeeper

A widower is left with two small children so he hires a housekeeper to help him. He gives her instructions as to what she shall cook, how she is to keep the house and how she is to dress and care for the children. He goes about the house from time to time to see that all is in order, and that she is properly obeying his rules. He watches her dominion over the children and corrects her in a manner befitting the relationship of master and servant. After a year or so he marries the housekeeper. Their relationship is now entirely changed. He no longer follows her around the house to oversee her work. He no longer tells her what to cook for dinner. Now she is his in a relationship of love. Now she delights to do his will. Now she seeks to find out his desires and to perform them. Now she asks him what he would like to have for dinner and goes to some trouble to prepare it. She is no longer under law but under grace.

It is necessary for the Christian to understand that the life of true righteousness comes not from law but from the love of Christ under grace.

Legalism

No Makeup

A college girl from my congregation met a girl who had almost no religious background. Child of a divided family, who had little concern with religion, she had reached college age with no church affiliation; she had not even attended any church services more than two or three times in her life. The Christian girl got her friend to attend church; the girl was saved during her senior year. Shortly after graduation the two girls went, with several others, on a trip to Europe. The girl from my church was to attend a Christian convention for a few days in Switzerland, while the others went on to Venice. On the morning she was to go to the convention, she appeared with no makeup. The new Christian cried out, "You have forgotten your makeup!" The older girl explained that the people at the convention did not wear makeup and that she was conforming to their practice. The new Christian was scandalized. If *that* was the essence of Christianity, she didn't want it. The girl from my congregation told me later, "I decided that if going without makeup would cause my sister in Christ to be scandalized, I would never go without it again."

More often than not the baby Christian, who has just come out of the world, is more scandalized by the narrow legalism of some believers than by the normal life of the so-called "worldly" believer.

No Stockings

Around 1928, I led a Bible conference at Montrose, Pennsylvania, for about two hundred young people and a few older people. One day two old ladies complained that some of the girls were not wearing stockings; these ladies wanted me to rebuke them. Looking them straight in the eye, I said, "The Virgin Mary never wore stockings." They gasped and said, "She didn't?" I answered, "In Mary's time stockings were unknown. So far as we know, they were first worn by prostitutes in Italy in the fifteenth century, when the Renaissance began. Later, a lady of the nobility scandalized the people by wearing stockings at a court ball. Before long, everyone in the upper classes was wearing stockings, and by Queen Victoria's time, stockings had become the badge of the prude." These ladies, who were holdovers from the Victorian epoch, had no more to say. I did not rebuke the girls for not wearing stockings. A year or two afterward, most girls in the United States were going without stockings in summer and nobody thought anything about it.

Nor do I believe that this led toward disintegration of moral standards in the United States. Times were changing, and the step away from Victorian legalism was all for the better. We should not be concerned about those who are well established not only in faith but in the rut of non-biblical legalism.

Looking at Christ

Seeing Nothing

An Eastern prince had difficulty with a riotous-living young man of his court. When the young man was given his choice between reformation and death, he complained that life was too hard—he could not reform. The prince ordered the young man to carry a shell full of oil through the city streets; two slaves walked beside him with swords drawn, ready to execute him if one drop of oil fell. When the young man came back, the prince asked him, "What did you see?" "Nothing," said the young man. "Nothing? Why it is the great market day. What did you hear?" Again the answer was "Nothing. For," said the young man, "I had my eyes fixed on the shell of oil. I could not look or listen, fearing my head might roll in the dust."

When we fix our gaze upon the Lord Jesus Christ we will be able to walk through the temptations of this life with safety.

The Upward Gaze

A young man called my hotel and asked for an appointment. I was busy but I told him if he could walk along with me to my next engagement, I'd talk with him. We had gone only a few blocks when the young man caught my elbow; I turned to see him gazing upwards. I supposed he had seen an airplane, or something similar, but just as suddenly he dropped my arm; we continued walking and talking. A few moments later he repeated the same gesture and look; again he said nothing of what concerned him or what guided his gaze. The third time, I asked him what was going on. He was greatly embarrassed, but finally he explained:

"A few days ago, I met a wonderful girl at a Bible conference. I knew at once that she was the girl I have been seeking for several years. I sat with her in meetings, played tennis with her, talked with her, told her I loved her. She told me that she liked me, but we would have to write to each other and get better acquainted. I have no picture of her, and I have been trying to remember as I think about her all the time. Well, yesterday I was walking along the street, and a pretty girl was coming in the opposite direction. I looked at her, as a fellow will, and then, a moment after she had passed I tried to think of the girl I love; to my horror she looked a little bit like the girl who had just passed me. I went over to the side of the curb and stood there, almost sick, and I asked the Lord to erase the memory of the girl who had just passed and let me see my true love again. I—I'd rather have *her* on the inside of my eyelids. Well, I got back the image of her so that I can recall her at will, but I determined not to look at anyone else who might even for a moment dim the vision of the girl I truly love. So, as we were walking along I was deeply engrossed in our conversation, but when I saw someone approaching who was pretty. I just looked up in the air, guiding myself as I walked, by touching your elbow. I wasn't aware that I had done it so strongly that you would notice."

I looked at him, and was filled with great delight, and I saw at once the spiritual application. The Lord Jesus Christ is the fairest of ten thousand and our vision of Him must be the spiritual vision from the Word of God, not the fleshy lineaments of some artist's concept, but our Lord, as He reveals Himself to each longing heart. We will, if we love Him dearly, be deeply grieved if our thoughts wander from Him, or if some vision of earthly things shall intrude to make us think of Him in the guise of some passing impostor.

Vista Vision

A picture on a small screen shows a mother, father and child walking along. The mother and the father slap and shake the child until the child's teeth rattle, and the child begins to whimper. They slap and strike the child; watchers say, "How cruel!" But look at it in wide-angle: it's forty degrees below zero in Dakota in the middle of the winter; the three have had to abandon their car to walk to safety. The child wants to lie down in the snow and go to sleep; the parents are striking the child to keep it from dying. They keep urging the child on.

When you look at God and the world and see the evil that is in the world, all you are seeing is a little eighteen-inch screen. But when you see it in the light of the whole of the Word of God, you see that the purpose is to know that in this universe God's methods are blessing through humility and yieldedness to Him.

Love, Human

The Crippled Sister

A crippled girl, living in the slums, underwent an operation that might enable her to walk again. When the operation was over, she needed a blood transfusion; her fourteen-year-old brother, a tough boy of the streets, volunteered. He was taken to the hospital, to the bedside of his crippled sister. He stared in tight-lipped silence while the vein in his arm was opened so that the blood might flow into the body of his unconscious sister. When it was over, the doctor put his hand on the boy's shoulder and told him that he was very brave. The boy did not comprehend; he had not understood the nature of a transfusion. After a moment, he looked up and said, "Doc, how long will it be before I croak?" As far as the boy was concerned he had been dying; slowly and willingly, he had stoically watched the blood flow—drop by drop, expecting his sister's life to mean his own death.

There, indeed, is the highest in human love. If this human love is to be seen in its highest degree, it will be through the words of Christ, who said, "Greater love hath no man than this, that a man lay down his life for his friends" (JOHN 15:13).

Marriage Requirements

A young man thinking about marriage had a list of requirements against which he checked every girl whom he met. Finally, he saw a girl who met most of his requirements, and he became engaged to her within five days. While they were driving to her parents' home, he slapped his foot on the brake, pulled over to the side of the road, and said, "Oh, I forgot to ask you if you are healthy." She was and the marriage was successful but the young man's meticulous caution was a standing joke among his friends.

Now, suppose that the man had put his list of requirements in writing: She is to keep the house clean, prepare the meals and wash the dishes. She will do the laundry. She will not allow herself to weigh over 125 pounds, and she will not cut her hair too short. One day the wife finds this list. She has been doing most of these things before she found the list, but it reveals to her some things that she has not been doing. As she reads the list, she ponders how to live up to his requirements; not because she must, but because she loves her husband.

We so sorely need: *love.* It cannot be pumped up, or forced. Love comes from knowing the Lord Jesus Christ. As we know Him thus, we learn to love Him, and as we love Him we love our neighbors. When we love Him thus, we shall delight to obey Him.

The Office Secretary

One day I was visited by a young man in his thirties, who had a personal problem. He told his story somewhat like this: "I work for such-and-such a company, and I have a private office. Several months ago my secretary was absent and I had to use another girl. One day she brought papers for my perusal; she got too close, and when she leaned over the desk, she let her hair trail across my face. I fought it down, but after all, I am a man, and toward the end of the day I put my hand on her and she came right back to be kissed. Even while kissing her, I was visualizing my two children running to meet me and my wife standing in the door. I hated what I was doing, but

I kept on. I had the greatest desire to push her from me, but I kept pulling her to me; my body was doing one thing and my mind was doing another.

"When I went home that night, I hugged my children so hard that one of them cried, and when we got him to laughing, I told them that it was because I loved them so much. I had tears in my eyes and my wife's eyes were shining. We all clung together in one of those moments that are indescribable. My wife was supremely happy, because I walked around the house that evening, touching familiar things that we had scrimped to buy, expressing my love for the home and for her, and before God I was never more true. Next day, the office intrigue began all over again. I was never more miserable in my life.

"Before a month had gone by I realized that my lust and my love were in a terrible battle. When I came home, there was everything that I wanted in life. When I went to the office, the machine of my body seemed geared to something terrible that was purely mechanical, and which I wanted to get out of more than any fly ever wanted to get off fly-paper. I heard my wife tell someone that I was becoming more and more of a homebody, and that all I wanted to do was stay at home. And it is true. I follow her around the house, talk with her in the kitchen where she is working, and watch her as she puts the children to bed.

"This morning, when I left the house, she told me that she thought she was the happiest woman in the world, because I showed so much that I loved her alone. I could hardly talk. In fact tears came to my eyes, and when I lifted a lock of her hair to dry them, I said to her, 'I love you more than life itself.' She cried and I crushed her to me until she screamed and smiled at the same time. Then I ran off to my train. But now what shall I do?"

With the husband's consent, I called the wife to my office and told her the story. Fear leaped to her eyes, but I reassured her. We took a taxi and went to his office. He was expecting us, and I stood by as they embraced and she said, "I know, I know, I understand, it's all right." Then I called the other girl into the office. The scene that followed typified the mortal struggle between the flesh and the spirit, both striving for the mastery of that body. But the wife was not striving; she knew that the mind, soul and heart of her husband had never been away from her. She understood the glandular warfare of his body, and that his lust had sprung to life in response to the lure of strange flesh. She looked at him with complete understanding and love.

The secretary stood there speechless. I said to her, "She knows all about it. She loves him and he loves her completely; he has never had any thought toward you except one of animal lust. You were never wanted except physically, and you are not wanted at all from now on. Do you understand?" I asked her to wait in the hall while I prayed with the couple. As I left, I saw the secretary dabbing at her eyes; I stopped and talked to her about her need of Jesus Christ.

The lust that draws you away from Christ may not be the carnal lust that attracted the man in my story. It may be some matter of the pride of soul, some inherent dishonesty, some ancient pattern of sin in which you indulged so often that it seems to bind you like a strong cord. The Holy Spirit can bring before you the thing that is marring your victory.

Love of God

The Baby Sitter

We went out one evening and left our children under the care of a baby sitter. When we returned about midnight, the girl was greatly concerned that our oldest child had been crying for about four hours. Nothing that the baby sitter could do would comfort her. I went to the child's room and found her flushed and sobbing, her face red with long weeping. When I picked her up, she threw her arms around my neck and sobbed, "Daddy, say it isn't true. You do love me." I replied that of course I loved her, and the child then said, "She said that if I was bad you wouldn't love me, and I know that I've been bad, so maybe you do not love me."

I pressed her to me, and said, "My dear child; I always love you. When you are good I love you with a love that makes me glad; when you are bad I love you with a love that makes me sad. But I love you, good or bad. I am always your daddy." The child was already more calm, and the dawn of a smile came to her face. I began to cover her gently with kisses, and then I told her that a good daddy had to be with her as the Lord was with Him, and with all of us who have become His children. She smiled and was soon asleep.

A man who has been made alive in Christ Jesus, but who has gotten out of the will of God is in Christ but he is not abiding in Christ. He is not cast forth as a son; he is cast forth as a branch. None of his actions please God, but this does not mean that God does not love him. God does love him, and is watching over him in every way, seeking to bring him back to the place of full fellowship.

The Daydreamer

Several years ago a young woman told me that nothing in her life seemed to make sense to her: she had passed her thirtieth birthday and she was still single; her faith was a distant, intellectual affair that did not seem to enter into her daily life at all; she was unhappy. To all questions on spiritual matters she gave answers that were orthodox clichés; I had the feeling that the truth had not entered deeply into her life. I questioned her about her work and about outside interests. She confessed that she spent most of her free time by herself. When I asked her what she did with her time, she was rather hazy. I accused her of spending a great deal of time daydreaming. She admitted that hours of her time were spent in that way. "And what is the pattern of your daydreams?" I asked her. She was obviously embarrassed and did not want to go on with the subject, but when I probed, she sat foward in her chair and answered me. What she said showed a pattern of interest in self and exaltation of self; I tried to bring her to the point of very definite trusting in Christ. I sensed that she needed an about-face in her thinking. I told her she had to face the fact that she might go on as her boss's secretary until they gave her the gold button for forty years of faithful service to the company, and that she might never know human love as she dreamed of it. She was shocked for a moment, as reality often shocks a dreamer, and then she said, "What shall I do?" I told her that she must realize that the most important things of life are the invisible things, and that there is a love from God that fills all the emptiness of life; it can satisfy even when human loves failed. "God is love," and "God is for us." I told her how to change the direction of her thinking from daydreams to meditation. As time went on her whole life was transformed. She began to meditate on what we are in ourselves and on how much God had stooped to love us. Above all she stopped thinking of faith in impersonal terms; instead of thinking of a distant God who loved a conglomerate world, she came to realize a very personal God who loved her, individually.

Thus it may be for every one of us. Life is planned by God to bring us to our sense of need of Him. The difficulties in your life, perhaps, are God's calling you away from things in order that you may understand how much He loves you.

Love Taken for Granted

A mother, in one of those delicious moments that make mothers what they are, drew her two-year-old daughter to her and said, "Oh, I love you!" The little girl, very much occupied with the whim of the moment, drew away and said, "Yes, I know." Love was taken for granted.

As early in life as the second year the Word was being illustrated: "Even a child is known by his doings . . ." (PROVERBS 20:11). Tragedy occurs when someone hears the voice of God saying, as He does from Calvary, and as He does from a thousand thousand circumstances of life, "My child, I love you," and is answered with an indifference that shows that His love is not really returned. Most of life's sadness flows from such an attitude. The windows of heaven are opened when we can learn to feel deeply: "We love him, because he first loved us" (I JOHN 4:19).

The Right Girl for the Son

A father and a mother love their son and want the very best for him. They hope he will find a girl outstanding in character and attainments, and that this girl will make him a good wife. They watch him pay attention to two cheap hussies, each of whom is seeking to capture the son for herself. The two girls may be jealous of each other in the modern sense of unpleasant fear and resentment, but the parents are jealous of their son in the Bible sense of the word. They are not jealous *of* him, nor are they jealous *of* either of the girls. They have a feeling of great love and desire for their son; they wish to protect him from any unworthy choice; they wish only that he will turn to that which will be best for him.

God has jealousy for us; He loves us so much that He does not wish us to waste our powers and our affections on the trivial and tawdry. God's whole purpose in the processes of life is to undeceive us, to turn us from hope or trust in ourselves and turn us back to all hope and trust in Himself.

Lying

The Group Method

General S. L. A. Marshall discovered that men interviewed immediately after battle are in such a state of shock that they can tell only the truth; officially it is called Group Method. General Marshall says that the average man cannot lie in the presence of comrades who would contradict him if he were telling an untruth; haunted by the memory of the recent dead, he will not lie. Whether this is completely accurate may be open to question.

We do know, however, that when the Lord arrays the lost before Him at the judgment of the great white throne there will be no lying. "Every mouth will be stopped and all the world be brought guilty before God," and all of the judgment of God will be according to truth. The way out is to come to Christ who is the truth.

Learning to Lie

A woman who had trouble with her daughter said, "I don't know where that child ever learned to lie." But the child had heard her mother say, "There's that horrible Mrs. Doakes coming; I wish that woman would keep her face out of this house." The mother cleaned up as rapidly as she could—straightening out, putting things in closets, getting everything out of the way. When the bell rang, the mother opened the door and cried out, "Oh, my darling, it's so good to see you, it's so nice to have you." Where did her daughter learn to lie?

Even a gray lie or a white lie is not justified in God's sight. Your little dears are going to learn more from the way you act and talk than they will ever learn from what you tell them.

Marriage

The Boss

A woman, interviewed about the secret of her successful marriage, insisted, "My husband is the Boss. I believe in letting him make all the important decisions."

The interviewer asked, "Who made the decision that he was to be the Boss?"

She replied, "Why, naturally, I did."

The TV audience was supposed to laugh, but this woman had hold of a profound biblical truth. God had long since made this decision (EPHESIANS 5:23,24); the woman had merely accepted the place for which she was created. That is why her marriage was a success. However, husbands should be warned that God has said that if a man doesn't have sense enough to know how to assume this great responsibility, God will not answer his prayers (I PETER 3:7).

Repairing the Electric Light

A wife asked her husband to repair an electric light over the kitchen sink, and he promised to do so. Next day she again asked him to fix the light and again he promised, but this time with some irritation. Two or three days later she asked again; "Stop nagging me," he shouted. The light was very necessary for her work at the sink, but if she called an electrician to do the job, her husband might explode. Having promised to do the work, he should have done it; his failure showed lack of understanding of his wife's problems. To her it revealed a great flaw in the man she loved—he did not have a proper sense of responsibility and integrity.

The way to avoid such difficulties in the adjustment of husband and wife is to have prayer together every day, asking the Lord to keep both in the way of grace. It is also good for each to be willing to face weaknesses in self and to ask the other, "Is there something that I do that annoys you?" When the answer is given in love, it is a small matter for love to remove the annoyance.

Meekness

The Winning Horse

What is meekness? Many people have a totally wrong idea of it, but they can learn the true meaning by listening to jockeys and horse-trainers after a horse race. The horse that wins the race is "the meekest on the track." This is the horse most under control, the horse that responds most quickly to the jockey's guidance. The self-willed horse, the factious horse, is frequently left at the post; when he does get started he may run faster than some of the others, but he does not finish with the leaders who were meek.

In the Word of God, meekness is presented to us as a vertical virtue, not as a horizontal one. Meekness is the way a man stands before

God—even as Moses was able to stand before Pharaoh—he is bolder than any man "The meek shall inherit the earth."

Millennium

On the Wrong Ferry Boat

About the turn of the century, a man rushed down to make a New York ferry; just as the ferry was pulling out, he jumped and landed on the rail of the boat. He sat there exhausted, breathing heavily. After a few minutes, he stood up and walked toward the center of the boat. A fellow-passenger said, "You almost missed it."

"Yes," he said, "but I'll get there now in time for the third race."

"The third race? Where do you think you're going?"

"Why, over to the race track."

"Well," said the other, "you're on the Methodist Church chartered Sunday-school picnic boat."

The man went over to the captain and said, "Captain, I'll give you $500, if you'll put me back."

The captain said. "Look, buddy, it took us twenty minutes to get out here; it would take us twenty minutes to turn around and go back, and another twenty minutes to get out here—that's an hour. There are 2,000 children on this ferry and that amounts to two thousand hours of their picnic time. You're on this boat till we get back at nine o'clock tonight."

"Oh," said the man, "where's the bar?"

"It's closed for the day," replied the captain.

No bar, nothing but children prattling and singing hymns—all day this man had to live in that atmosphere. When the boat docked at nine o'clock that night, the race-track man was first off—to get to the nearest bar.

This is a picture of what the millennium is going to be for millions of people on this earth. They hate; they do not want righteousness. Their hearts are deceitful above all things and incurably wicked.

All men will be as men here on earth; hatred will increase and multiply; curses will rise in their hearts against the Christ whom they see with their own eyes.

Missions

A Chinese Parish

A man I met spoke intimately of a certain section of China; he mentioned specific towns and villages, certain missionaries in various stations and the names of Chinese pastors. I asked when he had been in China, and he replied that he never been there. Years before, his college roomate had gone there as a missionary; they had corresponded regularly, writing once a month, and he had spent a great deal of time praying for his friend. He marked on maps the trips his friend described in his letters. He dotted his map with marks identifying churches and chapels; he memorized the names of believers about whom the missionary wrote. He supported the work with his gifts, sent special sums for special needs, helped to educate some of the young men of the region and daily lifted his heart to God in prayer for what had become his parish.

You, too, can travel with your gifts and your prayers; you can win some of that for which Christ died and lay it at His feet as a part of your own heart.

Mystery

My Secretary's Engagement

Many years ago, I had a wonderful, young private secretary. I was rather happy that as far as I knew she never dated any young man; selfishly I hoped that she would postpone marriage indefinitely so that I would have the advantage of her services. At the same time a young man, who was studying in one of the theological seminaries, was working in our church. He was in church often, but I had never known him to have a date with my secretary; I never connected them in my mind. One Sunday morning as I parked my car near the church, a young woman of our congregation came to me and said, "Max and Elisabeth are engaged." I was astonished—it could not be true. I walked fifty yards toward the side door of the church, and a young man on the steps said to me, "Max and Elisabeth are engaged." I shook my head in wonder and walked inside the door. Two young people were standing there and they said, "Max and Elisabeth are engaged." "Impossible," I answered, "but everyone is telling me so." I walked into my office and there stood the young lady in question; her smile proclaimed the well-announced subject. "Is it true?" I asked, and she answered, "Last night. We are going to be married and are going to Mexico as missionaries with the Wycliffe Translators."

Here was a true *mysterion* in the New Testament sense. It had been completely hidden, absolutely unknown, totally unsuspected. Suddenly it was whispered to one person, and the news spread like leaves in the wind.

New Birth

Found

At the Commencement Exercises of a Bible Institute in Canada, a young woman gave a testimony that will never be forgotten. She stood before the great audience and said, "I was found on a doorstep in a basket in Leeds, England, when I was six days old. I was found by the Lord Jesus Christ here in Canada ten years ago."

Many people might think it a great disadvantage to be abandoned by parents and left to the mercy of the world. To be found by Christ, however, is life's greatest experience because it is the beginning of eternity. You may have been born in the wealthiest of homes, been surrounded by loving care, but if you have never been found by Christ, you are lost indeed.

The Great North Road

Out in India I traveled on the Great North Road that runs up through the Punjab and the United Provinces. One side of the road was soft earth for the camels, the other side was macadam for the motor cars. In the rainy season the camel path was a miry bog. If a man was walking to Calcutta on the muddy side of the road, another might approach him and say that he had an experience to share with him: walking was easier on the paved side of the road. The man in the mud moves over to the paved road and cries out that his life has been changed. But I come along with my biblical desire for truth and ask two questions: Where were you going when you were walking in the mud? The answer is: Calcutta. And where are you going now that you are on the highway? And the answer is still, Calcutta.

You do not need your life changed, but you need it exchanged. You need an absolutely new life; this comes only from the new birth. Only then will you find yourself on a new road and traveling in a new direction.

The Intruder

A man and his wife telephoned from Philadelphia and said they had a great problem—could they come and talk to me? They did not know Christ, and as they began, I told them that here was the heart of their problem. I spoke to them of their need for Christ, and they talked about their good works—they were kind and charitable. I said to them that there was no other way. Then I said, "Where do you live?" and they gave me the number of their house. I continued, "Suppose someone came there at three o'clock in the morning and put a ladder up to the second-floor window and began to climb in, what would you do?" "Well," said the man, "I suppose I'd shoot him." I said, "What right have you to shoot a man. After all, can't a man come into your house in any way that he wants to come?" He said, "No." Then I said, "You are saying that you can get into God's heaven any way, any time—by any back window that you choose. God Almighty has made definite, positive and absolute rules for entering His heaven—rules as definite as our civilization makes—if you go to somebody's house you ring, you knock. As the Pennsylvania Dutch say, 'If the bell don't make— bump.' Make a noise and come up in the way that a house owner decides. If I approach your house and a sign says, 'Please go around to the side door,' I go around to the side door. This is your order. You have a right."

God has done the same thing. He says that anybody may come in, but they must come by the cross of Jesus Christ. "That's all," says God. "That is the one condition." And if man, in the stupid arrogance of his blind pride, says, "But I'll make me a little ladder; I've been working on my ladder for years. I painted a window on the wall; I put my ladder up to the window I painted and I want it to turn into glass so that I can break it and go through in my own time and my own way." God will not tolerate that.

The Large Bowl

Those who have seen training film made by the cartoon method may understand the following. A large bowl stands in the center of the picture; the bowl is broken into a hundred pieces and the pieces can be seen falling down. At the same time, the cartoonist draws a dotted line to show the form of the original bowl as it was before it was broken. A new bowl is then poured into the old outline—a bowl that cannot be broken. None of the old pieces are used in the creation of the new bowl. Finally, the old pieces are swept away and nothing but the new bowl remains.

If we are saved, we are bowls of wrath and have the power to break ourselves, but we do not have the power to put ourselves together again. God is not going to be frustrated by man's willfulness and sin; He pours new life into our molds. In His own time and in

His own ways, both unknown to us, He quickens us, makes us alive in Christ.

One of God's Fingers

Some one asked a Christian if were not afraid of slipping through the Lord's fingers. The reply was simple truth: "That is impossible, for I am one of the fingers."

By the new birth we become a part of the spiritual body of Christ.

The Reconstructed Hand

An orthopedic surgeon described how he restored the hand of a man who had lost his thumb and first finger. First, the surgeon took a roll of flesh—about the size of the handle of a valise—from the wall of the abdomen. The stump of the thumb was then attached to the flesh, and after a few months it had grown to the thumb, so that a further cut left a flapping tube of skin and flesh attached to the thumb base. Then a piece of bone from the tibia was placed inside the tube, and in a few months there was a complete thumb. The process was repeated on some of the fingers so that the man had his hand reconstructed, with 75 percent of the functions restored. I asked the surgeon if it would not be possible to use bones and tissues from bodies that had been killed in accidents. He hesitated a moment and then said, "It is very rare that we can get them soon enough." I pressed him for specific knowledge, and he told me that bones and tissues could be used providing they were secured within a few minutes after death. Then he said, "The whole body from head to foot is filled with a host of invaders that are held back by life. These invaders are everywhere and the moment death comes, they sweep out to destroy the body. Like runners that race from the starting point when the gun opens a race, these invaders sweep into the body. Within two hours the pathogenic organisms have carried their work of disintegration so far, there is nothing to do but dispose of the body."

The same law works spiritually. When Adam first sinned, death passed upon the race. In the spiritual realm, life was lost, and all of the spiritual invaders swept over the entire being of man so that his spiritual nature was completely disintegrated. Henceforth, nothing that was in man or from man could ever be used to repair or to regenerate spiritual life. The new life that is placed within us when we are born again is the workmanship of God.

Obedience

The Congo Serpent

In the Belgian Congo, the weather was hot and dank. No breath of air stirred; leaves hung from the trees as though they were weighted. In the garden not far from the missionary home a small boy played under a tree. Suddenly, the father called to him: "Philip, obey me instantly—get down on your stomach." The boy reacted at once, and his father continued, "Now crawl toward me fast." The boy again obeyed. After he had come about halfway, the father said, "Now stand up and run to me." The boy reached his father and turned to look back—hanging from the branch under which he had been playing was a fifteen-foot serpent.

Are we always as ready to obey? Or do we say: "Tell me why"? "Explain to me"? "I will after awhile"? Let it be, "Speak, Lord, Thy servant hears."

The Delayed Ferry Boat

A middle-aged man, who was a very young Christian, found in the Word of God that Christians are commanded to obey every ordinance of man for the Lord's sake (I PETER 2:13). Rushing to a business appointment that involved catching a ferry boat, he was tempted to do seventy in a fifty-mile-per-hour zone. He said to himself as he slowed down to the legal limit, "Lord, You wrote the Book; I didn't. I am going to obey, even if it costs my appointment." He thought he would have to wait half an hour, but to his amazement the ferry had been delayed ten minutes; he made it. He had never known it to be late before. He thanked the Lord who wrote the Book, learning that He holds all circumstances in His hand, and he thanked the Lord who had given him the heart to obey.

Old Nature

Bootstraps

Years ago, a family lived in California. The father had been born in Virginia, the mother, in New York. The Virginia grandfather had never seen his daughter-in-law or his grandchildren, so he determined to visit the West to see his family. His impending visit caused great joy and great preparation in the household. The house was painted; the curtains were cleaned; everything was pointed toward Grandfather's visit. Grandfather will be here in two months; Grandfather will be here in one month; in two weeks; in a week; in three days; tomorrow. And then he arrived. He was a handsome old gentleman of the South, with a white beard like General Robert E. Lee's, and a twinkle in his blue eyes.

The small grandson took a large share of the old gentleman's interest, and the boy was greatly impressed with his grandfather. The old gentleman's slippers fascinated him. The slippers had soft leather tops and loops in front and in back by which they were pulled on the foot. One day the five-year-old, put his feet, shoes and all, into the strange slippers, and reached down and put his fingers in the loops. The old grandfather said, "Pull hard, my boy, and see if you can lift yourself off the ground." The boy tugged and tugged, and the old man said, "Well, that's too bad. You'll have to eat some more oatmeal, and then we will try again tomorrow."

The little boy had stopped eating in the midst of his breakfast— there were more important things than food! The parents urged him to eat, and then the grandfather took charge. He reminded the boy that the slippers were waiting, and that there would be another trial when breakfast was over. If the movement of the spoon stopped for too long a period, the old man would wink at the boy, make a gesture toward his room where the slippers were, and the boy would speedily go to work on his oatmeal. When the breakfast was concluded, the pair, old and young, would go solemnly into the bedroom where another trial would be made. The little boy would pull and tug, but he could never lift himself off the ground. At a convenient moment the old gentleman would say, "Well, we didn't make it this morning, but we'll try again tomorrow."

This is the case of the sinner. He cannot lift himself, but the Lord Jesus Christ lays hold upon him and lifts him. We read it in one of the Psalms: "He brought me up also out of an horrible pit, out of the miry clay, and set my feet upon a rock, and established my goings. And he hath put a new song in my mouth, even praise unto our God . . ." (PSALM 40:2, 3).

Bubble Gum

A small boy, described as a "shy, second-grader, eight years old, a little owlish in spectacles," was guilty of committing a crime in a New Jersey school. It was Valentine's Day. He brought a Valentine and put it on his teacher's desk; then he went down into the basement and set fire to the school by lighting wastepaper in the boiler room. When the Fire Commissioner conducted an inquiry, evidence pointed to the boy. He readily admitted that he had set fire to the school. When he was asked why, he explained, as the news report put it, with childish simplicity, "In class yesterday, they took away my bubble gum."

The child says in effect, "I am on the throne in my life, and I want everybody else to bow down before me. I want to rule. When I want anything, I want it, and that is sufficient reason for my having it. If I want bubble gum, I am to have it. If anybody takes it away from me, I have a right to lash out and destroy anything that stands in the way of my whim and desire."

There is only one way to curb the fierce pride of the Adamic nature that rises even in a child. That is to plant the new life of the Lord Jesus Christ alongside it through the new birth by which we are made "partakers of the divine nature" (II PETER 1:4). Day by day we must submit our lives to the control of the Lord Jesus Christ, in order that He may keep the old nature crucified with Him.

The Cobra

When I was traveling in southeastern Asia, I reached a certain town early in January. After looking over some of the mission works, I went to the home of missionary friends for lunch. The thermometer registered over a hundred, and since it is customary to sleep for an hour or so during the period of greatest heat, my friends took me into their guest room. They apologized for the presence of a large packing case, filled with paper boxes and Christmas package wrappings. They said that the case had arrived from America full of presents for themselves and their children, and that it had come several days late. They had opened the presents and had put all of the boxes, wrappings and ribbons in the case to sort out later.

I went to sleep, but was awakened by a rustling noise; something was in the packing case. I dozed off and again I was awakened by the rustling of papers. Siesta time was over; I went out into the main room of the house and told them of the noise in the packing case. Instantly the atmosphere became tense. A quick call brought the servants running to the door; they stopped and looked at the box with wary eyes. The talk between missionaries and servants was in the native language which I did not understand, but the air of excitement needed no translation. A rake was hooked over the top of the case; it was pulled into the living room, then to the door and out onto the porch. It was then lowered, still being pulled from a distance, to the ground level of the yard. By this time a dozen servants had come running from neighboring houses. Each one carried a club, an ax, or a hoe. Finally, the case was turned on its side and out slithered a cobra about seven feet long. It was clubbed to death quickly, while the servants prodded the remaining litter carefully to see if the deadly serpent had a mate. The excitement among the natives continued unabated for more than an hour. They rummaged in every part of the room, including the bedclothes of the bed on which I had just been sleeping; they looked for holes through which the snake might have come, and for evidences that it might have been accompanied by a mate. The missionaries served tea, but the conversation revolved around snakes.

The point that I underline from this story is the tense attitude of danger that pervaded every man, woman and child in the group—missionaries and natives. They knew that something alive and very dangerous was there and they did not lower their guard for even a fraction of a second. No politeness toward a guest was allowed to turn their attention from the peril. There was no thought of avoiding the danger that was there; death was in the case—it had to be dealt with immediately.

The clear recognition of the aliveness of the old fleshly nature should cause every fiber of the new being to be alert to face the potential carnality in order that it may be delivered over to the death which is its proper sentence.

Five Pounds Lighter

A lady discovered that her bathroom scales registered five pounds lighter if she stood on her left foot instead of on her right. It made no difference to her that outside scales confirmed the right-foot weight. She wanted to be lighter than she was, so she took comfort in standing on the left foot.

Old nature always wants to believe the best of itself. Its pride is that of Satan, and it takes comfort in anything and everything that speaks well of it. Only in the Word of God do we get the true picture of what we are. Here are the scales that have no false springs and no positions that are off balance. Here we find the slaying of pride and the exaltation of the Lord Jesus Christ. Any other balance is false, and therefore, an abomination to the Lord.

My Own Way

One day, one of my children came out of the dining room with me and walked along to my study. There was a question about what was to be done in a certain matter. As I sat down at my desk I gave a clear and detailed answer. My child hesitated, then broke in with a question. I kept on at my work without looking up. "But, Daddy . . ." the child insisted, and phrased the matter in another way. Mother came along to find out what the delay was in fulfilling the command. The child answered, "I am trying to find out what Daddy wants me to do." At this point I broke in: "No. You are not trying to find out what I want you to do. You are trying to see if you can make me relent on the conditions so that you will be able to do what you want to do instead of doing what you know we want you to do. Now go and do it immediately."

How many times the Heavenly Father has to deal with us in this way. Our old nature is incurably addicted to having its own way. This is inherent in the statement that tells of the distance which separates the soul from God. "All we like sheep have gone astray; and we have turned every one to his own way . . ." (ISAIAH 53:6).

Heinz Nordhoff

Before the war Heinz Nordhoff was the manager of Opel, the German branch of General Motors. When the war ended he was forced to take a job as a manual laborer and existed on handouts from friends. The British knew his worth and offered him a job directing Volkswagen, a bombed factory that manufactured very small cars. He didn't want to leave the production of big cars, but had little alternative; under his leadership, Volkswagen has become one of the strong links in the great economic revival in Germany. Said Nordhoff: "The future begins when you cut every tie with the lost past."

All of us are born linked with the lost, Adamic past. As long as we try to salvage anything from it, we are in spiritual poverty and desperation. But when we come to Christ, the Holy Spirit begets us anew, and we become a new creation (II CORINTHIANS 5:17). The future begins when we cut every tie with the lost past. We can't do it, but Christ can.

The Naval Officer's Promotion

A young naval officer kept his promotion to lieutenant commander a secret, until he got his new gold-leaf collar insignia. He walked proudly into his home and waited for his wife's surprise and delight. An hour passed and she said nothing; he saw she was on the verge of tears. He put his arms around her and asked what was wrong. "You didn't even notice my new hairdo!" she sobbed.

The individual is, by nature, interested in himself. Perhaps this story can explain many a broken home and many a crisis in business. Only one remedy for such a situation—the love of Christ in the heart—can make us esteem each other better than self, and in honor prefer one another. Such a transformation is an evidence of the new birth.

Stolen Checks

A thief, who stole GI checks from mailboxes and cashed them, would not ordinarily make the front pages of the national press and be written up in the great news magazines. In one such case, however, the thief was the twenty-seven-year-old son of a high official in Harvard University. The judge, in imposing sentence of two years in prison, said he could not understand how a man of his "background and intelligence could descend to the level of a common thief."

The judge was ignorant because he thought that education, background and breeding could change the old nature. It is possible, of course, for culture and training to iron out certain wrinkles of sin, such as open thievery, but the heart of man cannot be changed by background or education. When the young thief said that he had stolen "because I like a good time," he was illustrating what God has said, that man has turned to "his own way." The cure is not education, but Christ.

Suspended Gravity

Tests made in a T-33 Jet trainer have made it possible to suspend gravity for as long as forty seconds. By flying the proper curve at high speed the occupants of the plane become weightless. A ball tossed from the hand does not fall; gravity is suspended. Half of the men tested felt pleasant, elated sensations. One wished he could live forever at gravity zero. There was a feeling of complete relaxation.

God describes the Christian life in terms of a double pull from the flesh and the spirit (GALATIANS 5:17). When we look to Christ and surrender to Him, we may know what it is to walk in the spirit and to have triumph for forty seconds, minutes, hours. . . . At times our old nature will make its downward gravitational pull known, but God has made it possible for us to return and rest in Him.

The Tonsillectomy

A minister friend of mine had trouble with his throat. He went to the doctor, who said to him, "You must have your tonsils removed at once." The minister replied, "But I have a big speaking schedule." The doctor relented and painted the minister's throat to fix him up for a few days. The climax came in Tucson, Arizona; the minister was stricken; he could hardly talk, and again he went to the doctor. The minister said, "You must paint my throat, you must help me get through." But the doctor said, "Look, if you don't take those tonsils out, your ministry is going to be finished entirely." Now when the doctor used that phrase, *if you don't take those tonsils out,* he didn't mean the man was to get a mirror and operate on himself. When he said, "If you don't take those tonsils out," he meant, "If you don't put yourself in the hands of a competent surgeon."

When the Bible says to put the old nature to death, it doesn't mean that you can do it, it means you are to deliver it over to Him for doing.

Perfection

A Dollar's Worth of Sugar

When I was a small boy in California, we spent our summers in Mount Hermon. For supplies we went to a little country store in Felton. In those days, there were no electric scales; bread was neither sliced nor wrapped, nor was sugar sold by weight—you bought a dollar's worth. The grocer scooped sugar from a barrel into a bag on one side of the scale while he placed weights on the other. When the magic moment came and the scales balanced, he left his scoop in the sugar barrel. The question is: How many pounds of sugar did we get for our dollar?

Someone may say, "I think there were twelve pounds because I once read in a book that at that time they sold twelve pounds of sugar for a dollar." Someone else says, "No, I think there were thirteen. I used to visit my aunt who had a grocery store in Vermont, and I personally weighed out thirteen pounds." A third person declaims, "Well, my father told me that his father told him that his father told him—and it's a strong family tradition—that there were twelve-and-a-half pounds of sugar for a dollar."

One person may argue on the basis of what he has read; another, on human experience, and the third on family tradition. But I say, "That grocer in the Felton county store put fourteen pounds of weights on the scales—two five-pound weights, one two-pound, and two one-pound weights. So, for a dollar we got fourteen pounds of sugar."

God says that He has a scale; in the Bible He reveals what He has put on His side. What has God set on His side of the scale? Perfection! God cannot admit anyone to Heaven who is not perfect. If God graded you, and 70 percent were passing, then Heaven would be 30 percent dirty; if He let anyone into Heaven with a grade of 99.44 percent, Heaven would still be dirty. So God must demand perfection.

Cutting Up the National Geographic

One day I was going through a pile of magazines, clipping various items, when my five-year-old daughter came in. She asked me if she could help. I smiled at the earnest look on her face, and wrote a little note which I told her to take to her mother. The note read, "Please deliver to bearer the small pair of unpointed scissors." A few moments later she came back into my study, carrying the scissors. I then turned over to her the pile of papers and magazines I had finished clipping and told her she might cut clippings from them. She was very pleased and set to work with great zest. A long time passed—perhaps half an hour—and no sign of fatigue with what she was doing, no word of interruption. I had become so engrossed in my work I almost forgot she was there.

I turned, and discovered that she was happily engaged in cutting to pieces the latest copy of the *National Geographic* magazine. If I had cried out at her or punished her, she would never have understood, for, in her heart, she undoubtedly felt, that she was "helping Daddy." There was no doubt that at best she was an unprofitable servant, at least so far as editorial help was concerned. Gently I took the magazine from her, told her the equivalent of "Well done, thou good and faithful servant," kissed her and said, "Now you go and help Mother for a while."

The true child of God is able to accomplish many things for the Lord Jesus Christ, and these things are accepted by the Lord even though they are not perfect in themselves. It is at this point that the operation of grace in our lives maintains us in our activities for God. We are surrendered to Him and we determine to do His will. We act, and the action is not perfect, but the perfect God looks at that action through the Lord Jesus Christ, and we are accepted in the beloved Saviour.

Plan of God

From Clinic to Zoo

In New York City, a high-school boy broke his nose. He was excused from school in order to go to a clinic to have it treated. Coming out of the clinic, he walked across the street to the Bronx Zoo, paid his fare and walked through the turnstile. He was immediately surrounded by officials of the zoo and photographers from the New York press. He was the 100,000,000th visitor to the Zoo since its foundation and was presented with a life membership in the New York Zoological Society.

Not only does everything that ever happens turn out for the best for the Christian, but, even more important, we know it in advance. The most significant part of the promise is the "We know," so come what may, the Christian knows the event has been planned by the Father and that it will bring good in the end, even if we may not see how at the moment of the event.

The Dismantled Clock

Small boys are always interested in finding out what makes things go. One day a boy took a clock apart to find out what made it tick. When he tried to put it together again, he seemed to have enough wheels and springs to make two clocks; he discovered that all of the parts must move in their proper way—certain wheels must move forward and certain ones backward. There are wheels that move quickly and wheels that move slowly. There is the large mainspring and the tiny hairspring; all of the parts work together to make the clock go.

In the life of a Christian, when events move forward we are very pleased with the progress. If events move backward, we are inclined to be impatient; we want them to move in the direction of our own will, not understanding the purpose that God has in our lives. There are matters that are great and very important to us—mainspring events in our lives—births, marriages, deaths, triumphs and tragedies. There

are matters as fine as a hairspring—petty annoyances, trivial happenings, that seem little and unimportant at times—that regulate the
course of our lives. There are events in our lives that move smoothly
and rapidly, and we rejoice at their action. Some things lag and incite
our impatience as we seek to speed them up to the tempo of our own
wills. But when all of these events—backward, forward; fast, slow;
great, small—are seen in their relationship to each other, we must conclude that to those who love God and who are called according to His
plan, everything that happens fits into a pattern for good.

The Mongoloid Child

Some years ago, a young minister in whose church I was holding
a series of weekly meetings, said to me, "I may not be able to attend every meeting because we're expecting a baby soon." About three weeks
later he came to the service, just before its close. Afterward I went to
his study; his back was to me, as I asked, "Well, which is it, boy or
girl?" He turned, and I saw tragedy written on his face. He said, "God
has given me a son, and I love that boy, but he is a mongoloid idiot." I
said, "At the very outset you must learn that God Almighty has honored you more than. He has honored many people. God does not give
the privilege of great suffering to every one of His children. He has
chosen you for this purpose."

Then I turned to the fourth chapter of Exodus, in which God
talks to Moses at the burning bush; I pointed to verse 11. Moses had just
said, "I am slow of speech, and of a slow tongue." And God replied,
"Who hath made man's mouth? or who maketh the dumb, or deaf, or
the seeing, or the blind? Have not I the Lord?" But I read the verse
thus: "And the Lord said unto Moses, Who has made man's mouth? or
who maketh him dumb, or deaf, or seeing, or blind, or a mongoloid
idiot? have not I the Lord?" He snatched the Bible from me and read
it for himself. "Oh," he said, "I never saw this before, but it's true, it's
true! It must be true! I believe it!"

To receive the Congressional Medal of Honor is not so great a
tribute as to be chosen, as one of God's children, to endure great

tragedy. This the Bible teaches everywhere. If you do not think that God has planned these things, then you must believe that there is a power greater than God, or that things happen from blind chance. If you have had tragedy in your life; if you have endured a physical defect or deformity, God planned it. If you are a man, God planned that you be a man. If you are a woman, God planned that you be a woman. If you are five-feet-two, or six-feet-five, God planned that height for you. If you are blind, God planned that you should be blind.

Shearing One Thousand Sheep

In driving from Glasgow to Edinburgh, we followed a road on the border between the Highlands and the Lowlands. As we drove down the road we saw a dozen men shearing a thousand or so sheep. We stopped the car, climbed over the fence, and walked about a hundred yards to watch. How fast the men worked! These sheep, had run half-wild on the moors of Scotland, shepherded mostly by dogs; they were not accustomed to men. Now they were deprived of the wide liberty of the moors; they were packed tight in the folds. We could hear them bleating. The man in charge of the gate let the sheep out one at a time; the next man grabbed the sheep and took it over to another man. The minute the third man flipped the sheep over on its back—all four legs in the air—the sheep became quiet. Snip, snip, snip went the shears, and off came the fleece. In the middle of the group of shearers stood a boy, twelve or fourteen years of age. He was hacking away at a sheep learning how to shear. I suppose it took him as long to do one sheep as it did each of the men six or eight, but he was learning, and his sheep was just as quiet as the men's.

"As a sheep before her shearers is dumb." I got a fresh picture of how my Lord submitted himself. I believe that God created sheep that way to illustrate exactly how the Lord Jesus did, because I am a great believer that we existed in the mind of God before the earth. In other words, before God created the heavens and the earth, He planned us;

then He planned the sun, and the moon, and the stars; then He planned this globe, and He planned Adam, and all the rest; He planned Christ, and we had been planned in Christ.

The Spanish Escorial

Just outside of Madrid I saw that architectural phenomenon, the famed Escorial—ancient monastery of the Augustinians, the order that produced Martin Luther. The kings of Spain have been buried there for centuries, and the church is a magnificent example of stately beauty. The architect who built the building made an arch so flat that it frightened the king. Supported by the power of his might the king ordered the architect to add a column that would uphold the middle of the arch. The architect remonstrated that it was not necessary, but the king insisted. The column was built. Years later the king died, and the architect then revealed that the column was a quarter of an inch short of the arch, and that the arch had never sagged in the slightest. Today guides pass a lath between the arch and the column, as mute proof of the rightness of the architect's knowledge.

The divine plan does not need human support. It may sometimes appear contradictory to human illusions. Men build their little columns, but God has a way of making them fall a bit short, so that in the end it can always be demonstrated that the column, like the arch, rests on its own foundation and needs no other support.

The Tangled Web

An elderly minister marked his Bible with a bookmark made of silk threads woven into a motto. The back was a tangled web of crossed threads that seemed to be without reason or purpose. When he had to call at a home where there was great trouble, sorrow or death, he would show this bookmark, presenting the reverse side with its unintelligible tangle. When the bereaved one had examined it intently, without finding any explanation for the seeming disorder, the minister would ask him to turn the marker over. Against the white silk background there was the phrase, in colored threads, "God is love." That side made sense.

It is thus with all of the tangled patterns of life for the one who has been called according to the divine plan. When we know this fact, we can be at peace with the world around us, because we are at peace within our own souls; and we are at peace within our own souls, because we are at peace with our Heavenly Father.

The Toy Boat

A small boy sailed his toy boat on a pond. The boat floated out of his reach, and he appealed to a larger boy to help him. This boy, without saying a word, picked up rocks and began throwing them out near the boat. The small boy pleaded with him not to hit his boat, but the big boy kept on. Soon the small boy noticed that each stone was falling on the far side of the boat, making a wave that pushed it nearer the shore. Then he realized that the big boy was planning the fall of each stone in order to bring the boat nearer to the shore. Soon it was within reach and the owner had his boat again.

We must never forget that God plans the fall of each stone within our circumstances, and that each storm and wave is calculated by Him in order to bring us nearer to Himself.

The Violinist

A man who loves violin music has the means to buy himself a very fine violin. He also purchases the very finest radio obtainable and builds up a library of great musical scores. He is able to take any piece that is announced on the radio and put it on his music stand so that he can play along with the orchestra. The announcer says that Mr. Ormandy and the Philadelphia Orchestra are going to play Beethoven's Seventh Symphony. The man in his home puts that symphony on his stand and tunes his violin with what he hears coming from the orchestra. The music that comes from the radio we might call foreordained. Ormandy is going to follow the score just as

Beethoven wrote it. The man in his living room starts to scratch away at the first violin part. He misses beats, he loses his place and finds it again, he breaks a string and stops to fix it. The music goes on and on. He finds the place again and plays on, after his fashion, to the end of the symphony. The announcer names the next work that is to be played, and the fiddler puts that score on his rack. Day after week after month after year he finds pleasure in scraping his fiddle along with the violins in the great orchestras. Their music is determined in advance. What he must do is to learn to play in their tempo and in their key; he must follow the score as it was written in advance. If he decides that he wants to play "Yankee Doodle" when the orchestra is in the midst of a Brahms number, there will be dissonance and discord in the man's house, but not in the Academy of Music. After some years of this, the man may turn out to be a creditable violin player; he may have learned to submit himself to the scores that are written and to follow the programs as played. Harmony and joy comes from this submission and this cooperation.

The plan of God is rolling toward us, unfolding day by day, as He has planned it before the foundation of the world. The score of God's plan is set forth in the Bible. In the measure that I learn it, submit myself to it, and seek to live in accordance with all that is therein set forth I shall find myself in joy and in harmony with God and His plans. Prayer is learning to play the same tune that the eternal plan of God calls for and to do that which is in harmony with the will of the Eternal Composer and the Author of all that is of true harmony in life and living.

Prayer

The Bank Account

You might see a sign in the window of a bank that reads: "If you present any checks according to our rules, we will cash them." That is a sensible announcement. But suppose I go into the bank, fill out a check for one hundred dollars, sign it, and ask for five twenties in cash. The teller looks at me, at my signature, and says, "Do you have an account in this bank?" I answer, "No—but I want you to know that I sincerely believe in cashing checks." Such folly would speedily land me in the arms of the law. It is not enough to believe in cashing checks; it is necessary to have an account in the bank.

It is not enough to pray in the name of the Lord Jesus; there must be the true deposit of saving faith. You can draw on this deposit of faith, if you are asking in the Holy Spirit. If He is praying within you, with groanings that cannot be uttered, then you may be sure your prayer will be answered. If you are merely asking for something so that you may consume the gift of the answer on your own desires, then you may be sure that God will not answer your prayer.

Father and Son

A father tells his college son what he is to do; the father also tells the boy that his needs will be provided for. The father does not draw a check in September for the school year and abandon the boy to himself. The father instructs the boy to write home and ask for money. The boy knows he is going to get it, the father knows he is going to give it, but both enjoy the fellowship of the letter, the asking and the answer. A yielded son will not spend beyond his budget, and a loving father will provide all that is in his power to meet his son's need.

The main function of prayer is to link us to God in fellowship and to prepare us in growth for further participation in His plan. In John 10, He made a certain and definite promise concerning the safety and keeping of the believer (vss. 27–29). Yet in John 17, He prayed seven times for the believers, that they might all be kept, though He had said that they would be.

If Two Agree

Many years ago, Mr. George T. B. Davis attended one of my Sunday evening services. Mr. Davis was a well-known leader in Christian work who was responsible for circulating several millions of copies of the New Testament in different lands and to different groups. I made a mental note that there was something I wanted to talk over with him, but he slipped out before I had a chance to speak to him. I went home, sat down and wrote him a note saying that I had missed him and I outlined an idea that we might collaborate on. I added a postscript saying that I was going out at midnight to mail the letter so that he would have it in the morning and could telephone me. In the next morning's mail was a letter from Mr. Davis. He wrote that he had not stopped to meet me after the service because so many others were speaking to me, but that the Lord had laid it on his heart to write me about a certain matter in which we might collaborate. It was exactly the same idea about which I had written him. He also added a postscript that he was going out to mail his letter so that I might have it in the morning. A few moments later my telephone rang, and he was on the phone to express his astonishment and joy that our letters had crossed in the mail during the night. I pointed out to him that here was the true meaning of spiritual agreement.

We had been the objects of this special grace of God and had agreed on earth; we could be sure that it would be done by our Heavenly Father. And it was.

The Missing Digit

In making a dial telephone call from memory, one number was missed and a wrong connection resulted. The call did not get through to the right person. One little mistake made all the difference.

In approaching God we must come in the way that He has designed. He has promised very definitely not to hear the prayers of those who do not come in accordance with the way He has determined. Christ said, ". . . no man cometh unto the Father, but by me" (JOHN 14:6). It is absolutely necessary that one believe in the deity of Jesus Christ and in salvation by the blood, in order to approach God. Anyone who attempts to climb up by any other way, though the devil may give him counterfeit answers for awhile, has a "wrong number" as far as God is concerned. A Christian cannot get through to God if he has unconfessed sin in his life. "If I regard iniquity in my heart, the Lord will not hear me" (PSALM 66:18). But if we pray for what is a good thing for us, and if we are walking in the will of God, we are sure to get the answer to our prayer. We have the "right number" and the answer is immediately forthcoming (PSALM 84:11).

The Request for Money

Every father who has a child away at school knows what it is to receive requests for money. When my younger son was in college, I had two letters, one following the other closely; both asking for fifty dollars. The requests were for different purposes, and the nature of the letters was quite different. The first letter was about three pages long; it was hedged about with explanations attempting to persuade me to grant the request. He recounted that he was on the Dean's list, and therefore near the top of his class and permitted to cut classes at will. A group of his companions, all with the same liberty of movement because of their high marks, wished to leave college for a five-day weekend; they wanted to drive a thousand miles to the home of one of the boys for a series of parties and good times. In short, his share of the expenses would be fifty dollars. He did not use the exact words, but the equivalent of "if it be thy will," appeared a half-dozen times. My answer was "No." My refusal crossed in the mails a second letter from my son, saying that he knew my answer would be "No"; he was making a substitute set of plans for the weekend. About three weeks later came a brief letter, roughly as follows: "Dear Daddy: There was an accident in the chemistry laboratory today, and the boy next to me broke a beaker of acid. I had to stop at the co-op and order a suit. They are making some alterations, but I need fifty dollars by return mail." There was no "if it be thy will" to that letter. A father may not have to give his boy a five-day party weekend, but he does have to keep him in pants. That is one of the obligations of fatherhood.

Some prayers need add no qualifying words. Some things are God's will so definitely that we need not hesitate, but may come with all boldness to the throne of His grace, expecting to find grace to help in time of our need. From such prayers the Lord God has never turned away His ear. Other prayers He will receive with kindness, and in His mercy He will not answer them, because He knows that we pray in ignorance, and that His answer would be far worse for us than we could ever imagine.

Promises of God

The Porter's Tip

Several years ago, a porter took me to my room in the Onesto Hotel in Canton, Ohio. He knew me well and we began talking about the promises of God. I had not yet given him his tip, and I asked him how much money he had in his pocket. He counted it, and found that he had $1.19. It was Tuesday; he would not be paid until Friday, and he had to live and support his family until then on tips, slender at best. I placed a fifty-cent piece in his hand, saying, "I give you this half dollar. Now how much do you have?" He answered, "$1.69." After I had discussed this with him, I took the coin and put it back in my pocket, asking him, "Now how much do you have?" He fell into the trap of faithlessness and answered $1.19." "Then am I a liar?" I asked. "No." "Did I give you that half-dollar?" "Yes." "Didn't you tell me it was yours?" "Yes." "Then how much money do you have?" He smiled and said, "I have $1.69, but fifty cents of it is in your pocket." It was in his before he left the room, and he had learned a little more about the certainty of the promises of God.

The Promise Box

When I lived in France in my student days, I was used of God to lead a girl to Christ. This girl later became the wife of one of the

French pastors in the south of France. She often came to our home and saw us taking verses from a "promise box"—a small box that held approximately two hundred promises from the Bible printed on heavy paper curled into cylinders. We used to take one out and read it when we needed a word of special comfort. This girl made a promise box by hand, writing these same promises in French. Throughout the years this box has been used in her home by her children, and they have been taught to trust in the Lord. She told us of an incident that happened to her during the war. No food was available except messes of potato peelings from a restaurant. Her children were emaciated; they cried to her for food. Their clothing was almost in rags, and their shoes were worn through. In one of her most tragic moments she turned to the promise box in desperation. She prayed, "Lord, O Lord, I have such great need. Is there a promise here that is really for me? Show me, O Lord, what promise I can have in this time of famine, nakedness, peril, and the sword." She was blinded by her tears, and in reaching for the box, she knocked it over. The promises showered down around her, on her lap, on the floor; not one was left in the box. She knew a moment of supreme joy in the Lord as the Holy Spirit suffused her with divine power and light; she realized that all of the promises were indeed for her in the very hour of her greatest need.

So it can be for you today. "Man shall not live by bread alone, but by every word that proceedeth out of the mouth of God" (MATTHEW 4:4). "Who shall separate us from the love of Christ?" You who have once known the love of God surely know that there is nothing in this world or in the world to come that can separate you from the love of Christ which passeth knowledge. "Therefore . . . be ye stedfast, unmoveable, always abounding in the work of the Lord, forasmuch as ye know that your labor is not in vain in the Lord" (I CORINTHIANS 15:58).

Prophecy

Climbing Mont Blanc

When we were living in Europe, we went with two young men for an excursion in the high mountains. We set out to climb Mont Blanc. From before dawn until after dark we worked our way up to that point on the shoulder of Europe's highest peak where there was a tiny cabin, half-buried in the midst of the eternal snows. The next morning, before daylight, we started out on the eight-or-nine-hour climb that would bring us to the summit. We knew from our distant view of the peak that the last miles were over great broad beds of snow, and at last we came to a slope that looked like the final slope. We congratulated each other on making such excellent time; we anticipated mounting the summit more than an hour in advance of our original schedule. Then we came out upon the rolling top of the peak and, much to our chagrin saw a slope down, a long flat valley, and another sharp rise that had to be mounted before the topmost height could be reached. We learned that the place that had deceived us was called in French, *Mont Maudit*—"cursed mountain." Undoubtedly many an Alpine sportsman has come to this place, thinking that the weary labor of the climb was nearly over, feeling the joyous sense of dominance and achievement that reaching the peak brings, blotting out the memories of perilous moments when footholds were precarious and when the rope that bound the party together was all that stood between them and death.

This is a perfect illustration of the Old Testament prophecies concerning the coming and work of Israel's Messiah. From a far distant perspective they were allowed to see the unrolling scene. Their minds fixed upon the summit of glory that lay before them and they forgot completely that they were to pass over the cursed mountain before they could reach the final object of their desire. For there could be no final redemption without the basis of the work of the cross where Messiah would be cut off for the sins of His people (DANIEL 9:26).

The Watch

Joe and John, were working with their father, one summer. The father said to the older son, "John, you have done an excellent job, and I am proud of the way you handled everything. At Christmas I want to give you a very fine gold wrist watch; I will give you this because you have been a good boy." Time goes on—October, November—the brothers talk about the watch a bit; and then about December 20th, Joe says to his brother, "John, I have seen the watch." That's all. The father had bought it and shown it to the mother and to the younger brother who says, "I have seen the watch." The promise made in August was just a promise, but now someone has seen the watch, and having seen the watch they know that when the time of fulfillment comes, it will come to pass.

In effect, Peter says in his second Epistle (1:16–21), "I've seen the watch. God made a promise in Isaiah, but I know it is going to be true for I've seen it. God lifted the veil and let me look upon it. The word of prophecy of the Old Testament is made more sure by the Transfiguration because we have been eyewitnesses of His majesty, and so we have the word of prophecy that is made more sure, a word whereunto you do well to take heed."

Public Confession of Christ

The Chinese Matriarch's Son

An old Chinese woman living in Java gave me a beautiful antique Chinese ivory. In the islands of the South Seas the Chinese have long been the principal traders, and some of them are immensely wealthy. I was preaching there for a few days and was entertained in the home of a Chinese matriarch, whose husband had left her a great business and a museum-like home. I had been told that although this woman was a fine Christian, her thirty-year-old son lived a life of debauchery. As I sat down to dinner, the young man came in and sat beside me. We began to talk, and before the meal was over he promised to come to the meeting at which I was speaking that afternoon. He came, and between that afternoon meeting and the evening meeting he talked with me seriously about his soul. He attended the evening meeting at which I presented Christ as Saviour; he left afterwards without speaking to me. The next day, however, he had cards printed and sent them out to hundreds of his friends and business acquaintances. I substitute another name, but this is the message the card bore: "Ah Wong, having become a Christian, wishes to announce to his friends and acquaintances that he will no longer be seen in his old haunts or living his old way of life."

The Chinese are not an effusive people and certainly are not given to showing their emotions. But I shall not forget the old mother as she stretched out her hands toward me, bowing low, almost looking away lest I see the tears that she could not keep back. When we left, she gave me *batik* sarongs fit for a princess, and an antique ivory that could grace the wall of the finest art museum.

The world understands a confession of Christ. When anyone has publicly confessed Christ, the world is astonished if the life is not changed.

Engaged!

Many years ago I rode the streetcar home from one of the suburbs of Los Angeles late at night. There were only half a dozen passengers in the car—all men—when a young man got on the car at an intermediate stop. The new passenger paid his fare, lifted his hands and cried out, "I'm engaged to be married. My girl just said 'Yes'." Everyone laughed; there was joshing and wisecracks. Love from his heart had found a response and he could not keep still about it.

Is it possible for an interchange of love between the Lord God and His creature without a great desire to acknowledge it?

The Young Man's Return Home

During the first world war, I had the opportunity of witnessing to the young scion of a family prominent for its social standing and wealth. The young man professed to accept Christ as Saviour; he made public testimony to that fact among the soldiers of his company. When the war was over and he was about to go home to one of the wealthy suburbs of a great city, he told me that he was afraid he would slip back into his old habits with his old friends. I told him that he would not have to give these people up—that they would give him up if he made a public confession of his faith in Christ. He agreed to tell the first ten people of his old set that he met, that he had become a living Christian.

He arrived at the suburban station near his home, he told me afterward, and almost immediately saw a girl whom he had known socially. She greeted him effusively and asked how things were going. He replied, "The greatest thing that could happen to a man has happened to me." "Oh," she said, "You are engaged to be married." He said, "Better than that; I have taken Jesus Christ as my Saviour." Her face froze; she mumbled some words of politeness and quickly went her way. A few minutes later a young man of his acquaintance passed by and shouted that now that the soldier was back there would be some good parties. The young Christian told about his new life in Christ. His friend mumbled some polite remarks and went his way. The same circumstances were repeated with a young couple and with two more individuals. But by that time the word had gotten around. A car passed with very close friends. They waved at him distantly, and that was all. They had heard the news: he had become "queer," "religious," who knows?—they may have called him crazy. But his public confession had aligned him with Jesus Christ; it had alienated those who did not want Jesus Christ and had established and strengthened him in his stand for Christ as his Lord.

Redemption

Fruit

I was born in a country of fruit in a little valley of California. It was a common sight to see tens of thousands of acres of blossoms in the springtime, and to look out on the vast and abundant harvest of the autumn. Without being conscious of the impression that was being made on me, the glory of the harvest became a part of my being. I still have a sense of solid satisfaction when I think of the thousands of square yards of apricots drying in the sun, of the freight-car loads of strawberries going off to market, of the hundreds of trainloads of apples that flowed through the little town. Fruit was the life of our community. I, like many of the boys in my town, spent many summer days cutting pits out of apricots, and I earned a great deal of money—for a boy—making thousands of apple boxes each season. It was thus we spent our autumn Saturdays.

The heavy black soil was clean and well cultivated, and the orchards stretched away for miles. For me, the North Star will always shine over a mountain peak—Loma Prieta—ten or fifteen miles away, with orchards stretching all the way to the foothills. Whether the wind blew from Del Monte by the sea, or from the fruited hills, the air was always redolent with the fragrance of the blossoms, the fruit, or the black earth, resting for its winter moment before springing into fruitfulness again.

This is the atmosphere of the Bible. The winds of God blow thus for the lives of His children. One of the most important purposes of redemption is that we might bring forth fruit unto God. We were transplanted out of death and rooted and grounded in His love so that we might bring forth fruit.

The Mother Hen

In the pioneer days of wood-burning locomotives, sparks from locomotives often set fires on either side of the railroad tracks. When the trains ran across the wheat fields, there was a ten-to-fifteen day period when the wheat was ripe enough to burn, yet not ripe enough to cut. Wheat fires sometimes burned for ten miles, sweeping great fields before them. A farmer saw billowing smoke in the distance; he knew the wind was coming toward him and that his wheat would burn right down to the edge of his barn, and that he might lose the house, the barn and all of his buildings. So he took a torch and ran to the edge of his own field; he lighted a fire, and the fire in his own wheat began to burn away one hundred yards, two hundred yards. It made a circle so that when the great fire came down on the wind and met the place that was burned over, it passed around and went on; with the backfire he saved his buildings, but he lost his crop. In great grief, he walked out in the burnt stubble and saw the charred body of a hen lying there. He thought that the hen had become confused and had been burned to death. Idly, he turned the body of the hen over with his toe, and out ran a dozen little chicks. The mother's body had been over them; she was burned, but they went out free.

In the day of Christ's dying, there was the dam of God's patience, and there was the flood of God's wrath; the day that Jesus Christ was put on a cross, God said that Christ was guilty of all of the law, having become a curse through being crucified. On the third day, God raised Him from the dead, and I ran out free, and you ran out free, for He was between us and the wrath of God. This is the atonement.

Prices for Paintings

The *London Times* publishes the prices paid for art objects in all of the salesrooms of the world. If a picture is sold in New York or Paris or Rome or London, the *Times* gives the full details of the sale. Suppose you are standing outside of a great auction room in London, and you hear a clerk say, "He paid $25.00 for a picture, another man paid $600,000.00 for one." You know quite a lot about the two pictures: The twenty-five-dollar picture, may be any one of 10,000 little dogs done by amateur artists who paint sunsets, trees and seascapes, hoping to get paid for them. The six hundred thousand dollar picture—was it a Gainsborough,

Rembrandt, Reubens, Franz Hals, Millet, Michelangelo, or Raphael? You can judge the painting by the price that is paid for it.

We can judge ourselves by the price Christ paid for us, the depths into which He had to reach in order to save us. Christ died for our sins, and when I learn the price that was paid for our redemption, I form conclusions that are justified from other portions of the Scripture—how great was my sinfulness, the depths of my nature and the height of His love.

The Prisoner's Confession

Governor Neff, of Texas, spoke to the assembled convicts of a penitentiary of that state. He finished by saying that he would remain to listen if any man wanted to speak with him. He further announced that what he heard would be held in confidence; nothing a man might tell him would be used against the man.

When the meeting was over, a large group of men remained, many of them life-termers. One by one they each told the governor that he was there through a frame-up, an injustice, a judicial blunder; each asked that he be freed. Finally, one man came up and said, "Mr. Governor, I just want to say that I am guilty. I did what they sent me here for, but I believe I have paid for it. If I were granted the right to go out, I would do everything I could to be a good citizen and prove myself worthy of your mercy."

This man the governor pardoned. So must it be with the great God who alone can pardon. The one difference is that we cannot say that we have paid for any of it. We can come and say, "Oh, God, I just want to say that I am guilty. I am a sinner, a rebel against Thy power and Thy justice, but I believe that Jesus Christ paid for my sin. If, in Thy mercy, because of Him, Thou wilt take me out of darkness into light, I will live as one who is alive from the dead." This, of course, is the man whom God pardons.

The Safety Pin

In one of the rescue missions of Philadelphia, a man had been saved. He had come from a good home, but had been reduced to misery through sin. He had sold his overcoat to obtain a drink; one bitter cold night he walked into a mission with his single coat pinned with a safety pin. On the second anniversary of his conversion he went into the mission to give his testimony. Well-dressed and holding a good position, he was able to give the glory to God. From his pocket he pulled out the safety-pin—plated with gold. Whenever Satan tempted him into thinking he was something, he pulled it out and looked at it.

When we remember the pit from which we have been dug, our desires turn toward God and we want to talk more closely to Him. Looking at the condition from which Christ drew us, we can realize the depths of His love in coming to redeem us.

Through the Mist

The *Saturday Review* published a portfolio of photographs that had won prizes at the Metropolitan Museum as the greatest photographs of the year. One photographer, who happened to be a Methodist minister, had photographed a ship coming through the fog; over the top of that ship he superimposed mists—mists so swirling you could barely see the ship below.

When I read that Christ died for our sins according to the Scriptures, I can peer through a mist and see the heart of God. I can begin to understand what He was and what He did and what motivated Him. It was love that caused Him to pay such a price. Christ died for our sins, and thus we see the inevitable glory of His grace in this simple phrase.

Responsibility to God

Two Young Robbers

Two young men were arrested robbing a service station. When the trial came up one of the men had four or five high-powered lawyers—his family was wealthy. The other boy had a court-appointed lawyer; he had been in reform school and had spent two years in Sing Sing. The two boys were obviously guilty; they had been caught in the act. The judge sentenced the boy who had been in Sing Sing to three years; the other boy was sentenced to ten years. The lawyers howled. The judge said, "This boy is a graduate of Choate Preparatory School and of Yale University. His father was an outstanding man in the community; this boy has sinned against his preparatory school and against Yale University. He has sinned against the whole American standard of ethics. Tremendous opportunities were made available to him, yet he turned against all that he knew to be right. He turned against the code of ethics of his family, his school, his university; he deserves a worse punishment." The judge acted in a biblical way, for God says, "To whom much has been committed, much shall be required."

The fact that we name the name of the Lord Jesus Christ increases our responsibility before God. The more education you have, the more you are answerable to God. The more knowledge you have of the Bible, the more you are answerable to God. The better your health, the more answerable you are to God. The minute that God gives you any advantage whatsoever, the more you are answerable to God.

Resurrection

The Locked Automobile Door

Like everyone else who has ever owned an automobile with a self-locking door, once I locked my keys inside the car. The ventilating window in the front was open so I thought I could put my hand through to unlock the door, but I couldn't make it. Three or four people tried and failed; finally someone with a small wrist tried it and he was able to reach through the window, unfasten the door and let me in.

You and I do not have a right to approach the cross of Christ unless we recognize that once there was a tomb that had the body of Jesus Christ in it, and that He was raised from the dead, and that the cross is on the other side. You and I today must reach our hand through the open tomb of Jesus Christ and grasp the cross on the resurrection side.

Wellington Defeated

When I was in my late twenties I went to Winchester, England, famous for its college and for its cathedral. The verger of the cathedral used to show people around the cathedral. He had been there for many, many years, and he loved to tell the story how the news of the battle of Waterloo came to England. There were no telegrams in those days, but everyone knew that Wellington was facing Napoleon in a great battle. A sailing ship semaphored news to the signalman on top of Winchester Cathedral. He signaled to another man on a hill and thus news of the battle was relayed, by hand semaphore, from station to station to London and all across England. When the ship came in, the signalman on board semaphored the first word—"Wellington." The next word was "defeated", and then the fog came down and the ship could not be seen. "Wellington defeated" went across England, and there was great gloom all over the countryside. After two or three hours, the fog lifted, and the signal came again: "Wellington defeated the enemy." Then all England rejoiced.

There was that day, when in the eyes of the world they put the body of the Lord Jesus Christ in the tomb. Men might have said, "Everything is ended, all is gone, sin has conquered, man is defeated, wrong has triumphed." But then three days later the fog lifted. Jesus Christ rose from the dead. The truth has come down ever since and Jesus defeated the enemy.

Righteousness of God

The Jammed Turnstile

A friend, who does not see well, entered a New York subway station and found that he needed change in order to get through the turnstile. The man in the change booth gave him the necessary coins, but to my friend's fingers one coin did not feel quite right. The changemaker brusquely brushed him on his way, saying that he knew what he had given in change. My friend put the coin into the turnstile slot, and the mechanism jammed. Quite angry by this time, the changemaker opened the turnstile box, and discovered a foreign coin. An American mechanism, geared for American coins, refused to accept the foreign coin which he had given the man who could not see well. Evidently, the foreign coin looked like an American one, but the mechanism rejected it because it was not an American coin.

Our own righteousness may pass for good coin here on earth, but the only currency that is acceptable in heaven is God's perfect righteousness.

Lace and Black Velvet

Along the Avenue Louise in Brussels are several stores that sell nothing but lace. I looked at the exquisite scarves, veils and handkerchiefs in the windows and decided to purchase a handkerchief for my mother. The two old sisters who ran the store showed me some handkerchiefs; I was rather astonished at the price and asked them if they could explain why they were so costly.

It was a few months after World War I, and I still wore my army uniform. The ladies had no other customers at that time of day and seemed pleased to tell the young American officer about their wares. One of them spread a roll of black velvet on the counter, and then began to show the lace against this contrasting background. I was initiated into the mystery of bobbin lace, and a few knots were tied for me in order to show me the method of making it.

Finally, they went to their safe and took out the marriage veil that had just been completed for the wedding of the Duchess of Brabant. Rather gingerly I took hold of the edge of it—the thing was valued at over ten thousand dollars—and began to look at it more closely. One of the ladies immediately lifted the black velvet that I might use the contrasting background to bring out the intricacies of this Brussels rose-point lace. From that day on I have always been interested in the beauties of lace, beauties which two old ladies taught me to comprehend against the blackness of velvet.

It is unquestionable that the glories of God's love and mercy and righteousness and goodness, and tenderness—all of the attributes of His grace—are known by the fact that God took the black velvet of man's sin and threw the web of His grace against it.

The Rock Display

In the Benjamin Franklin Museum of Philadelphia is a display of rocks, housed in a special room that is entered by a corridor shrouded in darkness. The darkness is necessary to accustom the eyes to a different light diffused in the special exhibit room. The light in the exhibit room is an indirect fluorescent light of rays that are ordinarily invisible to the human eye. In the darkness this light shines upon rocks that ordinarily appear gray and dun-brown; in the new light they glow with a brilliance and beauty that is incredible.

So it is with the righteousness of God as seen through the eyes of the world and as seen through the eyes of the Spirit. The world looks upon the righteousness of God as a drab thing, even imagining that it robs man of the happiness that the world promises so freely and gives so poorly. Around the shoulders of the poorest sinner shall be draped the robe of the divine righteousness, unto all and upon all who believe.

Saints

What is a Saint?

A little boy was accustomed to attending a church which had beautiful stained-glass windows. He saw that the windows contained pictures: "St. Matthew, St. Mark, St. Luke, St. John, St. Paul," and others. One day he was asked, "What is a saint?" He replied, "A saint is a person the light shines through."

Does God's light shine through you? Christ commands, "Let your light so shine before men, that they may see your good works, and glorify your Father which is in heaven" (MATTHEW 5:16).

Salvation

Drop It

When I landed at Makassar in the Celebes a few years ago, I was met by a little Malay boy who carried a bamboo cage containing tiny monkeys about six inches high—perfect little creatures, and very cute. The boy trailed me, saying, "Buy a monkey, Mister? One dollar; buy a monkey, Mister?" I looked at the monkeys and walked along; the boy followed, lowering his price as he pleaded, "Buy a monkey, Mister? Seventy-five cents!" and finally, "Fifty cents!" The missionary who had met me at the ship explained that we couldn't take the monkey; I gave the boy a tip and he went away happy. The missionary then told me how those monkeys are caught.

There is a gourd that grows long like a string bean and, upon reaching its full length, begins to swell. When the gourd is in the string-bean state, a boy ties a cord around half of it so that half stops growing; the other half continues to swell, and thus a narrownecked bottle is formed. Then the boy cuts off the gourd, hollows it out, drops in a couple of handfuls of rice, and ties the gourd to a tree. The monkey smells the rice, thrusts in his paw to grab it, but cannot pull his paw out. If he would drop the rice, he could get away, but so long as he holds on to the food his paw acts like a cork in reverse; he is a prisoner of his own greed. Although the animal chatters, pulls and tugs, he still holds onto the rice, and the boy slips a bamboo cage around him, then breaks the gourd. The monkey eats the rice and is sold down the river.

That is the picture of many people who have their hands full of sin, full of themselves. God says, "I will give you salvation to take you into heaven if you will admit that you have your paw full of something and if you will drop it. Admit that you are less than perfect, that you are the sinner that I say you are. Unless you open your hand and drop what you are clutching, I cannot give you my righteousness in Jesus Christ."

The Only Way

Many European towns still bear the marks of walls that surrounded them in the Middle Ages. Streets near these old walls are curved and sometimes wind up in a dead end. A man asked a stranger how to reach a certain address. When the stranger directed him, the inquirer was still a little dubious. "Is that the best way?" he asked. The stranger answered, "It is the only way. If you follow the other turning it will bring you back here."

That is a great illustration of the way to God. Go through Jesus Christ and His death on the cross. "Is that the best way?" someone might ask. The only answer to that is the truth: "It is the only way." Any other turning will take you—not back to where you are, but off into outer darkness of separation from God.

A Rocket Trip to the Moon

Let's suppose that we have reached the day that a rocket ship is ready for a trip to the moon. It has been built on the desert sands of southern California, about a hundred feet below sea level. It has not been built on top of the nearby Sierras, nor on top of Mt. Everest. A certain Colonel Eager Beaver, immensely wealthy and very egotistical, wants to go to the moon, but he declares that it is not becoming to him to go all the way down into the desert, below sea level. He is going to do the thing in a grandiose way. He is going to finance an expedition to Asia and get a party to climb to the top of Mt. Everest and take off from there. So Colonel Eager Beaver creates a great stir. Many men are willing to accept the high salary he pays to go to Asia on the expedition. Plenty of salesmen are willing to sell him all the equipment he wants; they pocket their profits with a smile. Finally the Colonel reaches Asia, and he and a small company of guides even reach the summit of Mt. Everest; they build a small shelter so that they can stay there month after month.

Then Colonel Eager Beaver hears that some skeptics criticize his plan. They know the reality of earth's altitude and the principles of rocket ships. But the Colonel is very proud and describes in great detail all that he has done. He argues that we must admit that he is closer to the moon than anyone else on earth. He is more than five miles above the level of the sea, and therefore five miles nearer to the moon than those poor creatures who have gone down to the rocket station to take off for the moon.

There is only one way to reply to him. In terse words, he must be told that he is a fool. There is no place for pride in an attempt to reach the moon. If any man is going to go to the moon, he must stop talking about mountain climbing expeditions, and go to the one place where there is a craft capable of crossing the reaches of space. Furthermore, when he gets to the launching area he must be willing to go through one small door into the rocket. Only then can he hope to achieve his purpose. By climbing high on the surface of the earth he is, in reality, farther from the moon than he would be by going low.

Some may think that my illustration is slightly fantastic, and I readily admit it, but the efforts of men to get to heaven are even more fantastic than those of the Colonel. There is only one way to get to heaven. That way was opened at one geographical spot on the earth—Calvary, outside the city wall of Jerusalem—where the cross of Jesus Christ was set up and where Christ, the Son of God, God the Son, died that He might become the Saviour of men. All over the world there are those who outfit their private mountain climbing expeditions of good works, and imagine that they can be nearer heaven because they have done this good deed or performed that philan-thropic act. But in reality the farther they are from Jerusalem the far-ther they are from God.

The Rubber Raft

An aviator, forced down in the middle of the ocean and drifting on a piece of flotsam, would not be concerned about the identification of the workingmen who had made a rubber raft that was being dropped to him from a rescuing plane. He would not stop to argue with nearby sharks as to whether the raft was made in Chicago or Detroit. With a last gasp he would wiggle on and be tremendously glad he was there.

So a soul in need will not be primarily concerned about who wrote the Epistle to the Hebrews or whether a Hebrew copyist made a false brush stroke in transcribing one of the letter figures which tell how many men fell in one day in a given battle. The soul in need sees in the Word of God: SALVATION. It is the Word of Life that is held forth to him (PHILIPPIANS 2:15,16). The believer knows that it came from God, that when it left God it was absolutely perfect, and that it will take him from death to life.

The Salvation Army Woman

The late Handley Moule, Bishop of Durham in the Church of England, was a very godly man. One day as he was walking along Princess Street in Edinburgh he approached a corner where a group of Salvation Army workers were conducting an open air meeting. He paused for a moment to listen and one of the young women of the group spoke to him saying, "Sir, are you saved?" The venerable Bishop looked at her with a kindly smile and twinkling eyes and asked her, "Do you mean . . . ?" Here he used three Greek words which were utterly incomprehensible to her. She showed her igno-rance by her stupefaction, and the Bishop continued in English, "Do you mean 'I have been saved,' 'I am being saved,' or 'I shall be saved'?"

True salvation is in all three of these tenses. In the past, the believer has been saved from the penalty of sin; in the present, he is being saved from the power of sin; and in the future, he will be saved from the very presence of sin. If any one of the three were left out, there would be no reality of salvation.

The Way to Iceland

During World War II, the late President Roosevelt used this particular expression in one of his great speeches. Poland, with some of the other countries of Western Europe, had been conquered by the German hordes and Great Britain was hard pressed. The battle of the Atlantic was about to begin. Addressing his remarks to England, the President said, "As for Iceland, we are determined at all costs *to keep the way* to Iceland." What did he mean? Iceland, situated strategically in the North Atlantic, was in the hands of the American government. Thus the sea lanes were assured of the safe transit of ships as long as Iceland remained in friendly hands. Roosevelt said in so many words that no matter what the cost, we would keep the way to Iceland open in order for shipping to make its course across the ocean unimpeded. The way was to be kept open.

God has not only provided a way, but He has seen to it that it shall be kept open in order that men might come to Him.

Sanctification

Cleansing

The difference between special cleansing and regular cleansing is the same as that between special and regular washing of the hands. A woman may work around the kitchen and go to the sink a score of times to rinse her hands because there has come some special need for cleansing. Or a student may get ink on his fingers and need special cleansing. But in the evening as we come to the time of retiring, we go through our regular cleansing even though there may not be any special dirt upon us.

Thus it is with the life that is brought to the Lord day by day. There may come special outbreak of sin, some rising surprise of the old Adamic nature, and for this we will need to rush back to God for special cleansing and restoration to full fellowship. But at the end of a day when nothing of special evil has touched our lives, we still need to return to Him and ask forgiveness for the faults which He can see and which we may not recognize.

Sanctified Peaches

In August the streets of China used to be filled with fruit sellers, in village as well as in city. A huge assortment is on display—half a dozen kinds of melons, varieties of peaches, apples, grapes, and other fruits. To one accustomed to eating fruit freely, it was a distinct disappointment to see this wealth and be unable to eat any. In those days the methods under which the fruit was grown and the filth involved in the handling made it impractical for a foreigner to spend a few coppers, rinse or peel the fruit, and enjoy it. Before the fruit can be eaten, it must be sanctified. Strawberries and peaches had to be washed in a solution of potassium permanganate, then dipped in boiling water and carefully pared. If the skin was broken the pieces had to be cut out meticulously and discarded. If the skins of tomatoes had been broken, they could be eaten only after they had been cooked. Travelers in the Orient learned to take sanitary precautions they never dreamed of at home. All of these preparations correspond to sanctification.

We live with a terrible source of infection. Radical treatment is necessary. The cause of infection has to be delivered over to death. As peaches and fruit must be prepared with chemicals, and open spots cut away with a knife, so the old nature must be delivered over to the Lord Jesus Christ for crucifixion death. This is the meaning of the "I die daily" of the apostle. It is the moment by moment disinfection of sanctification.

Satan

The Black Eye

Suppose a man has angered a group of men who are standing with the world's champion heavyweight boxer. One man says, "You are going to get a black eye!" The offender says, "Well, if I am to receive a black eye, please let the world's champion give it to me. I can at least boast about that!" But they reply, "No, you will get it from the water boy, who is the weakest one here."

So Jesus Christ, made lower than the angels, was to inflict ignominious defeat upon the most powerful of all created beings. How did He do it? In Deuteronomy, Christ answered Satan, "It is written, 'Man shall not live by bread alone, but by every word that proceeds from the mouth of God.'" No wonder Satan hates the books of Moses and does all he can to bring them into disrepute! Christ wielded the Sword of the Spirit, and the flashing power of the Word of God inflicted the first wound on Satan.

Inflated Decoys

The Army has revealed that it misled the foe by the use of pneumatic decoys. In the middle of the night soldiers inflated rubberized tubes and painted fabric so that enemy aircraft, flying over our positions on reconnaissance, would think they saw fleets of tanks and masses of artillery when, in reality, they were looking upon inflated decoys.

There is nothing new under the sun. The devil has been using this device for ages. How many Christians have been afraid of what they thought they saw and felt, when, in reality, they were faced with the ruse of a foe who was defeated at Calvary. There the Lord Jesus "spoiled principalities and powers, he made a shew of them openly, triumphing over them in it" (COLOSSIANS 2:15). From the moment Christ died, Satan was left with inflated decoys instead of power. True victory is available for those who lay hold, by faith, on the spiritual weapons of our warfare, which are mighty, through God, to the pulling down of strongholds (II CORINTHIANS 10:4).

The Overblown Balloon

I once saw a small child playing with a toy balloon. When it had no air in it, it was a small thing that could be hidden in the palm of the hand. When it was blown up it was a frightening thing; it had a devilish face painted on its side. The child had blown and blown until the face was quite large. The child did not know the technique too well, so a great deal of spittle had gone into the balloon. Suddenly it exploded; all the child held in his hand was a messy little bit of rubber, with the distorted face reduced to little or nothing. The child attempted to stretch this out but the face had lost its power to frighten.

When I thought of this in retrospect, it reminded me of what happened to Satan when Christ died. The devil and his principalities had been filled with pretentions, but Christ had disarmed them and made a show of them—a public example. We can thank God that Satan was effectively put to an open shame, exposed publicly. His overblown balloon burst, leaving him nothing but the messy remains of his grinning pretentions.

Steaming the Ocean

Duveen, the famous English art connoisseur, took his little daughter to the beach one day, but she would not go into the chilly water. After persuasion failed, Duveen borrowed a tea-kettle, built a fire, heated a little water until it steamed beautifully; then, with a great flourish, he poured it into the ocean. His greatly impressed daughter went in without a murmur.

Where can we find a better example of one of Satan's tricks? He dilutes an ocean of unbelief with a steaming teakettle of Christian ethics and people go wading in, self-satisfied but unaware that they are bathing in unbelief.

Second Coming

Black Sand

When I was a little boy, I sometimes went down to the beach, five miles from our home in California, and played on the sands of Monterey Bay. Some little distance up the beach there is a great stretch of black sand; it is black because it contains a great deal of iron. I can remember taking a box of sand and drawing a magnet through it. Fine black grains clung to the magnet—particles of iron. I put these grains in another box, and drew my magnet through the sand again. Each time I got some more grains, I removed the particles of iron until nothing was left in the box but sand. Though I could not tell the difference between the sand and the iron on the beach, the magnet could tell the difference immediately. Had I been able to use a stronger magnet, I could have taken all of the iron out of a large box of sand in a moment.

The day is going to come when the Lord Jesus Christ will rise from the throne of God where He is now answering the attacks of Satan upon us, by telling the Father that we belong to Him because of His work on the cross. When He rises from that throne, it is time for judgment to begin. But God tells us that before judgment comes, He is going to do a wonderful thing—like the work of the magnet picking the grains of iron out of the grains of sand. He is going to remove from the earth all who are trusting Christ, and take them to be with Himself.

The Coming Friend

Did you ever get a letter from some friend or relative announcing that they were coming to your home for a visit? You don't know when they will arrive. You keep looking for them at any moment. Suddenly the doorbell rings; you go to the door and find the baggage man with the trunk and valises of your coming guest. The door closes. You stand looking at the baggage in the hall. Surely it will not be long until you see your loved one in person.

So the Christian waits for Christ. The events of current history are but the baggage that mark the nearness of His coming. Our Lord is at the door.

Our Clubhouse

When I was a boy, I lived on a street that came to a dead end a block from my home; beyond a fence across the street lay an undeveloped tract of land. One day the fence was taken down, and the street was extended. Soon a contractor built many houses there and families moved in. One house remained unfinished. Workmen came for two days and then absented themselves for a week or two; they returned again for several days, then were absent for another long period. My father explained that the contractor was using that house to occupy his men when they were not needed on some other house in the tract. That house became the headquarters for a group of us boys. We retrieved every discarded scrap of board, every short end, every fallen nail. Before the floor was laid, we had enough pieces to cover several square feet of bare joists; a good length of two-by-four served as the upright to which we nailed other pieces. Finally, we had a clubhouse big enough for a couple of Newfoundland dogs, or four or five boys. It was our delight for many days. One day after school we heard hammering and sawing and knew that the job was going forward. At five o'clock when the mill whistle blew the men left the job. We swarmed in and discovered that they had knocked our clubhouse apart and thrown the whole thing through a window opening. It lay, disjointed and wrecked, on the ground outside. The work proceeded with some steadiness for many days. The floor was laid and on top of the first, rough pine flooring, quartered oak boards for the finished floor were laid. One piece, cut and ready to put in place, had been left lying there, and the idea came to us that we could nail it into place. Carefully, we examined the other pieces to see how they had been nailed in: We wrapped a rag around the nails and tapped lightly with the hammer lest we leave some scar. It took us almost an hour to secure one piece of board. We wondered if it would be allowed to remain; we marked the board and the wainscot so that we could tell whether "our" board had stood the test. The next evening we entered the house and were thrilled to find "our" board in the center of the finished floor.

Three or four years later, passing that house at night when the shades were up and one could see the warmth of that room with its lights and curtains, I stood outside for several minutes, recalling with pride that I had helped place a quartered oak board in that floor.

When the Lord Jesus Christ comes again we shall account for the materials we have used. Some buildings—some lives—are like a patchwork doghouse built on open joists, destined to be destroyed. But some will endure as part of God's eternal structure. Let us bow before God and ask Him to wreck everything in our lives that results from our own efforts apart from Him. Ask Him to confirm everything that is being built according to the plans and specifications of His Word.

The Fishing Fleet

In a city near Edinburgh, a large fishing fleet goes forth each year on a long expedition to the Newfoundland banks. When the fleet returns, the whole town is notified, and as the boats come over the horizon, everyone is at the dock waiting for loved ones who have been away for two, or three long months. On one such return, as the fleet approached the shore, the captain stood on the deck of one of the ships with his field glasses, reporting to the sailors. Naturally, they were all wondering about their loved ones. The captain said, "Jock, I see your Mamie and the two bairns there; Bill, there is your Freda; John, I see. . . ." As he told each man of his family and wife, each was relieved to know that all was well—there had been no sickness, no death. One man came to the captain and asked, "Do you see my wife there?" The captain turned and said, "I'm sorry Angus, I don't see her; she's not there." Angus began to worry because his wife was not in the crowd on the wharf. When the ship docked, the men greeted their loved ones, but Angus moved through the crowd looking everywhere for his wife; he could not find her. Her passed quickly through the village to his house on a hill. With hurried step he opened the door—there was his wife. She said, "Oh, Angus, I've been waiting for you." He replied, "The wives of the other men were watching for them."

Believers in the Lord Jesus Christ should not be only waiting but also watching for the Lord to come.

John's Homecoming

The atmosphere of the believing church should be that of the mother and father who have been told that their son at the war front has received his rotation papers—he will be home any day. In this day of airplanes they know it is possible for him to get on an airplane and be in Philadelphia and at the front door perhaps quicker than a cablegram and telegram could be delivered. So the house is gotten ready. John is coming home; he may be there any moment. You may be sure his fiancee is thinking with great joy of the imminence of his return. Every stop on the stair, every ring of the bell, every ring of the telephone, may be news from John, he may be there in a moment.

Now that is undoubtedly the psychological atmosphere in which the early church lived. The thought of His coming should be before us like the returning of the son and the loved one. He has said he will come back.

The Plane Ride

Some years ago I had to go out to Los Angeles on a plane from New York. The hostess seated a girl twenty or twenty-one years of age beside me. Obviously the girl had never flown before. Over the loudspeaker, the hostess said, "Fasten your seatbelts"; the girl did not know what a seatbelt was. I helped her and asked, "You've never flown before?" And she said, "No, this is my first time." As I spoke to her, she opened her pocketbook, and there was a picture of a GI, a fine, rock-ribbed New England face. I said, "You're going out to see him?" "Yes," she said, "he's coming home. I'm going to see him." I talked to her. They had gotten married a year and a half before, had a honeymoon of just a few days, then he had gone to the coast and left for Korea. Now he was coming back home; she was going to see him, and that meant more to her than anything else. Nothing else counted for her; her whole soul was in her eyes. As I told her how to fix the seatbelt, I said, "Now don't be worried, the engines are going to whirl and you'll think that something is going to happen, but it isn't. They're just testing the engines and when they quiet down, then there will be the moment of pull and you'll feel the takeoff." She was interested in everything she was doing, but most of all in the young man in the cellophane-bordered picture in her pocketbook. He was her bridegroom; she was his bride; she was going to see him.

You wonder sometimes why Christians live as they do and make the choices they make. They are on their way to see their bridegroom, yet they go right out and live in the world as though it made no effect in their life at all. Why do people live the way they live in the light of the fact that Jesus is coming again? This is the blessed hope. We are going to see Him.

Separation

Divided Allegiance

Louis Adamic, a Yugoslavian boy, came to the United States at the age of fourteen. He became absorbed in writing and eventually mastered a vivid prose style in his adopted language. His first book, *Dynamite,* was a history of the American labor conflict in its more violent phases. *The Native's Return* made him famous; he wrote this book after a visit to the land of his birth. From that time on the author's allegiance was divided. He wanted to do something for Yugoslavia; thinking that Stalin was Yugoslavia's best friend, he abandoned our democratic ways, fought against granting Trotsky asylum in America, and little by little became more interested in Balkan politics than in American democracy. When Tito broke with Stalin, Adamic followed Tito. Louis Adamic was found dead at his New Jersey farm below Easton. It was widely suspected that he had been murdered by a member of an anti-Tito Slavic party. One commentator said, "The moral seems to be plain: divided citizenship, divided national loyalties, can mean terrible tragedy in the modern world."

The spiritual analogy is just as plain. God will never accept a compromise. The world and the flesh seek to draw the allegiance of a believer in a thousand subtle ways, but God demands separation. The separation is in the heart, while the activity is in the midst of the market place, the church organization or the social whirl.

Doubtful and Dirty

A newspaper comic once showed a man dressing in a hurry for an evening engagement. He called out to his wife, "Mary, come and see if this collar is clean enough to wear." The answer he received was, "If it's doubtful, it's dirty."

God says, ". . . come out from among them, and be ye separate . . . and touch not the unclean thing . . ." (II CORINTHIANS 6:17).

Many Christians are worried as to whether or not they should partake in this or that form of the world's work or play. A very good rule for the Christian who is really seeking to follow the Lord closely, is that the doubtful thing is generally unclean. The doubt in our mind probably comes from the presence of the Holy Spirit who is warning us. The closer we come to yieldedness, the more quickly doubt will turn to certainty.

The Great Albatross

Ornithologists now know that the great albatross flies around the world several times in the course of its life. These birds can stand buffeting by ocean gales for days, but they become seasick if they stand on the deck of a moving ship.

The true Christian can go across the face of life, buffeted by all the winds of time and space, as long as he remembers that he is in the world but not of it. When he comes down and becomes a part of the movement of this world he loses his Christian joy and power, because he is entirely out of the element for which God created him.

Tops and Marbles

A boy does not give up playing with tops and marbles. Tops and marbles give him up. He may be playing marbles one day when the older boys come by; if they are short a man for a ball game, they may ask him to play. He covers his field as if his life depended upon it; when he is at bat, he swings hard enough to break himself in two. When the game is over, he walks—struts—with the older boys; he sees the "little fellows" with whom he had played so recently, playing marbles. His lip curls contemptuously as he says, "Kid stuff." He has not given up marbles, marbles have given him up.

The believer in the life of Christ does not have to give up "things." The new life of Christ will push off the old, dead habits and these "things" will give him up.

Sin

A Splash Under the Light

A person, walking on a dark night, gets splashed by a taxi going by. Oh, he says, "I got some mud on me." In the reflection of a light about fifty yards away, he says, "I don't think it is too bad." As he gets nearer the light, he says, "It's worse than I thought." Right under the light, he says, "I'm going to have to go back to the apartment and change."

The nearer you get to the Lord, the more you are going to see what sin is in your life. The nearer we get to God, the more we will see what we really are.

Automobile Laws

Back in the early days of automobiles there were no laws against speed. A man who had learned the joys of fast driving bought one of the fastest cars available and took it out on the roads, driving as fast as road conditions allowed. He crossed the border into another state, and was confronted by a large road sign stating that the state speed limit was 35 miles per hour. Every mile or so he found another announcement of the speed limit. The law infuriated him, so he broke it at every opportunity. As he sped he passed still another sign reaffirming the speed limit; it further announced that the road was patrolled and that the law would be strictly enforced. The law had not created his desire for speed—that had existed long before the law was enacted—but the law made him conscious of his fierce desire to speed, and it also made him conscious of his rebellion against the restraining demand of the law. Each succeeding sign brought the same swift rebellion. His foot moved from accelerator to brake, from brake to accelerator as his mind veered from desire for speed to fear of arrest. The coming of the law brought out both the desire to have his own way and conflict with authority that sought to restrain him.

Before the law, sinful desire had occasionally cropped up; but with the law, rebellion became open, and the sinner determined to satisfy his desire at all costs. If we are to live in triumph, with righteousness reigning through Christ, we must pass through the experience that is set forth here in order to be brought to God's own method for victory over sin's thrust from within us.

The Blackboard Marks

A little girl, coming home from her first day at school, asked her mother where the marks on the blackboard went when they were rubbed out. The mother answered that they disappear. "But where do they disappear to?" the little girl questioned. "They vanish," her mother told her. "But where do they vanish to?" the child insisted. The mother used all the words she knew to explain but she could not make it clear to the child.

This story illustrates what God has done with our sins. He goes so far as to say that He, who is all knowledge, will remember our sins against us no more.

Broke

A young man in college was so engrossed in preparations for final examinations and in extra-curricular activities, that he neglected to write home for five weeks. Then his parents received a letter, which said, "The inevitable consequence of not writing for five weeks is that I am now broke."

The inevitable consequence of not keeping in close communication with the heavenly Father is that the child becomes spiritually bankrupt. It doesn't take five weeks, either. A day will destroy fellowship. It is sin which cuts the communication lines and anything which cuts them is sin.

Extinct Flowers

During World War II, great bombs fell right in the center of London, and buildings were completely leveled. When the debris was cleared away, there was earth in the center of London, and flowers sprang up in the bomb craters. Botanists had thought these flowers died a hundred years ago, but their seeds had lain dormant under the city, and now flowers came back that men had thought extinct.

When men face tragedy or complex crises in their lives, seeds of sin rise up from their dormancy and strike out. Occasionally you hear of men of exemplary character becoming murderers or thieves because the seeds are there. Unhappy is the man who does not know that every seed of sin lies in him. Only by the grace of God in Christ and by the building of the edifice of faith over the top of it, can the light of day keep the explosions of life from bringing the subsoil out with all the horrors that are there ready to spring into growth, if they are not curbed moment by moment.

The GI's Loan

An ex-GI went into the Chase Manhattan Bank in New York to get a loan from their small loans department. The Chase Manhattan is one of the largest banks in the world and negotiates loans of millions of dollars with great industries. But they also have a small loans department that lends a few hundred dollars to a working girl or a laboring man. The former soldier had to fill out a lot of forms because the government was guaranteeing the loan; it was necessary for him to come back a second day.

When the GI returned he was kept waiting for quite a while. Finally, the president of the bank came up to the GI, introduced himself, and asked him if he'd mind being photographed. The day before, the bank records had shown that sometime on the following day the total monies loaned by the small loans department would reach the sum of one billion dollars. The bank authorities decided to publicize that fact by granting a "free" loan to the customer who appeared at the right moment. The soldier was the fortunate man—the department had just reached the billion-mark. He had signed all the papers and had obligated himself to repay the sum of six hundred dollars in installments, but now, before the news cameras, he was *given* the sum of six hundred dollars; his note and other papers were returned to him. The bank, of course, got much more than six hundred dollars' worth of publicity on the transaction, but we might well say, "O the blessedness of the GI to whom the Chase Manhattan Bank will not impute or charge his loan." The bank had effectively said, "This one is to be placed to our account. You will never have anything to pay."

God has declared that it is His sovereign plan to charge to the account of Jesus Christ the sins of all who will admit that they are personally bankrupt spiritually, and who will throw themselves upon His grace to save them.

The Gossip

A woman received a juicy bit of scandal on the telephone one Sunday morning. She was eager to communicate the news to another close friend and tried to reach her by telephone. The line was busy and she could not get the call through. Again and again she tried, but without success. Her impatient husband was waiting to take her to the communion service. The woman reluctantly went to church, but she hoped that no one would tell her friend the morsel of gossip before she got home to relay the news.

The woman reached for the bread and the cup with the definite knowledge that she was planning sin as soon as the church service was over. She thus eats and drinks unworthily, and is eating and drinking condemnation to herself, not discerning the Lord's body.

The Hunter and the Bear

As the hunter raised his rifle, the bear called out, "Can't we talk this over like two sober human beings?" The hunter lowered his gun. "What's to talk over?" he asked. "Well, for instance," said the bear, coming closer, "what do you want to shoot me for?" "Simple," grunted the hunter, "I want a fur coat." "All I want is a good breakfast," smiled the bear. "I'm sure we can get together sensibly on this." So they sat down to work out an agreement. After awhile the bear got up—all alone. They had reached a compromise. The bear had secured his breakfast, and the hunter had on his fur coat.

There has never been any other result in the warfare between the flesh and the spirit when the spirit permits any compromise with the flesh. Sin is deceitful and will always destroy even while putting forth a pretense of fair words. The Word of God gives us only one possible course of action, "FLEE."

The Income Tax

A man working on his income tax forms, does not get the job accomplished on Saturday evening; he plans to continue on Sunday afternoon, following the communion service. He knows that he is juggling figures and claiming invalid deductions to cheat the government.

When he takes the bread and the cup he is announcing to the world that there is no course of action in his life that is wrong and that is not surrendered to the Lord. It is a public lie. The proper state of mind must be that *as far as a man knows,* Christ is Lord of every area of his life. He must be living after the Spirit, and surrendering the deeds of his mortal body for mortification—putting to death—by the work of Christ. God will continue throughout life to reveal new areas for the growing Lordship of Christ, but at the moment of taking communion properly, the man has surrendered every area of which he has an awareness of conflict.

Iron Out of Ore

In Venezuela there are great iron mines, from which ore is shipped to the largest iron works in the world, near Philadelphia. If a man were to try to get iron out of ore with a hammer, he could not do it, because iron is not a mechanical agglutination; it is a chemical union. The ore must go into a great furnace; as the temperature rises, the iron within the ore turns to liquid, and the pure metal runs out.

This is exactly how God works in your life and mine. This is why we must be salted with fire. You and I cannot hammer sin out of our lives. Rather, we must recognize that God loves us and that He will salt us with fire until the slag is burned away and only pure metal remains. So, if you and I desire to be delivered from sin, we must be willing to go into the flame. There is no other way.

Kicking His Shins

A little girl was very mean to her younger brother; she treated him so badly, he went crying to his mother. When the mother learned what had happened, she said to the little girl, "Mary, why have you let Satan put it into your heart to pull your brother's hair and kick his shins?" The little girl thought it over for a moment, and then answered, "Well, Mother, maybe Satan did put it into my heart to pull brother's hair, but kicking his shins was my own idea."

The evil in the earth does not all come from Satan; much of it comes from the heart of man. To be sure, Satan tempts man to sin, but a great deal of sin is man's own idea.

Meerschaum Pipes

When we were in Holland, we wanted to spend Sunday at Marken, a beautiful little island northeast of Amsterdam. Since there was no hotel there, we stayed in a town four miles away in order to take the ferry over in the morning. The women of the town wear turned-up caps, and the men wear big, baggy trousers and wooden shoes, and smoke meerschaum pipes—great big pipes about as big as a saxaphone. In the morning, while we waited for the ferry we noticed several hundred villagers gathering for the Catholic church service across the street. The bell began to ring, and little girls began to scurry into the church. Then followed the teen-age girls, the young matrons, and finally the older women. None of the men moved; they went right on talking and jesting, as stolidly as though there had been no motion at all. When the last old woman had gone in, there were two seconds of breaks; then the little boys went toward the door, and successively the teenagers and the older men. As the smokers approached the church, we noticed something we had not seen before. In front of the church were large wooden racks with number holes. The men came up, hung their pipes in those niches in the racks and went on into the church. When the last man had gone inside, we saw 75 or 100 meerschaum pipes. Not a man was in sight. Of course, when the Mass was over, they would come out, each man would reach for his pipe and light up.

I said to myself, "I wonder what we would see if out in front of our churches, we had a rack for our little packages of sin—something we were doing, a nice neat little box, Christmas-wrapped. As you entered you hung your package on number 18, went inside and took communion, said, 'I surrender all,' and hurried back to that box."

Never Got Caught

A man filling out a job application blank came to the question, "Have you ever been arrested?" His answer was "No." The next question, asking "Why?", was meant for those who had answered the first part in the affirmative. Nevertheless, the applicant answered it with, "Never got caught." That was the truth.

He had sin in him, but he did not have it on him simply because a policeman hadn't been there at the opportune moment. But the sin that is in us in the sight of God is also on us, as we are answerable to God. That is, the sin is on us unless it is on the Saviour, and then it can never be on us again, since He bore it for those who put their trust in Him. There are not three places in the universe where sin can be. Your sin is either on yourself or on the Savior.

Radioactivity

One of the most terrible aspects of atomic energy is the terrific lingering radioactivity imparted to anything nearby. Human beings go near the place where an atomic explosion has taken place at their own peril.

What an illustration of the effects of sin! Someone may think that their loss of temper or their crisis of passion lasted for only a moment, but corroding effects may continue for months in the life of a Christian and the wages are death in the life of a non-Christian. The death that proceeded from Adam's sin is still causing casualties.

The Testimony Exhibition

During my late teens I observed the corruption of sin in a rescue mission in Los Angeles. I listened to the testimonies of men with criminal records: The first said that he had been in prison three times, and had lived a life of sin; the next had been in prison four times, and had sinned even more; the third man had had six imprisonments, and added dope to the alcohol of the first two. I was uneasy; these men seemed to be exhibitionists, though I did not know the meaning of the word at that time. If the man who had testified first had waited till last he might have remembered a few more convictions, and have found a deeper black for his portrait. Finally, I could not contain myself any longer. I rose to say that I had a greater testimony than any man who had spoken. There was an intense silence as these men, eroded with cancerous sin, turned to look at the beardless youth who was seemingly raising their bid to take the game. And then I cried out that the reason I had a testimony greater than any that had been given was that I was able to say that Jesus Christ had saved me from all these horrors, and He had kept me from them. I can remember a very dirty old man bursting into tears. Perhaps looking upon me conjured up the memory of his youth and what he might have been.

But although I had such a testimony, and still have it, I am able to look down through the electronic microscope of the Word of God and see the corruption of the nature which is mine by inheritance, and to acknowledge that all of the seeds that brought forth such corruption in these men were and are within my being, as they are within yours. It is in the light of this truth that the true Christian will be very humble, and will desire to grow in compassion toward those who are out of the way.

The Treacherous Creek

Just outside the town in California where I was born is a creek that winds across the country, eventually flowing into the Pajaro River. Many a spot along this creek would make a magnificent swimming hole, but no boys are ever seen there. It is not even necessary for parents to tell their boys not to go near these waters. Were any new boy to suggest a swim, others would quickly tell him that the name of the creek is *Salsipuedes;* Spanish for "Get out if you can." There are quicksands in the creek. Legend has it that a man attempted to cross and was caught in the terrible grip of the sand; a Spaniard, coming by, called out to him, *"Sal si puedes,"* and that is how the creek got its name.

Nothing could be more terrible than the locking of that invisible power that catches a man and pulls him down steadily to suffocation and death. This is the picture that God Himself has given us of the force of sin that holds every man and woman in this world until the redemption provided by Christ Jesus has been made effective in their lives.

The Whine of the Shells

During the first world war the soldiers near the front line trenches learned to know the whine of the different types of shells as they screamed their way over to bring death. When a shell was heard, men flung themselves into the nearest hole without any worry as to what kind of filth or death might be in the hole. Nothing in the hole could be as bad as the exploding steel.

So it is that men run away from life when God speaks to them. He uncovers their sin and tells them of their need and immediately they run for cover. There is no honesty behind the evasions, and this Christ will not tolerate, but where there is an honest doubt, He will meet it.

Sons Of God

The Dirty Beggar Child

If you were walking down some important street in the midst of great crowds, and should see a dirty beggar child holding out his hand toward you, your heart would be moved to pity. But if that child kept running after you and called out to you "Mother," or "Father," when you have never seen the child before, you would be stirred to righteous indignation. What right would that child have to attract attention to you and turn the gaze of all the passersby from the child's filth to you? Desire on the part of a child cannot create a parental relationship. If you go to the child in the street and lead him to your home, give him new cleanliness and new clothing, and adopt him into your family, then he has the right to call you father, and the law will recognize that right. But the right and authority must be given by you.

In the divine relationship God has made full provision for sonship. If we are to become sons of God, the first step is that we must realize that we are not sons of God, and cannot be except through the channel which He himself has opened up to us through Christ.

Spiritual Life

The Christian Student

A Christian student must understand that it is sin for him to be lazy, for mental laziness is a sin. If a student has a brain capable of earning a grade of A, it is a sin for him to get only a B. If he is capable of earning a B, it is a sin for him to get only a C. If this be true in our mental life, it is also true in our spiritual life.

We are not to be lazy in our spiritual life. Man is a soul; he has a body and a spirit. We must spend much time on the body, keeping it fed and clothed, and letting it sleep in order to recuperate. But we are not to be lazy. Spiritual laziness is the cause of spiritual defeat.

Corot's Pond

While Jean François Raffaeli, the French art critic was walking near the village of Barbizon he saw the renowned Jean Baptiste Corot painting a meadow, with woods in the background. Raffaeli saw that Corot had put in a small lake, although actually there was no lake in the field before him. "But, Monsieur Corot!" he exclaimed, "is it permissible to paint a pond where there is no pond?" Corot retorted, "Young man, it is eleven o'clock. I have been here in the field since six this morning. I became very thirsty, so I put water in the picture to refresh myself."

Therein we recognize our own thirsts and hungers, our need for refreshment; so Paul expresses his need of refreshment and gives the clue as to how we are refreshed.

The Submerged Bottle

If you submerge a bottle in water, what happens? Some will say, "The air bubbles out and the water flows in." But I have seen a bottle submerged in water and no air came out nor did any water flow in. There was a cork in the bottle, which must be pulled out if the bottle is to submerge.

God is like that with us. He has the purpose and the power, but He will not ravish our beings. Love can never be commanded, and He wants us to love Him, so He woos us by creating all the qualities which go with emptiness and frustration. But when we tell Him to go ahead and do His work, outcome the obstacles which keep Him from filling our beings, and in comes the power of the Holy Spirit, so that life at once takes on abounding quality. There is no abounding without the pressure of His power behind it. Nothing can overflow from us until we have first been filled. And we cannot be filled until His power comes in with the enabling.

Time and Patience

Fabre, the greatest naturalist who ever lived, began the main part of his work at sixty; he was able to give all his time to it when he was seventy; and he was discovered by fame at the age of ninety. He had done all of his work without a laboratory; all of his insects had been raised in old flower pots and sardine cans. He always referred to his two best instruments as *"time"* and *"patience."*

God tells us that He uses these two things in developing our spiritual lives. How many times we are told to wait upon the Lord! The flesh does not want to take time, but God does, for He is dealing with eternity. And, too, patience is to have her perfect work.

Standards

General Pershing's Parade

In a certain mountain village about a hundred miles from Paris, a group of American soldiers, consisting of a lieutenant and about forty men, guarded an ammunition dump. The lieutenant received permission to go on leave for two weeks, and he left the group in charge of the master sergeant.

A few days afterwards a motorcycle messenger rode in from General Pershing's headquarters stating that 2,700 men were to be chosen to march in the peace parades of London, Paris, Brussels and Rome. But as they read the order, they discovered that there were two conditions imposed as standards for selection. The first brought them no difficulty, for it stated that every candidate had to have a clean record—no man would be chosen who had been court martialed. But the second condition gave them pause. The order stated that every man applying had to be at least one meter and eighty-six centimeters tall.

The corporal looked at the sergeant and the sergeant looked at the corporal and then one of them asked how much one meter and eighty-six centimeters was. There was no answer. Then the corporal said, "At any rate, Sarge, I am taller than you."

When mess time came and the news spread around the group, it was the same thing over again. No one knew the metric system. The men got into an argument as to their relative heights, and soon they were standing up, back to back, to see who was the tallest man in the company. Finally, they knew their comparative heights, all the way from Slim down to Shorty.

The officer returned, heard the news, and asked if there were any candidates. The sergeant replied, "The trouble is, Sir, that we do not know what one meter and eighty-six centimeters is." The lieutenant knew enough French to go out into the village and bring back a meter measure. Soon a mark of the required height was made on the wall. Now the men no longer measured themselves against themselves. They measured against a mark on the wall that was unchanged and unchangeable according to the orders from headquarters. One or two men backed up to the mark, and their companions told them that they were an inch or so short of the requirement. Some men merely looked at the mark and knew that there was no hope. Finally a call was made for Slim and he came to be measured. He puffed himself up to his greatest possible height and stood there, rigid and swollen as they measured him.

When the ordeal was ended, it was discovered that he, too, was short, even though he was short by no more than a quarter of an inch.

Of course, General Pershing got his 2,700 men. I saw them that day when they came under the Arch of Triumph on Bastille Day, the fourteenth of July, in what must have been one of the greatest parades of all history. These men, all in new uniforms, with American Beauty roses tied to their bayonets, made a proud sight as they marched down the Champs Elysees, each one of them 186 centimeters tall at least-more than 6 feet one-and-a-fifth inches.

The rule God has made for entry into heaven is that men shall measure up to His glory and be as perfect as He. This rigorous standard is to be found expressed throughout the Bible, and it is to be found exemplified in the man, Christ Jesus. The Old Testament was built around the command of God: ". . . ye shall be holy; for I am holy . . ." (LEVITICUS 11:44).

Nine Feet High

A little boy came to his mother, saying, "Mama, I am as tall as Goliath, I am nine feet high." "What makes you say that?" asked the surprised mother. "Well, I made a little ruler of my own and measured myself with it, and I am just nine feet high!" said the boy.

There are many people who follow the little boy's method, measuring themselves by some rule of their own. God tells us of those who, "measuring themselves by themselves, and comparing themselves among themselves, are not wise" (II CORINTHIANS 10:12).

God has the standard measurement and He tells us: ". . . all have sinned, and come short of the glory of God" (ROMANS 3:23).

Out of Tune

Several years ago, musicians noted that errand boys in a certain part of London all whistled out of tune as they went about their work. It was talked about and someone suggested that it was because the bells of Westminster were slightly out of tune. Something had gone wrong with the chimes and they were discordant. The boys did not know there was anything wrong with the peals, and quite unconsciously they had copied them.

So you will tend to copy the people you are most with; you will borrow your thoughts from the books you read and the programs you listen to, almost without knowing it. God has given us His Word, never out of tune, to set the standard for our song. Here is the absolute pitch of life and living. If we learn to sing by it, we shall easily detect the false in all of the music of the world.

Standing and State

The English Heir

The younger son in a certain family in England disgraced his name and family by outrageous conduct. The family told him that if he would leave the country, he would receive a check each quarter that would permit him to live in some comfort, but that he would be refused all income if he remained in England. He emigrated to Canada and received his check every three months. He spent it within a few days, and the rest of the time he lived the precarious existence of a semibum. He drifted down into the United States, after making arrangements for the Canadian bank to send him his money at a certain time and place. In the meantime his father died suddenly, and his older brother was killed in an automobile accident, all within a matter of hours. By British law, he became heir to the title and estates. But he had dropped from sight in the United States and could not be traced. His wife left England, arrived in New York, and undertook the search for her husband. He had just drawn a remittance and supposedly would not be heard from for another three months. The best detectives were employed to locate him and within a few days he was traced to a small town not far from Chicago where he was eking out a precarious existence as an elevator operator in a cheap hotel. His *position* was that of a noble earl of England with access to the House of Lords. His *condition* was that of an underpaid starveling in a cheap job in a midwestern town. His wife flew to meet him and flew him back to New York. It was then that the newspapers discovered the story and printed the details. The man was in New York, in the process of acquiring a new wardrobe; he was awaiting passage on the steamship that was to take him back to his ancestral castle, his estate and his new life.

Old John

Years ago in Scotland a simple fisherman was bound by strong drink; on too frequent occasions he took the money from his catch and spent it on liquor while his wife and children suffered miserably. They lived in a little hovel off at the end of the fishing village, out of sight of most of the villagers. But one day there came a great change. Old John, as he was called, came to the knowledge of the Lord Jesus Christ as his own personal Saviour. There was an immediate transformation. He brought his full money home and gave it to his astonished wife. He worked more steadily, and soon they had more money than they had had in years. The wife bought new clothes and new shoes for the children, and new dresses for herself. There was food on the table, coal for the fire and all was going very well. After a few weeks of this, his wife said to him one day, "John, if you are going to keep on like this we should begin to think of moving out of this miserable place and taking a better place."

"Right," said John, "I shall go and see the landlord about a new house at once." He made his way through the town to the landlord and asked to rent a good house which was available. The landlord said, "I would never rent a good house to you."

"Why do you say that?" asked John. "You don't know me at all, and I am quite sure that I am able to pay the rent and that I would be a model tenant for you."

"Of course I know you," said the landlord. "You are old drunken John, the fisherman."

"I know you are quite mistaken," said John quietly. "You have never seen me before. Old John is dead and I am new John, a new creature in Christ Jesus." He opened his purse and poured out a good handful of gold coins on the table before the eyes of the astonished landlord. I do not know whether the man was convinced by the testimony of the new John, but he was convinced by the sight of the gold coins. Soon new John was living in a new house.

From our perfect standing under justification, the past life of every born-again man has ceased to exist so far as God is concerned. I suppose that there were people who lived in that village who still remembered, even after years and years of calm sobriety, that new John had once been old John. The world has a tenacious memory for past sins.

The Rich Beggar

A lawyer in New York received papers from a Texas lawyer, asking him to look up the next of kin of a wealthy client who had died in the southwest. Evidence showed that a rough but strong character had emigrated to the west at the close of the war between the states. He settled on land that later brought in great gushers of oil; he died leaving a tremendous estate, and no will. His movements were traced back to Philadelphia, and it was discovered that a sister had lived in that city. She had died leaving no heir except a grandchild who turned out to be a beggar. That beggar, we will say, is attempting to wheedle a few coins out of passersby. The lawyer begins to investigate; after considerable checking, doublechecking and triplechecking, he becomes convinced that the beggar is the rightful owner of the estate in Texas. He communicates this knowledge to the attorneys in Texas, and they arrange that a considerable sum of money shall be arranged for the immediate use of the heir. You walk downtown with the lawyer until you locate the beggar. "That man," says the lawyer, "is worth approximately thirty million dollars, and I have just deposited one million of it in the bank for his drawing account." The observer might say with some justice that the man certainly did not look like a man who was worth millions. And not only was it certain that he did not look like a millionaire, he was not acting like a millionaire. His condition was that of a beggar; his position was that of a millionaire. The lawyer informs the man of his new position and estate. The man, who has some memory of his grandmother and has heard tales of a great-uncle who went out to the new frontiers and struck it rich, acknowledges his identity with great joy. He is overwhelmed by the prospect of his riches.

Let us face the fact that there are many Christians who live a life that is not far from such a condition. They have been given all things in Christ, but they do not joyfully avail themselves of the riches and go on to live in the power and possession of the wealth which has become theirs in title.

The Scotch Lady

A young minister came to visit a woman who was dying. Just out of theological seminary, he had more theology than Bible in his head; he had not experienced much of the experimental joys of long and close living with the Saviour in the knowledge and power of the divine love. Appalled at the apparent joy and certainty of the patient, he began to counsel her to give diligence to make her calling and election sure. But the dear old saint had been walking with the Lord for many a year and was long past the stage of learning the ABC's of the gospel. She gave a testimony so clear that the young man was frightened; he pressed her to go back and be less presumptuous with God. She answered, "Young man, if I should nae be in Heaven the guid Lord would lose more than I could ever lose." This amazed him more than her first attitude and he asked for an explanation. The old lady answered, "If I should nae be in Heaven all that I could lose would be my own soul, for that is all I have to lose. But if I should nae be in Heaven the guid Lord would lose His name and honor, for He has promised to save them to the uttermost that come to Him by Christ, and that is the way which I have come."

If we come to that place where we are aware of our position in Christ, we will be like this Scotch lady whose answer to her young minister showed such clear faith and realization of the truth of her position in Christ.

Stewardship of Time

Time

A city employee or a former city employee, mailed Frank J. O'Brien, city treasurer of Albany, New York, a $100 bill marked "money for stolen time."

We are stewards of our time as much as we are stewards of our money. We are going to give an account of our moments as well as of our words. One of the most terrible thoughts ever devised by man is that which is inherent in the common phrase that this or that occupation is engaged in as a "pastime." Usage may have dropped the second "s" from the spelling, but the idea is that we must find something to pass the time away. May God help us to change our thinking that the idea of "pass time" is to "steal time." That is more true, and in stealing it, we rob both ourselves and God.

Suffering

A Polished Shaft

In the British Museum in London, Mrs. Barnhouse and I visited one of the Egyptian rooms containing a magnificent collection of flints. Instruments of all sorts had been chipped from the hard rock. Certain arrowheads, even under the microscope, defied detection of the manner of manufacture. Yet we knew that somewhere, sometime, a workman had patiently chipped particles from the rough rock until a polished shaft was ready for the quiver of the huntsman or warrior. Read the text from Isaiah: ". . . he hath . . . made me a polished shaft; in his quiver hath he hid me" (ISAIAH 49:2).

When Isaiah tells us that God had turned him into such a shaft, he is telling us that he had undergone the cutting of the chisel. It was a process that was filled with pain, but when it was completed Isaiah tells us that he was a polished shaft. What is more, the Lord had made of him a useful instrument; he was hidden in the Lord's quiver, under the shadow of His hand, so that when an instrument was needed, he was available for the Lord's purposes.

Language Study

Our school systems include the study of languages because of the effect of a second language on the mind. If one knows but one language one is tempted to think that everything is understood; in reality the sound and pattern of words and syntax go through the mind, bringing forth reactions, ofttimes without bringing forth thought. If it is necessary to translate an idea from one language to another, it is no longer possible to fool oneself. The translator is forced to think the thing through. He is forced to understand.

In this may be found some of the reasons why God permits His people to suffer. Long ago we read. "To have suffered much is like knowing several languages; it gives one access to so many more people." Many of God's children have found, in the midst of suffering, that things which they had allowed to flow normally in life, without giving serious consideration to their meaning, must be thought through in suffering. Those who have not lived with suffering cannot understand the crystal-clear thought of the sufferers. To them God has revealed Himself in a way that they would not give up for anything.

Praying For Patience

A young man came to George Goodman of England one day and said, "Mr. Goodman, I wish you would pray for me that I might have patience." Mr. Goodman answered, "Yes, I will pray for you that you have tribulation." "Oh, no, sir," the young man replied, "it is patience that I want." "I understand," said the Bible teacher, "and I will pray for you that you may have tribulation."

The astonished and disturbed young man was shown a passage in the Bible: "And not only so, but we glory in tribulations also: knowing that tribulation worketh patience" (ROMANS 5:3).

Some of the people of God have patience—a resigned patience that cannot honor Him very much. But there are instances, and they constitute a real testimony to the faithfulness and goodness of the Lord, where the joy of the Lord is the strength of His suffering child. Life is lived, one breath at a time, in a patience so mixed with the joyfulness that only can be seen in the midst of suffering. That life is seen as the life of God.

Supplying Man's Need

Inlay Procedure

When a dentist fills a cavity with an inlay, he first grinds out all of the decayed matter, then he takes an impression in wax or some other substance into which the inlay is cast. If the work has been properly done, the inlay will fit the cavity perfectly; it will fit no other cavity in the world. Its contours, exact to less than a thousandth of an inch, fit the contours of the cavity.

It is thus that God's supply is able to meet man's need. Your particular need is as individual to you as your tooth cavity. God alone can meet every contour of that need. The perfection of His ability is seen in the amazing completeness of His perfect supply. All He asks is that you let Him cut away the dead matter of your sin, then He will meet your need completely.

Raisins

A small boy in a grocery store was told to take a handful of raisins from a large box. He shook his head and refused. Finally the grocer took a handful and filled both the upturned hands of the little boy, who received twice as much as he could have taken for himself.

If you are missing the best in the Christian life, why not try turning your hands over so that God may fill them? He reserves the best for those who leave the choice with Him.

Tactlessness

"Are You Saved?"

On Sunday evenings our young people's services are attended by many college students. One evening some years ago, during a social time before the meeting, I was greeted by a young woman who made it her business to approach every stranger and ask, "Are you saved?" She so greeted a brilliant young woman—a teacher of mathematics in a Philadelphia high school. In answer to her question the newcomer replied, "I do not believe in the divinity of Christ." The tactless Christian proceeded to introduce the young teacher to one and all with the words, "I want you to meet Miss Blank; she does not believe in the divinity of Christ." When Miss Blank was introduced to me in this manner, I shook hands and merely remarked, "Oh, she will some day." Then I brought other people into the conversation in order to relieve her embarrassment. After the meeting I stood near the door while the young people were leaving. I smiled at Miss Blank and said, "I should like to talk with you sometime." We made an appointment, and when she came to my office she remarked, "When that girl introduced me to you, I was about to leave. I just could not take any more. When you waved her aside and got me out of her clutches, I decided to stay."

As a result of our conference that day, Miss Blank trusted Christ as Saviour and Lord, and within a year she enrolled in a Bible training school. Three years later, she was teaching on a foreign mission field, where she led many students to know Jesus Christ as Lord and Saviour.

An attitude of love on our part is quickly detected by those who do not think as we do; they also detect any lack of love! We must be careful not to alienate people who express unbelief they really do not mean. I suppose that "doctrine detectives" would have flailed this young woman with arguments; they would have given her a hard time with apologetics trying to convince her of the deity of Christ. Beyond question, that doctrine is central to the Christian faith; but there are many on the fringes of belief who are unsure, but who can be won to our Lord when they see Him in us, holding out His hand to them in love.

Temptation

The Knock at the Door

A little girl was asked what she did when she was tempted. She replied, "Well, when I hear Satan come knocking at the door of my heart, I just say to the Lord Jesus, who lives within my heart, 'Lord Jesus, will You please go to the door?' And then, when the Lord Jesus opens the door, Satan draws away and says, 'Oh! Excuse me, I have made a mistake.' "

God has given us Himself to dwell within our hearts. The Living Word is there with a full command of the Written Word. When we let Him meet the temptation in our behalf we shall know the joy of positive victory. We are fortunate that one victory does not help us to win another, for our hearts are kept from feasting upon an experience so that we may gaze upon the living Lord Jesus Christ.

Passing a Truck

We had been following a big truck for several miles up a narrow mountain road. It seemed that every time there was a place to pass, a car was coming in the opposite direction. Finally the moment seemed propitious. We were almost ahead of the truck when an oncoming car appeared. We tramped the accelerator to the floorboard, and the rush of reserved power practically pushed the car to safety.

It is precisely this rush of reserve power that God has promised the Christian with every spiritual emergency. With every test there is a way of escape (I CORINTHIANS 10:13). The accident (the spiritual defeat) takes place only when you are passing on a blind curve (out of the will of God). No defeat was ever caused by any lack in Him.

The Piano Mover

A newly-arrived pastor of a large church in Arizona did not know that many people live in that desert climate for their health, until he called upon a stalwart passerby for help in moving a piano. Without a word, the man disappeared. Friends told the pastor, "You must never ask that man to do any work; he is here for his lungs. If he had pushed that piano, he would have used so much strength that he would have had to go to bed for a week." The pastor said, "I have to be careful whom I ask to do certain tasks."

God sees the heart and knows our strength. He will never permit us to be tempted above what we are able, but will with the temptation make a way of escape, that we may be able to bear it. We can praise God that "he knoweth our frame; he remembereth that we are dust" (PSALM 103:14). Therefore, He provides for all our need and makes His strength perfect in our weakness.

Tongue

Whales Jumping the Rope

At the trainer's signal a 16-foot whale, weighing 34,000 pounds, leaped straight out of the water until his tail was a foot above the surface; he opened his mouth to receive the handful of fish and fell back into the pool with a splash. A second whale took one end of a rope from another trainer and carried it 100 feet down the pool to the first trainer. When the two trainers pulled the rope so that it was six feet above the surface, the second whale broke the water and jumped the rope. For an hour, whales, porpoises, sea lions and seals went through their paces at Marineland, near Pacific Palisades.

Here before our eyes was a striking illustration of James 3:7: "For every kind of beasts, and of birds, and of serpents, and of things in the sea, is tamed, and hath been tamed of mankind." When I saw this truth, I was forced to admit the truth of the next line: "But the tongue can no man tame. . . ." I asked the Lord to keep mine cleansed that it might praise the Lord in holiness.

Total Depravity

The Amnesia Victim

A young man, suffering from amnesia, lived a new life amid old surroundings; he could remember nothing that had happened before he fell off of a haywagon. As he fell he had cried out, "Hand me that pitchfork and I will. . . ." He was eighteen when the accident occurred; ten years of his new life passed. One day he got into a fight, and received a sharp blow that knocked him to the ground. His head struck a stone and he cried out—finishing the sentence he had started ten years before—". . . spread the hay." He arose, thinking that he was still eighteen years old, still on the haywagon.

The blow that struck the race in Adam made all his sons unconscious of the true nature and being of God. In that unconsciousness we were born; and in that unconsciousness we live until the moment we are saved. Immediately we are made aware of the holiness of God. We go back to a comprehension of our own creaturehood and of our total dependence upon the Saviour.

The Canoe

Human goodness may be likened to a canoe. A canoe is a lovely little boat for its purpose—to be used on rivers and lakes in calm waters. It is admirably suited for young people on a beautiful day or evening in June. But the canoe is not suitable at a seaport or to cross the ocean. It is a totally unfit boat for such a purpose. The trip from New York to France cannot be made by a canoe, even in the month of June when the ocean is generally calm.

So the human character is admirably suited to take an individual around the daily course of life in the midst of a sinful world, but it is a totally depraved thing for the passage from earth to heaven. If a canoe be adjudged by all canoeists to be the best canoe that was ever made, it is still insufficient for the ocean passage. If a human character be adjudged by all men to be the best human character that ever developed, it is still insufficient for the passage from death to life, from earth to heaven.

The Grand Canyon

Several years ago, I motored across the continent with my family. One summer day we saw some of the beauties of the national parks in southern Utah; we drove on to the north rim of the Grand Canyon of the Colorado, arriving there after sunset. We found our rooms for the night and ate our dinner; then we walked down the path to the wall that guards the edge of this mighty chasm. There was no moon and we looked out into pitch darkness. I told my children what lay before them, but it was impossible to see anything whatsoever in the inky blackness. Far to the south we could see the lights of the hotel on the south rim of the canyon. I told the children that between us and those lights was a distance of many miles, and that separating us from the lights was the greatest canyon in the world, going down a mile to the great river which lay hidden beneath us. I suppose that the children accepted what I said on faith, and that they formed some sort of mental picture of what I described to them, but if we had left the place and driven on, they would never have really understood what the canyon really was.

In the morning we arose early, before sunrise, in order to see the coming of the dawn. The canyon was still invisible beneath us, but far to the southeast we could see the great range of the San Francisco peaks. At first, they were but a faint shadow; then they became etched in outline, and soon the first rays of the invisible sun touched them. The canyon remained invisible beneath us. The line of things that we could see descended from those peaks to the rim of the canyon near us, and then to the distant rim to the south, but the depths of the canyon were still not visible. After the brilliance of the new day broke, our sight began to pick up the walls of the canyon, and little by little we were able to see farther and farther—to the very depths of the canyon.

My own awareness of the total depravity of my being and the incapacity of my fleshly nature is a close parallel to the experience we had on the rim of the Grand Canyon. At first I was aware of the biblical statement concerning my nature just as a man might be aware of a geographer's description of the Grand Canyon. Then as time passed I stood on the brink of my own sinfulness without knowing it was there in reality. At last, I saw, not the canyon of my depravity, but the distant mountain peaks of the cross of Jesus Christ, brought to my vision by the illumination of the Holy Spirit. Only then did I begin to see the edges of the abyss that is in the human heart, and as the years have passed my sight has gone deeper and deeper into that sinful depth. I discover from the Word of God the statistics of my depravity without having known at close range the depths of its capacity. Every Christian must come to this knowledge for himself.

"I'm a Captain"

A young man who had been brought up in one of the worst slums of New York, rose to fame and fortune in the theatrical field through his literary talents. He bought a yacht, and although he hired a man to run it for him, he himself assumed the title of "Captain." He got himself a resplendent uniform—complete with gold braid and brass buttons—and invited his old mother to go for a cruise. His mother had come to the United States from eastern Europe, and she had retained the native common sense that many such immigrants have. The boat stood out from the harbor, and the young man went below to change into his uniform. A few moments later he came out on the deck to parade before his mother. "Look, Momma," he said, "I'm a captain." The old lady surveyed him calmly and then, as one accustomed to deflating the ego of a bumptious child, she answered, "Sammy, by you, you is a captain, by me you is a captain, but by captains you is no captain."

Many people need to realize the importance of this illustration. By you, you're a good man; by your neighbors, you're a good man; but by God, you have no goodness. ". . . all our righteousness are as filthy rags . . ." (ISAIAH 64:6).

The Stream

A spring comes forth from the side of a hill—clear, cold, limpid, and containing a certain metal content from the earth. As the stream flows down through the countryside it becomes polluted. Each time man builds on its shores the stream becomes more foul. If it passes through a village or town it becomes undrinkable; if it passes through a city, it bears the germs of death for anyone who drinks of it. Yet there are traces of its original state for the chemical analysis still shows the presence of the original values. Even in its depraved state the stream still has its uses—its flow can carry away the sewage that would mean pollution if left in the city, although it becomes more polluted itself in performing this task.

So is the goodness of mankind. Adam came fresh from the hand of God, and there was no sin within him. When he chose to follow his own will instead of remaining in creature submission to the will of God, death entered into the human stream, which, under the analysis of the great chemist is seen in all its component parts in Romans 3:10–18. This is God's analysis of sin.

The Trinity

Heat, Light and Air

Any one of you may hold your hand before you and look at it. Between your eye and your hand are three things which are one, and which are also three. Each may be studied separately, but it is impossible to have one without the others. Between your hand and your eye at this moment are light and heat and air. Your eye can see your hand because of the light waves that are in the visible spectrum. Even when there is no visible light, there are invisible rays below the red and beyond the violet—infrared and ultraviolet. Darkness is only a matter of human eyes—that which stimulates the rods and cones of our retina we call visible light; the rest, no less real, is invisible light.

Before you in the light that you see there is also air. If you blow on your hand you can feel the air. You breathe it in; you breathe it out. You live by it. And there is heat between you and your hand; take a thermometer and measure it—see its variations as you go from a warm room to the winter snow without. You cannot have heat, or light, without having them in some relationship to our atmosphere. And you cannot have heat or air without having them in some relationship to our atmosphere. Science can use any one of them apart from the others, but can never separate them totally. To all intents and purposes they are three, and they are one.

We Christians do not believe that there are three Gods, but that there is one true God who is in three persons.

Trust

The Farmer and the Nest

A farmer watched a bird building her nest in a heap of branches pruned from the apple tree beside the farmhouse. All day long the bird toiled; in the evening the farmer destroyed the work she had done—

scattering the tiny twigs about and trampling them beneath his feet. The next day the bird, undaunted, began her building once again. Again at evening time her work was destroyed. Judged by the feeble standards of the bird, ignorant of all beyond the cycle of her instincts, the man was cruel and not to be called good. The third day she began her nest once more, but this time in the rose bush beside the kitchen door. In the evening the farmer smiled upon the bird and her work remained. Day after day she continued her cyclic round; the nest was completed; the eggs were laid and warmed beneath her bosom. But long before the time for hatching, the pile of branches from which she had been driven had been removed. Had the farseeing farmer allowed the bird to have her way, all of her nest, her little ones, and her hopes for the season would have been destroyed. She did not see beyond one summer; he saw the end from the beginning.

So our God knows the end from the beginning, and the true believer who has submitted himself to God in Christ has received a new set of senses by which he learns to trust God in all things, even those which he cannot understand. The Lord Jesus said to His disciples, ". . . What I do thou knowest not now; but thou shalt know hereafter" (JOHN 13:7). The simple child of God has learned this lesson well and goes on in confident trust in Him who worketh all things after the council of His own will.

Trusting The Unknown

A college girl once said to me, "I have never trusted anyone in my life. How can I trust the Lord Jesus with all the problems of my daily life?"

Since it was Easter vacation, I asked her how she was going back to college. She said, "I am going to fly."

"Do you have your ticket?" I asked.

"No," she said, "I have to find out what time I can get a plane."

"How are you going to do that?" I inquired.

"Well," she replied, "I am going to telephone the airline and find out what time the plane leaves and reserve a seat on that plane. Then I shall take a taxi out to the airport and board the plane."

I said, "Do you know the reservation clerk at the airline?"

She replied, "No, I don't."

I asked, "Are you going to taxi to the airport, trusting the information of this unknown clerk?"

"Yes, I am."

"Do you know the pilot of this plane?"

"No, I don't."

Then I said to her, "You trust the word of an unknown clerk at the airline office, and put your life into the hands of a pilot whom you do not know and probably will not even see. But you will know what real trust is when you take the word of the Lord Jesus Christ who died for you and rose again, and allow Him to pilot your life by His resurrection power."

Truth, Searching and Owning

The Ornithologist's Discovery

An ornithologist discovered a new plant in Scotland which had never before been found in the British Isles, and botanists immediately traveled to see the plant in its natural habitat. The plants were growing on two little rocky crests, composed of a slightly richer rock; they were surrounded on all sides by miles of nothing but wilderness. An ornithologist discovered the plant because any normal botanist would have despaired of the whole mountain long before he came in sight of its one rewarding acre.

Many men go their way in the search for truth. There are few who find it. Wandering in the wilderness of their human reason they will not go to the Word of God which appears from the distance to be but a barren outcropping. The Lord Jesus Himself said: ". . . I thank Thee, O Father, Lord of heaven and earth, because thou hast hid these things from the wise and prudent, and hast revealed them unto babes" (MATTHEW 11:25).

Umbrellas

Many of us own more umbrellas than we possess. We have bought them, but they have a habit of disappearing. They are ours, but they cannot keep us dry when it rains. They are as though we did not own them.

This simple illustration should be sufficient to remind us that we own truth which we do not always possess. The title has been put in our name, but we do not enter into its possession.

Unbelievers

Bargains

The world is always looking for a bargain. Many a storekeeper has made money by taking an 89-cent article that no one would buy, marking it up to 98 cents, and saying it is something very special. Once we were attracted to a pile of advertising folders on the counter of a railroad ticket office. There in large letters was the interesting offer, "$5,000 for 25 cents." This looked worth investigating. But like many of the world's offers, and like all of Satan's offers, there was a hitch to it. If the whole truth had been printed, it would have read, "$5,000 for 25 cents and your life." Or else, "$5,000 for 25 cents and two eyes." Or again, "$5,000 for 25 cents and both hands." The money part of the offer was less attractive by the time the details were known.

The devil comes with the word, "The whole world for just a bit of worship of me." It sounds attractive, but the omitted words should be added: ". . . and the loss of your soul." This is what Christ indicated when He said: ". . . what shall it profit a man, if he shall gain the whole world, and lose his own soul?" (MARK 8:36). Yet there are many at Satan's bargain counters, willing to pay the present price, but unmindful of the second payment.

The Bayonet

If you were out on Guadalcanal with a rifle and a bayonet, and an enemy soldier approached you and said, "Oh, how well you are equipped, what wonderful shoes, what a magnificent gun, but that bayonet I really believe is soft rubber and a Hollywood prop." "Well," you might say, "If you really believe that it is soft rubber and a Hollywood prop, I guess I had better put it over here against the tree. I can't use it, if you don't believe that it is real steel." "Now," says the enemy soldier, "we are ready to fight with judo," and over his shoulder you go and land in the jungle.

The devil wants to get you off guard and to abandon the weapon that God has given to you. If a man comes and says, "I don't believe that your bayonet is steel," the best way to convince him is to cut the button off his shirt and perhaps nick him slightly. He will be convinced immediately that it is not soft rubber. The Lord Jesus cut deeper than the button on the man's shirt—He penetrated right through to the heart. What are you going to do with somebody who says, "I don't believe that the Bible is the Word of God"? I answer that the only way to deal with him is exactly what the Lord Jesus Christ did, He deflated Satan with the sword of the Spirit.

The Blackout

At the beginning of the second world war, I was holding a union meeting in the city of Belfast in Ireland. The great hall in which the meetings were held was roofed with a skylight, had it been lighted by night, it would have shot a beam like a searchlight over the darkened city. Each evening the chairman of the meeting announced that at the blackout hour the lights would be put out. One night in the midst of the sermon, someone pulled a switch that lighted the great hall. I immediately stopped speaking. There was great consternation; ushers ran to rectify the error. One man clawed at his companion, crying out in fear, "What's the matter? What's the matter? Why did he stop?" The companion replied that the lights had been turned on. Need I say that the reason this man had to be told that the lights were on was because he was blind? The coming of the light meant nothing to him.

That was why it was necessary to send John the Baptist to tell the world that the light had been turned on. God sent His light, lighting every man that cometh into the world. But the effect of that light was not to bring sight to blind men, but to bring condemnation to men who thought that they could see, and who were therefore doubly blind.

The Ferryboat Ride

Michael Patrick O'Brien, got on a ferryboat in Macao, without a passport; he could not get off in Hong Kong, nor could he get off in Macao when the ship returned. For weeks he went back and forth between the two cities while his case was shuttled between various embassies; some called him a Hungarian, others an Irishman or an American.

How many people are there in this world who shuttle back and forth between one opinion and another—spiritually stateless—because they refuse to abandon all earthly citizenships and build their hope in the Lord Jesus Christ. Ever learning and never arriving at the knowledge of the truth—this is the ferryboat upon which men go back and forth in their futile lives because they have refused to own the Lord Jesus.

The Foundering Ship

If a ship were foundering at sea, and if the crew had taken to the water, we would recognize their peril at once. If rescue boats came near and ropes were thrown to the struggling survivors, we would hold our breath in the hope that they might be rescued. How would we feel if we saw one swimming man catch hold of the rope with a free hand and fling it from him with a gesture of defiance? We would find the sight incredible, and we would wonder if the man's reason had tottered, and if he were unaware of the consequences of his act.

There might be some rational explanation for a swimmer refusing to come into a rescue boat, but there can be no such explanation from the divine point of view for men refusing to heed the Word of God and come to salvation through Christ.

Hammering A Shell

At Fremicourt, near Baupaume, France, two farm workers found a World War I artillery shell in a field. One of them began hammering on it with the hope of salvaging the copper. Suddenly it exploded, killing one man and injuring the other. How terrible to think of a man hammering away on something that will destroy him.

Yet how many people in daily life keep clinging to that which will destroy them for eternity, thinking that they can gain a little pleasure, a little self-satisfaction. "Then desire when it has conceived gives birth to sin; and sin when it is full-grown brings forth death" (JAMES 1:15, RSV).

The Indian And Fear

If we had no more knowledge of God than as Creator, we should be possessed by terrible fear, like the savages in the heart of Africa and along the banks of the Amazon. Their whole existence is one of great fear. An Indian told a missionary that his people never know a moment without fear. "We are afraid when we rise in the morning, and when we go to sleep at night," he said. "We are afraid when we sit down to eat and when we rise to work. We are afraid of the jungle, and when we are in our dugouts, of the river. We are always within an arm's length of death, and we see an evil spirit in every tree and plant, in every snake and animal; yes, in every other man, woman and child."

That would be the condition of us all, were it not for the Lord Jesus Christ. But when we read His assurance, "He who has seen me has seen the Father," we enter into His rest. For the Lord Jesus Christ revealed not only that the God of Heaven is His Father, but also that He wants to be our Father and invites us to come to Him through His Son, Jesus Christ.

The Lost Hunter

The newspapers carried the story of a hunter who got lost simply because he was stubborn. The man had a compass with him, but he was so confident that he was woodsman enough to find his way without consulting it, that he neglected to look at it until it was too dark to see. He had no matches and was forced to bed down in some leaves in the shelter of a rock. In the morning he decided again to trust his own gift of woodsmanship. The day wore on and he made little progress. He decided he had played the fool long enough, so he pulled the compass from his pocket and was soon on the right road home. This man was lost until he admitted that he was lost and only then was he able to find his way.

If a man will come to the place where he admits to God and himself that he can do nothing for himself, the Lord will immediately reveal to him the way of salvation and will plant new life within, making the man a partaker of the divine nature (II PETER 1:4).

The Lost Ship

Legend has it that Prince William, son of Henry I of England was aboard a ship that was lost at sea; only one or two survived the catastrophe. The story says that the nobleman in charge of the young prince was a very proud man. He went into the captain's room and discussed the course with him. The captain said he was sailing his ship in a certain direction because, on his last voyage, he had discovered a rock at a certain point. The nobleman pointed to the chart and insisted that there was no rock because it was not charted and ordered the captain to go straight on, under pain of death. The captain was forced to obey, but the ship went aground on the rock and was lost.

This legend shows the tragic position of those who blindly reject the truth that is revealed in Christ Jesus. Unbelievers may say that the rocks of judgment do not lie in the path of the future, but the wreck will prove the truth of God.

Montgomery Street

Signor Guiseppe Bartolo flew in to the New York airport and took the bus into Manhattan. He loaded his baggage into a taxi and said, "Montgomery Street." The taximan took him to such a street and Bartolo pulled out a picture of a house and tried to find it—it wasn't there. He left the cab and started to walk. An hour later the cabby took the baggage to the police. That evening the police brought Bartolo in, still insisting that the house was gone. There was the picture of his son's house—on Montgomery Street, San Francisco! The father wouldn't believe the "New York" on the policemen's badges, until they got his son on the telephone. Only then was he convinced, only then did he consent to start on his way west.

How many people there are who think they are in a place of spiritual safety when in reality they are lost souls! They have some vague trust in religion of some sort and are far, far from Christ. The only way to be sure is to have the definite assurance of the Bible—the Word of God—a full commitment to the Christ of the Bible, backed up by the Holy Spirit's witness with our spirit that we are the children of God, and a definite knowledge of spiritual growth in likeness to Christ.

Now

A great hotel publishes a little booklet of chatter for its guests. Whoever prepared it needed a line to fill up space and inserted this sentence: "On the great clock of time there is but one word—NOW." The hotel probably thought the phrase was a good one for salesmen who need to be about their business, and a good maxim for others who are likely to let important matters slip.

Every sinner should realize that this time is going by most rapidly. "... behold, now is the accepted time; behold, now is the day of salvation" (II CORINTHIANS 6:2). The sinner must realize that NOW is not only the single word on the clock of time; it is also the word on the door of eternity. Fail to enter in while you have NOW to do it, and you will find that the door is closed to you forever.

Testing the New Automobile

Glenn Leonard, a bulldozer operator driving to his home in the country, decided to test the acceleration of his new automobile. He passed the side road to his farm, made a sharp U turn at the next road, sped back and turned in the far road. Meanwhile, the driver of a station wagon observed the rapid turn and burst of speed; he mistook the light-blue machine for an unmarked police car, and turned into the road to Leonard's farm to escape detection. The station wagon driver was closely followed by Leonard, who was only interested in getting home. The alarmed driver continued at high speed to the dead end of the road, where he abandoned the station wagon, which was loaded with stolen coffee, cigarettes, and shotgun shells.

The Bible says, "The wicked flee when no man pursueth . . ." (PROVERBS 28:1). How often it is that men run away from nothing more than their own conscience, carrying it with them all the time.

Union With Christ

Backstage at the Met

I once had the privilege of going backstage just before a performance at the Metropolitan Opera House in New York. Before the curtain went up, dozens of individuals walked about in the wings, doing vocal exercises. Completely oblivious of others, each singer concentrated on his own voice; the result was piercing discord. We are all familiar with a similar effect in the tuning-up of orchestra instruments before a concert.

Too often the bystander in the world looks upon the church as a group of frivolous amateurs, each concerned only with his little part. But the Lord Jesus Christ prayed, "That they all may be one; as thou,

Father, art in me, and I in thee, that they also may be one in us: that the world may believe that thou hast sent me" (JOHN 17:21). Some may "view with alarm" a movement to join believers in divine oneness; nevertheless, the Lord intended such a union.

The Forest of Redwoods

On the coast of California are great forests of redwoods—*sequoia sempervirens*. The manner in which these trees grow is unlike that of any other tree. Two trees of this species may grow up year after year, a few feet from each other. Finally, sometimes after fifty or a hundred years, the trees touch, and the bark begins to overlap and fill out, so that the two trees ultimately become one. There have been cases where a dozen trees, springing up from the outer roots of a tree that has fallen, have formed a perfect circle. After a century or two, all have grown together so that one may walk between two trees into the empty heart of a great tree, and the ultimate outward appearance will be that of a single giant tree. Near Santa Cruz are two trees: one grows at an angle to the other, yet contact has been made a hundred feet in the air, and from that point upward two trees become one—a single top growing from two totally different trunks.

God looking down into time from His eternal vantage point, saw us in Christ—grown into Him, one plant with Him. We had been of the root of Adam, and Christ, in becoming sin for us grew into us so that our death became His death, and His death became the death of our death.

Meeting at the Corner

Several years ago a fad among teen-agers was a series of jokes—a play upon words or lines spoken by one inanimate object to another. One day one of my children came to me with this one: "Do you know what one wall said to the other?" As a good father should, I did not attempt to guess the answer, but replied dutifully, "No. You tell me what one wall said to the other." The answer came crisply, "I'll meet you at the corner."

I can say to every man in Christ, "I'll meet you at the Lord Jesus Christ." If we can come to an agreement as to who He is and as to what He has done for us, we should meet there with Him.

Universal Brotherhood

The Carpenter's Children

A missionary in Central America once preached on the subject of universal brotherhood. At the close of his address, two professors from a local school said that they thought they had found a flaw in his reasoning. Were not all individuals of the human race descended from Adam and Eve? And did not God create Adam and Eve? And therefore, were not all individuals thereby the children of God? The missionary pointed to the benches in the room and asked, "Who made these benches?"

The man replied that they had been made by the local carpenter.

"And do you, therefore, call these benches the carpenter's children?" he asked.

"Of course not," they answered. "They are not the carpenter's children because they do not have in them the life of the carpenter."

"And do you have the life of God in you?" was the searching question that revealed the reality of man's departure from God. No one can be called a child of God, if he does not have within him the life of God.

Will of God

The Bird and the Butterfly

A large home had fine plate-glass windows that looked out on a beautiful garden. A bird outside tried to catch a butterfly that was inside; the bird flew against the window while the butterfly flew up and down trying to get away. The butterfly could not see the glass and expected at every moment to be caught; the bird did not see the glass and expected at every moment to catch its prey; yet the butterfly was as safe as though a wall of stone were between them.

We who are Christians must not forget that the invisible presence of Christ is between us and every difficulty of life. There is nothing that can touch us unless it passes through the will of God in Christ. Our Lord has shown us that we are between His hand and the Father's. ". . . neither shall any man pluck them out of my hand. . . . no man is able to pluck them out of my Father's hand" (JOHN 10:28,29). This is why the believer is so sure.

Formulas Not Understood

Revelation of the production methods of the atomic bomb is bringing to light some remarkable stories. Time and again companies were asked to design a machine according to a "mathematical formula which they did not fully understand." Out of this amazing gadgetry have come scores of new products and processes that have nothing to do with atomic power, such as new ways to dehydrate foodstuffs. Factories that followed the uncomprehended will of the atom staff learned that they had been working smoothly in an overall plan that was for the honor of their nation.

God's will is not comprehensible to many; therefore they refuse it. But those who take it, even as "a formula they do not understand," and work conscientiously to its fulfillment, find the results above and beyond all they could ask or think. Christians who will to do the Lord's will, who definitely make up their minds to do the Lord's will, learn to know the inner meaning of the truth that is of God and not of man.

Gothic or Roman Missals

One of the oldest Spanish proverbs is: *"Alla van leyes do quieren reyes,"* or "Laws go the ways that kings desire." It arose when Alfonso VI, at the beginning of the twelfth century, had to decide whether his country should use Gothic or Roman missals. The king resolved to leave the matter to chance; he threw both into the flames, saying that the one that came out unburnt should be chosen. But when the Gothic missal survived the ordeal, he threw it back into the flames and decided in favor of the Roman. From this act the proverb became popular throughout Spain.

Many people treat the will of God in just this way. They will put a choice up to God and will keep on trying until the matter turns out to suit them. Unless a person is a surrendered Christian, it is correct to say that actions follow the will of the flesh. The only way to have the will of God is to be willing to do it, and 90 percent of knowing that will consists in being willing to do it before you know it.

No Fog on the Bridge

Terrified passengers lined the railing of a Mississippi River steamer, as it sped through a dense fog. A committee, sent to remonstrate with the captain, for going too fast, discovered that it was clear on the bridge. The fog was dense for about twenty feet above the water so that the passengers, on their level, could see nothing, but the captain could see everything.

The next time you are in a fog remember that God is not and never has been in a fog. He knows all things and is in complete command. Nothing can ever touch you until it has passed through His will.

The Pin Cushion

A little girl acknowledged a gift from her aunt: "Thank you for your present. I have always wanted a pin cushion, but not very much."

Many Christians act this way about the will of the Lord. They are so filled with their own desires that they do not want what He sends. The whole Word teaches us that He reserves His best gifts or those who delight to do His will.

Scientific Instruments

Every science has its own instrument. The geologist uses a hammer to take his samples from the rock. A biologist uses a microscope. An astronomer uses a telescope. You would laugh if a geologist left his work with rocks, and hammer in hand, and said: "I am tired of studying rocks. I am going to study astronomy." Not with a hammer! You cannot learn astronomy with a hammer! You would laugh at the astronomer who sought to turn his great telescope down into a meadow to look at a daisy. You cannot learn anything about a daisy from a great telescope! No, the telescope is made to look at the stars; the microscope for the small daisy; the hammer for the rock.

In the science of God, theology, there is an instrument that belongs to Christianity and it is the surrender of the will to the will of God before you know it.

The Texas Cow

I often think of a certain cow I saw along the road in Texas. As we were driving by one of those ranches where they have 500,000 acres and very fine fences, a cow came through a hole in the fence. The cow wandered into the road; when it heard the engine of our car, it started to run. By the time we caught up to the cow, she was some 400 yards away from the hole in the fence, and still going. Finally we passed her. If that cow was ever going to get back into the field with those strong fences, she was going to have to go back to the place where she got out.

That is exactly how you are going to get back into the will of God. If you keep running down the road, you won't find it. You go back and get in the will of God at the place where you got out of the will of God. This is God's method.

Three Signs in Line

During the war, I was invited to the Panama Canal Zone where tens of thousands of troops were guarding that most important link in our communications. Our meetings were held in the baseball park, and thousands of people received blessing from God. A general in the United States Army came to me after one of the meetings and asked if there was anything that I would like to see or do while I was in the Zone. I told him that I wanted to see the working operation of the canal from the bridge of a ship. He whistled and made a gesture of doubt, telling me that only one civilian had gone through the canal since the beginning of the war and that he had been a brother of a cabinet member. But the general said he would try.

The next day he came back with permission from the commanding general, and the following day I spent several hours on the bridge of a ship, with the chief pilot of the canal. When we had gone through the first locks, moving from the Pacific towards the Atlantic, we came out on the great inland lake which had been created by a series of dams. The pilot pointed out the locks by which we were to leave the lake. I asked the natural question: Why did we not steam directly toward that point? He told me that in the beginning of canal navigation the channel had been dug in a direct line, but as time went on the inflow of jungle rivers brought so much silt that the channel was being filled in. A survey of the bottom of the lake showed that a zigzag course across the lake would follow the lines of least silting. But how can a ship find its bearing for a zigzag course? Ahead of us was a series of markers. The first, just above the surface of the water, was a large sign, several times larger than an outdoor advertising billboard. Across it was a black line, while a vertical line split it in the middle. A hundred yards behind this sign there was another, exactly like it, but considerably higher. A third sign stood another hundred yards away—again much higher above the water. As we moved toward these signs the vertical marks on the three signs appeared to be exactly in line with one another. Far away to the right we saw a similar set of signs. The vertical marks, of course, were not in line with each other; but as we approached the first set, there was a moment when the vertical marks on the second set came in line, one with another. At this point the order was given and the ship turned directly toward this new indicator. The same process was repeated again and again until we finally came in line with the exit locks, and moved on into the canal.

I told the pilot that the lining up of the markers was a good illustration of the way in which a Christian must live his life. There are three things which must be in line if we are to know the will of God and remain in it. First, to be in the will of God any step of faith must be in accordance with the Word of God. Second, we must be surrendered to the Lord so that we are willing to do His will before we know what it is. Finally, the Holy Spirit working in our lives shows us through circumstances, exactly what the Lord wants us to do.

The Young Wheelman

A confident young man walked into the captain's cabin of a Mississippi riverboat, and asked for a job as a wheelman.

"What experience have you had on the river?" asked the captain.

"Five years, sir."

"Do you know the location of all the shoals and snags?"

"No, sir, but I know where there ain't any, and that's where I calculate to steer." He got the job.

In the Christian life the path of safety in Christian living is not in knowing all the nature of sin, or the path of wickedness, but in knowing the will of the Lord and in being willing to stay in it. The obedience of the saints in Rome at the time Paul wrote to them had become famed throughout the Christian world. Paul complimented them: ". . . I am glad therefore on your behalf: but yet I would have you wise unto that which is good, and simple concerning evil" (ROMANS 16:19). We must steer where sin is not.

Witnessing

Carlisle Castle Prisoners

Carlisle Castle has slits in its walls that used to serve as windows; an iron bar stretches from top to bottom. In the sill you can see and feel grooves worn into the stone by the fingers of men who were imprisoned in the castle. When the Scotch border was a place of feud and skirmish, the prisoners looked out toward the hills of Scotland. They so longed to get back to their homes that they literally pulled at the stones with their fingers. Perhaps in their spirits, this made them feel that they were escaping from prison, and away to Scotland.

I wonder if Christ in your heart is straining to get out in love and mercy to those around you. Perhaps He cannot get out to live His life through you. Christ liveth in me to indwell and to possess to the full, in order to shine out, to live out, to flow out. That is the normal experience of the Christian when he is right with God.

The Elephantiasis Convert

A disease known as elephantiasis is a terrible scourge in tropical countries. The skin of the diseased becomes very thick, very hard, and fissured like an elephant's hide; the part affected is enormously enlarged. I have seen unfortunate people whose lower legs—running from above the knee down to the foot—were from twelve to fifteen inches in diameter. One poor sufferer from this disease heard the gospel of Jesus Christ and was transformed. He became a radiant Christian and did nothing but tell people of the grace of God, which He had showed in sending His Son, Jesus Christ, to die for them. This man lived in an African village; he was determined that every soul in the village should hear the good news of salvation. Although it was extremely difficult for him to walk on his monstrous legs, he thought nothing of the pain and toiled from hut to hut telling those who dwelt there about the Saviour who had come into his life. Each evening he returned to his own hut, where he was maintained in life by the kindness of his relatives. At the end of several months he was able to tell the missionary that he had visited every hut in the village; now he was starting to take the gospel message to a village about two miles away. Each morning he started out painfully, walked the two miles to that village, went from hut to hut spreading the gospel, and returned the two miles to his own hut before sundown. Having visited every hut in the neighboring village, he remained at home, but after some weeks, he began to be more and more restless.

He asked the pastor and the missionary medical doctor if the gospel were being taken to a village that lay ten or twelve miles through the jungle. As a boy, before he had become afflicted, he had traveled the jungle path to that village; he remembered that there were many people there, and he knew that they needed the good tidings of the Saviour. He was advised not to go to the village, but day after day the burden grew upon him. One day the man's family told the missionary that the man had disappeared from the hut. He had slipped out just before dawn; they had heard him go, but supposed it was just for a moment. He did not return, and the family was concerned about him.

Afterwards, the full story became known. Step after weary step the afflicted man dragged his leathery legs and gigantic feet along the path that led to his goal. The distant villagers said that he had arrived after noon; his feet were swollen, bruised, and bleeding. He was offered food, but before he would eat, he began to tell the people about Jesus. Up and down the village he went, to the very last hut, telling them that the God of all creation was Love and that He had sent His only Son to die that their sins might be removed. He told how the Lord Jesus had been raised from the dead and had come into his heart, bringing such joy and peace.

There was no shelter for him in that village, so though the sun was low, he started on his way down the jungle path toward home. The darkness of Africa is a terrible darkness, and the night can bring forth many jungle creatures. The sun went down and the poor man dragged himself along the dark path, guided by some insight which kept him from going astray. He told the pastor later that his fear of the night and the animals was more than balanced by the joy he felt in his heart, as he realized that he had told a whole village about the Lord Jesus Christ.

About midnight the doctor was awakened by a noise on his front porch. He went to the door with a light and there was the elephantiasis victim, his legstumps wounded and bleeding. The doctor and his helpers lifted the almost unconscious man into one of the hospital beds. Seldom had any of them seen such a frightful sight as those bleeding feet that had come back from such an errand of love and mercy. Unashamedly, the doctor told how he had ministered to those feet—cleaning and dressing them—and how his own tears had fallen into the ointment he put upon the stumps. The doctor ended by saying, "In all my life I do not know when my heart was more drawn out to another Christian believer. All I could think of was the verse in the Word of God, 'How beautiful are the feet of them that bring glad tidings, that publish peace.' "

Here was a man who had been sent by God to tell the story of what Christ had done for him. Although he did it at the cost of much personal agony, he had not flinched; he had gone through to the end to tell needy men the good news of salvation for their souls.

Haste, Post, Haste!

Not many people who use the word "posthaste" realize that the word goes back to the time of Henry VIII. During the reign of "bluff King Hal," postmasters and relays of horses for carrying messages were established at the principal towns in England. The postmasters endorsed each letter with the exact time each missive was delivered to them. The messengers were sometimes rather irresponsible people who delayed to play games with acquaintances in inns or to waste time in some other way. On this account a very drastic law was put into effect—every dispatch carrier should "ride for his life"; this had a literal meaning, for the penalty for delaying *en route* was hanging. Letters of the sixteenth century were often ornamented with a drawing of a dispatch carrier suspended from the gallows; beneath the figure was the admonition, "Haste, post, haste! Haste for thy life."

This law held good for many years, and there were numerous hangings. Gradually opinion changed, and the penalty for delay was lessened; hanging was only for those messengers who were bribed or coerced into allowing someone else to read a dispatch. Later, a still lesser punishment was adopted: imprisonment for a short time, or a period of confinement in the stocks or pillory. Not until the nineteenth century was simple dismissal applied in such cases; but the old expression "post-haste" still lingers with us.

So our King has given us a message that must be delivered to all men. The King's business requires haste (I SAMUEL 21:8). Let us be out with it. "Go ye into all the world . . ." He has said, and to those who go, He has added, ". . . and lo! I am with you . . ." (MATTHEW 28:20). There is no death penalty, but there is a reward for obedient servants and for those who do not obey, even though they be saved, there is "the terror of the Lord . . ." (II CORINTHIANS 5:11).

Indirect Advertising

Near the Kingsport Press in Tennessee a southbound bus makes a scheduled midday stop of twenty minutes so that passengers may freshen up and get a bite to eat. One driver said, as he brought his bus to a stop: "Folks, we'll be stopping here for twenty minutes. This line makes it a strict policy never to recommend an eating place by name, but if anybody wants me while we're here, I'll be eating a wonderful T-bone steak with french fries at Tony's first-class, spotlessly clean diner directly across the street."

Indirect advertising is indeed important and often more effective than the direct pitch. So is the indirect witness for Christ. The believer who reveals Christ by the way he lives, moves, walks, talks, eats, reads, pays his bills, keeps his garden free of weeds and a thousand other details of life, will probably do more than the fanatic with the sandwich board that reads, "Prepare to meet thy God."

The Lost Race

To the participants in one of the Olympic games, loss of the four-hundred-meter relay race for women was a tragic incident. The Germans were far in the lead when the next-to-the-last girl came to pass the baton to the last runner. With a clear five-yard lead and the race as good as won, the baton was dropped. Pictures showed the despair on the face of the last runner as she realized what had happened. We sat one evening in Berlin looking at an illustrated magazine that showed pictures of the Olympics. The magazine had texts under the pictures in several languages. The English read: "They muffed the baton"; the French read: *"le temoin,"* the French word for "witness." The idea was that the runner who reached the tape had to have the baton as a "witness" that the full distance had been covered by each of the runners.

If the witness is lost, the race is lost, provides a great spiritual lesson. These girls had made the Olympic team and had the honors attendant upon their prowess. They were eligible to run the race. They lost the prize, however, by losing the witness. They were castaways from the medals.

So it is in the Christian life. All who are born again are eligible to run the race. No one can run the race until he is made eligible through saving faith. All who are received into salvation in Christ will be in Heaven, but not all will receive the prize in addition to salvation.

Toadstools Versus Mushrooms

A woman risked her life and that of her family on a page from the *National Geographic Magazine,* when her husband brought some strange-looking things in from the fields. The family was undecided whether they were mushrooms or toadstools, until someone dug up a *Geographic* that showed plates of edible varieties. Their harvest was pictured, under the name of "Shaggy-mane," definitely "edible." With this as the basis of their faith, they prepared and ate the mushrooms. Nobody suffered.

Here is a perfect illustration of "receiving the witness of men." But God has said that "If we receive the witness of men, the witness of God is greater . . ." (I JOHN 5:9). You can risk your life ten thousand million times more securely on the Word of God than on the pages of the *Geographic.* You can even risk your eternal life on the Word of God. In fact, if you do not risk your eternal life on the Word of God, you will have eternal death. ". . . these are written, that ye might believe that Jesus is the Christ, the Son of God; and that believing ye might have life through his name" (JOHN 20:31).

Witness of the Spirit

Going to Princeton

A young man from the west, got off an express train at Trenton, New Jersey. He wanted to go to Princeton, and he had been told that at that hour of the day, his best connection would be to walk a block or two from the railroad station and take a streetcar. It was his first time in a city of any size, and he was proud enough to wish to get along without asking for information. He walked to the car tracks where he saw a car marked "Princeton." He boarded it, and paid his fare. After fifteen or twenty minutes the conductor came through the car, collecting another fare for the next zone of travel. The young man paid this fare also, and another at the next zone change. He realized they were nearing the end of the line, when the conductor began turning the seat backs to face the opposite direction. As the young man picked up his valise he finally asked, "Which way is the campus of Princeton University?" The conductor looked at him, dumbfounded, and asked, "Did you want to go to Princeton? You should have taken this car going in the other direction. You are in Hamilton Square."

The important point in this story is that the young man *felt* as if he were going to Princeton. He had traveled for ten miles in quiet confidence that he was going where he thought he was going; suddenly, he was miles away in another direction.

I am quite sure that there are many men and women in this world who are on their way to the lake of fire, without hope and without God, but who *feel* as if they are going to heaven. The witness of the Spirit is always based on the Word of God and is in tune with the sacrificial death of the Lord Jesus Christ. It, therefore, follows that the witness of the Spirit is not a mere feeling, in the sense of some spine-tingling emotion, or vague, sense movement. It is definitely an intelligent, controlled and related work of God in our hearts.

Handsprings

Several years ago I was preaching for a few days in Portland, Oregon. At the close of one of the evening meetings a young minister invited me to drive with him the next day, to view the noble grandeur of the Columbia River Valley. I never like to go to the Northwest without seeing this, for I believe it to be the most beautiful river valley in the world. The next morning he and his wife picked me up at my hotel. The wife remarked on the blessing of the service the evening before when I had preached on the joys of being joined to the Lord Jesus Christ. Her exact words were, "Oh! Doctor! That message last night was such a blessing to me. All the way home my heart was just turning handsprings at the thought of all that we have in Christ." I replied, speaking rather slowly, "Turning handsprings? Cartwheels? Somersaults? Well, that is a very interesting way of describing it; but the Bible gives it in different terms. There we read, 'The Spirit himself beareth witness with our spirit that we are the children of God.' "

Sittin' Pretty

One Sunday I was preaching in Philadelphia. My subject was a rehearsal of the verses in the Scripture in which God treats His work concerning our sin. As I preached this great message of deliverance, I noted a boy about twelve years old. He was sitting in the gallery, and he leaned forward, holding the rail, listening with great intentness. When I came to my summing up I put all of the promises into a single sentence. Our sins are forgiven, forgotten, cleansed, pardoned, atoned for, remitted, covered; they have been cast into the depths of the sea, blotted out as a thick cloud, removed as far as the east is from the west, remembered against us no more forever, cast behind God's back.

After the closing hymn, I went to the back of the church to greet the people as they were leaving. In a few moments the people from the galleries began to come down, and the boy came toward me. He caught my sleeve and said, "Good sermon, Doc!" I smiled and he continued, "Gee, we're sure sittin' pretty, aren't we?" And then he went on his way.

I looked after him for a moment and a great joy came in my heart, because I knew there had been in his heart the witness of the Holy Spirit.

Work of God In Us

The Artist and The Brush

An artist who plans to exhibit a painting inspects every brush stroke, adding a slight touch here, deftly changing a shade there, until the very day of exhibition.

The Lord God is working that way with us now. The differences between Him and human artists is that when He finishes we shall be like the Lord Jesus Christ. There is no doubt about that.

Binding Guy Ropes

A balloon cannot ascend as long as a single rope binds it to its moorings. If every cord but one is cut, it may struggle, but it cannot rise. Not until the knife severs the final stay will it arise. Nor does it ascend of itself. It would remain as heavy and inert as the earth beneath it were it not for the gas within it.

Have we gladly taken the knife and with one decisive stroke forever severed the last guy rope that binds us to the sensuous things of earth and time? Or have we at least said, "Lord, I am willing that Thou shouldst cut that rope for me. I find it impossible to do it myself." That is enough for the Lord. He has lifted many a soul into the heights, by the breath of His Spirit, who was unable to say more than that at first. A mind, willing to be made willing by Him is all He asks.

The Flaw in the Marble

The great Italian sculptor, Benvenuto Cellini, told of receiving a vast block of marble with one flaw. Because of this flaw, no artist would submit a design—except one.

In the public square of Florence a fence was built around that piece of marble, and a little shack was erected for the artist. For two years the sculptor labored; then the fence was torn down, and the shack was taken away. All of Florence beheld the result and marveled. Since then, Italy and all the world has marveled at Michelangelo's "David."

In that block of marble was a statue; others did not see it, but Michelangelo did.

In the lump of clay which is you, God sees an image too—the image of Jesus Christ. And God wants to form the image of His Son in you.

The Grand Lama

In Tibet, the government used to be a theocracy and the ruler was the Grand Lama. When he died, it was believed that his spirit entered into a boy baby who was born at the very instant of the lama's death. The high priests of the religion cast horoscopes, wandered over the land and pounced upon a child whom they declare to be the Grand Lama. The choice might be a boy living in filth, in a herdsman's tent, far removed from any culture or education. In an instant this child, with matted hair and filthy body, was declared the Grand Lama of Tibet. In that instant he is as much the Grand Lama as he is, years later—enthroned in his palace in Lhassa, in undisputed control of the entire forces of the country. Between the moment of his choice, which was totally apart from him or his people, and his rule, has been a long period of training; but from the first moment the priests who surrounded him have bowed before him and accepted him for what he was declared to be.

There is a great similarity here to the work of God. For us He stooped from Heaven and found us in our sin. It was He who declared us to be His sons. It was He who declared us to be justified.

He said that He saw us righteous, the reign of death broken. He said that in that instant we were the possessors of eternal life and that we were His heirs and joint heirs with Jesus Christ. All of this occurred simultaneously and instantaneously, apart from any merit in us. It was on the basis of sheer grace. The process of training us for the throne life began at once. He will keep on perfecting us until the day of Jesus Christ.

My Vase

Years ago in France, as I watched a potter at work, he asked me if I would like to try my hand at making something. So I took a lump of clay, wet my hands, shaped the clay and threw it against the wheel. As it began to turn, I pressed my hand against the clay and it rose up into a pillar. Then I put my finger into the middle and made an opening.

I had formed a lovely vase with a flange at the bottom. Then it bellied out and narrowed to a neck.

Thinking that it should be just a little narrower above the flange, I put my fingers there. Suddenly the vase broke.

Looking at it, I asked, "What can be done with that?"

Smiling, the potter took the same bit of clay and made a beautiful vase. Then he put it in his kiln to bake. When it came out, it was beautiful.

God works like that in our lives. We mar them but He makes them beautiful. When God takes a life deformed by sin and molds it into the image of Jesus Christ, all heaven rejoices. We are to the glory of His grace.

Works

A Copper Penny

In 1947, a rumor spread that the Ford Motor Company would give a Ford in exchange for every copper penny dated 1943. The rumor spread so fast that Ford offices throughout the country were jammed with requests for information, and in spite of a telephone strike, thousands of inquiries came in by telephone as well as by telegram and mail. Washington also reported that a large volume of queries had been received at the offices of the mint. It all turned out to be a joke. The statistics of the mint show that in 1943 there was no copper available for coinage and that 1,093,838,670 pennies were minted of steel-zinc, but that the number made of copper was exactly zero.

There has been a rumor abroad in the human race for centuries that entrance into heaven could be obtained by presentation of works. The fact is that there are no works made on earth which are acceptable in heaven. They all show the counterfeit of having come from the mold of the human heart. God has declared that He will accept only the work that bears the image of the Lord Jesus Christ performed on Calvary in dying for sinners. There is no hope apart from this. "Not by works of righteousness which we have done . . ." (TITUS 3:5). "Not of works, lest any man should boast" (EPHESIANS 2:9).

A Drink

If I ask if you would be willing to take a drink of the finest spring water—the purest water that could be obtained by any chemical standards of analysis—you might answer that you would certainly be willing to drink such water. Then suppose I tell you that I have not said a word about the glass into which the water is to be poured. That should give you pause, for the glass in which that pure spring water is conveyed to you has just been emptied of diphtheria culture from a medical laboratory, and multitudes of deadly germs are spread through the water. Now will you take a drink? You refuse, of course.

It is even so with God. You may argue or boast about the works which you have produced; you may even think that by your standards of analysis your works should be acceptable to God. But the Word of God comes bluntly to tell you that your good works are contained in a glass of your sinful Adamic heart, and that they have infected every part of your being so that they are an offense to God because they have touched you.

The Half-Baked Pancake

I have a venerable friend who has a sweet spirit that reflects long living with the Saviour. While he was staying in a large hotel in the South, he spoke to his waitress about her soul and she began to justify herself before him. She told him about her character, how hard she worked, and how she took care of an aged mother. Day after day as she waited on him, three meals a day, she would tell him more about her good deeds. After about two weeks of this, my friend said to her one morning, when the rush was over and few people were left in the dining room, "Mildred, will you bring me something special from the kitchen?" "Why, certainly, I'll get you anything you want." The old saint of God then carefully described his order. He wanted a pancake that was cooked on one side and not touched on the other. She expostulated that it would be terrible, and that he wouldn't want to eat it. He insisted, and she went out to the kitchen. My friend heard the chef talking in loud tones, and it took a definite repeating of the order to get what had been asked for. Finally, the waitress came into the dining room bearing the pancake cooked only one one side; the chef followed her to the door to watch what happened. My friend looked at her in great kindness and said, "Mildred, for the past two weeks you have been telling me how good you are; how you take care of your mother; what a fine character you have. I will admit that humanly speaking you are well-done like the under side of this pancake. But as God sees you, you are this uncooked mess of runny dough, unpalatable and nauseous. What you need is Christ and Christ alone." The woman looked at the plate and saw herself as God declared her to be; she was broken down by the force of the illustration. It was the means of bringing her to the knowledge of her own sinfulness in the sight of God, and to trust in the Lord Jesus Christ as her Saviour.

Perhaps you need to see yourself thus today, as a half-baked pancake. For, as J. B. Phillips puts it, "This, then, is what has happened. Sin made its entry into the world through one man, and through sin, death. The entail of sin and death passed on to the whole human race, and no one could break it for no one was himself free from sin" (ROMANS 5:12). Multitudes of believers praise God that the Lord Jesus broke the power of canceled sin, and set them free forever.

The Pharmacist's Mate

Aboard a United States submarine in enemy waters of the Pacific, a sailor was stricken with acute appendicitis. The nearest surgeon was thousands of miles away. Pharmacist Mate Wheller Lipes watched the seaman's temperature rise to 106 degrees. His only hope was an operation. Said Lipes: "I have watched doctors do it. I think I could. What do you say?" The sailor consented. In the wardroom, about the size of a pullman drawing room, the patient was stretched out on a table beneath a floodlight. The mate and assisting officers, dressed in reversed pajama tops, masked their faces with gauze. The crew stood by the diving planes to keep the ship steady; the cook boiled water for sterilizing. A tea strainer served as an antiseptic cone. A broken-handled scalpel was the operating instrument. Alcohol drained from the torpedoes was the antiseptic. Bent tablespoons served to keep the muscles open. After cutting through the layers of muscle, the mate took twenty minutes to find the appendix. Two hours and a half later, the last catgut stitch was sewed, just as the last drop of ether gave out. Thirteen days later the patient was back at work.

Admittedly this was a much more magnificent feat than if it had been performed by trained surgeons in a fully equipped operating room of a modern hospital. Study this analogy and you will know the real meaning of Christ's words: "Greater works than these shall he do; because I go unto my Father" (JOHN 14:12). For Christ, perfect God, to work directly on a lost soul to quicken and bring out of death and into life is great, but for Him to do the same thing through us is a greater work.

Too Wide for the Door

In his mission field, a certain missionary had to do many things for himself and his family. When the baby grew too big for the carriage he started to build a bed for the child. After he prepared the wood, he glued the mortised pieces and was ready to complete the bed. His wife thought it too cold to work in the shed so he brought the materials into the kitchen and started to work. When the bed was finished, the baby was brought to the kitchen and placed in it while his parents gazed admiringly. Suddenly the father had a disquieting thought. Suppose the bed would not go through the door! Quickly he measured bed and door and found the bed one inch too wide to pass through.

There are many people who spend their time building their lives according to the plan of this world. They take great pride in their work, but they make it broader than Christ. The day will come when they suddenly realize the measurements will not allow it to pass Heaven's door. "... strait is the gate, and narrow is the way ..." (MATTHEW 7:14), and no human works can take us through. Christ alone can bring us to God, and when we get there we will find that He has been gracious enough to bring some of our works along, not as the price of our entry into heaven, but as a part of His love for which He will reward us.

The Visit with the Ward Patient

A Christian visited a hospital and paused at each bed to say a word of prayer and give out a gospel or devotional tract. At the close of the visiting hour he came to the last bed in the ward and spoke to the patient very briefly: "Dear man, when you come to the end of this life, will you go to heaven?"

In a tone of defiance the man replied, "Oh, I think I shall get to heaven all right."

"What do you think they do in heaven?" asked the visitor.

Taken aback, the man hesitated, then said, "Well, I hadn't thought about it, but I imagine they sing a great deal."

"That is right," the visitor said, "and we have the words of the song in the Bible." He opened the New Testament to the book of Revelation and read:

> and they sang a new song, saying,
> "Worthy art thou to take the scroll

and to open its seals,
for thou wast slain and by thy blood
didst ransom men for God
from every tribe and tongue and
people and nation,
and hast made them a kingdom and
priests to our God,
and they shall reign on earth" (5:9, 10 RSV).

The visitor said, "I must go now, but I leave this New Testament with you, and ask you to consider this question: If you were taken to heaven tonight, could you sing heaven's song?"

Next day the Christian returned and went straight to the bed of this man, who greeted him with the words, "I read those verses fifty times, and I shall never talk about my good works again. In heaven they sing praises to Christ for redeeming them by His blood. I have been trying to get to heaven without a Saviour; but now I know heaven's song, and I have trusted in His blood so that I can sing that song now!"

How many people are like this man! They rush through life without a thought of what will certainly follow, hoping against hope that somehow they will reach heaven. They advance reasons for being received on the basis of their good works, fulfillment of religious rites or ceremonies, or their superiority of character over others. But none of these can avail. The refrain of heaven's song is, "Thou wast slain and by thy blood didst ransom men for God." If you do not learn to sing that song on earth, you will never sing it in heaven.

Worship

Worship God

As we were leaving Beaumont, Texas, we saw a large sign along the highway calling upon people to acknowledge God. "Go and worship God in the church of your own choice," we read. We pulled to a stop in front of a red light. Another car drew alongside us. A child's voice read the sign and said, "Daddy, what does worship mean?" The father replied, "It means to go to church and listen to the preacher preach." Could there be a more horrible definition? Worship—three or four hundred years ago it was pronounced worth-ship—means the acknowledgment of the worth that is in our God.

Worship in heaven is described in terms of God's angels and sons falling before Him, saying, "Blessing, and glory, and wisdom, and thanksgiving, and honour, and power, and might, be unto our God for ever and ever" (REVELATION 7:12).

Yielding The Body To Christ

The Accelerator Foot

I was riding with my wife whom I consider a very good driver. She is a better driver than most men, and her life is so ordered that she drives many thousands of miles each year. We came to a small town, and she slowed down to 35 miles an hour, then to 25 miles as the signs indicated. I believe that most drivers go 30 in a 25-mile zone, 40 in a 35-mile zone and 55 in a 50-mile zone. This Christian woman was going exactly 15 in a school zone and I commented on her driving. I knew that her overall time from one city to another was approximately the same as my own, and I had not been as careful as she to obey the letter of the law. Her answer was something like this:

"I can think of three reasons why a Christian should obey the law. The first is because the law has a penalty. The second reason is that our own personal safety is involved, and we should take care of ourselves. The third reason," and this was the reason which concerned my wife, "is the fact that the Bible commands the Christian to keep even the petty ordinances of the municipality. We read in Peter's first epistle, 'Submit yourselves to every ordinance of man for the Lord's sake....' " She then continued, "I prayed about this a great deal when I came to this verse in the Bible, and I concluded that since I delight to worship God, since He has told me that we are to obey him, and since He tells us to submit ourselves to every ordinance of man *for His sake,* I would consider that I was worshiping the Lord with my accelerator foot." I had to admit in my heart that I could find no way to excuse improper driving when the matter was considered as an act of worship of our Lord. The whole of the passage reads: "Submit yourselves to every ordinance of man for the Lord's sake; whether it be to the king, as supreme"—that would correspond to our federal laws—"Or unto governors"—that would correspond to our state laws—"as unto them that are sent by him for the punishment of evil-doers, and for the praise of them that do well. For so is the will of God, that with well doing you may put to silence the ignorance of foolish men: as free, and not using your liberty for a cloke of maliciousness, but as the servants of God" (I PETER 2:13–16).

There is one other detail of this same story that merits recording. I lamely explained that if I sometimes speeded it was because my mind was on other things, and my foot grew heavy on the accelerator; that when the road was clear I drove by road conditions, and I did not mean to break the law. My companion answered: "That's like the story of the little girl who was reproved by her mother for something she had done. The little girl said, 'Mother, I didn't mean to do it.' And then after a moment she said, 'But mother, I didn't mean *not* to do it either.' " It is the meaning *not* to do it that really counts.

The next time I was driving was on an eighty-mile trip into New York. I started down the road and found myself consciously keeping the car at exactly 50 miles an hour—not 51. In my heart I was saying, "Lord, I have a good car and am a good driver; I could do 58 here without difficulty, but I am submitting myself to the 50 ordinance for Thy sake." And I found myself feeling good about it. Then came a 35-mile zone to test me and a 15-mile-school zone. I poked along, doggedly determined that I was going to worship the Lord with my right foot on the accelerator. I soon found that I was getting a great joy out of this; beyond any question the Lord was answering me within my heart. But the thing that amazed me most was that I found myself making very good time. It seemed also as though there was an opening in the traffic at every turn. When I finally swept into the Lincoln Tunnel and out into Manhattan, I found I had almost tied my best record for the distance—a record I had made without thought of anything except the car I might see in my rearview mirror.

Thus it may be that we, as true believers in the Lord Jesus Christ, may help solve the terrible problem of traffic deaths by taking this text in the epistle to the Romans and listening to it as though it read, "I beseech you therefore by the mercies of God that you present your accelerator foot as a living sacrifice, holy, acceptable unto God, which is your reasonable service."

Selling the House

A friend of mine bought a house for $11,000, and lived in it for about five years. Then he had to move to another city. Knowing that prices had gone up, he hoped to get $13,000 or $14,000 for it. He advertised the place for sale, and almost immediately a prospective buyer came to see him. When he was asked the price, the owner said, "Make me an offer." Without batting an eye the visitor replied, "$17,000." Hiding his amazement, my friend replied, "Well, I would like to get $20,000 for it." The buyer pulled out a checkbook and said, "Let's split the difference, I'll pay you $5,000 on account. I've got to catch a plane and get back home to get ready to move." So the deal was concluded on that basis. $13,000 or $14,000 would have been acceptable; $17,000 was agreeable; the final price of $18,500 was very well-pleasing!

The Lord God planned our redemption, and Jesus Christ accomplished it by giving Himself for us. When we understand this and present our bodies to the Lord as living sacrifices it is not only acceptable to Him, it is agreeable, it is well-pleasing to Him. In return He shows us His will for our lives, and then we learn by experience that His will is good, well-pleasing and perfect.

The Young Man

A man was going with a girl who, some of us thought, was not at all worthy of him. Some breathed a sigh of relief when he went into the army and was gone for two or three years. The girl drifted around with other fellows, and the worthy young man met a worthy girl in a distant city, fell in love with her, and married her. When the war was over, he returned to his home with his bride; one evening the first girl drove by the house and dropped in to see her old flame and to meet his wife. But the wife was not there. The first girl made no attempt to hide her affection; the man realized that he had but to reach out his hand and she would be his. He told me about it afterwards. There was within him all that goes with male desire, but there was something more within him also, and he began to talk about the wonderful girl he had married. He showed pictures of his wife to the first girl and praised his wife to the skies, acting as though he did not understand the obvious advances of the girl. It was not long before she left, saying as she went, "Yes, she must be quite a girl if she can keep you from reaching." The young man was never more joyful in his life. He said that in that moment all of the love between him and his wife was greater and more wonderful than ever; he could think of his wife in a clean, noble way. A philanderer might have scoffed at him, derided him for "sacrificing" his pleasure. But there was not the slightest hint of sacrifice in the generally accepted sense of the word.

There was, however, every sacrifice in the sense of Romans 12:1, "I beseech you therefore, brethren, by the mercies of God, that ye present your bodies a living sacrifice, holy, acceptable unto God which is your reasonable service." The turning of his heart and mind and soul, yes, and body, to the love of his true wife was the living sacrifice which praised her and made him all the more noble because of it. It is in this sense that the believer in Christ presents his body as a living sacrifice to the Lord.

Illustrating Great Themes of Scripture

The Bible

Bible Reading for Busy People

Many people complain that they do not have time to read the Bible as much as they would like.

In Boston, Lydia Roberts provided readers of *The Globe* with this excellent summary of "How to Get Time to Read a Book":

1. Talk less.
2. Carry a book in your bag.
3. Put a book under your pillow at night; if you can't sleep, read.
4. Wake up 15 minutes earlier every morning and read.
5. Keep a book handy to pick up while in the kitchen, dressing, or on the telephone.
6. Have a book ready when meeting unpunctual people.
7. Take along your own book when going to the dentist, doctor, or lawyer. Why read their old magazines?
8. Keep an unread book in your car in case of traffic jams or a wait for repairs.
9. Never go on a journey without a book; you might not like your seatmate.
10. Remember that a book in the hand is worth two in the bookcase.

If a literary columnist can give such suggestions for those who are interested in reading the ephemeral titles that pass across the book counters, how much more is such advice valuable for a Christian and his Bible. If you are determined that you shall know the Scriptures, you will find the time. You will make it.

How to Read the Bible for Profit

Read your Bible slowly. Take time, even if you have but little time. Give God the opportunity to talk back to you. This is the most important part of Bible study. When you merely plow through the Scriptures, letting your brain have full play over the text, making decisions as to what it means, and incorporating it into the *corpus* of your theology, it is comparatively worthless for spiritual results.

A great mathematician once said that if he were given only two minutes to solve any problem he would spend one of those minutes in deciding the method by which he would reach the solution.

This is excellent advice. If possible never be pressed or hurried when you approach the Word of God. He has said, "Be still, and know that I am God" (Ps. 46:10). He is the God of all holiness, and it behooves us to approach Him with reverence.

The Word of the Lord is the burning bush out of which comes the flame of fire. The Word of the Lord is the mount from which the Lord of Hosts shows Himself. In it God speaks to us; in it we hear the words of everlasting life. We must be sanctified and wash our garments and be ready to hear the Lord. We must strip away all earthly affections and set them on things which are above. We must fall down before Him with godly fear. We must know who it is that speaks; even God the maker of heaven and earth; God, the Father of our Lord Jesus Christ; God, who shall judge the living and the dead, before whom all flesh shall appear.

And when we have that attitude, He suddenly whispers to us that we are not to remain afar off, but that we are to come near to Him. I once was reading in an English hymnbook and came to that verse

> Father of Jesus, Love's reward,
> What rapture it will be,
> Prostrate before Thy throne to lie,
> And gaze and gaze on Thee.

I tried to put myself in that frame of mind, and felt my heart to be prostrate before the Lord, looking at Him from afar. Then in my heart the Holy Spirit brought me a message from Christ, "Not there, but up here. By faith, come up here." And I remembered that it was written that God has raised us up together with Christ, in the ascension, "and made us to sit together in the heavenly places in Christ" (Eph. 2:6).

And I began to learn more of the Bible than I had known in a long time. It is not a shallow process that spreads over a wide bed, but a deep process that digs a well, and then another, and then another, and still another. But the water in each well is fresh and cool, and He holds the cup to our lips.

How to Understand the Bible

The shortest road to an understanding of the Bible is the acceptance of the fact that God is speaking in every line. The shortest road to the knowledge of the will of God is the willingness to do that will even before we know it. If we expect the voice of God to speak to us when we open the Bible, and have asked the Holy Spirit to bless it to us, we will find that He will undoubtedly answer that prayer. The Holy Spirit cannot feed us, though, if we have allowed known sin to come between us and Him.

Unless an author can give you his meaning within the pages of his book, he has failed. The reason the Bible is the universal Book is that one does not need a tremendous background of knowledge in order to understand it. The Book speaks to the heart of both the sinner and the saint. Anyone who tells us that we must have a full knowledge of Gnostic philosophy in order to understand the Gospel and the Epistles of John is making himself ridiculous. "If any man willeth to do his will he shall know the doctrine, whether it be of God or whether I speak of myself" (John 7:17). This is the criterion for comprehension of Biblical truth. The governor of the feast did not know the source of the wine in the second chapter of John, but the Scripture says that the servants knew. The truly yielded heart of the child of God would rather be a servant and know what God is doing than be a governor and not know what God is doing.

An old Scotch lady, when asked if she enjoyed reading commentaries, replied somewhat dubiously, "Yes . . . I like to read them sometimes. The Bible throws a great deal of light on them." There may be scholars who think that this attitude toward the Bible is wrong, but this is the reason why some simpleminded folk know more about God and His ways than some professors will ever know. The yielded heart, the certainty that God is speaking, and the willingness to listen, are the sum and substance of the "methodology" of Bible study.

How to Interpret the Bible

The Word belongs to the Lord and He can use it as He pleases. He can expand it and so use it to give it new depths of meaning as time passes. A Christian asked if it were possible to get blessing out of verses that, in their literal interpretation, did not apply to present circumstances at all. I answered:

When you get a blessing out of the Word, which is a blessing from God with full maintenance of His character and being, you may be sure that the question of the primary interpretation does not enter into the matter. Providing there is no violation of spiritual principles, you may give the Holy Spirit the widest latitude in interpreting the Word as He sees fit. But if a voice bids you take something out of the Word that would violate another clear principle of the Word, then you may know that the voice is from the enemy. If, for example, a voice told anyone that Philippians 2:12 meant that we must work for salvation and that it is not necessary to believe in Christ, that would be a devilish voice. But if some young man got pulled out of a rut of sin by reading Galatians 6:7, "Whatsoever a man soweth that shall he also reap," when the context clearly shows that the primary interpretation has to do with Christian giving of money for the teaching of the Word, we would not be astonished that the Spirit had thus used the Word. There would be no violation of spiritual principles, though this verse deals with giving and has nothing to do with the sowing of wild oats.

You will note that the Holy Spirit takes verses of the Old Testament and quotes them in the New Testament with what we might call a new twist. For instance, in Habakkuk we read of the vision, "It will surely come, it will not tarry" (2:3). But the Holy Spirit changes *it* to *He* in Hebrews and says, "He that shall come will come, and will not tarry" (10:37). The progressive revelation of truth is sufficiently advanced by that time that all should know that Christ, not an impersonal "it," is the answer.

So trust yourself to the Word of God; throw yourself upon it, and expect that the Lord shall speak to your heart in clear and definite ways, guiding you and leading you and teaching you the way you should go.

What Does It Really Say?

Be careful, in reading the Word of God, to find out what it really says. How many people there are who have false ideas of the Bible simply because they believe that the Bible says something it does not say at all! If one could speak to the average man in the street he would probably say that if there is such a being as the Devil, he is to be found in hell; yet the Bible teaches that the Devil has never yet been in hell. The man would probably say that the Devil in hell is occupied as chief torturer of the wicked, yet the Bible clearly shows that when the Devil is finally cast into the lake of fire, he will be the chief victim.

Scores of like instances are to be found in people who have picked up casual impressions as to what the Bible is supposed to say. A science professor in one of our great universities once asked me how to answer the criticism of non-Christians who laughed at the Bible because it taught that disease was communicated by demons instead of by germs, as science has demonstrated. I pointed out that the simplest answer is an emphatic denial that the Bible teaches anything of the kind.

Never bow to an agnostic's argument against the Bible without checking the facts, for agnostics are often notoriously ignorant concerning the Bible. I once discovered that a group of liberal theological students knew practically nothing about the Bible, yet some of them were ready to deny that certain things were in the Bible until they were shown several passages from the Scripture. One of them even turned to the title page of the Bible that was held before him to see if it were a standard version, as he thought that, since he had never heard of them, such things could not be in the Bible.

The Reader's Digest carried the condensation of an article about the death of William Jennings Bryan. It told how Clarence Darrow had put him on the stand in the famed Scopes trial in Dayton and had flustered him by demonstrating the impossibility of some of the Bible stories. "You believe the story of the Flood to be literally true?" "I do, sir." "Mr. Bryan, the Bible says every living thing that was not taken on the Ark with Noah was drowned in the Flood. Do you believe that?" "I do." "Including the fishes that were left behind?" The writer says that Bryan winced, but replied: "It says every living thing, and I am unwilling to question it." The writer went on to say that the thought of fishes being drowned startled the loyal audience, and concluded that Bryan's death was hastened by his defeat to Darrow.

Without casting any aspersions on the late champion of the commoner, we wish that Darrow had read his Bible a little more closely. For as a matter of fact, when he stated, "The Bible says every living thing that was not taken on the Ark with Noah was drowned in the Flood," he was simply showing his ignorance of what the Bible really does say. Further, when Bryan answered, "It says every living thing, and I am unwilling to question it," he was admitting a weakness in the Bible which is not there at all.

The Bible, in fact, states most definitely that the effects of the Flood were limited. "And all flesh died that moved *upon the earth,* both of fowl, and of cattle, and of beast, and of every creeping thing that creepeth *upon the earth,* and every man: all in whose nostrils was the breath of life, of all that was in the *dry land,* died. And every living substance was destroyed which was upon *the face of the ground,* both man and cattle and the creeping things, and the fowl of the heaven; and they were destroyed *from the earth.* . ." (Gen. 7:21–23).

Make a habit of finding out what the Bible really says. If you do not understand what it means, ask someone who knows. There is always an answer that is satisfying to both faith and reason.

What Shall We Read in the Bible?

Peter wrote that the brethren were to be put always in remembrance of certain things, even though they knew them, so that they might be established in the present truth (2 Peter 1:12). It is a great phrase, and one that needs to be understood if there is to be true growth in the life in Christ from day to day.

I thought of this when I read an essay written a generation ago by an Edinburgh professor of theology on "The Practice of the Spiritual Life." After speaking about the necessity of reading the Word of God the professor asks, "What shall we read in the Bible?" He then answers his question: "First, read what feeds your soul: which means that as you get older, new and before unappreciated portions of the Bible will disclose their value. Certain parts probably will come to no harm if you leave them alone altogether. But let first things be first: make the Psalms and the Gospels central."

That paragraph may be plausible to the unthinking, but there are two spiritual errors in it that account for much that is wrong in today's great, spiritually dying churches. The first error is the denial of Christ's own words: "Man shall not live by bread alone, but by every word that proceedeth out of the mouth of God" (Matt. 4:4). It is true that the parts will not come to harm if you leave them alone, but you will come to harm, for you will have a vitamin deficiency by neglecting some of the truths which God has given you in various parts of the Scripture.

The second error is in thinking that the Psalms and the Gospels take priority over the Epistles. The Christian must learn to live by reading the Epistles. The Christian must learn to live by reading the Epistles. We do not believe that any Christian life will develop very rapidly if it is confined to the Psalms and the Gospels. Even when we read the Gospels we must think of them constantly in terms of the truths that are revealed in the Epistles. Our Lord said, "I have yet many things to say unto you, but ye cannot bear them now. Howbeit when he, the Spirit of truth, is come, he will guide you [in the Epistles] into all truth" (John 16:12, 13).

The proper method of Bible study is to enter into the Gospels through the Epistles, and to enter into the Old Testament through the New. And the prerequisite to any of this study is that the truth which is revealed in the Epistles, as to the nature of the new birth, shall have entered into you.

Truth

At the time of the tercentenary of the death of George Herbert, a literary critic wrote of this great Christian poet: "As his experience develops, he realizes increasingly that the more we love the truth, the less inclined we are to obscure or decorate her features."

This is the path of every true child of God. As our experience develops, we realize that God uses the truth alone as the instrument of regeneration (1 Peter 1:23). It is the truth by which we grow (1 Peter 2:2), and truth is the means of our spiritual progress (John 17:17). Paul realized this when he wrote of spiritual matters, saying, "which things also we speak, not in the words which man's wisdom teacheth, but which the Holy Spirit teacheth" (1 Cor. 2:13).

Believers must make the definite choice, with respect to God's Word, to put truth into a proper perspective. To give truth its proper position—the position that God Himself has given it—is to subordinate every human opinion to the truth and to live one's life within the sphere of God's revealed Word. This is the meaning of David's phrase, to delight in the law of the Lord; to meditate therein day and night. With Paul, the result affected even the choice of words in his vocabulary.

Those who obscure the features of truth do so because they have something to hide, "for every one that doeth evil hateth the light, neither cometh to the light, lest his deeds should be reproved" (John 3:20). Those who decorate the features of truth are living a life of self-glorification, and the truth, in its great simplicity, is not great enough for them. "He that doeth truth cometh to the light, that his deeds may be made manifest, that they are wrought in God" (John 3:21).

In the early days of oil painting, artists like the Van Eyck brothers painted with microscopes, and it is possible to count the tiny pearls on the robe of one of their queens, the hairs of an angel's head, or the stubble of a man's beard. This was one form of "truth" in art. By the end of the nineteenth century, the Impressionists were taking blobs of paint and smearing them upon canvas with a broad brush. Close at hand, the effect was meaningless. Standing across the room, with the proper light upon the picture and with eyes half closed, one could get a distinct impression of what the artist was trying to convey. These later masters insisted that theirs was another form of "truth" in art. The Word of God combines all that is reality in both of these methods without any of the drawbacks attendant upon either. Truth is written so plainly that a wayfaring man, though a fool, need not err therein. The message is so insistent that he who reads must run to tell it. Therein is all that the most realistic mind can desire in preciseness and exactitude.

Without obscuring or decorating the features of truth, there is also an impressionism that grows and develops with long companionship with the Word of God. One of the most elementary examples of this is the Bible teaching of the doctrine of the Trinity—nowhere stated and everywhere taught. We are able, as Coleridge so discriminatingly said, to apprehend that which we cannot entirely comprehend.

Owning Truth

Children learn early in life the rights of property. "That is mine," and "That is yours," are words which in every nursery must be well understood. Many lessons can be learned from knowing that certain things belong to us and that we must care for them if we would keep them for proper use.

"The secret things belong unto the Lord our God: but those things which are revealed belong unto us and to our children forever" (Deut. 29:29). The word *belong* is not from the Hebrew, but was added by the translators to make the meaning of the original more clear.

Nevertheless, there is a great truth involved in this verse. God has revealed truth unto us by His Spirit (1 Cor. 2:10). That truth belongs to us.

The question that we need to face is whether or not we possess that which we own. Many of us own more umbrellas than we possess. We have bought them, but they have a habit of disappearing. They are ours, but they cannot keep us dry when it rains. It is as though we did not own them. This is, indeed, a very simple illustration, but it is sufficient to remind us that we own truth which we do not always possess. The title has been put in our name, but we do not necessarily enter into its possession.

When the patriarchs entered the promised land, they were ordered to go in and possess it. The promise was given that they should possess every place where the soles of their feet should stand. North, south, east, and west—all they had to do was to walk in faith, and God Almighty became bound to fulfill His promise and to keep them while they were walking. In like manner, the Word of God has been given to us. It is a promised land; we are to enter in and possess it. Some Christians camp in the four Gospels with an outpost barracks in the Psalms and never get any further in the possession of Christian truth. The great well-watered plains of the Epistles and the crowning heights of prophecy are foreign lands to their timidity. Let the Christian realize that the entire Word of God belongs to him. Each truth within its pages is waiting to speak to the heart.

We

Great embarrassment can arise if you include yourself in a "we" that someone else has used for a group that has no place for you. "We are going to drive to California," someone might say, but when you get into the car you will be told that you were not included and that there is no place in the plans for you.

I thought of this when I saw on a sign outside a church a part of a great verse: "If we confess our sins, He is faithful and just to forgive" (1 John 1:9). Crowds were passing and I wondered at the possible reaction of individuals to the text. Did some unbelievers get the idea that God was a sort of good grandmother who would condone and overlook any offense for a spoiled child who would say, "Grannie, I'm sorry"?

And then, in my mind, I reworded the text for use in front of a bank: "If we present our checks, the bank is faithful and just to cash them." Immediately it is seen that the "we" is not a universal one, but is strictly limited to depositors, and that the promise is limited by certain rules for the cashing. Certainly if you have a deposit in the bank and present a check for an amount that is covered by your deposit, the bank will be faithful and just to cash your check. But if you are not a depositor, you may not expect the check to be cashed. In fact, if there is even the attempt to present a check where there is no account, you can be arrested and sent to the penitentiary.

One of the most important facts in Biblical interpretation is that the Bible is restricted for much of its meaning to those who are definite believers in Christ. Apart from the universal offer of salvation to the lost, there is not a line in the Bible for the Hindu, the Muslim or the unregenerate Protestant. There is not one word of comfort in time of sorrow, of consolation in bereavement, or of strength in time of weakness, for those who have not been born again. Three verses farther on from the verse that we quoted from the sign in front of the church, the relevancy of the promise is strictly limited. "If any man sins" (and you will see that it does not mean any human being, but any born-again believer), "we have an advocate with the Father, Jesus Christ the righteous: And he is the propitiation for our sins: and not for ours only, but also for the whole world." There is a definite distinction between the "we" and the "our" of the believer and the "world" which has not believed. Be careful to teach these distinctions lest men be lulled by false hopes. "Ye must be born again" (John 3:7). "We know that we have passed from death unto life" (1 John 3:14).

Doubts and Certainties

While leafing idly through a student's reference book, I was struck by the inscription on the flyleaf. It read, "As long as you have any doubts whatsoever about the 'meaning of life' or the 'destiny of man' you can hold only opinions, never 'truth,'—and you can never brand another man's opinions as 'false.' Be true to your own ideals, and be kind to those who differ with you."

Many people, especially young people, are coming to grips for the first time with the world of ideas, ideals, opinions, and "comparative" religions, and think in line with this inscription because they are not possessed by the great certainties that may be ours in Christ.

The believer, by definition, has received into his life the Lord Jesus Christ, who said, "I am the Truth." Having received Christ, how can we hold any truth as an "opinion," when He has set it forth in terms of Himself? In knowing Him who said, "I am the Life," how can we have any doubts about the "meaning of life"? The unbeliever cannot understand this; but the believer must grow in spiritual discernment until his attitude toward all life reflects the attitude of Christ. The gift of spiritual discernment to know what is true and what is false is perhaps the rarest of the gifts of God. It is the ability to lay every opinion alongside the Word of God. If the opinion proves level and straight by this measurement, it has passed the test and can be taken as truth. If it does not conform to this absolute, it must be rejected.

As for "the destiny of man," we know by God's Word that this, too, is fixed. If a man is out of Christ, he has no destination other than that of being out of Christ. If he is in Christ he has an advance destination—a predestination—to be conformed to the image of God's Son (Rom. 8:29). The destiny of the unsaved is to remain forever in their own self-created confusion. When a believer knows these facts he has arrived at complete truth in so many areas that there is no room for an opinion that conflicts with complete truth. The truths of God, salvation, and eternity, to mention but three, have been acknowledged as absolutes. Only where there is no direct teaching in the Word of God on any matter may we hold opinions, subject to change.

If you attempt to be true to your own ideals you will soon discover that you are not capable of doing so. No person has ever lived up to all the light that God has given him, and that is why we need the Lord Jesus Christ to redeem us and to take up His dwelling place within us. Only when He lives within us can He furnish us with increasing power to live His life. This, of course, will include being very kind to those who differ with us. We have become the servants of the Lord, "And the Lord's servant must not be quarrelsome but kindly to everyone, an apt teacher, correcting his opponents with gentleness. God may perhaps grant that they will repent and come to know the truth" (2 Tim. 2:24, 25).

Two Great Needs

There are two things of which the world is totally ignorant. One is the fact of sin, and the other, the fact of God's holiness. These are spiritual truths, and being spiritually discerned, they become known only by the work of the Holy Spirit in our hearts. When this occurs, progress in all Christian truth becomes simple and steady.

In the preface to a theological work published in England a century ago, the author speaks of the help he had received from a certain British nobleman. He writes of him: "For years he had found the emptiness of the world, and had begun to seek the better part. His religion was no sentimental religion; his fear of God was not taught by the commandment of men. His faith was drawn directly from the inspired fountain of divine truth. The origin of that carnestness and attachment to spiritual things which he manifested in his last years was the perusal of the tract entitled 'Sin no Trifle.' Deep was the impression that tract had made. He read it and reread it, and continually carried it about with him, until it was entirely worn away. Under the impressions springing from such views of sin, he said to an intimate friend, when in the enjoyment of health and vigor: 'It is easy to die the death of a gentleman, *but that will not do!*' "

Sin is no trifle. It is the cause of the death of the human race and of every ill that we know. This understanding is the first step in spiritual growth. It is only when we accept God's verdict about sin and look to the Lord Jesus Christ that we can grow in spiritual knowledge. No wonder, then, that this same author was able to continue to write of his noble friend, "From the time the claims of God to the homage of his heart had laid hold on him, the Word of God became his grand study, and few men have I ever known who held with a more firm and tenacious grasp the great truths that the Word of God, and that Word *alone,* is the light and rule for the guidance of Christians; and that every departure from that Word, alike on the part of churches and individuals, implies going off the rails, and consequently danger of the highest kind. As his religion was Scriptural, so it was spiritual."

All this goes to prove the great declaration of Scripture that "faith cometh by hearing, and hearing by the Word of God." As one steeps himself in the teachings of this Book he sees himself more clearly in all his sin and unworthiness. He sees, too, the matchless worth of the Lord Jesus, our God. He sees the cross and all that it means. Faith feeds upon these great teachings and grows because it is rooted in the Word of God.

God

His Existence

The Bible says that anyone who wishes to draw near to God must believe that He *exists,* and that He will reward them that diligently seek Him (Heb. 11:6). This is why the Bible always takes God for granted. In the beginning of Genesis Moses did not attempt to prove the existence of a God. Setting forth proof for God would have been superfluous, for by Moses' time there were already too many gods. Nor did Moses begin with nature, attempting to go step by step the long, laborious path through the desert of logic to the person of the one true God. Instead, Moses boldly began with God and then, like a plummeting eagle, dropped down to the lesser things of creation. There is never any attempt to prove God by creation, but rather there is the explanation of the creation in terms of God. He is the axiom upon which all truth is built. He is not carried by any other truth but carries all truth with Him.

Thus it is that the Word of God starts with the majestic statement, "In the beginning God." Nothing else is needed. All will be logical that begins with the truly *theo*-logical. The Bible would not be what it is if Moses had attempted to begin his work with an anthology of little syllogisms, building block by block with neat little packages of wisdom, attempting to reach the heavens with the building blocks of earth.

The only mind that demands a proof of God other than the little mind, the small, the carping mind, is the mind that has thrown up a barrier of sin and rebellion and will not admit the existence of God for fear that it will be necessary to bow before Him.

"That which may be known of God" (Rom. 1:19) in nature destroys the vain excuses of man, and that which may be known of God through His revelation builds us in Jesus Christ. Do not attempt to go to God by way of nature. The path winds too much, and He has purposely built in too many detours that come to dead ends. Go to God through Jesus Christ and you are at the end of the road at once. It was Christ who said, "No man cometh unto the Father, but by me" (John 14:6). And just as truly He said, "Him that cometh to me I will in no wise cast out" (John 6:37).

So it is: you will never get to God if you try your own roads, but you can get to God at once if you submit to His road.

His Faithfulness

Man is always subject to error. He can be mistaken without knowing it because he is fallible; he can also be mistaken wittingly because the seed of sin is in him and he loves the "darkness"—untruth, rather than the "light"—truth. But God, the great, unwavering one in whom is no variableness, does not confuse us by changing His ways. Every statement is sure; every prophecy is secure; every promise is certain; every fact is verified by the nature of His being. He is the one who can say, "Let God be true, but every man a liar" (Rom. 3:4). We may build upon His facts, promises, and prophecies, since they are His, and because He is the same yesterday, today, and forever. A generation after the promises of the Books of Moses had been recorded, Joshua was able to say that God had proven Himself true. "There failed not aught of any good thing which the Lord had spoken . . . all came to pass" (Josh. 21:45).

God's faithfulness, however, endures more than a generation. The wisest man known to the ancient world was wise because he knew God and had built upon His Word. At the dedication of the temple, Solomon was able to say to the people, "There hath not failed one word of all his good promise" (1 Kings 8:56).

It was upon this faithfulness of God to His Word that Solomon based his appeal to the people to be faithful to God. The Word never fails; therefore, walk according to the Word. This is the logic that Solomon used.

Finally, after Joshua's witness of a generation, and Solomon's witness of centuries, came the Lord Jesus, the source of Joshua's strength of leadership, and the spring of Solomon's wisdom. He sealed all God's Word with the seal of finality and gave Himself, not only as the sacrifice for sin, but as the pledge that there should fail "not . . . one word" of all that had been promised and given. The Holy Spirit tells us, "All the promises of God in him are yea, and in him Amen, unto the glory of God by us" (2 Cor. 1:20).

Why do we not believe God more? Not one word of all His good promise has failed; not one soul, trusting Him for salvation, has ever been lost; not one stumbling saint has not known the undergirding of His power. The foundation of God standeth sure. He must be faithful or He would cease to be God, and we cannot conceive of God's becoming "not God." His Word is settled in heaven, and though heaven and earth pass away, it shall never cease. His Word is as eternal in the past as is God and as enduring for the future. Build upon it without fear.

His Garments

From the dawn of civilization people have been interested in clothing. The writings of the classics are full of allusions to and descriptions of dress. The art galleries pass before us, a veritable fashion review of history. The textile museum of Lyons contains remnants of cloth from ancient Egypt, the Orient, Greece, Rome, and thousands of costumes of the Middle Ages, not to speak of the myriad samples of modern fabrics. Silks and satins, wools and cottons, linens and laces; royal purple and dun burel; tunics of kings and robes of queens; the splendor of courtesans, the chasuble of popes; the gay and somber pageant of vanity unrolls before our eyes.

The Bible speaks of those who are clothed in "purple and fine linen" or in "soft raiment," but certainly there are garments more wonderful than these. Isaiah sings, "I will greatly rejoice in the Lord, my soul shall be joyful in my God; for He hath clothed me with the garments of salvation, He hath covered me with the robe of righteousness, as a bridegroom decketh himself with ornaments, and as a bride adorneth herself with her jewels." There is no doubt that the Scripture teaches that God has provided His own righteousness as a covering so that we may be able,

> Dressed in His righteousness alone,
> Faultless, to stand before the throne.

"Christ is made unto us . . . righteousness." We are to "put on the Lord Jesus." Man is to be clothed with God.

But there is another truth about spiritual garments that is often overlooked. God clothes Himself with vestments; He is covered "with light as with a garment"; He is "clothed with honor and majesty." We sing of Him as "pavillioned in splendor and girded with praise," but the deeper truth is that God clothes Himself with a man. That the Spirit of God "came upon" this man or that man is a phrase used often in the Bible. The Hebrew word is used in a double sense, and is the same word that is used in the Scripture for "clothed." The translation of the Rabbi's version of the Old Testament in these passages is always "the Spirit of God clothed him," but the greatest Hebrew authority, Gesenius, renders it, "The Spirit of God put him on." God is a Spirit, yet He works in the world, working through men. He wishes to clothe Himself with you. Do not confuse this penetrating spiritual truth with the more familiar truth that we are clothed with Him. Get it rather in all of its strength, that He wishes us to be yielded to Him so that He may take us and use us as His cloak. We are to adorn Him. His omnipotence is to enter into our weakness, and He will be arrayed, adjusting us as suits Him best. The world will see God at work in those who are His redeemed. Then we will realize that all that is done in the realm of Christian work is done by our Lord, fully dressed in one of His own saints. We need only recognize the spiritual principle that underlies His working and be willing to be draped as a piece of cloth to cover Him.

His Intolerance

God is the only being in the universe who has a right to be intolerant. In fact, if He were tolerant He would not be God. Tolerance, in one of its shades, is the supine allowance of that which is evil. Crabb, in his great work on synonyms, says, "What is tolerated is bad in itself, and suffered only because it cannot be prevented; a parent frequently suffers in his children what he condemns in others; there are some evils in society which the magistrate finds it needful to tolerate."

We can well understand, therefore, why God must be intolerant. To admit any deviation from good order, to allow any wrong practices or thoughts, would be to permit that which the nature of God must reject. Therefore, if God were tolerant there would be chaos in the universe. Anything that is not in absolute accord with the will of God is necessarily wrong, and to permit it would be to abdicate the throne of the universe, suffering Satan to take control.

God is sovereign. Without a doubt, this is a doctrine that is even more important than the truth of redemption. In His sovereignty God will have no partner on His throne and He will not share His royal seat. We shall reign with Him only because our wills will have been brought absolutely into line with His will, and we must recognize at every step that all our power and our life is derived from Him and that we are utterly dependent upon Him forever. God will not give His glory to another (Isa. 42:8). You waste your time if you invite Him into a temple that is already fully occupied with self. God requires all of the room in our lives.

What would be your thoughts and actions if you were suddenly asked to surrender all of the world that you hold dear? God will never share the throne of life with some other claimant. The second Adam will never accept the first Adam as a partner.

When we read in the Scriptures, "The Lord thy God is a jealous God" (Exod. 20:5), we understand it only because of the noble intolerance of God. The Greek word for jealousy means, literally, to be filled with a burning desire. God, as a jealous God, is filled with a burning desire for our holiness, for our righteousness, for our goodness. Thus He is jealous for us, though He could never be jealous of anything or any being, for only good is found in Him.

The day shall come, after the testing time is over, that the intolerance of God will come to its final fruition, and all things that offend

Him shall be plucked out of His kingdom (Matt. 13:41). While we wait for that day let us see to it that we do not have any divided allegiance. All that we have and are belongs to Him alone.

His Justice

For several years radio stations have broadcast the proceedings of court cases. Commonest of these broadcasts have been those of traffic courts, and the principle of such broadcasts has been hotly debated. A Chicago judge spoke out against the practice, quoting some pertinent figures in support of his argument. In one court, of those tried when proceedings were not broadcast, 31.6% were convicted; of those tried during broadcasts, 87.5% were convicted. The average fine when there was no broadcast was $10.63, but when the judge had a radio audience, the average fine was $36.25.

The conclusion from these figures is most interesting. The judge, instead of judging according to principle of justice, was judging for effect. This may be called "justice," but it is human, fickle, and in reality, unjust. The increase in convictions and the heavier fines before a radio audience are indicative of the fact that the judge did not care as much for the high principles of law when he was alone with his conscience as when he realized that he was not only judging, but being judged by other people.

When God judges, He judges according to the principles that are inherent in Himself. He will "by no means clear the guilty" (Num. 14:18). Though He will pardon freely those whose debt has been paid by His Savior Son, "He repayeth them that hate him to their face, to destroy them; he will not be slack to him that hateth him, he will repay him to his face" (Deut. 7:10). He "regardeth not persons, nor taketh reward" (Deut. 10:17). "He hath prepared his throne for judgment; and he shall judge the world in righteousness. He shall minister judgment to the people in uprightness" (Ps. 9:7, 8). "Shall not the Judge of all the earth do right?" (Gen. 18:25).

The Psalms are, in large part, filled with praise to God, and it is remarkable to note how often the righteousness of God's forthcoming judgment is the reason for praise to God. It is noteworthy that He calls upon the whole universe to witness His judgment. "Our God shall come and shall not keep silence. . . . He shall call to the heavens from above, and to the earth, that he may judge his people. Gather my saints together unto me; those that have made a covenant with me by sacrifice. And the heavens shall declare his righteousness: for God is judge himself" (Ps. 50:3–6).

Unlike the radio judge, the Lord God would administer righteous judgments with or without witnesses. He tells us, however, that there will be witnesses, and His character draws us on to long for His speedy return and His just judgment.

His Patience

The fact that God is slow to anger (Neh. 9:17) may lead us to believe that He will occasionally condone sin. God can never condone sin. He can place our sin upon the Lord Jesus and deal with it in death; He can in faithfulness and righteousness reach into a life and cleanse it from all unrighteousness on the basis of His Word (1 John 1:9), but His nature will not permit Him to overlook sin.

To presume upon the grace of God and continue in sin that grace may abound (Rom. 6:1) draws an exclamation of horror from the apostle, and puts that sinner in grave danger of judgment.

The Lord gives His people time to judge themselves and promises to withhold judgment if they turn from sin and repent. If they do not repent, however, they are in danger of "withering" and of being cast into the fire (John 15:6). The casting forth as a branch and the withering have no reference whatsoever to the loss of salvation; the passage is one on fruit-bearing. The entire passage is applicable to the realm of our Christian testimony.

Withering is a slow process, barely perceptible at first to either the one who is being withered or those who look on. The holly with which we decorate our homes at Christmas is a good example. At first it is green and bright, even though separated from its source of life; then it begins to wither, dries out and crumbles, and is finally thrown into the fire.

The believer is no longer among the fools who make a mock of sin (Prov. 14:9), but he is always in danger of dealing too lightly with himself. Let us never forget that slowness does not imply a lack of movement. Our God is a consuming fire, and if we will not allow Him to place our sins on Christ for judgment, He must proceed to wither us and finally save us by casting our works into the fire (1 Cor. 3:15).

His Plan

No small part of God's plan is the triumph of individual righteousness during the present lifetime on earth, in the midst of all the surrounding unrighteousness. God purposes to bring righteousness into life so that it shall be the dominating characteristic in the believer. We were "created in Christ Jesus unto good works wherein God hath before ordained that we should walk" (Eph. 2:10).

It should be understood, of course, that when we thus emphasize personal righteousness, we are not speaking of a system of salvation by that righteousness. The believer's righteousness is an effect of the reign of God's grace within his heart, and certainly not a cause of that grace. God never does anything for us because we are good, but because He is good. "We love him because he first loved us" (1 John 4:19). We work righteousness because He has wrought righteousness in us. "What the law could not do in that it was weak through the flesh, God, sending his own Son in the likeness of sinful flesh, and for sin, condemned sin in the flesh, that the righteousness of the law might be fulfilled in us, who walk not after the flesh but after the Spirit" (Rom. 8:3, 4).

Every day we are the objects of the grace of God. All that He does is through grace. Even the rewards that we shall receive are ultimately because of grace, for even at best "we are unprofitable servants" (Luke 17:10).

It is a very great sin, a sin of presumption, to think that it is possible to live in sin because there is a great abundance of grace. Against such a thought the Spirit cries out through Paul, "God forbid!" (Rom. 6:2). Grace is not merely to abound; grace is to reign (Rom. 5:21). To the ear of the Greeks who heard this verse the first time the message would have been: "Grace is to king it! But, note well, grace must reign through righteousness."

The world may hold the mistaken idea that the end justifies the means, but God's method is such that the means are holy. He will never work His grace through unrighteousness, though He sometimes is gracious in spite of unrighteousness. But the Lord wishes to work righteousness through us by working righteousness in us. That is His present work in His own people.

His Power

A well-known biologist spent his whole life studying a beetle. To the one who knows little about these things it seems impossible that there should be enough in such a tiny animal to occupy a brilliant mind for a lifetime. But when this man had come to almost the end of his lifetime of study, he stated that he had made a mistake in taking a beetle as his unit of study, that he should have confined himself to the wing of a beetle!

We should never tire of the thought of God's power. Our minds can go out into the limitless distances of space and wonder at the infinitely great, or turn to the jostling life which appears to us under the lens of the microscope, and everywhere find the manifestation of God's power. "Great is our Lord, and of great power; his understanding is infinite" (Ps. 147:5).

But as great as is God's power in these things, we see its climax neither through the telescope nor under the microscope, but in one great act, the resurrection of Christ. All the words for power in the Greek language are used in Ephesians 1:19, 20, in speaking of this greatest exhibition of what God can do. "And what is the exceeding greatness of his power to us-ward who believe, according to the working of his mighty power, which he wrought in Christ when he raised him from the dead . . ." Resurrection is always an exhibition of power. When Elisha, speaking for God, called the son of the Shunammite back to life, when the Lord Jesus turned back the forces of death and raised the widow's son, the daughter of Jairus, and

Lazarus, it was a mighty work of God's power. But the resurrection of Jesus Christ was more than the resurrection of a dead man. It was the act which was an answer to His death for our sin. He died under the condemnation of God, for He was bearing our sins. But in His death, God finished His dealing with the sin question, and was able to raise Him from the dead, because the full force of His wrath against iniquity had been spent. His resurrection showed that He had paid the full price of the penalty of sin, and that the condemnation was finished.

There is also a power that flows from His resurrection itself. We who believe are united in Him, and we share in His resurrection life. From Him, the resurrected one, comes power. Nothing that can touch us is outside the reach of this power, the power of the knowledge of Christ and of His resurrection. All of God's might and authority and strength is put at the demand of the feeblest of His children who have come to Him through the resurrected Son. It is ours, if we simply take what is offered us through Him.

His Presence

God is *with* us; God is *for* us; God is *in* us. If we understand the nature of these prepositions we shall grow indeed in the graces of Christ.

The very name of our Lord Jesus was Immanuel. *God with us* (Isa. 8:10; Matt. 1:23). The meaning of the incarnation is that the Lord came to us from Heaven, the Word being made flesh to "dwell among us." "All we like sheep have gone astray; we have turned every one to his own way" (Isa. 53:6). This disobedience caused the loneliness that characterizes man and highlights his greatest need. But suddenly, Christ came, and God was *with us.*

Then He went to the cross and through the tomb, and perfect reconciliation was provided. Now, God is *for us.* He not only tells us so but adds, "If God be for us, who can be against us?" (Rom. 8:31). Here is the all-pervading, breathtaking statement that the Creator of the universe, Author of all life, is *for us.* If He had not told us this Himself, it would be the height of arrogance and presumption to think that it could be so, but He Himself has said it, and has confirmed it by explaining, "He that spared not his own Son, but delivered him up for us all; how shall he not with him also freely give us all things?" Rejoice! God is *for us*.

Then He rose from the grave and poured out the Holy Spirit, and God was *in us*. The Lord Jesus had announced it, "He dwells with you and will be in you" (John 14:17). Then the day came; "He breathed on them and said, Receive the Holy Spirit" (John 20:22). Ever since, it has been for each and every believer, "Christ in you the hope of glory" (Col. 1:27). Rejoice! God is *in us*.

The unbeliever should know that God is beside him, calling him. He should realize that God holds out His hand to him and is willing to support him. But only the believer knows the fulness of the power of the indwelling Lord. Only when His presence within us becomes indescribably everything—life and awareness of life, and so much more—can we enter into the life that is to be lived "more abundantly" (John 10:10).

His Program

There are different kinds of judges. In our day the word has only one meaning—one who rules in a court and decides the merits of a case in accordance with the points of law that are involved. In the Word of God there is another type of judge. In the Book of Judges, the Hebrew word translated *judge* means to *put right* and then *rule*. The world is in need of this type of judge.

Many men desire to rule, and there is an abundance of dictatorship in the world today; but there is no man with the power to put things right. Ten thousand men will give you ten thousand different explanations of all that is wrong, and will add as many remedies that are sure to correct everything. Nothing works out, however, for no man has the power to deal with sin in the human heart and its effect on the world. Until a man comes who can do this, the world must wait in agony.

In our age, God is not putting everything right. This is still the time of His patience; He is working in individuals. Perhaps the best expression of His purpose in this age of the church is to be found in James' summary of Simon Peter's speech at the council of Jerusalem: "God at the first did visit the Gentiles to take out of them a people for his name. And to this agree the words of the prophets; as it is written, After this I will return, and will build again the tabernacle of David, which is fallen down; and I will build again the ruins thereof, and I will set it up; that the residue of men might seek after the Lord and all the Gentiles, upon whom my name is called, saith the Lord, who doeth all these things" (Acts 15:14–17).

It is very important that we, as Christians, go along with God's program and not seek to have one of our own that is contrary to His. We cannot put things right and rule; the Lord Jesus alone can do this. It is not even in line with His purpose and grace to do this now, for when He *puts right* it will be with a "rod of iron." The Christian's business is "to serve the living and true God" by doing only what He wants done. He has revealed His purpose, which is "taking out a people for His name." If we work in line with this purpose, success will crown our efforts and we shall be blessed. Individuals will come to the knowledge of Jesus Christ as their Savior; that very knowledge will transform their lives and bring untold happiness in the midst of this world of sin. When the last individual is brought out of the world—the last living stone added to complete the edifice—then He, the Lord Jesus Christ, the righteous *Judge,* will come to put right and *rule.* He alone can do it, and He can do it alone.

His Promises

Our relationship to Christ must be intensely personal. If it is not, the deepest longings of our soul can never be satisfied. Augustine prayed long ago, "O God, Thou hast formed us for Thyself, and our hearts can know no rest till they rest in Thee." It is the personal contact with the Lord Jesus that will cause us to grow in Him. No one can thrive spiritually on mere church membership, sacraments, ritual, or formality. Stained glass windows and soft music, beautiful and permissible as they may be, will cause a soul to forget itself for a moment, and will lift the soul up aesthetically, but they cannot feed the soul that is hungry.

God our Father wants us to be very personal with Him. He desires that we should appreciate His promises and use the riches He has unlocked to us in Jesus Christ. Several years ago I was preaching for several weeks just outside of London. A woman noted for her saintliness lay at the point of death. Everyone spoke of her great joy in life and of her joy in death. She heard of our meetings, and asked, just before she died, that her study Bible, with the Newberry references, be given to me. A few days later her earth-life span ended and life indeed began for her.

Today her Bible lies on my table. Her marginal comments have often delighted me and I have discovered the secret of her power and joy. *She believed it was all for her, personally.* On the blank pages at the back of the book she has lists of promises gathered together over the years. The headings of the lists are alive with meaning. "How was I saved?" she wrote, and underneath, "2 Cor. 5:21." Then, for the deeper Christian life: "A definite act, July 9, 1894, S.E.H." Following this, she has "Gal. 2:20; Rom. 6:19, a *slave* of God's righteousness." Then are listed together "Power Tests," "The riches of God's grace," "The root of holiness," "The Lord's call to praise and joy," and also groups of verses for "Hours of darkness" and for "Shields against the legal spirit."

She had fortified her soul through God's *revelation*. One feels that here was holy ground where a soul met God. It breathes the atmosphere of personal contact. It would be a real blessing to many of us if we would, alone with God, take these headings and beginning with "How was I saved?" seek the answers in His Word.

We would discover that God has made two kinds of promises. He has bound Himself to us conditionally and unconditionally.

One line of promises throughout the entire Word is made upon certain conditions. If we fulfill the conditions the resultant blessing is ours. If we fail to meet the conditions, we do not receive the blessing.

Still other promises are absolutely unconditional. They are ours because God says they are ours; nothing that we do alters the situation in the least.

This is illustrated in the life of Abraham. Certain blessings were conditional upon his remaining in the land, and when he left the land he forfeited the right to the promises. God made him other promises— that his name should be great, that his seed should be made as the stars of the sky and the sand of the sea. God has accomplished this. Abraham is one of the universal names and his descendants cover the earth, in spite of the fact that they have broken every ordinance of God.

The same is true for the child of God today. Scores of promises are conditional—to receive we must ask, to know the power of His strength we must recognize and acknowledge our weakness. But there are unconditional promises for us as well, and one of them is "My God shall supply all your need according to his riches in glory by Christ Jesus." This does not mean that God is going to give us everything we *think* we need, and herein lies the true explanation: as God sees our need He will meet it. Who has not heard a father or mother say to a child, "You need a spanking"? Very often the child does. If the heavenly Father sees that we need discipline, He will provide it. The supply of our need does not mean merely that of material or spiritual blessing, but includes the discipline as well, and every other care that a heavenly Father can bestow upon His children so that they should grow toward the measure of the stature of the fulness of Christ.

Yet someone will point out that some believers who give every evidence of being born again are in the midst of terrible testing. Some of them are receiving charity as their only means of livelihood. How does one explain the promise of God's supply of every need in the light of such experiences of some true believers?

We must be very careful with the Word of God, that we do not interpret it to mean other than what it really does mean. Every promise must be judged in the light of the entire Word. It is true that we have a definite promise. "My God shall supply all your need according to his riches in glory by Christ Jesus" (Phil. 4:19). This promise was spoken well within the age of grace and there is no means of getting around the fact that it must apply to all believers in the age in which we live. Furthermore, it is not a promise that is conditional upon our righteousness, as are certain promises of supply which are to be found in the Old Testament and in the Sermon on the Mount. It is a promise that is conditioned on God's grace alone. Like that other great promise in the eighth chapter of Romans, it is based on the blood of the cross. "He that spared not his own Son, but delivered him up for us all, how shall be not with him also freely give us all things?" (Rom. 8:32).

Such a promise would seem to indicate that the believer had a universal store of material blessings, and that he could count upon an unfailing supply from God. Yet only a moment's thought would take us through history and we would realize that there have been thousands of believers who have had their lands confiscated, their loved ones torn from them, their bodies racked with torture, their homes and possessions destroyed, all because they trusted in the Lord Jesus Christ. Why did God not supply their need? The answer is that He did supply it. They needed strength to resist, and He gave it to them. Lack of food was merely the means of their passage to His presence. Our mistake lies in defining our need as being what we think it to be. The passages of Scripture refer to our needs as they are measured by God's omniscience.

The proof of all this lies in that same eighth chapter of Romans. If we would always read the context of our promises, we would not make so many mistakes. For in the same paragraph with the great promise that He would give us all things with Christ, He continues to show that nothing can separate us from our Lord. The apostle writes, "Who shall separate us from the love of Christ? shall tribulation, or distress, or persecution, or famine, or nakedness, or peril, or sword?" (Rom. 8:35). Notice two of these words, *famine* and *nakedness*. These cover the lack of the elemental things of life. Food and clothing. We know that believers have been deprived of these things before and have left a fragrant testimony to the supplying power of the Lord.

> The body they may kill,
> God's Word abideth still,
> His kingdom is forever.

There are times when food and clothing are essentials in our need as God sees our need. Then they will be supplied. There are other times when these are secondary to the testimony He wants us to bear. Then He will supply strength and sweetness in the midst of want. The attitude of Christian people who suffer is a condemnation of the attitude of many others who suffer while cursing God.

Nothing that we have said here, however, should be construed as diminishing our responsibility to give to the welfare of those who are our brothers and sisters in Christ. If a man seeth his brother in need and does not give unto him, how dwelleth the love of God in him? Not at all.

His Provision

God never asks anything of us that He has not already provided. It is a great thing when we learn this principle of God's dealings with His creatures. Do we have anything of our own to give God when He asks something of us? If we think we do, we are beside the mark and are in spiritual poverty. God's requirements are so many, so varied, and so great, that a man who tries to meet the call on his own will certainly fail.

The unsaved man will look to the Creator, wondering what he must do, do, do—seeking to provide a deposit balance to his credit that may satisfy some of the demands of God. The result of such hopeless attempts is that "the wicked are like the troubled sea when it cannot rest, whose waters cast up mire and dirt; there is no peace, saith my God, to the wicked" (Isa. 57:20, 21). But when the unsaved man realizes that God must require perfection—absolute holiness like His very own—he also realizes that as imperfect beings we cannot attain that end, and that therefore God must provide it. When he looks to the cross and sees that the revelation of God's righteousness may be had as a gift to meet God's requirements, then he will know peace with God for the first time. His own struggle to furnish the unattainable will cease, and he will recline in the joy and rest of full confidence and trust.

He will know that God has provided for him that which He had to demand of him. That is justification!

Then the child of God, day by day, will also realize that the strength for the daily life is provided in Christ. The Christian life is one of countless requirements, but every one of them is met in Christ. The Father asks that we let our light shine, but we look at the burned-out wick of our lives and cry with Paul, "I know that in me, that is in my flesh, dwelleth no good thing." I have no light. Then the Father points to the fact that before He ever said to us, "Let shine," He had already said, "Ye are the light of the world," and that He had already placed within us a light that can never go out.

He requires in us the reflection of Christ, and He polishes our lives that we may give back that reflection. He wants increase through us, but it is He who sows the seed in a field that He ploughs, harrows, and waters, that the field may indeed bring forth fruit. He wants our lives to be fruitful with the graces of the Spirit, and so He adorns the life with the Spirit's gracious fruit, and "love, joy, peace, longsuffering, gentleness, goodness, faith, meekness, and self-control" appear within us.

Show me more and more what God requires of me, and point again and again to the Lord, that He is a hard Master, reaping where He has not sown, requiring a high rate of interest. Reiterate my responsibilities, contrasting them with my infirmities. Each time I will point you to the Lord Jesus Christ. As each need or each lack is demonstrated, Christ is therein magnified, for He is the fulfillment of each need. "I will glory in my infirmities that the power of Christ may rest upon me." I will revel in my nothingness, that Christ may be all in all. For God has never asked of us anything that He has not already provided—the full and free provision is in Christ.

I thought of this provision when the telephone rang and a Christian lady asked for advice. Her physician, who with his healing gift had changed her outlook on life, had died suddenly, and she felt very alone in the world. She had come to Philadelphia and was calling me from the station. As I sat by the telephone during the prolonged conversation I began to write down some of the phrases that came over the wire.

"I need most to be among Christian people and under Christian teaching," she said.

"No!" I replied. "If you needed that, the Lord would provide it, for He has promised to supply all your need (Phil. 4:19). He will bless you in your lonely place."

"But I can gain confidence by talking with someone who has more confidence," said the voice.

"But that is not God's way," I answered. "Confidence is another word for faith, and we read that 'faith cometh by hearing, and hearing by the Word of God' " (Rom. 10:17).

"Yes, but I am not the steady kind. God has provided strong ones to bear the burdens of the weak, and we who are weak need those strong ones."

"God may indeed use some of His own to help others, but He is only pouring Himself through them. It is not those individuals who can strengthen you. You must get all your strength from God alone. He has said, 'My grace is sufficient for thee; for my strength is made perfect in weakness' (2 Cor. 12:9), and if you recognize your infirmities and accept them as an opportunity for God, He will make His strength perfect in your weakness."

"Oh, I feel so desperately frightened," said the voice, "but I don't want to admit it."

"Do you not realize," I answered, "that you are dishonoring God by failing to appropriate that which He has provided for you? If God causes a little fire of testing to break out, He has also provided a little water to quench it. There will always be a pint of water for a pint-size fire and a gallon of water for a gallon-size fire and an ocean of water for a fire of that proportion. God has told us that He will never permit us to be tested above what we can endure (1 Cor. 10:13)."

All I could say to this doubting one was that the provision was there, but that it must be appropriated. A teacher or a pastor may be used of God, but he will always work toward weaning all of his hearers from himself so that they will be resting only on Christ. Then they will learn that they can work out the solutions of their own problems, perhaps with fear and trembling, but also with great confidence, for God is dwelling in their hearts from the moment they are born again. Paul has noted: "Work out your own salvation (i.e., the solution of your problem) with fear and trembling, for it is *God* which worketh in you . . ." (Phil. 2:12–13).

His Responsibility

Remind God of His entire responsibility. This is the advice of a devotional writer in commenting on the cry of Asa (2 Chron. 14:11 ASV), "Lord, there is none beside thee to help." There are things that God must do, simply because we cannot do them ourselves. That is why our security, day by day, must come from God. "O foolish Galatians, who hath bewitched you . . . having begun in the Spirit, are ye now made perfect by the flesh?" (Gal. 3:1, 3).

The old Scotch lady was right. When she was visited by a very young minister who was short on experience, she held fast to her firm assurance of her safety in Christ. "But just suppose that after all God should let you sink into hell?" said the minister. "He would lose more than I would," came the firm answer of faith. "All I would lose would be my own soul, but He would lose His good name." Yes, she was right. The security of the believer does not depend on the individual ability to hang on, but on the eternal power of our God and Savior, Jesus Christ.

As God must be responsible for our salvation and security, so He must take care of us in our difficulties. "Lord, there is none beside Thee to help." "The arm of flesh will fail you, ye dare not trust your own." It is in this extremity, when there is no power in others or in self, that we must remind God of His responsibility. How often the Scriptures give us the examples of men who were pushed into a corner, cried to God, and He delivered them. He is "the same . . . today."

We must also realize God's responsibility for our growth. "It is God that giveth the increase." "To whom shall we go? Thou hast the words of eternal life." All progress in spiritual life comes from Him.

"He that hath begun a good work in you will perform it until the day of Jesus Christ."

The Scriptures seem to indicate by their tone that God desires to be reminded of His responsibility. This presupposes, of course, a yieldedness on our part, a submission to His will and a daily obedience. But He will ever furnish all the strength.

His Sovereignty

With God nothing is impossible. When our hearts lay hold on that fact and feed on it until our souls have absorbed it, we will know a great personal blessing.

The hymn writers of the centuries have found this to be true, and have given us a series of word combinations that are unique in our language. They show how souls in search of spiritual food have found all-sufficient supply in the Lord and His grace. "My grace, all-sufficient, shall be thy supply." This line from "How Firm a Foundation" includes the "all" which swells the sufficiency of divine grace to its proper proportions. Go on through hymnology:

> He with all-commanding might,
> Filled the new-made world with light.

> See Israel's gentle Shepherd stand
> With all-engaging charms . . .

> 'Tis God's all-animating voice
> That calls thee from on high . . .

> O that the world might know
> The all-atoning Lamb!

> The name all-victorious of Jesus extol;
> His kingdom is glorious, and rules over all.

> He ever lives above, For me to intercede;
> His all-redeeming love, His precious blood to plead.

> One ray of Thine all-quickening light
> Dispels the clouds and dark of night.

> Peace on earth, good will to men,
> From Heaven's all-gracious King.

> Jesus, Thine all-victorious love
> Shed in my heart abroad.

If the words are taken together they begin to form a picture of our Lord, all-powerful, all-gracious, all-sufficient, and all in all. And when there are sorrows which overtake us, we may be sure that they have been measured to our need and our ability to endure.

> Obey, thou restless heart, be still
> And wait in cheerful hope, content
> To take whate'er His gracious will,
> His all-discerning love, hath sent.

His Trinity

The word *Trinity* is not found in the Bible, but the truth of this doctrine is in every part of the Book. Though Christians have been talking about and believing in the Trinity for two thousand years, there are many Christians who cannot name the persons in the Trinity correctly. As a result of this error certain cults have an easier time gaining a foothold in some minds which are not established in the truth.

This thought came out of a statement of the Russelites (who call themselves "Jehovah's Witnesses") who deny the doctrine of the Trinity, holding that Christ was a created angel. The Russelites quoted the passage in Timothy (1 Tim. 6:16), and said that only God had immortality. A young Christian was confused and asked us about this verse.

We answered by asking him to name the persons of the Trinity. He replied, "God, Christ, and the Holy Spirit." Immediately we saw the root of his confusion. He had not put the second and third Persons of the Trinity in the place which is rightfully theirs. We answered, "No, you are wrong! If you are going to begin with God, then you must say that the members of the Trinity are God, God, and God. This is the only possible way of being correct in the matter. The Trinity is (not *are*) God the Father, God the Son, God the Holy Spirit."

We should be careful not to think of God as being only the Father and as being distinct from the Son and the Spirit. God is the Son, and God is also the Spirit, but the Father is not the Son, and the Father is not the Spirit.

Christ

Biography

The author of a biography begins at the birth and follows through to the death of his subject. But to understand any life story you must go back from the end to the beginning. What a man became is what makes his growth and development significant.

If this is true of a man, how much more is it true of our Lord Jesus Christ, the God-Man. This is why God did not give us a biography of Christ. The four Gospels are far from being biographies; they are portraits of various phases of His revelation of God. The meaning of the whole story can be determined only by seeing Him at the end, enthroned at the right hand of God the Father. It is this enthronement that gives significance to His resurrection. It is His resurrection that gives significance to His death, and it is His death that gives significance to His life.

Does this mean that we can dispense with the story of His birth and childhood? One school of thinking tends to believe that Jesus' ministry began with His baptism. For all intents and purposes they leave out the important first thirty years. Another school of thinking, especially in the Roman Church, overemphasizes the birth of Jesus and the exaltation of His mother. It lessens the importance of His later work, practically concluding with His death, and putting little emphasis on the resurrection.

Resist these trains of thought and take the whole story from glory to glory. What do we find? We see the whole Christ, who came from the throne of the Father and is back on that throne now. We see Him confronting us as the living God, born for us and crucified for us. His redemptive work and the power of His resurrection lead us to faith in His divine birth by the work of the Holy Spirit.

When we know Him in this light, we find ourselves identified with Him, as He becomes identified with us. His virgin birth makes us realize that our own new birth is divine. His pure boyhood beckons us on to purity, and growth in Him. Seeing Him as He is leads us on "until we all attain to the unity of the faith and of the knowledge of the Son of God, to mature manhood, to the measure of the stature of the fullness of Christ" (Eph. 4:13).

Nativity

This is by far the best name for the day of joy which we celebrate as the birthday of our Lord. "The Word was made flesh and dwelt among us, (and we beheld his glory, the glory as of the only begotten of the Father) full of grace and truth" (John 1:14). This is the nativity.

That was the incomparable day. The people that had once walked in darkness (Isa. 9:2) were by now sitting in darkness (Matt. 4:16), but God sent the great light to illuminate the darkness of our hearts and to lift men from the abyss of eternal darkness. No human eye could pierce those shadows. The sin of Adam and Eve had caused this darkness to roll over the world and the night would have been eternal without the coming of the Light of the world. The prince of darkness reigned; but the Prince of light was born and sent into this world. The prince of death ruled; but the Lord of life had come. The power of mortality thrusts every generation into the graveyard; but the Baby was born who will banish all the powers of the enemy and bring immortality through the Gospel.

God's love seems all the greater when we realize what He left in order to come here. Everything that is of earth can be contrasted with that which is of Heaven. Yet He left it all for our redemption.

This is why the greatest thought of the nativity must ever be: "Let this mind be in you which was also in Christ Jesus; who, being in the form of God, thought it not robbery to be equal with God; but made himself of no reputation, and took upon him the form of a servant; and was made in the likeness of men" (Phil. 2:5–7).

How great a sin to live in darkness after the Light has come. If the Lord Jesus Christ has not saved you from your sin and then become Lord of your life, the darkness of sin is still upon your soul, your eyes are still blinded, and your life is empty of all that God wants you to have.

Today He says to you, "I am the light of the world; he that followeth me shall have the light of life" (John 8:12).

Incarnation

With the passing days I find that I dislike any pictorial representation of our Lord Jesus. Especially do I abominate the pictures which show Him long faced and long bearded, with a faraway look in His eyes.

It is too bad that we have become accustomed to thinking of the Lord as dressed in a long robe. In His day all men were so dressed, so that there was no difference in His dress from that of any other man. If we would truly think of Jesus as He was when He was on earth, imagine Him in a Sears Roebuck suit and a five-dollar hat, walking through Times Square, not attracting a second glance from anyone. No one would ever have given Jesus Christ a second glance if God had not sent John the Baptist to announce Him. "There standeth one among you whom ye know not" (John 1:26), was the message of the forerunner, while the Holy Spirit tells us, "He was in the world, and the world was made by him, and the world knew him not" (John 1:10). It was only when He was proclaimed and had begun to perform wonders that the crowd came after Him. Even the crowds did not follow Him for anything in Himself though, but only because of the food that He gave them to eat (John 6:26).

If anyone is hurt by my description of the Lord as an unknown, common man, let him read the Word of God which tells us that "He hath no form nor comeliness, and there is no beauty that we should desire him" (Isa. 53:2).

It had to be thus. If the Lord had come in a form that was worthy of Him, every eye that looked upon Him would have been seared blind in its socket. Every nerve that touched Him would have withered and died in a moment. It could not have been otherwise. He is God.

When God gave the specifications for a wilderness tabernacle in which He should be worshipped, He chose a prefabricated house with a few dozen boards that could be taken apart and set up again where the Spirit led through the cloud and the fire. A few badger skins, dyed red, were flung over these boards, and a curtain was hung before the door and another one before the holy place. It had to be that simple. If God had put a temple on this earth which was worthy of His honor, it would have been a weight on this globe that would have outpulled gravity, and the sphere would have gone wobbling through the universe. So God was content with the tabernacle. And when the Lord came He was content to occupy a body that was ordinary even by human standards. Thus we know that He can understand our needs and sympathize with our littleness.

The Word was made flesh and tented among us—for thus the Greek reads (John 1:14). And this is the glory of the incarnation.

Atonement or Crime?

The New York papers on a Monday morning after Palm Sunday carried a report of a sermon by a well-known minister. The headline over the sermon report stated that the noted minister viewed the "Crucifixion as Greatest Crime," and the article carried on the thought by saying that the preacher had declared that Christianity was the only religion which began with the martyrdom of its founder.

This, of course, is absolutely false. Christ was not a martyr, though He Himself has inspired many martyrs. Yet Satan has had his martyrs, too, and many thousands have died in the fanaticism of the faith of Mohammed or other false religions. There is a vast deal of difference between a martyr and the Savior. There could be millions of martyrs, but there has been only one Savior. A martyr dies for a cause, the Savior dies for sinners. "When we were yet without strength, in due time Christ died for the ungodly" (Rom. 5:6). No martyr ever did this. "God commendeth His love toward us, in that, while we were yet sinners, Christ died for us" (Rom. 5:8). No martyr ever did this.

The crucifixion was not a crime. The sinful heart of man crucified Christ, and that sin not only produced hearts that cried out, "Crucify Him," but in this instance has produced a preacher who denied the meaning of that crucifixion.

If someone states that an act that involves the death of a man is by definition a crime, we answer that this may be true from the standpoint of men in acts against other men, but this was not the case in the death of Christ. He was "delivered by the determinate counsel and foreknowledge of God" (Acts 2:23). Though He was taken by wicked hands and crucified and slain yet, nevertheless, "it pleased the Lord to bruise him, he hath put him to grief" (Isa. 53:10).

No man has a right to speak of the crime of the crucifixion if he is not speaking first of the atonement provided by the Father in offering up the Son.

Resurrection

The principle of life out of death is the central principle of the Word of God. That our Lord is life, and that He alone has the power of bringing life out of death is the basis of the Christian faith and of our personal salvation.

When the Lord was going to judge the earth with the deluge, Noah believed that God could sustain life in the midst of death, and entered the ark, the symbol of that power, in order that he might be carried from the damned creation to the new creation.

When Abraham was a hundred years old, he came to close grips with the God who gives life to the dead, and calls into existence the things that do not exist. He looked not at his own body, neither at the deadness of Sarah's womb, "but was strong in faith, giving glory to God; and being fully persuaded that what God had promised he was able also to perform" (Rom. 4:19–21).

Our God, by this same principle of life out of death, brought forth the sinless Savior from the womb of the sinful Mary. It is interesting to

note that a Roman Catholic Pope pointed this out long before the
existence of the modern heresies of Mary's impeccability and quasi-
divinity. Pope Innocent III (A.D. 1199) said, "Mary was produced in sin,
but she brought forth without sin."

At Easter time we celebrate the central illustration of this divine
fact, as we remember that God declared Jesus Christ to be His Son,
with God's own authority and power by His resurrection from the
dead (Rom. 1:4).

Our own salvation is in the belief that God can implant divine life
into the midst of the death of our fallen Adamic nature, making us partakers of the divine nature. It is our triumph that we believe that God
is able to give resurrection life for us to live at the present time, knowing Him in the power of His resurrection (Phil. 3:10).

It is the political hope of this world that the Lord Himself shall
come to bring peace to a world of men of ill will. Only His life can
bring peace and justice to the nations of the world today.

When the last judgment has been completed the Lord will speak
the word that will end the existence of our universe, rolling it up like a
scroll. He will then speak the word that will form the new heavens and
earth in which His resurrection righteousness will exist forever.

The Face of Christ

Two parents were at their work one day when their little daughter came into the room. She wanted to help father and mother who
were at opposite ends of the room, and she asked for something to do.
She went happily about her little "work," which was, of course, not important, but the mere handling of scraps of paper. She was happy, however, because she was "helping."

Then, as children do, she tired of her occupation and went about
her play, returning from time to time to the room where the quiet
work was going on. Finally, she came with a piece of paper and said,
"Please write a letter on this paper." The father smiled, took the paper
and wrote on it and said, "Now please take this note to Mother." The
child carried it across the room and, at first, the mother did not want

to be disturbed, but finally took the paper and read it. It said, "Mother: Look closely at the face of the bearer of this note and tell me just what you think of it!" The mother smiled, swept the child into her arms tightly, and said, "What do I think of this? I think this is precious." The child returned the mother's kiss and went on again to play.

The father continued his work, but could not help thinking of the peculiar relationship of parents and children. What is it that causes the heart to surge with joy at the sight of the child? It is a feeling, an instinct, all a part of that which God has given the human race. Such things have been called "the vestigial remains of the image of God."

Then we think of the Father's love for His Son. The Bible is full of it. It is our guarantee in Heaven at the present moment. We are saved to the uttermost because the Son is there pleading in our behalf. Wesley has written:

> The Father hears Him pray
> The dear anointed One.
> He *cannot* turn away
> The presence of His Son . . .

Here, then, is our assurance. It is Christ in the presence of the Father. Look on the face of Thy Son, O God, and tell me what Thou dost think of Him! And the Father looks, and the answer comes: "I think so much of Him that I sweep Him into My love, and with Him all those 'many sons' whom He brings with Him."

The Finest View

The host always seats his guests so that they can get the finest view. If there is a beautiful vista into the garden, the guest is not seated with his back to it, but is placed at that side of the table which will allow him to lift his eyes from time to time and see the beauties that lie outside. If a guest is taken to some famous hotel, or to some magnificent beauty spot, the host sees to it that the visitor gets the seat with the finest view.

Have you ever stopped to consider how the Lord has placed you when seated at His Table? We come to the communion service and sit as He has placed us. It does not make any difference whether the church faces north, south, east, or west, or whether your seat is in a high gallery, straight out from the pulpit, or to one side in a transept. There is, in spite of any place in which you may be seated, a spiritual vision that has been definitely designed by the Lord. If we fail to look up to see the view that He has placed before us, it is our own loss.

There are three things to take into consideration as we think of the Lord's Table.

First of all, it is generally observed on the first day of the week. This is not the Sabbath of the Law of Moses; this is the Lord's day, the day of resurrection. So we approach the Table on the grounds of the work of the risen Lord Jesus Christ.

Secondly, we are seated with our backs to the cross. Calvary was a judgment for sin, and when we come to the Lord's Table, judgment is behind us. It is God, Himself, who has said that the believer shall not come into judgment but is passed out of death and into life (John 5:24). This is why "there is no condemnation to them who are in Christ Jesus" (Rom. 8:1).

Finally, as we lift the bread and the cup to our lips, we look out across the Table to the view that He has prepared for us "until He come" (1 Cor. 11:26). What a glorious view this is. Not only is judgment past, but glory lies before us. We lift our eyes to His coming; the Lord is at the door. We see Him, no longer the suffering Messiah, no longer in intercession for sinning saints, but in all the glory of the Father, the glory of the adoring angels, and in all His own glory.

When Clemenceau visited the United States, he said at the moment of his return to France that the most wonderful thing he had seen while in America was the view from his dinner table overlooking the Grand Canyon of the Colorado River. Impressive as that view is, it is a view of erosion and death. No abyss, be it ever so deep, no mountain, be it ever so high, can compare with the grandeur and the glory of the scenes that the Lord has placed opposite us as we sit at His Table. Lift the cup high and drink all of it; the glory lies before us. It is "till He come."

True Freedom in Christ

No chains remain when Christ sets a man free. One of the most amazing statements ever spoken by our Lord is that sentence to the Pharisees, "If the Son, therefore, shall make you free, ye shall be free indeed" (John 8:36). Elsewhere He has told us that the one who claims freedom but is yet bound in chains is lying, and is not in the truth (1 John 1:6).

A short story, "How Does It Feel to Be Free?" by the Russian author Manuel Komroff, gives us a vivid illustration of false freedom. We can contrast this story with the reality of freedom that is in Christ. Komroff tells of a convict released after many years in prison. As he walked down the street outside the prison wall, the guard on the tower waved at him and called, "How does it feel to be free?"

Upon returning to the home of his children he was given a room to himself, but found its spaciousness oppressive. He curtained off half of it, replaced the bedsprings with boards, and took the pictures from the walls of the room so that his surroundings would be more like those to which he had become accustomed.

The climax of the story lies in one incident of the "free" man's life. "He amused himself by collecting old bits of wire that he found on old picture frames and in the basement of the apartment house. It gave him great pleasure to send the wire down the neck of a bottle and watch the odd twists and coils it would make in the bottle—as though it were life itself going through its many painful convulsions. He kept the bottle on the open fireplace in front of his window ... By this time the bottle on the window was packed tight with bits of wire. He carried it down to the basement and broke it over the ash can. The heavy wad of iron wire was freed from its container. It was nothing but a rusty, solid mass, the same shape as the bottle that now was scattered in fragments. He turned it in his hand and examined it closely. Was it an experiment that had failed? Did he imagine that the tough springy wires would jump back to their former state once freed? No. It was a rusty solid mass, brown as a cough mixture, and shaped like a bottle. If he had a label, he could paste it on and mark it—'Free!' "

This is precisely what Jesus Christ does *not* do in a life. The entrance of new life is not the breaking of a glass which leaves the old life in its imprisoned form. It is rather the implanting of a new Life that is more powerful than the old. The figures used in the Scripture are those of growing childhood, a spring of flowing water, a living and powerful idea.

On the life which Christ Jesus sets free, it is possible to put the label "Free indeed."

Water of Life

All blessings are to be found in Christ. God tells us very definitely in Ephesians that He has blessed us with all spiritual blessings in Christ. In Romans we have the great promise that "He who spared not his own Son but delivered him up for us all, how shall he not also with him freely give us all things?" (Rom. 8:32).

Christ realized this very distinctly. He also knew that the world's entire need could be met only through Him; in fact, any portion of the world's need would go unmet if He were not the source of supply. This realization appears not only in His great declaration, "Without me ye can do nothing," but also in His general attitude toward the men and women with whom He had contact. We think of Him beside the well, talking to the Samaritan woman and telling her that her great need of the water of life could be met only in Him. In the most simple manner possible, He makes the startling announcement that He is the Messiah.

This announcement is made more majestically in the Gospel of John, when Jesus went up to the Feast of Tabernacles. We find in the seventh chapter that "About the midst of the feast Jesus went up into the temple and taught," and in verse 37 we read, "In the last day, the great day of the feast, Jesus stood and cried, saying, 'If any man thirst, let him come unto me, and drink.' " These words are most significant when we realize the details of the observance of the Feast of Tabernacles. The feast was commemorative of the wilderness march of the children of Israel and of their final entrance into the Promised Land. The feast lasted eight days. During the first seven days, water was drawn from the pool of Siloam, brought up to the temple area, and poured out. This was symbolic of the fact that Israel had drawn water from wells during the wilderness wanderings. On the eight day the water was brought, clear as crystal, from one of the springs of the city. This spring water was symbolic of the fact that after the wilderness march Israel had come into the Promised Land, drinking from springs that would never run dry as long as the people were faithful to God's covenant.

How significant then, that on the last day of the feast, when the source of water had been changed and wells had given way to springs, that Christ should have stood and cried so boldly before all Jerusalem, "If any man thirst, let him come unto me, and drink. He that believeth on me, as the scripture hath said, from the innermost being shall flow rivers of living waters."

We must also record the results of this declaration of our Lord, "There was a division among the people because of him." Strange but true. The presence of Christ reveals the true heart of man. Happy are those who learn to come to Him and drink.

Discipleship

The worst that can be known about eternity and about the Christian life is to be found in the Word of God. When one has seen all that is forbidding in the Scriptures, there is nothing left hidden that can come forth as a surprise. Every new thing which we shall ever learn in this life or the next to come will be a delight. The worst has been told us.

Men often wonder about eternity and about death, and hesitate even before the struggles of life, though our Lord has said, "If it were not so, I would have told you" (John 14:2). The implications of this verse are amazing. He has been careful to underline anything in His service that is cold or forbidding. All that might reflect unfavorably upon Him or the life He calls us to lead has been scrupulously written down. He has held back no accounts of disappointments; He would have told us if there had been anything more to fear than that which has been revealed.

Whenever the disciples were tempted to dream dreams of future grandeur, Christ immediately brought them back to reality. Their discipleship was not the preface to coronation, but to crucifixion. When they talked among themselves concerning places of honor, He told them that they must deny themselves, take up their crosses daily, and follow Him.

Christ was constantly showing men what it would cost to follow Him, but at the same time He invited the whole world to come to Him. It was as though He was saying to them, "I have told you the worst, and the best is not possible to describe. The path through time and eternity will be thus and so," He implied. "If it were not so, I would have told you."

The worst has been told; the best we cannot know now. One of the verses of one of our great hymns says:

> But what to those who find? Ah this
> Nor tongue, nor pen can show,
>
> The love of Jesus, what it is,
> None but His loved ones know.

We knew the worst before we came to Christ. We are now learning the best.

Demons and Deity

Christ asked men questions about Himself. Of unbelievers He asked, "What think ye of Christ; whose Son is he?" Of His own He asked, "Whom say men that I, the Son of man, am?" and again, "Whom say ye that I am?" Yet it was not from men that the true answer first came, though the Pharisees answered well that Messiah was David's Son. When Peter came out with his great confession, Christ declared it to be a supernatural revelation and not the result of man's mental processes.

The reason the true answer concerning the person of Christ did not come first from man is easily understood by the reaction to Peter's confession. It was to be expected that the unbelieving Pharisees would not own Him, for "the natural man receiveth not the things of the

Spirit of God, for they are foolishness unto him, neither can he know them, for they are spiritually discerned" (1 Cor. 2:14). But from those that followed Jesus we would have expected more. Nevertheless, the answer is the same, "Flesh and blood hath not revealed it unto thee." Man's deductive or intuitive faculties are incapable of spiritual discovery, even if one is a follower of Christ. Even the Christian is dependent upon God for spiritual revelation by the Holy Spirit.

Who then was the very first to proclaim His deity after His ministry had begun? Not man, unsaved or saved—but two demons. "They cried out, saying, 'What have we to do with thee, Jesus, thou Son of God?' " (Matt. 8:29). Of course they knew this through God's permission; it is clearly indicated in Scripture that Satan and his host are aware that judgment is awaiting them because of Jesus Christ. The whole of Satan's force was alive to the attack upon Christ from the time of His birth. "Art thou come hither to torment us before the time?" we hear them screech. And though it was wrung from them, it was nevertheless a confession.

Yet there are men today—men of blinded eyes and blinded hearts—who dare deny the Deity that not even demons could deny. All who deny that Deity will one day be forced to bow the knee before it—but they will then be in the lake of fire. All Unitarian tongues, though today they may be satisfied with calling Him the wayshower, the great example, or the perfect man, must one day confess, though too late, that He, Jesus Christ, is Lord Jehovah of all.

But now, today, "If thou shalt confess with thy mouth Jesus as Lord, and shalt believe in thy heart that God hath raised him from the dead, thou shalt be saved" (Rom. 10:9).

No Creed but Christ

There are those who cry out that they do not want any creed but Christ. We answer, "What Christ?" And the answer to that question is, of necessity, a creed.

A minister once said that it was a shame that the church could not follow Paul on the road to Damascus. He had not been bothered with questions of theological dogma. He had simply said, "Lord, what wilt thou have me to do?" The minister evidently had not read the Word of God very closely. If we realize that the Greek word for Lord was undoubtedly the same as the translation of the Hebrew, *Jehovah,* we have the beginning of a creed in the very question.

Further, we must realize that before Paul asked for orders he had previously asked another question, "Who art thou, Lord?" Take it any way you like, the answer to that question is a creed, and the Lord wants us to be clear and plain in our concept of that answer. He keeps questioning until the relationship is firmly established.

As the disciples were discussing the roadside gossip, the Lord came to them and broke into their thoughts. "Whom do men say that I, the Son of man, am?" The answer to that question is a creed, and the disciples' answers showed the varying creeds of the world, all of them false. This did not satisfy our Lord. He kept on questioning. The "but" in His phrase of inquiry is luminous. "But whom say ye that I am?" The "but" shows that Jesus Christ was not satisfied with the thought of the world. Indeed, how could eternal Truth be satisfied with Satanic error?

It was Peter who answered, "Thou art the Christ, the Son of the living God" (Matt. 16:16). This answer satisfied the Lord and He immediately explained to the disciples that the answer was a divine revelation, not merely a thought that might have equal value with other opinions. This was truth. Everything else is to be excluded. *Christ* is the translation of the Greek word that is equivalent to the Hebrew *Messiah.* "Thou art the Messiah!" This embraces the whole of the Old Testament. This is indeed a creed. "Thou art the Son of the living God!" This embraces the heart of the Godhead.

The second Psalm shows us one of the many sides of the creed of Christ. In this Psalm, the Father answers the rebellion of the world with this prophetic statement about the coming of Christ, "Thou art my Son; this day have I begotten thee." And He continues to show that this Son is to be His final answer to the world. What a creed! And we have every right to say that this is Christ's own creed.

The Love of Christ

The Word of God tells us that we were loved before we were capable of loving in return. "When we were yet without strength, in due time Christ died for the ungodly ... God commendeth his love toward us, in that while we were yet sinners, Christ died for us" (Rom. 5:6, 8). "We love him because he first loved us" (1 John 4:19).

When a man and a woman truly love each other they spend some time talking over the wonder of their acquaintance. "When did you first know you loved me?" "Do you remember the first time we met?" "What did you think of me when we were first introduced?" These and a thousand similar questions make up the ever-fragrant conversations of true love. There can be no such questions about the relationship between our Lord and ourselves. It was when we were lost that He found us. It was when we were dead that He brought life to us. It was when we were without strength that He came as the strong one to deliver us. It was when we were unlovely sinners that He manifested His grace by stooping to love us.

If there is any true love on our part toward the Lord, it is because we have learned to know who He is and what He has done for us. "We love him because he first loved us." We know the verse, but we do not love Him as we should. If we find that our love is cold, it is because we have not spent time with Him, for how could we gaze upon Him and not be entranced with Him? How can we see Him moving among men and not be touched with His compassion?

It does not suffice to have learned all the verses that recount His praise. There are those writers of the Word who have spoken of Him as "the fairest among ten thousand," "the lily of the valley," "the altogether lovely," or "the bright and morning star." All this is but a trick of the memory if we do not show in our lives the love that we bear for Him in our hearts.

It may be well for the child of God to spend time asking and answering the question concerning our love for the Lord. Do we not overestimate what we think of the Lord? We cannot overestimate what He has done for us nor how deeply He loves us. The Lord came to Peter who had boasted of his great love for the Master, and asked him twice if he really did have a great all-encompassing passion for Him. The chastened disciple twice answered that he did have an *affection* for the Lord. The Savior then came down to the lower level of Peter's word and asked, using the Greek word *phileo,* "Hast thou this affection for me?" Peter was grieved because the Lord came down to this lesser word, and cast himself upon the Lord with an abandon of emotion that showed how much chaff had been taken away in Satan's sifting. The Lord made no effort to claim more than the renewed heart knew was there. Peter knew that the Lord had planted love within him, and he knew that the Lord knew it. "Lord, thou knowest all things; thou knowest that I love thee."

The Savior knew that He had begun a good work in Peter which He could continue to perfect until His return. So in His great grace He did not turn away from Peter because the disciple's love was small. Instead, the Lord gave him his commission for service, and began a lifelong work in His servant.

Thus our confidence must be in our Lord. In all of His grace, He will not turn us away for failing Him.

Our Providence

Worldlings have very strange ideas about Providence. Insurance companies list, under acts of Providence, all the great catastrophes. If a combination of circumstances gives a happy result, men say that the matter is providential.

The Word of God tells us not that Providence is the Author of all the sinister tragedies that come upon men, but that He is none other than the Lord Jesus Christ. We know from the Book of Job that it was Satan who, when he was granted the permission, brought war, lightning, rapine, and the great wind from the wilderness, all of which left a trail of death. We also know that it was Satan who, when he was granted further permission, brought disease upon Job. So, in saying that the Lord Jesus Christ is Providence, we are not charging Him with the ills of mankind.

It was Isaac Watts who wrote:

> His very Word of grace is strong
> As that which built the skies;
> The voice that rolls the stars along
> Speaks all the promises.

Do we have Biblical authority for that statement? We are convinced that we do have such authority. If we turn to the first chapter of the Epistle to the Hebrews we find God's great description of His Son, Jesus Christ. Our Lord has been appointed Heir of all things. It is by Him that God made the ages. He is the brightness of God's glory; He is the express image of God's person. We can understand the meaning of this if we think of the relation of the image on a coin to the die which stamps the coin. Christ is elsewhere spoken of as the image of the invisible God (Col. 1:15). The die may be invisible, but our Lord is visible.

After this great series of statements concerning the eternal Son, Paul says of Christ that He is "upholding all things by the word of his power" (Heb. 1:3). Is this not a perfect description of Providence? What is it that keeps the stars in their courses? The Lord Jesus Christ. What is it that keeps us from being whirled off into space by the force of this spinning earth? It is the Lord Jesus Christ. What is it that makes all of the atoms obey the laws which chemistry is charting? The Lord Jesus Christ. What is it that holds the seas in bounds, orders the seasons, causes the trees to bud and the flowers to spring, and brings life from generation to generation? The Lord Jesus Christ.

There is none other that is Providence. Is there another way we can *know* that all things work together for good to those who love Him? The one who orders the universe is none other than our Redeemer.

Our God

An old poem has recently reappeared. Like a hardy perennial it comes up again and again, and the undiscerning will find it good, since they read it through sentiment and not through the Word of God.

Richard Watson Gilder wrote:

> If Jesus Christ is a man,
> And only a man, I say
> That of all mankind I cleave to Him,
> And to Him I will cleave alway.
>
> If Jesus Christ is a God,
> And the only God, I swear
> I will follow Him through Heaven and hell,
> The earth, the sea and the air.

According to the truth of God it would be necessary to change the first verse to read something like this:

> If Jesus Christ is a man,
> And only a man, I say
> That of all mankind He a liar is
> For leading so many astray.

Let us apply the simple method of choice between two alternatives. Jesus Christ certainly claimed to be God. That claim is either true or false. If it is true, and we know it is true, then He is God, and all things are subject unto Him. If it is false, then either He knew that the claim was false or He did not. Let us take these propositions and analyze them.

If Jesus Christ made a false claim to be God, knowing that the claim was false, He was a liar of the first order. If He made a false claim to be God, not knowing that it was a false claim, He was simply insane. In such a case we would have to classify Him with those in asylums who think they are Napoleon, Hitler, or God, as some poor creatures do. There is no fourth possibility. Jesus Christ is God, a liar, or a lunatic.

The Christian knows on grounds of inner conviction that Jesus is his Lord, both in clear title and in the Lordship of life. He is our God.

Our Standard

There was a day when men were not worried if weights and measures were only approximate. The inch was the measure of the large joint of the king's thumb. The foot was the length of the royal foot and the yard was the distance between the king's nose when he was looking straight front, and the end of his thumb when his arm was extended to the side.

Of course these standards are now much more exact than they used to be. In 1926, when Mr. John E. Sears was the leading British authority on metrology, he reported to the Royal Institute of Great Britain that the standard yard of Queen Elizabeth's reign had still been in use as the standard in 1824. During the interval it had been broken and "crudely repaired by dowelling and binding the two pieces together with two strips of sheet brass and copper wire." This is enough to make any self-respecting scientist's hair turn!

Is it not astonishing then, that when men are willing to spend vast sums of money and great time and energy to measure the millionth part of the width of a hair, that they are so lax in their desire for moral and spiritual measure? Yet God has given us standards more exact than any yet devised by man. The Book and the Man do not vary the decillionth part of a millimeter in their unchanging standards.

Do you wish to know what God requires of you? The law will measure you to show how far short you fall. Do you want to learn what God's possibility of manhood really is? The matchless Lord Jesus will reveal every shade of this perfection. Do you want to know the cost of bridging the distance between your fallen heart and the white holiness of God? The cross will measure it to the last infinite cent. Do you want to know the speed with which God can bring you from the infinite depth of sin to the infinite height of the glorious position of the sons of God? The justifying grace of the loving Father can be the measure of that infinitesimal moment that brings you out of death and into life.

It took an expedition of French scientists more than a year to find the length of the meter. They described it as one forty-millionth of the earth's circumference measured on the equator at sea level. When they returned to Paris with their results, they were challenged by some scientists who said that the meter could not be exact because of contraction due to the change of temperature, and by others who said that the equator was a circle, and a section of an arc could not be as exact as the section of a straight line.

No one can question our divine measures, however, for Christ never faileth: "but whether there be prophecies, they shall fail; whether there be tongues, they shall cease; whether there be knowledge, it shall vanish away . . . And now abideth faith, hope," . . . and Christ, but the greatest of these is Christ. His expedition to earth to confirm the divine measures can never be called into question.

Our Sovereign

It is not astounding that the world often makes itself foolish. The world works by the rule of knowledge, and God clearly tells us that if the world leaders had "*known,* they would not have crucified the Lord of glory" (1 Cor. 2:8).

We have a right, therefore, to pity those who go against God's plan. "The god of this age hath blinded the minds of them which believe not, lest the light of the glorious gospel of Christ, who is the image of God, should shine unto them" (2 Cor. 4:4). Man is most pitiful, however, when he is blind while playing with that which could give him sight and light. A deaf mute at an orchestra concert or a blind boy fingering a scalpel which might be the means of giving him vision excite more pity than they would under other circumstances. So the worldling quoting Scripture is, perhaps, the saddest sight that this world can offer.

Across the square from the Capitol in Washington stands the magnificent Union Station. Above its entrance we glance at the inscriptions carved in the stone. The first panel reads *"Thou hast put all things under his feet."* Instinctively comes the thought of the return of our Lord Jesus, and His destruction of death, the last enemy that is to be destroyed. In the great glorification chapter in First Corinthians the climax of the whole sweeping revelation is in this great triumph of Christ, when God "hath put all things under his feet," after death, "the last enemy," has been destroyed.

These thoughts flash through our minds before we read any other part of the carved inscriptions. Then, in the next panel, we read, *"The truth shall make you free."* This, of course, is part and parcel of Jesus' great message of Himself as the Light of the world.

The third panel announces boldly, *"The desert shall rejoice and blossom as the rose."* We recognize this as Isaiah's magnificent prophecy of the miracle of the Lord's return, when, just as we shall be transformed by seeing Him, so shall the very earth be changed by the brightness of His presence. "Instead of the thorn shall grow up the fir tree, and instead of the brier shall come up the myrtle tree" (Isa. 55:13). All this shall take place in the moment when the groaning earth shall see her returning Lord come to make all things right.

But what on earth are these three verses doing, cut into the stone facade of Union Station? After looking more closely, we realize that we have read from left to right, reading merely the three Bible verses that are separated from the body of their inscriptions by a long line. Then we read the inscription itself. We need not read far before we know that poor, blind man has been very foolish once again. The first inscription is, "Fire—Greatest of discoveries—Enabling man to live in various climates—Use many foods and compel the Forces of Nature to do his work—Electricity—carrier of light and power—Devourer of time and space—Bearer of Human speech over land and sea—Greatest servant of man—itself unknown—*Thou hast put all things under his feet.*" Under whose feet? Why, under man's feet. Better still, we should write it, "Under *man's* feet." In the Bible, the passage refers to God placing all things under the feet of Jesus Christ. In the Washington inscription all things were placed under *man's* feet.

Poor man! This is man's day. We cannot expect anything else than that he would attempt to rob the Lord of some of His glory. The other inscriptions are similar in thought. Man has achieved; man has wrought. Glory be to man.

But in this world the Lord Jesus has His own. We delight to confess that this world is enmity against God; we acknowledge that the world by wisdom knew not God. We admit that nothing of permanent good can come from man.

> From the best bliss that earth imparts
> We turn, unfilled, to Thee again.

Our Hope

The prism is a light breaker. The pure, clear light passes through the varied facets of the prism and is broken into red, orange, yellow— all the shades of color. Science has studied it all out and found that it all works according to cold law. The sun shines through the warm spring rain; the drops of water catch the light, break it to pieces, and throw it across the sky in the glory of a rainbow.

The rainbow is more than the mechanics of physical law, though. God set it as the sign of a covenant and the surety of His promise. Man has made the rainbow a symbol of hope.

In the Scriptures we learn to realize the full meaning of hope. Man is born in sin, with his face turned toward the lake of fire. One of the most terrible phrases in the revelation that God has given us is that man is "without hope." Draw the shades of night. The sun is gone, the moon is blotted out, the clouds have curtained out the stars; no light seeps through to show the way to the lost wanderer. Man is without hope. And then "in due time" Christ appears. "The light of the knowledge of the glory of God (is) in the face of Jesus Christ" (2 Cor. 4:6). What does that light reveal? "His visage was so marred, more than any man" (Isa. 52:14). It shows us tears, the tears of God, running down His face like rain, and mingling with His blood. What a prism for God's eternal light! All the colors of Heaven were broken up in those tears when the hours of darkness were over and the light of God's holiness broke forth anew; out across the blackened sky was flung a rainbow. Hope for the lost was won by the cross. Hope for the past—the blood has washed it away; hope for the present—the Lord is risen to reflect His light in us; hope for the future—blessed hope. He has won the right to return as conqueror and to bring His myriads with Him. This rainbow reaches from the solid rock of the cross to the eternal abiding place, and man is forever secure.

The Tempter and Temptation

The Creator and the Creature

Enmity was put between Satan and the Lord Jesus (Gen. 3:15). Whenever we contrast these two, the creature and the Creator, the wonders of our Lord Jesus shine out as in no other comparison.

This thought occurred to me while I was studying the meanings of some of the names of Satan. He is called "the accuser of the brethren," but our Lord is "the Mediator for the brethren"; Satan is called "the slanderer," but the Lord will find something to praise even in those who at the best are unprofitable servants. Satan is called "the wicked one," while our Lord is "the Holy One"; he is "a liar" and the Lord is called "the Truth." He is called "the old serpent," subtle and deceiving, where Christ is presented as "the Lamb without spot or blemish, guileless and atoning."

In the fourteenth chapter of Isaiah there is a picture of Satan which furnishes us with probably the greatest contrast in the Scripture. Satan said in his heart, "I will" (Isa. 14:13). When Christ came into the world He said, "Lo, I come . . . to do thy will, O God" (Heb. 10:7). In Satan's remark we have the simplest definition of sin, "I will." This phrase on any lip or in any heart is a tangent drawn away from the straight line of God's truth, the distance ever widening as the willful one persists in any will that is not the Father's.

The five "I wills" of Satan in this passage are a cry of greed. "I will ascend . . . I will exalt . . . I will sit . . . I will ascend . . . I will be like . . . ." All of these are covetousness, which is idolatry (Col. 3:5).

The last of the declarations of Satan was "I will be like the Most High." Why did he choose to be like that particular phase of God's nature? There are almost four hundred titles for our Lord in the Word of God. Each name or title reveals a different aspect of the Creator. It is significant, however, that Satan desired to be like the Most High.

When Abraham returned from the Battle of the Kings, he was met by Melchizedek who was priest "of the most high God, possessor of heaven and earth." Through pride, Satan wished to exalt himself to that manifestation of God which seemed to carry with it authority in the realm over which he had been placed as prince, having been set in authority by God (Ezek. 28:14; Luke 4:6).

With Satan it is "I will go up; I will be more; I will seize; I will possess." Our Lord Jesus "being in the form of God, thought it not robbery to be equal with God: but made himself of no reputation, and took upon him the form of a servant, and was made in the likeness of men: and being found in fashion as a man, he humbled himself, and became obedient unto death, even the death of the cross" (Phil. 2:6–8). It is this contrast that so reveals the heart of our Lord. In Him there is no self-seeking. Though Satan cries, "I will go up," Christ cries, "I will go down." "Thou madest him a little lower than the angels" (Heb. 2:7). It is for this that we fall at His feet and praise God that He has once again been made high above the angels, and been given the Name that is above every name. Gladly we worship Him as Lord of all.

The Snake's Head

It was a startling headline, but the article that followed told a startling story. The Associated Press dispatch was from San Antonio, Texas. The headline was "Snake's Head Bites Man." The news item was as follows:

"The severed head of a rattlesnake bit a man here. Olin Dillon, snake handler at a local reptile garden, severed the snake's head yesterday. When he attempted to remove the snake's head from the chopping block, the fangs struck one of his fingers. He was hospitalized. Jack Davenport, garden director, said the bite resulted from muscular reflex action and that Dillon received more venom than from the usual bite."

There are many important passages in the Bible which compare the workings of Satan to those of a snake, and he is particularly identified as "that old serpent, called the Devil, and Satan" (Rev. 12:9). Not the least interesting are those passages which refer to the crushing of Satan's head and his activities after that crushing. It is for this reason that the news item arouses interest.

In the Garden of Eden, the Lord addressed the following prophecy through the serpent to the devil, "And the Lord God said unto the serpent, Because thou hast done this, thou art cursed above all cattle, and above every beast of the field; upon thy belly shalt thou go, and dust shalt thou eat all the days of thy life; and I will put enmity between thee and the woman, and between thy seed and her seed; *it shall bruise thy head,* and thou shalt bruise his heel" (Gen. 3:14, 15). We know that this was accomplished at Calvary, for we are told that the purpose for which Jesus Christ took a human body was "that through death he might destroy him that had the power of death, that is, the devil" (Heb. 2:14). It is correct for us to say that all of the work which Satan has been doing since the time of Christ's death may be likened to the lashings of the body of the serpent. The believer is safe while he is conscious of his position *in* Christ; it is only as he moves out of that condition, relying on his own strength, that Satan can touch him. It is wonderful to know that "the God of peace shall bruise Satan under your feet shortly" (Rom. 16:20).

The time is to come—it is a time definitely fixed in the plan of God (Hab. 2:3; Heb. 10:37)—when Satan shall be cast out of Heaven into the earth (Rev. 12:9) where he shall agitate briefly before he is dealt with eternally. Just as the Texas snake gave more venom in the bite after his head was severed, so the Scripture tells us that Satan's last activities shall be his most furious. "Woe to the inhabiters of the earth and of the sea! for the devil is come down unto you, having great wrath, because he knoweth that he hath but a short time" (Rev. 12:12).

But the Lord, who has provided protection from all of the fiery darts of the wicked one (Eph. 6:16), has planned the ultimate and eternal removal of this defeated foe and the day will come when the universe shall know his work no more.

Enemy Strategy

The nation was horrified when it learned that Japan had sent ambassadors of peace to talk peace while the aircraft carriers were moving into place for the bombing of Pearl Harbor. The enemy had tricked us with a very old strategy. He had made us think that his intentions were good when they were really bad, and he had hidden his presence from us in order that he might more effectively strike at us. There is an ancient proverb which says, "Beware of Greeks, bearing gifts." The same trick that deceived us had been used often in ancient times.

The origin of that trick is not the work of men, though. The Bible gives us a very clear picture of the enemy of souls at that same kind of work. Paul says, speaking of Satan, "We are not ignorant of his devices" (2 Cor. 2:11). Certainly there is no need for ignorance concerning the devices of the devil, for they are set forth plainly in the Word of God, and they are also visible all around us.

Yet if you should go down the street on a sidewalk quiz program, Mr. Average-man might tell you that he is not even sure that there is such a being as a real devil. Such a man should say to himself, "Remember Pearl Harbor." It was when they got us to thinking that they were not there, that they were able to hit us hardest. Satan is not spreading the idea that he does not exist because he is modest, shy, and retiring, but because he is the enemy of souls.

Another one of his characteristic stratagems is to give those who believe that he does exist an entirely wrong concept of what his true nature and character really are. In the Middle Ages, when there were no radios, no magazines, no newspapers, no movies, no telephones, and none of our modern means of passing the time, the people were frequently amused by the miracle plays. These were a sort of religious pageant in which religious stories were acted out on the stage. The audience learned to look for one character on the stage who was always dressed in red, wore horns on his head, and a tail dangling out behind him. His hoofs were cloven, and he had a pitchfork in his hand. The onlookers were quite thrilled when they saw this figure sneaking up on the hero or the heroine. The idea arose that Satan could be called the "old Nick," or "his satanic majesty," and that he was a slightly comic character.

It is always dangerous to underestimate the enemy. The Bible gives us the true picture of this being: that he really exists, and that he is the enemy of men. We need, religiously, to get over the idea that Satan is a comic character and realize that he is a malignant being of great power who hates men. He hates us because God has said that He is someday going to replace the rule of Satan by the rule of righteous man, under Christ. We will do best to submit ourselves to God, and to realize that the death of Jesus Christ was the means whereby the Lord conquered Satan. We must submit ourselves to the Savior who will enable us to live lives of victory over the enemy.

Do We Rush On?

Hundreds of millions of people pray each week, "Lead me not into temptation." But there are many Christians who pray this prayer, either intelligently or unintelligently, and immediately rush into temptation and force themselves to live and act in its shadow.

I was once taking a walk at sunset in a North India hill station. My host led me on a path that followed the flank of the mountain, and to one side was a vast panorama of beauty. Here and there smaller, private paths led from this main path to the homes that were dotted over the hillside. At one of these junctions was an odd sight. The owner had planted a post on either side of his private path and between these posts had placed a gate. The posts were strong, the gate was heavy, a chain held it shut, and a padlock secured the chain, but the posts were not connected to any fence. Within a step of one of the posts was a well-worn path that led around the gate, and anyone who wished could have walked on the path and gone his way as readily as if the postholes had never been dug or the gate planted across the path.

Is this not a picture of much of Christian effort toward a life of victory? The forms of religion are well-planted; ideas of sanctification may be securely locked into the framework of proper doctrine, but these are not joined up to life, and are not living. Too often we make provision for the flesh, in direct disobedience to God's command (Rom. 13:14).

The heart that has accepted God's verdict concerning the old nature and the weakness of the flesh will ever be ready to cry, "Lead me not into temptation; do not put me to the test." But what is more, this believer will constantly realize that the fence is there, that the old nature has been crucified with Christ and will always be on the far side of the main path. The believer will keep the Lord between him and the temptation, and will put his eyes on the view whose beauties the Lord is so eager to point out to him.

The dust of the dead in the catacombs of Rome has a greater influence in the world today than the bodies of many Christians who are still warm with life. It is not enough to be physically alive; there must be a positive witness in life. When this witness has been lived, death cannot end it. Abel "being dead yet speaketh" (Heb. 11:4).

There is a great difference between believing with the mind and believing with the heart. Psychologists may laugh at this, but the Scripture and experience will tell us that there is a difference. "If people see a lion, they run away," says Stevenson in one of his essays. "If they only apprehend a deduction, they keep wandering around in an experimental humor." He goes on to show that a good writer must convince like nature and not like books. The mind of a man walking down a railroad track may become mentally convinced that a train is coming. Faith with the heart moves him to get off the track. It is "with the heart man believeth unto righteousness" (Rom. 10:10).

There is a great deal of difference between oratory and evangelical preaching. Beecher and Moody were contemporaries, and both moved their generation. A few years after the end of Beecher's ministry, unbelief had settled down in his pulpit, with death following in its train. Moody had done his main work in a mean part of his city, yet his work has grown with the passing years. The one had made an irruption like the Parthian hordes who dashed away again, shooting while they retreated; the other had conquered like a Roman and had settled colonies.

So frequently we hear Christians, speaking of those who hold false doctrine, say that they are such great personalities, apparently believing that personal charm excuses error. Charles of Orleans clashed frequently with his cousin, King Louis XI, over the discipline of enemies of the state when these enemies were his personal acquaintances. "No matter what treason he may have made or meddled with," says a historian, "an Alençon or an Armagnac was sure to find Charles reappear from private life, and do his best to get him pardoned. He knew them quite well. He had made rondels with them. They were charming people in every way. There must certainly be some mistake." But Louis XI cut their heads off and saved France from civil war. He could see treason through charm.

God tells us that every mouth will be stopped and that all the world will be brought guilty before Him (Rom. 3:19). Mrs. Samuel Pepys wrote out a list of her just complaints against her husband, recounting in plain English his infidelities. Mr. Pepys, in an agony lest the world should come to see it, brutally snatched and destroyed the telltale document. Then, strange to say, he immediately went to his diary and wrote out a full account of all her charges, admitting their truth, so that the world knows him for what he was, but in his own handwriting. Thus the conscience and memory of man will war against him when he comes to face his Judge. Only the blood of Jesus Christ can take away the burden of sin and remove it even from the memory of God.

William Penn and Samuel Pepys were near neighbors, and Pepys was much disturbed when the Quaker wrote his "Sandy Foundation Shaken." Stevenson says of the incident, "Pepys had his own foundation, sandy enough, but dear to him from practical considerations, and he would read the book with true uneasiness of spirit; for conceive the blow if, by some plaguey accident, this pen were to convert him! It was a different kind of doctrine that he judged profitable for himself and others. He writes in his diary, 'A good sermon of Mr. Gifford's at our church on "Seek ye first the kingdom of Heaven," a very excellent and persuasive, good and moral sermon. He showed like a wise man, that righteousness is a surer moral way of being rich than sin and villainy.' It is thus that respectable people desire to have their Greathearts address them, telling, in mild accents, how you may make the best of both worlds, and be a moral hero without courage, kindness, or troublesome reflection; and thus the Gospel cleared of Eastern metaphor becomes a manual of worldly prudence, and a handybook for Pepys and the successful merchant."

Ruskin points out that we posses a fatal power of equivocation through the fact that we possess words from Greek and Latin sources on the one hand and from Saxon on the other. He uses as an example the word "bible" which comes from the Saxon. We use the Greek word with a capital letter when we want to dignify one book, and translate it into English in the common instances. He says, "How wholesome it would be for many simple persons if, in such places as Acts 19:19, we retained the Greek expression instead of translating it, and they had to read—'many of them also which used curious arts, brought their bibles together, and burnt them before all men; and they counted the price of them and found it fifty thousand pieces of silver!' Or if, on the other hand, we translated where we retain it, and always spoke of 'The Holy Book,' instead of 'Holy Bible.' It might come into more heads than it does at present, that the Word of God by which the heavens were, of old, and by which they are now kept in store (2 Peter 3:5–7), cannot be made a present of to anybody in Morocco binding; nor sown on any wayside by help either of steam plow or steam press; but is nevertheless being offered to us daily, and by us with contumely refused; and sown in us daily, and by us, as instantly as may be, choked."

Run Away . . . and Fast

The devil may yell "Coward!" after you, but do not be afraid to run away. There is only one method of meeting temptation—flee to the Lord. If it is necessary, the Christian can flee to the Lord in the very midst of a great temptation, but it is better for him to flee even from the situation where the temptation will be greatest.

In other words, a Christian who knows that he has been tempted (whether or not he has yielded) to pilfer small amounts in a job as cashier would not only have the right but the duty to ask for transfer to another job, not being afraid to state the reason why. Such a testimony would increase confidence rather than destroy it. Men or women who know that they are possessed of a very strong appetite for drink will properly avoid invitations to gatherings where liquor will flow freely. Knowledge of our weakness should give us an indisposition to put ourselves in a place of temptation. A high school girl once came to me and said that she had frightful temptations to "pet" with all her dates and asked if it were cowardly to avoid all but double dates. I told her that the Lord had given her that desire to avoid temptation and that she should follow it.

The Lord is able to keep money out of the hand of the one who knows the roots of pilfering are in him, and is able to do it right on the job where opportunity for sin abounds. The Lord is able to keep abstinent the one with appetite for drink, even though he finds himself in the midst of many drinkers. The Lord is able to keep the girl or boy clean even in the face of the clamant desires of the flesh. But the Christian who knows what the Word of God has to say about the weakness of man's nature will not flaunt that nature in the face of temptation.

I have a letter written by one who had been invited into a situation where there would be great attendant temptation. Its example is worth following. The person wrote, "I am afraid. I know that I have been growing in the Lord and that He is furnishing strength above measure. But I do not want in any way to pray 'Lead me not into temptation' and then walk straight into it. I am afraid. I know you will understand. Therefore I am going to do the only thing that is consistent with a Christian's position when he finds himself in such a situation . . . run away. The devil may cry 'Coward,' but discretion is not only the better part of valor, but it is the better part of Christian living."

This believer was obeying the command of the Lord to make no provision for the flesh (Rom. 13:14). The Christian who has shown the Lord and himself that he hates sin will find increased strength and power when he suddenly finds himself in a place of temptation which he knows he did not place himself in by his own premeditated choice. The Lord put him in that place, and will with the testing, make a way of escape that he may be able to bear it (1 Cor. 10:13).

Fretting

One of the great tests of our spiritual advance is the way in which we "take" criticism. Some Christians cannot stand any criticisms of themselves or their work, and become fretful in the face of it.

Some time ago I had a telephone call from a man well known in his profession and active in his church where, as a layman, he carries on an earnest work of teaching. He made an appointment to see me, and within a few moments was at my doorstep, greatly perturbed. Something had happened to disturb his peace of mind. An incident had occurred which caused some people to criticize him. Someone had failed to consult him in a professional capacity at a time where his position and attainments would have made him the logical man to consult. He was disturbed and agitated; his feelings were ruffled. He was hurt. What should he do about it?

When he had finished pouring out his heart, I sat and looked at him in absolute silence. After a moment—and a moment can seem long when there is absolute silence—he started to talk again, but I silenced him with a gesture. Then I said quietly, "God has said, 'Be still and know that I am God' " (Ps. 46:10). There was another moment of silence.

I then told him of an incident which had made a profound impression upon me in my earlier life. There was a time when there was real persecution. Bitter words had been spoken against me and my work, and I was on trial over a long, dragged-out period. Worst of all, on advice of counsel I was forbidden to say a word about it to any other person. Over the course of a year or two that can really have an effect! I was learning what it was to "answer not again." During that very trying period I was walking down one of Philadelphia's principal streets when a godly man, an official in one of the great denominational headquarters, came up to me. He started to speak of the events which had received publicity and I answered that I could make no comment. He understood and put out his hand with a strong grasp, saying, "They haven't spit in your face yet, have they?" The answer was "No." "Well, then, you have a long way to go before you are like Christ, for that is what He got."

Those words have been of great comfort to me through the years, and I was able to give them to my visitor. Then I pointed out that all that was hurt was in his old nature. He was defending that which Christ had said should be kept crucified with Him. If the incident which had upset him had been cast upon the Lord there would have been great peace. My visitor became calm as soon as he understood this. He stopped twisting his handkerchief, and was filled with inward peace.

Fretting is the caressing of the old nature. Peace is the gift of the Heavenly Father to those who put everything on Him.

Danger Signals

God had danger signals long before the railroad developed them. Railroads are making their signals safer and safer, as they wish to avoid accidents, but God has already perfected His.

In the history of railroading, danger signals began with the flagman and the red lantern. Swift trains received their only intimation of coming danger from such imperfect sources. Then came petards on the track, hand block signals, and electric block signals. Now the Pennsylvania announces the "electric eye." In the cab of the engine will be an electric reproduction of wayside signals miles ahead. If the signal is "Stop," there will be a loud warning whistle in addition, that will not cease until the driver acknowledges, mechanically, that he has received the signal. Trains hurtling along the rails at eighty miles an hour can pick up these delicate signals and record them unerringly. Thus the engineer, regardless of the snow or fog, always has before him the track conditions ahead, as indicated by the wayside signals.

The Christian goes through the world beset with greater spiritual dangers than any material dangers that lie in the path of a fast limited. "We wrestle not against flesh and blood, but against principalities, against powers, against the rulers of the darkness of this world, against spiritual wickedness in high places" (Eph. 6:12). Satan or his minions may bring us temptation, or something may come from the flesh itself to war against the soul. God has a perfect signal system against any such spiritual danger. "There hath no temptation taken you but such as is common to man: but God is faithful, who will not suffer you to be tempted above that ye are able; but will with the temptation also make a way to escape, that ye may be able to bear it" (1 Cor. 10:13). Note this precious promise. God is faithful. He who keepeth us neither slumbers nor sleeps. Every time a temptation of any kind is put in your path, He provides a way of escape. A factor of nature might endanger the track of a railroad, but the signal could not pick up the peril and transmit it to the oncoming train. God is faithful; He has never failed and never will. He plants within us His Holy Spirit, who is so sensitive to the presence of sin that every intimation of its approach is recorded. Sanctification is the process whereby God trains us to heed the Spirit's signals.

The Lord Jesus lived His life *as a man,* but He was so spiritually alive to every onslaught of the enemy that the signals were in every case heeded. "He was tempted in all points like as we are and yet without sin" (Heb. 4:15). If we are to be like Him, it must be in the path that He trod. The dangers will not diminish, but if we will to do His will, we will heed the signals that God gives us every time the enemy of the flesh brings any temptation. Thus we will be able to bear it.

Set in Safety

A friend recently asked what I felt was my greatest spiritual need. I replied that I was conscious of very many lacks but that I felt that one of my greatest was to know more of the Word of God in order that I might know Him better. My friend was astonished, saying that he knew I had lived my life within the horizons of the Bible and knew a great deal about it. I replied that I knew enough to know how much more there was to know, and that I sometimes felt like a man who had been running for a long distance—chest heaving, lungs pulling for more oxygen. It is possible to long after God with such panting.

In answer to this need there is a great promise.

There is a verse in the King James Version which is meaningless because the translators could not compass the Hebrew, but which is luminous in the more modern versions. In Psalm twelve we read, "'For the oppression of the poor, for the sighing of the needy, now will I arise,' saith the Lord. 'I will set *him* in safety *from him* that puffeth at him' " (vs. 5). The words in italics show that the translators were on unsure ground and added words to make what they thought was sense.

The American Standard Version reads, "I will set him in the safety he panteth for"; and the Revised Standard Version reads, "I will place him in the safety for which he longs."

What a wonderful promise this is! Here is true safety. It is the safety that we long for, that we pant for. When we feel any oppression whatsoever in our spiritual poverty, the Lord undertakes for us. When, because of our need, we sigh, the Lord arouses Himself in our behalf. When we are out of breath in our running, the Lord intervenes. It is well to remember that the idea that is imbedded in the name of the third Person of the Trinity, the Holy Spirit, is in reality, the Holy Breath. How blessed, then, that when we are out of breath for Him, He can answer by breathing Himself upon us. Then it is that we have the safety we pant for.

When we have learned this truth we need not be in fear or anxiety for anything. When we are fiercely beset by the conflict with the flesh, the Lord will arise in our behalf and give us the safety of victory that we long for. When some sudden sorrow comes to us that would ordinarily plunge us into gloom, He intervenes and brings the light that He is and places us in the safety that we long for. He uses this wonderful method to supply all our needs even as He has promised (Phil. 4:19). The supply is Himself. He arises; He breathes; He sets us in the safety for which we sigh.

"Blue Devils"

It is a wonderful thing to know that the Lord is greater than our earthly circumstances. No matter what they may be, He can overcome them and dominate them so that the Christian shall be in true joy.

I have a friend who, in early life, was a trained nurse. She married, and with her husband went into a poor section of one of our great cities in order to do missionary work for the Lord. The couple opened a little store in order to get acquainted with their poor neighbors, and about a thousand customers a week came in and out, many of whom received "a word fitly spoken." Widowed, this woman still carried on this work for the Lord, and the whole neighborhood thus had a witness of the love of the Savior.

An experience of this child of God may be a blessing to many who read it. She wrote, "One very rainy night, a little over a year ago, I locked my store and started home. There was a pouring, drenching, chilling rain and a high wind. An umbrella was useless. The cars were blocked, and I waited on the corner for three quarters of an hour. I was soaked to the skin, and chilled to the bone. Then I had to ride in two cold cars. When I reached home there was no dry clothing laid out for me, there was no warm supper, the fires were banked and the house was cold. Now the Lord has been good to me, He has blessed me with a happy disposition—the 'blue devils' do not trouble me often. But they were there that night. I thought: I will feed my kitten, I will not bother with any supper, I will go right to bed and cry it out. I began to remove my soaked clothing, and as I did, the Lord brought these words to my mind:

> There is never a day so dreary,
> There is never a night so long,
> But the soul that is trusting Jesus
> Will somewhere find a song.

And I began to sing:

> Wonderful, wonderful Jesus,
> In the heart He implanteth a song,
> A song of deliverance, of courage, of strength . . .

The singing warmed my body; soon supper was ready, the house was warm, my kitten was purring joyously, there was not only the cheer and warmth and brightness of home, but something far greater, the glory and joy of the presence of the Lord Jesus in my own being. 'And the glory of the Lord filled the temple of the Lord, so that there was no room . . .' for the 'blue devils.' There have been and will be other cold rainy days, but the memory of that victory through Christ will preclude the possibility of defeat in similar circumstances."

You can know this triumph. It may not be a cold rainy day for you, but the "blues" may be upon you for some reason or another. The

Sin

How Far Did Man Fall?

Some time ago, while teaching a Bible class on the Book of Genesis, I came to the third chapter and the account of the fall of man. In the course of the study I said that many of the great differences in theology which divide men and churches arose out of the question as to how far man fell in the sin of Adam. To my astonishment, the crowd laughed. I was not expecting it at all, and had a flash of stunned silence, but then I immediately saw that the laughter came from a shock of something so unexpected. The audience had never heard the matter expressed in that way, and their minds were totally unprepared for the statement, and did not comprehend it. The combination had touched off laughter.

Yet in no small sense the statement is historically true and Scripturally revealing. One of the fundamental differences between the Catholic and the Reformed theologies is the question of the distance of the fall. Or, to put it in another way, of what is man capable at the present time? Rome would teach that man is quite capable of storing up merit by a system of good works. Every religion which believes that salvation is through human character holds that man has not fallen very far. Some think, indeed, that he has fallen upwards! The great difference between the Arminians and the Calvinists again lies in this question, How far did man fall?

It is a matter that is of great importance to all who carry on any kind of witness to unbelievers. I remember a preacher who once said in a private conversation that if he thought there was a spark of the divine left in fallen men, he would counsel putting electric fans in the pulpit to fan the spark to flame, rather than preachers to proclaim the miracle-working Gospel. Facetious? Perhaps, but there is a great deal of truth in his remark.

There can be no doubt that New Testament theology is based on the fact that man fell all the way. He fell so far that he could fall no farther. He fell so far that there was no life left in him. He is "dead" (Eph. 2:1), and must be "quickened" by the Spirit before he can have even the remotest semblance of faith, but even that must be the gift of God (Eph. 2:8). The natural man receiveth not the things of the Spirit, neither can he know them (1 Cor. 2:14); in fact there is no one that understandeth, not even anyone that seeketh after God (Rom. 3:11). The carnal mind is enmity against God and is not subject to the law of God, nor indeed can it be; they that are in the flesh cannot please God (Rom. 8:7). When we realize this, we will learn to rely less on anything that appeals merely to the natural man and his understanding. Instead we will send forth the Word with the knowledge that we are preaching to dead men, whom only the power of God can quicken. All praise will be to Him.

The Curse Upon Man and the Earth

Satan is interested in anything which can take the minds of people away from the Word of God, and in anything which can get people to disbelieve the Biblical account of the Fall and God's curse upon man and the earth. *The International Journal of Religious Education* recounted the story of a regional conference of the United Christian Youth Movement.

An altar was erected with a cross and candles in the background, and a pile of fruits of the earth and dishes of soil on a white altar cloth occupied the foreground. The young people had a service that was called "The Ceremony of the Soil." There were special prayers written for the occasion, including the following: "Grant us . . . strength . . . courage and intelligence . . . to the end that the land shall blossom as a rose and in all Thy holy earth none shall be hungry nor be afraid."

Immediately, the Christian thinks of Cain and his offering. Here is the hatred of the blood of Christ and the hatred of God's curse manifested in a religious act which is Satanic in origin. The prayers are prayers to Satan, even though there is a cross on the altar. The land, according to the prayer, is to blossom like the rose as a result of strength given to men, rather than by the return of the Lord Jesus Christ, as the Bible teaches. The earth is referred to as "Thy holy earth," though the Scripture teaches, "Cursed be the ground for thy sake . . ." (Gen. 3:17).

The very soil has been smitten with the curse which came because of the sin of man. Thorns, thistles, and deserts are on this globe because they reflect the heart of man. The erosion of our top soil (20 percent of the top soil of America has already gone toward the oceans), keeps up with the spiritual erosion of our population.

Christian eyes and Christian hearts can look out upon the cursed earth only when they know that the thorns which pressed into Christ's brow were a prelude to the removal of the curse of the thorns, and that "The whole creation groaneth and travaileth in pain together until now . . . waiting for the adoption . . . of our body" (Rom. 8:22). God can never accept the offering of fruits unless the offering of the blood has come first.

The Total Depravity of Man

The great theological doctrine of total depravity has had many enemies. Yet we find it hard to understand how anyone can take cognizance of the atrocities perpetrated by the Nazis against the Jews and fail to see what roots of sin are in the human heart. To call the instigators and perpetrators of these crimes "bestial" is to insult every animal that ever walked the face of the earth. If we should see a lion bound upon his prey and tear it to bits, it would be only proper to say, "He eats almost in a human fashion."

We find it hard to understand how men can fail to fully recognize the fallen position of the sons of Adam. Their inability to see it is more proof of that total depravity. Those who look at the human race through the pages of the Bible will bring both the stories of the German atrocities and the noble deeds of courage which were manifested on the battle front, into a perspective of spiritual truth.

The Bible does not teach that there is no good in man; the doctrine of total depravity does not mean that. The Bible teaches, rather, that there is no good in man that can satisfy God. This is why the Lord Jesus Christ had to come from heaven to accomplish man's redemption, and why man can never accomplish it for himself. We would be willing to accept, for the sake of argument, that the monsters of Buchenwald and Dachau may have been loving fathers who wept in their beer when they listened to Brahms and Beethoven. We must also realize, though, that the heroes of noble deeds are men with flaws in their characters. It is God who tells us that in the heart of every one of us are the roots of those abominable evils which flowered in the annihilation camps of Germany. Jeremiah 17:9 is much stronger in the original tongue than in English; we read "the heart is deceitful above all things and incurably wicked." When God calls a thing incurable, we may be sure that it is.

If preachers everywhere would constantly emphasize the fact that there is no good in man which can satisfy God, the need for the Gospel would be seen much more clearly. We believe that apart from this declaration there can be no thought of salvation in the heart of any man. Let us therefore boldly and unflinchingly declare the doctrine of total depravity, though it is undoubtedly the most unpalatable truth which can be presented to the natural man.

The Goodness of Man

It is strange that thinking men so often fail to see beyond the glittering generalities to the solid foundation of truth that lies beneath. Almost every error has a basis of truth, but men see the scaffolding rather than the building because their eyes are blinded, either by self or by a more sinister power.

When delivering the graduate lecture to the Royal Military Academy at Woolwich many years ago, an English writer of some distinction talked to the young officers on the honor and high integrity of human nature. He gave as two examples a captain who had gone bravely down with his ship and a mother who had suffocated her own child under a mattress. The first, he claimed, was human nature, and the second was not. He called upon his audience to choose their creed in life as illustrated by these two incidents. "Which of them has failed from their nature, their present, possible actual nature, not their nature of long ago, but their nature of now?" He later went on to say, "You have had false prophets among you—for centuries you have had them—solemnly warned against them though you were; false prophets who have told you that all men are nothing but fiends or wolves, half beast, half devil. Believe that, and indeed you may sink to that, but refuse it, and you may have faith that God made you upright, though you have sought out many inventions. So, you will strive daily to become more what your Maker meant and means you to be . . . and you will say, 'My righteousness I hold fast, and will not let it go.' "

There are two root errors in this whole treatment of the great problem of human nature, or perhaps one root error that has two branches. This is the failure to see that man is fallen from God's perfection, that even our righteousness are as filthy rags in His sight (Isa. 64:6). It is the failure to recognize the implications of the holiness and justice of God. The two branches that grow out of this error are easy to trace. The first is that even the highest and best that man may have, his strongest heroisms, his noblest acts and aspirations, cannot measure up to the perfection that God's righteousness requires. The other branch, so often neglected by Christian theologians, is that there are some naturally good elements in the human heart—high character, stern honesty, noble honor—that have ever been ingrained in the best of the human race. Without it we would not have chivalry and the splendid literature that has grown out of knightly doings. Without it we would not have the magnificent traditions of fair play and justice which are the component parts of the righteousness which exalts a nation.

By all means, coin as much of this local currency of honor and integrity as human nature can spend, but do not forget that God has said that He will not accept this currency toward the entrance fee to Heaven. The only coin that will pass at that gate is the righteousness of Christ, which He is ready to place in the account of anyone who will approach Him in a true attitude of humbleness and adoration.

The Minister and the Murder

A literary review in the London *Times Literary Supplement* complained that American writers of detective stories do not keep to the proper rules of the game. "In the traditional English story the author—unless without a sense of craftmanship—does not have the murder done by a clergyman; he does not extract skeletons from the cupboards of those who are to live happily ever after; within the limits of the genre his characters observe the conventions of their social position to the point that where they disregard them they are marked down as suspects. But in the American story, spotting the culprit is more difficult because anybody may have done anything."

This may not measure up to English literary standards, but it most certainly does measure up to the Biblical standards of truth. The roots of sin—all sin—are planted deep in the human heart. The Word of God teaches us that they can never be uprooted, and that therefore God counts the old heart as "incurably sick" (Jer. 17:9 ASV). The divine manner of dealing with the sin of a believer is to condemn it, then to create through Christ a new life alongside the old.

"There hath no temptation taken you but such as is common to man" (1 Cor. 10:13). Culture and education may keep some men from some sins, but these cannot deal with the root from which sins grow. Frequently enough there are outbreaks of every type and kind of sin in every type and kind of individual. These sins are consistent enough to show that sin lurks everywhere. The world has invented phrases to cover it, and so speaks of "black sheep" or "skeletons in closets." The truth is that the "white" sheep have the same hearts as their relatives who have broken out of the fold. The skin does no more than cover the skeleton that has become a world symbol of death.

Perhaps the unbeliever will point out that sin also crops out in the hearts of believers. We are the first to recognize this as truth, and to count it as a proof of our assertions. The believer has an old nature within him just as surely as he has bones beneath his flesh. We shall never know, though, how many believers who would otherwise have broken forth into open sin have been kept from sin by the power of

God. It is through faith in the power of the blood of Jesus Christ that we can have a victory over root sin and the fruit of sin.

Pleasant Curse?

Martin Luther was a zestful man, and at the table often spoke words that he would have revised carefully before putting into writing. Friends and acquaintances recorded many of these utterances, some of which have been greatly misunderstood. One day he flung out a sentence which may seem absurd on the surface but which will stand close examination.

"The curse of a godless man," he said, "can sound more pleasant in God's ears than the hallelujah of the pious." On the surface the remark seems blasphemous; illustrate it and it becomes plausible, possible, and even certain.

Take a man who has a form of godliness, but who denies the power of God. When such a man utters a pious hallelujah, it is a raucous screech in the ears of God. Remember Christ's words, "Beware of the scribes, which desire to walk in long robes, and love greetings in the markets, and the highest seats in the synagogues, and the chief places at feasts; which devour widows' houses, and for a show make long prayers: the same shall receive greater damnation" (Luke 20:46, 47). We can be certain that the hallelujah from the lips of these "pious" ones is hateful to God.

But what about the curse of the godless man? Luther meant, of course, that God hates the sanctimonious hallelujah more than He hates the godless curse. It is not that the curse is acceptable, but that the heart that expresses it is not as far from God as the heart that is corroded by pious hypocrisy and hypocritical piety.

When religion is simply a cloak, it is an infected and filthy rag encrusted by the suppuration of the wound it bandages. God accepts a hallelujah from none but redeemed lips; for an unregenerate man to praise Him while denying His Son is an offense to His holiness.

This truth must be examined closely, for its implications are tremendous. It means that God does not accept the "grace before meals" offered by unbelievers. Even when people simply say, "Thank God, Amen," the omission of the name of the Lord Jesus is an attempt to come into God's presence without acknowledging their need of redemption. Into the same category falls the lodge prayer that omits the name of Jesus Christ and attempts to approach God with thanksgiving apart from redemption through the cross. These religious hallelujahs are not acceptable. Christ has stated the indispensable condition that "No man cometh unto the Father but by me" (John 14:6).

Luther's language was a little extravagant, in that it might make the unwary think that a curse would be pleasant to God. He would have put it better if he had said, "The curse of a godless man can be less offensive to the ears of God than the hallelujahs of the religious man."

Black and White

A magazine article, in discussing the techniques of making moving pictures, pointed out that sorrow, misfortune, or difficulty must be shown in black and white, never in color. If coolies laboring in China are shown in color, the background is so beautiful that the viewer gets the idea that their life is one of romance and prosperity. Only when the scene is shot in black and white are the squalor and misery seen for what they really are.

This is also true when sin is depicted. Done in color, it has a beauty that seduces the viewer into thinking that it is not sin. When a woman down a back alley leaves her husband to have a child by another man, the scene is done in black and white. When a motion picture actress leaves her husband to go to Italy and have a child by another man, the scene is viewed in technicolor, and the actress is lauded by society as having done the right thing. Editorial writers announce that she has been "rehabilitated," "vindicated," and "reestablished."

God reserves His colors for sunsets and spring blossoms. He always describes sin in black and white. This is why the Bible is such a remarkable book, and why it is so hated by those who wish to escape its implications. "The wages of sin is death" (Rom. 6:23). "It is a fearful thing to fall into the hands of the living God" (Heb. 10:31).

One of the worst effects of the fall of man was that man was fitted with rose-colored glasses. This is described in the New Testament, where we are told to "exhort one another every day, as long as it is called 'today,' that none of you may be hardened by the deceitfulness of sin" (Heb. 3:13).

Take a good look at your own life today. Try to see in black and white all that you have been looking at in color. It might even be well to reserve the color for those around you, and to use only the black and white for yourself.

Born-Again Rascals?

One of the characters in *Lanterns on the Levee,* a popular novel that was once on the best-seller lists, asks a minister why so many good church members are rascals six days a week. The minister's reply is that it is because they have been born again! They are sure of salvation, so they can do anything they want to do.

Such doctrine, needless to say, is far from the Biblical truth. Paul answered that same charge, for it was being made as long ago as his time. "What then, shall we continue in sin that grace may abound? God forbid!" (Rom. 6:1), and he answers, "How shall we that are dead to sin live any longer therein?"

The thing that the world often fails to take into consideration is the level from which the Christian has been brought, the level on which he lives now, and the level on which he would be living were he not a Christian. Let us make a scale from one to one hundred and measure all men in their "goodness" against that scale. We discover that many who were born with a natural background of twenty, thirty, or forty, are saved and henceforth live on a scale beginning at fifty and moving up to the sixties, seventies, and eighties. A cultured, refined unbeliever born at the scale of seventy or eighty, may rise in good works to a mark of eighty or even ninety. He is the rare bird whom those of the world choose as their standard of what a non-Christian should be, and they ask if he is to go to hell while the Christians who live on the fifty-eighty level are to go to Heaven. They never compare the progress of the Christian who began at the twenty level with that of the non-Christian who remains at twenty, or has fallen to ten. They do not talk about the great number of those who begin at sixty to eighty and have fallen to forty without Christ. Somehow they feel that sin in silk is not quite so horrible as sin in rags. They look upon a prostitute in rags as being far worse than the velvet-clothed mistress of the corporation executive.

The fact remains that those who are really born again are not the rascals. The life of God in the heart of one who has passed from death unto life will always bring that person up on the scale. Even the hypercritical world is forced to confess that they are far better than they would have been if Christ had not touched them, and the quiet-living Christians who work hard, pay their bills, and live for Christ seven days a week are not even seen by the critics who notice nothing beyond the superlative.

Nonetheless, the world's criticism should cause every born-again believer to look more closely at his personal life, in order that he may obey the word of the Lord, and "provide things honest in the sight of all men" (Rom. 12:17).

Christian Sins

There is no doubt of the fact that Christians often indulge in sin. God has told us that if any of us deny the existence of the old nature we are deceiving ourselves, while if we admit the presence of the old nature but believe that the incurable sins are curable, "we make him a liar, and his word is not in us" (1 John 1:8, 10). Those two searching statements found in the First Epistle of John are like the darkest of settings to bring out the precious stone of grace that lies embedded between them. For set exquisitely between the two verses that keep us from the false teaching of the denial of the old nature and the false teaching that finds any hope in the old nature, God has given us the great promise that "If we confess our (the Christian's) sins, he is faithful (to the mercy displayed at Calvary), and just to forgive us our sins, and to cleanse us (Christians), from all unrighteousness."

This very fact that forgiveness for our sins is provided in advance is the greatest reason why we must yield our lives to our Lord, so that He may furnish the power to keep us in our proper sphere. The second chapter of 1 John begins, "My little children." This is one word in the original language that really means "born ones," but the nearest we can approach it is by the use of the Scotch word *bairns*. "My born ones," the Holy Spirit tells us, "these things write I unto you (Christians), that ye sin not. And if any (born-again) man sin, we have an advocate with the Father, Jesus Christ the righteous: and he is the propitiation (atoning sacrifice) for our sins (i.e., Christian sins), and not for ours only, but also for the sins of the whole world" (1 John 2:1, 2).

What a contrast! Let us see what this means, practically. Two men stand before you. One is an unbeliever and the other has been born again through belief in the blood of Christ. They are both tempted, and both of them fall. Which sin is the worst in God's sight? The sin of the unbeliever is merely one more spot on the filthy rags that God can never accept (Isa. 64:6), but the sin of the believer is far worse. This is shown by a penetrating remark made by a Chinese Christian. He was asked, "How do you differ from the heathen?" The keen reply throws a floodlight on our text. "We Christians wear a white robe on which every spot is visible."

True, the sin was forgiven before it was committed; Christ bore it and it is a part of the "all things" from which we have been justified (Acts 13:39). But that is all the more reason that our God would deal with it severely—not with a judgment that involves our eternal salvation, but with a discipline that may shake our lives now, and may affect the remainder of our lives here on earth.

The Greatest Christian Sin

Many writers, secular and religious, talk about the failure of the church. But since the church is made up of the totality of its members, the failure of the church is the failure of its members. Let us leave out of our consideration, for the moment, the question of the mixture of tares in the midst of the wheat. It is simple to explain the failure of the church on the basis of the mingling of the unregenerate with those who have been born again.

Let us look at the church as an organism and consider the failure of those who are truly saved, for there is a sense in which the true church does fail. Christ said, "As long as I am in the world, I am the light of the world" (John 9:5). But now that He is not in the world He is no longer the light of the world except by reflection through those of whom He said, "Ye are the light of the world" (Matt. 5:14). What is wrong with the believers? What is the chief sin of the Christian?

The world says that "familiarity breeds contempt." This may be true in some situations, but familiarity also breeds something entirely apart from contempt. In multitudes of Christian lives familiarity breeds indifference, and indifference is the characteristic sin of the believing church today. Several million Christians go to church each Sunday and hear evangelical sermons; they are not lacking across the country. Although there are areas where there may be but one building in fifty miles which houses a group of true believers of the Lord Jesus, there are vast areas where the doctrine is impeccable but the people are indifferent. Honest preachers who have cried to God in the loneliness of their studies will hold forth the faithful Word, but many wonderful people will only smile at them and say, "I certainly did enjoy it." The preaching was meant to probe, to prick the heart, to burn the dross, but people go back instead to their conversations about neighbors and friends and all the pettiness of life.

The reason for this indifference seems to be that these people only have time for God from eleven to twelve on Sunday morning, and fifteen seconds of grace before a meal and sixty seconds of prayer before sleeping. There is no feeding upon the Word, yet growth comes from the Word (1 Peter 2:2). We must steadfastly hold forth the Word and call people to it. There is no other cure.

The Pull of the Old Nature

We cannot on our own help God, but we may be employed by Him. One of the greatest mistakes men make is in thinking that their energetic fussing will aid God in the accomplishment of His plans.

He is the Eternal; we are creatures of time. Even when we have been born again, and the supernatural, eternal life of the Lord Jesus has been planted within us by that miraculous work of regeneration, the friction of the presence of our old nature still ties us to a framework of time, and tends to give us man's viewpoint instead of that of God.

One may be accustomed to the speed of an automobile moving seventy miles per hour over our superhighways, but the first time one takes off in an airplane and feels the surge of power and the release from frictional drag, a new concept of speed and motion is instantly experienced.

The spiritual parallel will be known when the Lord comes to change these bodies of our humiliation, that they may be made like unto the body of His glory. In the meantime, His desire for us is that we be as free as possible from the pull of the old nature.

To this end we must learn God's methods. We cannot help Him out. He will not allow anything we do in our own strength to come to fruition, lest we be lulled into the false hope that our own strength is sufficient. Building apart from God is worse than building a house of paper. When paper falls it does not wound.

Abraham and Sarah tried to help God out. They had received a promise that they would have a child; God would see to it. Abraham believed God. But there was a lapse of faith, for the fulfillment tarried. The natural thought came first to Sarah's mind. Why not help God out? If God is slow, can we not do something that would be equally as acceptable? The error here lies in the failure to see that God is never slow. A second error is in the thought that anything we are, apart from a fully yielded will, could be useful to God.

Only when we have yielded ourselves to Him can He use us, working through us. Even then it will be "not I, but Christ." We will be channels through which He can flow, but His is the power. We will be employed by Him, and His will will be paramount. The world simply cannot reach through Christ to the yielded heart. The battle may rage about us, but the peace of God that passeth all understanding keeps our hearts and minds in Christ Jesus. This is undoubtedly why those who are the busiest in Christian work can usually be counted upon to do the little extra things when it is necessary, for they have learned to make haste slowly with God.

The Sins of Presumption

It is a terrible thing to be executed—more terrible when God Himself is the executioner. Among the many stories found in the Bible, there are several which tell of men whom God struck dead. In none of the instances recorded where God visited punishment of death upon one of His own was the sentence passed for any moral sin. No violation of what we call the Ten Commandments has ever been followed by death imposed by God.

Nadab and Abihu, in Leviticus 10:1, 2, brought ordinary fire, perhaps a kitchen stove fire, into the tabernacle of God to light the incense, which is a symbol of worship. God struck them dead immediately. The fire should have been taken from the brazen altar, from the fire which had originally been lit by fire sent down from Heaven. Here was the great sin of worship on a basis of human works. In this awful manner God taught that worship, to be acceptable to Him, must be on the basis of His works and His grace.

Hophni and Phinehas (1 Sam. 4:11) were struck dead by God, and their father, Eli, died (when he heard the news) because the fattest cuts of meat were served to these boys by their doting father during the distribution of the food to the priests. Once for all, the principle is brought out that there is to be no favoritism in the ministry of the Word, but that all is to be equal on the basis of the gracious infilling of the Holy Spirit. These corpses of the sons of the high priest testified against favoritism or the advancement of friends in the work of God.

Ananias and Sapphira were struck dead because they pretended to be fully surrendered to God when they were consciously holding back a part of their possessions. Their sin was precisely the same as that of church members who sing, "I surrender all" when they do not mean it.

In other words, spiritual sins were punishable by death, whereas moral sins were not only covered over by the grace of God, but those who had committed these sins were restored to fellowship and used by God in the carrying on of His work. It would appear that lying, swindling, murder, adultery, betrayal, and stiff-necked stubbornness do not merit penalties as great as sins of worship in self-will, personal favoritism in the things of God, and hypocrisy in surrender. The significance of this statement is to be found in the fact that God knows what the old nature is like, and that it can never be anything else, but spiritual sins involve the holiness of God Himself.

One strong word of warning is called for here. If the old nature should take undue liberty because of God's grace and the second chance given to men who have sinned morally, then that presumption would become a spiritual sin involving more disaster than the actual commission of an overt act of sin. God's Word says, "What then, shall we continue in sin that grace may abound? God forbid." This is probably the meaning of David's statement, "Keep back thy servant also from presumptuous sins." A better translation would seem to be, "Keep back thy servant also from sins of presumption." In other words, because God's character is so gracious and loving, we must not sin against that grace.

The Sin of Slander

There is, in the Book of Jeremiah, an arresting word spoken by the enemies of the heroic prophet. "Come," they said, "and let us smite him with the tongue" (Jer. 18:18). On the surface the threat is absurd. A man would have a hard time killing a fly with his tongue! In actuality, however, that threat of Jeremiah's enemies expressed a terribly real danger. With the tongue, a career may be smashed, a reputation blasted as by a charge of high explosive, or a life withered, shriveled, and finally killed.

We have called attention more than once to the danger of evil-speaking among Christians. Let us use this vivid phrase from Jeremiah to bring up the subject once again. It is a sad fact that the tongues of professing Christians are often all too busy doing the devil's work. There is, for instance, a self-righteous use of the tongue that is particularly deadly as it smites the reputation of others. Take slander; some people think that as long as they are technically truthful in talking about another, they are not guilty of the devastating sin of slander. This matter appears in an entirely new light, however, when seen through the words of General William Booth, the founder of the Salvation Army. This paragraph appeared in *The Bible Today:*

"To slander a brother means talking about his faults—or 'what may be considered his faults'—to his brethren or to others, and talking about him when there is no necessity to do so, or when no good end will be served by it. Many think that, in order to slander a man, something that is false must be said about him, but in that case it would be lying as well as slander. Slander is a very serious sin. By one hour's slander, a man may inflict a greater injury on the Kingdom of Christ than he will do good by twelve months' hard work. Slandering is very cruel. It is very unkind to spread forth a man's faults and infirmities, thereby doing him incalculable injury, merely from envy or some other uncharitableness, or for the mere pleasure of talking evil. Slander is cowardly. No one should say behind a man's back what he dare not, or would not, say to his face. Slander is unscriptural. It is in direct contradiction to the command of our Lord, who said, 'Speak evil of no man.' Slander is senseless. The Devil and his followers will be ready enough to revile, and persecute, and say all manner of evil falsely against (true Christian) soldiers, without their comrades joining in this vile business."

Few things could work toward more true unity in the Lord's service than for every Christian worker to read these words, ponder them, and make every effort to live accordingly.

The Sin of Willfulness

One of the worst of all sins, worse than theft, adultery, or murder, is the sin of wanting one's own way. It is the desiring of one's own way which leads to every other sin in the world. The shortest definition of sin is "I will," and when Lucifer spoke those words (Isa. 14:13, 14) sin thereby entered the universe. Whenever man says, "I will," with a desire which is in opposition to God's will, he, too, is in the midst of sin.

How this willfulness is manifested is shown by an item which appeared in the public news media. A small boy, who was described as a "shy second-grader, eight years old, a little owlish in spectacles," was found guilty of committing a crime in a New Jersey school. It was Valentine's Day. He brought a valentine and put it on his teacher's desk, then went down into the basement and set fire to the school by lighting the wastepaper which was in the boiler room. When the Fire Commissioner conducted an inquiry, evidence pointed to the boy, and he readily admitted that he had set fire to the school. When he was asked why, he explained, as the news report put it, with childish simplicity, "In class yesterday they took away my bubble gum."

The newspaper reporter may have smiled when he heard this. It was one of those items which is sure to fill three or four inches on the front page of a newspaper under the guise of what is known as "human interest." The depths of horror which are in it would not be perceived by those who look upon the matter merely as a childish prank. Only those who know the Word of God could realize how terrible such a manifestation is. Analyze it in the light of the Word of God, and it becomes the fierce pride of the Adamic nature which rises even in a child.

The child said in effect, "I am on the throne of my life, and I want everybody to bow down before me. I want to rule. When I want something I want it, and that is sufficient reason for my having it. If I want bubble gum, I am to have it. If anybody takes it away from me, I have the right to lash out and destroy anything that stands in the way of my merest whim and desire."

This can be explained on the basis of a psychosis, a neurosis, or a complex of some sort, but it is actually a plain manifestation of original sin. If it is allowed to develop, it can put a pistol in the hand of this same lad and make him a murderer. There are not many convicts in prison today who did not, in childhood, do something analogous to the act of this small boy. The fierce self-desire of the Adamic nature manifests itself not only in those tendencies which lead men to prison, but also in those which lead men to the ruthlessness of ecclesiastical leaders who will destroy a church rather than yield a matter of personal pride.

There is only one way to curb the Adamic nature. That is to plant the new life of Jesus Christ alongside it, through the new birth by which we are made "partakers of the divine nature" (2 Peter 1:4). Day by day we can then submit our lives to the control of the Lord so that He may keep the old nature in submission. Not even the Christian is safe for a moment unless his old nature is yielded to the Lord for the crucifixion death. No life is safe, no home is secure, unless Christ is made preeminent and the old nature is kept in its place of death.

The Path of Sin

A controversy once raged in the columns of a British newspaper as a result of an article by a well-known clergyman, who said that there are times when we have to choose a path of evil, that sometimes there is no right choice to be made. He gave several examples. "A close friend gives me a present for which I have no liking or use. Shall I wound his feelings by saying so, or shall I, if not by words at least by actions, deceive him? A trifling clash between the duty of truth-telling and the duty of love, but nonetheless a clash."

Another example: A friend of the minister was in South Africa in the colonial days, and his house was attacked by members of the Matabele tribe. The man's wife stood behind him, loading the guns so that he could fire as fast as possible. "You won't let them get me?" she asks. "No," answers the husband. "I am saving two cartridges—one for you and one for me." There were three alternatives. He could kill as many human beings as possible; he could kill his wife and himself; or he could surrender, only to die by horrible torture while his wife would have been left to an even more awful death.

The third example is that of a woman who, in a moment of infatuation, has been false to her husband, and upon awakening from that brief madness knows that she still loves him and her children. What shall she do? Shall she break her husband's heart, disgrace her children, and break up a home by telling the truth, or shall she embark on a lifetime of lies and deceit? "Choose which alternative you please as the better one, or rather as the less evil. One thing you must not do. You must not talk of her acting rightly, for she has left herself no right course to choose."

We do not propose to go into the details of argument as to possible actions in the above cases. We wish instead to point out the *Christian's* course of action in all cases. First, it is impossible to live a long course of sin and then be in a position to act nobly. When desire has conceived, it bringeth forth sin; and sin, when it is finished, bringeth forth death (James 1:15). In other words, sin leads men into paths from which there is no escape. The choice is merely a choice of evils. But for the Christian, there is a way out. The dilemmas that are caused by sin, when confessed to the Lord, are covered by the blood of the Savior and put behind us. The past is past and need not be dragged out to plague us. The present is under His direction and need not bring us fear. Whatever circumstances may come, of peace or tragedy, we know that they have been sifted by our Lord, and we are content.

The Escape from Sin's Penalty

The *Manchester Guardian* once ran a literary contest which involved writing a new ending for Shakespeare's famed tragedy *Hamlet.* Contestants were to present a synopsis for "a better last act." All of the contestants kept Hamlet alive, and some had the heroine return after her "death" in the previous act and state that she had only been in a trance, or that she had been feigning death to see if Hamlet really loved her. Each of the entries involved some artful device to insure a perfect, happy ending.

Thus man seeks to change life and make it something different than it really is. In real life there are tragedies, and the greatness of Shakespeare is that he was able to reproduce real life in his dramas. When man amuses himself, he wishes to escape from life for a while and give himself unreality; therefore, the majority of the world's make-believe stories end with everybody living happily ever after. Although men may live in the illusion of an "escape mechanism" for a while, life comes to an end in its own bitter way unless there is true redemption in Christ. The world may create an illusion of forgetfulness for a time, but beneath the surface remains the intense despair that must break out in the end.

Another column of this same British publication was an editorial comment upon the suicide of a brilliant cartoonist. The *Guardian* remarked that those who make other people laugh are, themselves, frequently sorrowful. A famous story is often used to illustrate this. A famous nerve specialist on London's Harley Street once received a visitor who requested an examination. The doctor completed his diagnosis and told the patient that there was nothing really wrong with him. "You need to get out among people and laugh." The doctor then told the patient that he himself had been, just the night before, to see a famous Italian clown who was causing all of London to roar with laughter. "Go and see Grimaldi," said the doctor. "He will take you out of your doldrums." The patient looked at the doctor steadily and said, "I am Grimaldi."

The only way to change the last act of your life is to permit the Author of peace to deal with your sins at the cross of Jesus Christ. Then He, who is Peace, will come into your life and bring His own peace with Him. All future scenes are rewritten from that point; there is a new creation.

The Concern for Sin

Some time ago a Christian approached me after a meeting and said, "I am worried because I am not worried about my sins."

The phrase is a startling one, and should lead each of us to examine our spiritual status before the Lord. Worry, in itself, is a sin, because it is a lack of faith. The Quakers recognized long ago, however, that there is a spiritual emotion which is not exactly worry that is perfectly proper in the life of a Christian. The Quakers called this "a concern," and it is common in their circles to hear them say, "I am concerned about this or that."

If a sin comes into the life of a believer, he should immediately become concerned about it. It should cause him to rush to the Lord in confession and repentance, and it should cause him to build every bulwark possible against the recurrence of the sin.

This proper concern is described by St. Paul in the Second Epistle to the Corinthians, where he recounts the effect of his scathing denunciation of their low estate. He writes, "For godly sorrow worketh repentance to salvation not to be repented of: but the sorrow of the world worketh death. For behold the selfsame thing, that ye sorrowed after a godly sort, what carefulness it wrought in you, yea, what clearing of yourselves, yea, what indignation, yea, what fear, yea, what vehement desire, yea, what zeal, yea, what revenge! In all things ye have approved yourselves to be clear in this matter" (2 Cor. 7:10, 11). This is the attitude we should take toward ourselves when we have knowledge that we have grieved the Holy Spirit.

We come now to a very solemn question, the question that was brought to mind by the statement of the man who was worried because he was not worried about his sins. The question is this: Do Christians today fear sin as they should? Are Christians really concerned when sin comes into their life? Is there a godly sorrow that worketh repentance to a daily triumph that is not to be repented of? I am frank to say that from my contacts with many people, I have gained the overall impression that there is not deep cutting distress on the part of Christians when they grieve the Holy Spirit. There is not even a concern that they are not concerned about their sins. The man who is truly concerned about the matter will undoubtedly be led by the Holy Spirit to repentance and forsaking of that sin.

We then ask ourselves why we have this indifference. There are several answers, one of which rises from the fact that we are living as a minority in the midst of great masses of people who no longer look upon sin as the Word of God has taught us to look upon it. Many forms of sin are not only popular, but respectable, and are shrugged off with the excuse that the sinner is human, so nothing else can be expected. This attitude rubs off on many Christians. Secondly, many Christians have a head knowledge of some of the truth without its ever dominating the heart. When the Lord told His disciples not to pull up the tares, lest they take some of His wheat, He was saying that some Christians are so much like unbelievers that other Christians could not tell the difference. We are certainly thankful that God sees through to the heart. The preaching of the doctrine of justification has caused many people to say that they have eternal life, and then do nothing about it. If a person sins and is not concerned about it and is not concerned that he is not concerned about it, it may be seriously questioned whether he has ever been born again. We must never believe in eternal presumption.

The only remedy that we know is for the child of God to stay inside the Word and to contemplate the finished work of the cross. The love of Christ controls us, and regeneration comes through the Word. We must have a definite determination of practical holiness, a determination that will carry us forward with every part of our being surrendered to the Lord, so that He may do what we cannot do.

The Excuses for Sin

The human being, with all of his inheritance from Adam, is incurably addicted to making excuses. This was forcibly brought to my attention by a news item from Vancouver, British Columbia. A man was sentenced to jail for one year for breaking into a cafe in the middle of the night. He was caught red-handed inside the cafe with the cash register open. Nevertheless, he protested his innocence in court, and even when he was sentenced, departed for jail claiming that he was the victim of circumstances.

His defense was that as he was walking along the street he had stumbled and fallen into a window, which had broken. When he saw the two panes of glass had been destroyed, he opened the window and entered in order to leave his name and address, so that he could make good the damage. Having no pencil, he went to the cash register to look for one, and was in the middle of the good deed when he was arrested. The story was just a little too much for the jury and the man went to jail!

I immediately began to think of Adam, who, when he was caught running away, tried to cast the blame back on God, saying in effect, If you had given me another kind of wife, this wouldn't have happened—"the woman thou gavest me . . ." (Gen. 3:12). The woman excused herself by putting the blame upon the serpent. When Abraham was caught in a lie by Abimelech, he stumbled around making it worse by the flimsy excuses he presented. The Lord Jesus told the parable about the men who would not come to a feast. One had "married a wife," and could not come. Another had bought a yoke of oxen and had to test them. A third had bought a field and had to go to see it. The first man could have brought his wife with him, the oxen could have been tested the next day, and the field would still have been there at any later date.

There is a vast difference between an excuse and a reason. There may be some validity in the latter, but not in the former. We are told that in the judgment day, "a hail shall sweep away the refuge of lies" (Isa. 28:17).

I have often remarked throughout my ministry that most people, when overtaken in sin, are more concerned with public opinion than they are with God. Since the time of Adam the effects of the Fall have been more marked from generation to generation, and "saving face" is just as important in one part of the world as it is in another. One of the holiest exercises that any Christian can perform is that of getting down on his face before God and asking to be shown a clear revelation of himself in such a light that no excuses can be offered to lighten the explanation of his folly.

The True Repentance for Sin

A Sunday School teacher once asked a class what was meant by the word "repentance." A little boy put up his hand and said, "It is being sorry for your sins." A little girl also raised her hand and said, "Please, it is being sorry enough to quit."

There is, indeed, a vast difference between the two. That is why the Lord said through Joel, "Rend your hearts and not your garments" (Joel 2:13). In the Orient, the tearing of clothes and the wearing of tattered garments was a sign of mourning. The people of Judah had gone far from the will of the Lord, and He had sent a plague of locusts upon the land to devour the crops. Following this, a drought had come and the fields had been burned brick-dry. Joel preached to the people, telling them that they deserved all that the Lord had sent upon them, and that they should repent. But he also warned them that they were to repent from the heart, and not with mere outward show. It is not enough for stubborn men to go on inwardly in their sins, with a sanctimonious show of mourning on the outside. "Rend your hearts and not your garments."

It is so easy to put responsibility off on someone else—even on God. I once saw a cartoon which showed a little boy down on his knees saying his prayers. The caption read: "Please, God, try hard to make me a good boy." There is no doubt that the Lord is more than willing to cooperate with us, but He will not force His way within and mesh the gears of righteousness for us. There are things which we must do ourselves. We have to be willing, and if we find ourselves unwilling, we must pray, "Lord make me willing to be made willing." In all cases, there must be a persistent, intellectual affirmation of our own guilt and our own need. Then we must look at the cross of Jesus Christ until the need and the provision come into the same focus. The sorrow for sin will get out of our heads and into our hearts, and we will not only be sorry for sin, but sorry enough to quit. It is the cross and the realization of the love that was manifested there which will ultimately bring the sorrow, the victory, and the blessing.

The Victory over Sin

In an issue of *The Atlantic Monthly,* a kleptomaniac wrote anonymously of her experiences in shoplifting. After a realistic description of the methods of stealing and of the fear that grips the heart of the thief, the article concludes with the "cure" of the habit. The thief was caught on two different occasions, but because of her genteel appearance, was merely forced to pay for the goods stolen at that moment. The fear of punishment gripped her and she wrote, "I wrote a compact with God today, promising quite a sum of money to the church if He would save me from this mistake . . . I am glad God allowed me to be caught, for it was the only way to stop me. My will was not enough. The medicine had to be bitter to be effectual. I know that I shall never try shoplifting again. I am not superstitious, but I am afraid to be caught for the third time . . . The evil of the crime has been branded on my heart, not by the eighth commandment, but through fear of the consequences to my health and professional standing . . . It has now been a year since I signed my compact with God. He has kept His part of the compact and I shall keep mine . . . ."

It is improbable that the writer of that article will read these lines, but there may be some other person who is sorely tempted with this or any one of a thousand other sins, who will need more than "a compact with God" to keep from sin. We have no way of checking up, but we are sure from knowledge of human nature, and above all, from knowledge of the Word of God, that this poor woman will be tempted and will fall into the same sin again. The despair that will come will be all the more horrible since it will follow a period of comparative victory during which the soul will have been led to trust its own strength.

There is only one way to victory over sin. That is a constant reliance upon the cross of Jesus Christ, and a moment by moment committal of life to His keeping. It is by grace, not law. The woman's "compact with God" was merely a repetition of the covenant of Israel which was never kept by man. When the law was given Israel said, "All that the Lord hath said, we will do" (Exod. 24:7), yet they did not do it. God has definitely told us that the law—covenants, compacts, vows—is absolutely ineffectual—"what the law could not do, in that it was weak through the flesh . . ." (Rom. 8:3). Christians are not to make vows to God. Sometimes the devil tempts us along this line, but it is only a shrewd attempt to get us back on the ground of law where we can be dealt a heavy blow.

The truth about victory over sin is that it is found only in Christ. "What the law could not do, in that it was weak through the flesh, God sending his own Son in the likeness of sinful flesh, and for sin, condemned sin in the flesh, that the righteousness of the law might be fulfilled in us who walk not after the flesh, but after the Spirit." There is God's way of dealing with habitual sin. It is the only way that works.

The Antibiotic for the Old Nature

There is a word which holds out great hope to many suffering from physical ailments, and there is a principle in this word which illustrates admirably one of the greatest truths in the Word of God. The word *antibiotics* has been derived by doctors from *antibiosis*, meaning "an association between two or more organisms which is detrimental to one of them." The best known of the antibiotics is penicillin; another is streptomycin. The prefix *anti* means "against" and the root word *bios* (as in biology and biography) means "life." Against the living bacteria, other living organisms are released in the body which fight the disease-bearing bacteria. Good life fights evil life. The life in penicillin feeds upon the life of some disease-bearing bacteria and destroys them. In test tubes, streptomycin has destroyed the bacilli of tuberculosis and leprosy, and the bacterium of tularemia.

The great spiritual illustration that can be shown is the principle of warfare between the flesh and the Spirit. We have an old nature of sin. Left to itself, it grows and multiplies like the splitting of bacteria and the spread of malignant tissue. But when we are born again, the life of God is released in us as an antibiotic. "The flesh lusteth against the Spirit, and the Spirit against the flesh; and these are contrary the one to the other, so that you cannot do the things that ye would" (Gal. 5:17). The life of the Holy Spirit within is the antibiotic that fights against the living death of the old nature.

This is clearly expressed in the eighth chapter of Romans. If we follow the Greek, leaving out the last ten words of the first verse and then going on in the continuing tense, we read, "There is therefore now no condemnation to them which are in Christ Jesus. For the law (the antibiotic) of the Spirit of life in Christ Jesus makes me free from the law of sin and death" (Rom. 8:1, 2). If we will deny ourselves those fleshly lusts which feed the old nature and give ourselves the food of the Word which nourishes the new life of the Spirit, we shall be "strengthened with might by his Spirit in the inner man" and shall be "filled unto all the fulness of God" (Eph. 3:16, 19).

Sanctification and Sin

In August the streets of China are filled with fruit sellers. A variegated assortment of a half-dozen different kinds of melons, many varieties of peaches, apples, grapes, and other fruits, is most tastefully displayed. To one accustomed from childhood to eating fruit rather freely, it is a distinct disappointment to see all of this fruit and to be unable to eat any of it. The conditions under which they were grown and the filth accompanying their handling all along the way make it impossible for any foreigner to do what he might do in an occidental country—spend a few coppers, rinse or peel the fruit, and enjoy it.

Before we can eat the fruit, it must be sanctified. Strawberries must be washed in a solution of potassium permanganate, peaches must be treated likewise, then dipped in boiling water and carefully pared. Any place where the skin has been broken must be meticulously cut out and discarded. Tomatoes whose skins have been broken cannot be safely eaten unless they have been cooked. It is all rather complicated and somewhat annoying. All of these preparations for eating fresh fruit correspond to sanctification. We recoil from the filth as we see it, and take every precaution that the deadly germs which cause uncomfortable or deadly diseases shall not infect us.

If the effects of sin were as visibly disastrous—if pride and lying and other sins produced as much dread and carefulness in us as does the sight of village sewage being shoveled onto strawberry beds—would we not be more careful to enter into the deeper knowledge of sanctification? Is not this same idea behind Paul's cry, "Ye have not yet resisted unto blood, striving against sin" (Heb. 12:4)?

We live with a terrible source of infection. Paul exclaims, "O wretched man that I am! Who shall deliver me from the body of this death?" (Rom. 7:24). Radical treatment is necessary. The cause of infection must be delivered over to death. As peaches and fruit must be prepared with chemicals, and open spots cut away with a knife, so the old nature must be delivered to Jesus Christ for the crucifixion death. This is the meaning of the apostle's statement, "I die daily." It is the moment by moment disinfection of sanctification.

Salvation

Changing Places with God

Burton Stevenson, in his *Home Book of Quotations,* gives the following epitaph from an old English churchyard:

> Here lie I, Martin Elginbrodde;
> Hae mercy o' my soul, Lord God,
> As I wad do were I Lord God,
> And ye were Martin Elginbrodde.

As a matter of fact, if God and any one of us were to change places things would be exactly as they are now, providing we received all that God is, and He became all that we are. The blasphemy which underlies such an epitaph as this is the implication that Martin Elginbrodde has more lovingkindness and tender mercy than God Almighty. The real truth, of course, is that man has less holiness, less justice.

There is a striking line in the Psalms, "Thou thoughtest that I was altogether such a one as thyself" (Ps. 50:21). Here is the greatest tragedy in human thought. It is the failure to recognize the truth of the Word of God, "My thoughts are not your thoughts, neither are your ways my ways, saith the Lord. For as the heavens are higher than the earth, so are my ways higher than your ways, and my thoughts than your thoughts" (Isa. 55:8, 9).

The born-again Christian, looking upon his heart, is forced to say: If I were but the justice of God, I would send myself to eternal separation from God. If I were but the holiness of God, I would separate myself eternally from that holiness. Then we can understand that only by that redeeming love which came to the cross and bore the stroke of that justice and the separation of that holiness, is it possible for love to redeem us and draw us to Him.

It has been said that Christianity can be expressed in three sentences. The three sentences are: I deserve Hell. Jesus Christ took my Hell. There is nothing left for me but His Heaven. When we analyze those three sentences we can see that every doctrine in Christianity is included under one of the three. Under the first are the doctrines of the nature of man, of the fall, and of the holiness and the justice of God. Under the second are the doctrines of the love of God, the atonement, propitiation, and redemption. Under the third is the doctrine of assurance and our future hope.

We are delighted to side with God against Martin Elginbrodde and against ourselves, and to ascribe all praise and glory to Him.

Chemistry and Bread

A Christian worker spoke of the narrowness of some believers who were not willing to consider others as worthy of Christian fellowship. "They are so bad," said our friend, "that according to them there would be only about five hundred people who are saved." This statement, though an exaggeration, makes us to think about the essential elements of our salvation.

What is necessary in order to be saved? What is necessary in order to eat bread? At first the two questions, side by side, may seem irrelevant, but there is a closer connection than appears on the surface. Imagine three hungry men sitting before a table with a plate of sandwiches. One of these men is a noted chemist, another is a famed anatomist, and the third is an illiterate farmer. The bread is passed. The chemist turns to the doctor and tells him of the latest experiments in biochemistry. Science is now convinced that it is on the track of real knowledge in this field. Experiments have shown that the energy that is to be found in electrons may be life itself. The air is thick with big words, of which the illiterate knows the meaning of none. The doctor tells the chemist of the latest research in the field of endocrinology. Scientists now believe that they know how food is transmitted into blood, muscle, and bone, how the cells are broken down and built up, and how the various glands function in their marvelous work of rehabilitating the human body.

While the two scientists are talking they become engrossed in their conversation, and they are somewhat annoyed upon finishing their first sandwich, to find that the farmer has quietly eaten all of the remaining sandwiches. The scientists know all about the chemistry of the bread he has eaten and all about his body which is assimilating the food; he, on the contrary, knows nothing of these things. But they are still hungry and he goes from the table satisfied.

There are faults in our analogy, but there is sufficient force in it to show the great principle of salvation. There are some people who will talk in theological terms that only a few can understand. Others will hedge Christianity around with all sorts of obstacles, making it hard for souls to come to Christ, when God has made it easy. In the meantime, there are simple souls who are turning away from self and are looking to Christ alone for salvation. They are being satisfied with the living Bread from Heaven. It is this simplicity of trusting Christ that God honors by implanting within the believer eternal life.

Some people might say, "Why do you go into theological argument and accuse some men of being unsaved, just because they do not happen to believe exactly as you do about some of these doctrines? Can we not leave the theological terms aside and go in the simplicity of Christianity? The definite answer is, yes, you can go on in the simplicity of the Christian faith, providing you truly know that faith. If I present a loaf of bread to a scientist and he examines it from afar, insisting it is made of *papier-mâché* and that it is not bread at all, then I have every right to believe that the man has not profited by the bread, even though he may contend that he greatly admires the loaf as a work of art.

Believing that Christ is just a good man, or merely a great teacher, is admiring the loaf without feeding upon it. True faith turns away from any thought of providing its own food. It turns to the cross of Jesus Christ where it accepts God's verdict that the death of His Son eternally satisfies every claim that divine justice could ever have against the trusting sinner. The Lord Jesus is God's Bread for a lost world.

Self

St. Augustine prayed, "O Lord, deliver me from the lust of always vindicating myself." There can be no doubt, for we know it from the

Bible as well as from experience, that self always wishes to vindicate itself.

In the Bible self is called "flesh." We are clearly taught there is only one way to deal with it; it cannot be trained, it cannot be reformed. Its heart is incurable, its mind is hatred. The whole message of Scripture is a general declaration that God will not deal with man apart from the cross of Jesus Christ. It was self that caused the death of our Lord. Yet in that death we may find self's crucifixion, and learn to have the life that flows from the Lord Jesus Christ.

Augustine has undoubtedly put his finger on one of the principal characteristics of the flesh. It wants to defend itself. If we combine this with the fact that it always wishes to exalt itself, we have its true nature. It thinks all good of itself; it thinks no bad of itself. One of the reasons a Christian is left on earth after he is saved is to bring him into the frame of mind that will admit that so far as his relationship to God is concerned, there is no good in the flesh, and that, conversely, there is all evil in the flesh. "For from within, out of the heart of men, proceed evil thoughts, adulteries, fornications, murders" (Mark 7:21).

Salvation is the admission that we cannot save ourselves and that we are willing, before God, to turn our backs upon self, to despise and reject it, and to turn instead to the Lord Jesus Christ, who formerly was despised and rejected, and to put all of our trust in Him, believing God's verdict about self and Christ.

An English devotional writer said, "Beware of refusing to go to the funeral of your own independence." This has nothing to do with our independence towards men, but is concerned with an attitude towards God. The Christian life is meant to teach us that we must be utterly dependent upon our Lord, and that therefore we must be willing to go daily to the funeral of our own independence. This is exactly what Paul meant when he said, "I am crucified with Christ" (Gal. 2:20) and "I die daily" (1 Cor. 15:31).

Banking and Salvation

I once came upon a very good illustration of salvation while talking with a member of the board of directors of a small town bank.

When I mentioned a mutual acquaintance who is a member of the same board, my friend told me of the canny shrewdness which had made this man successful. "I don't know the extent of all his deals," he said, "because I am not on the loan committee, but as a member of the examining committee I see enough to know how clever and fore-sighted he is." We discussed the functions of a bank director and then I had my illustration.

God is His own loan committee and He lends every man every-thing that he is or has. God has loaned you your physique, whatever it may be; God has loaned you your intelligence, whatever its quotient; God has loaned you your very breath. (Remember the line of the hymn? "I'll praise Thee as long as Thou lendest me breath.") But God is also His own examining committee. Furthermore, we are all de-faulters and faithless to every trust that God has given us. "There is none righteous, no, not one." Our shortages will show up before Him more surely than the falsifications of a banker could be detected by the examining committee.

I pointed out that Jesus Christ on the cross gave up His life as our bond and security. Then we discussed a case well known in that part of the country, where a young man, thinking that his wealthy father was dying, forged his name for approximately a million dollars. The father got well, discovered the shortage, made it good, and disinherited his son. But our God, knowing all too well our shortage, made it good in the death of Christ, and instead of disinheriting us, gave us His in-heritance. What we must do is admit our guilt, throw ourselves on the mercy provided at the cross, and accept by faith the fact that *God is sat-isfied with the death of Christ instead of our death.* With acceptance of these great facts comes such a change of life that we should henceforth live a life of gratitude.

Wesley understood this. Knowing that he was a defaulter, and that his case would come before the examining scrutiny of God, he sang,

> Arise, my soul arise; shake off thy guilty fears,
> The bleeding sacrifice in my behalf appears.
> Before the throne my surety stands!
> My name is written on His hands.

Eternal Security

A noted Christian leader, well known to many thousands of God's children for his wonderful messages on the deep spiritual life, passed through a time of great testing. He was old and his life span had nearly run its course. Illness had attacked his brain, just as it might attack the eyes of one or the knees of another, and he imagined that he was lost. He, who had spoken many times on the wonderful security of the believer in Christ, said to the few friends who entered his room that a cloud had passed over his faith, and that his old nature was so terrible that he was sure that he was lost. We do not doubt for a moment that he was saved. We can be certain that he will be in Heaven, for we know that our entrance into Heaven does not depend upon anything other than the fact that Christ has washed our sins from us with His own blood.

Very frequently, though, Satan comes to those who are not old Christians and who are not touched by physical infirmity of the mind and seeks to tell them that they are now lost. The first flush of joy that comes with the knowledge of forgiven sin has been lost by the outcropping of the old nature. Perhaps the young Christian was deceived by some well-intentioned Christian worker who informed him that if he would accept Christ everything would be lovely and all his struggles would be over. The truth, of course, is that the new nature is put in with the old nature and that the two struggle against one another. The greatest struggles that life can know are not within the unsaved, but within the saved. When one of these great struggles breaks out, ending either in defeat, partial defeat, partial victory with great weariness, or full victory, the young Christian is often an easy prey for the voice of the one who is called the accuser of the brethren. He insists that there was really no miracle creation, no new birth, and that everything is the same as it was before.

In times like this there is but one thing to do. Run to the cross! The young Christian will go to the Lord in the midst of defeat, saying, "O Lord, here is Thy child. I did the best I knew how in coming to Christ, and if there was any failure on my part, I come over again to the cross. My hope is built on nothing less than Jesus' blood and righteousness. I must just stay at the cross." Satan will tempt many times, but if this course is followed each time, we will discover that Satan will leave the tactics that serve only to drive us closer to the Lord Jesus and make us more sure of our foundation on Him.

The promise in 1 John does not say that if we confess our sins He is *merciful* and just to forgive. . . . When we came the first time we obtained mercy. Now whenever we come as Christians confessing our sins—so different from the sins of the world though they may be the identical acts from all outward appearance—we find that the Word of God says that "He is *faithful* and just to forgive us our sins, and to cleanse us from all unrighteousness" (1 John 1:9). This faithfulness is His own faithfulness to the covenant of salvation which He gave us at the cross. When we have come there for salvation He has justified us once for all—looked upon us as being in Christ, and so being as ready and fit for Heaven as Christ is. This is our position in Him, and when we get out of fellowship with Him the way back is to acknowledge our position and enter into the fruits of Christ's work as applied to us moment by moment through the faithfulness of God.

If We Confess

Governor Neff, of Texas, visited the penitentiary of that state and spoke to the assembled convicts. When he had finished he said that he would remain behind, and that if any man wanted to speak with him, he would gladly listen. He further announced that he would listen in confidence, and that nothing a man might say would be used against him.

When the meeting was over a large group of men remained, many of them life-termers. One by one they passed by, each telling the governor that there had been a frame-up, an injustice, a judicial blunder, and each asking that he be freed. Finally one man came up and said, "Mr. Governor, I just want to say that I am guilty. I did what they sent me here for. But I believe I have paid for it, and if I were granted the right to go out, I would do everything I could to be a good citizen and prove myself worthy of your mercy."

This, of course, was the man whom the governor pardoned. So must it be with God, who alone can pardon. The one difference is that we cannot say that we have paid for any of it. We can come and say, "O God, I just want to say that I am guilty. I am a sinner, a rebel against Thy power and Thy justice. But I believe that Jesus Christ paid for my sin, and if, in Thy mercy, Thou wilt take me out of darkness into light, I will live as one who is alive from the dead."

This, of course, is the man whom God pardons. Anyone who would attempt to stand before God and make a plea of self-righteousness would hear words of sternest condemnation. One thing that God cannot stand is man's justification of himself, or man's measurement of himself in terms of his relationship with other lost sinners. The greatest insult that a human being can offer God is the thought that human character, human righteousness, or human efforts can fit any man for eternal fellowship with a holy God in a pure Heaven. Such an idea denies both the sinfulness of sin and the holiness of God, and constitutes the surest proof of the depravity and uncomprehending mind of the carnal being who is enmity against the God of righteousness and true holiness. The sinner who comes to God must come as a sinner; only then can he see his God as the Savior, and only then can he see himself as a pardoned sinner. So it is with us; we shall never be anything more than pardoned sinners. Yea, though we claim for ourselves all of the marvelous titles that are rightfully ours as redeemed ones, we shall never be anything else than redeemed ones. Sons of God, heirs of God, joint-heirs with Christ, priests and kings, all these things we are; sitting on the throne of Christ with Him in glory, judging the world and judging angels, all of these we shall do. Perfect, holy, righteous; these things we are in position and one day we shall be in actuality. But nevertheless, we shall never be more than pardoned sinners. Our song in heaven will be, "Unto Him that loved us and washed us from our sins. . . ." Or else we shall sing, "Thou art worthy . . . for Thou has redeemed us . . ."

These are the words that will cling to us for eternity. Washed . . . redeemed . . . The detail of the picture shall fade from our memories and we shall not blush with horror as we do now when we look back upon some of the things that we have done, dishonoring God. But we shall always remember that we were sinners.

Lucifer was filled with pride because of his power and beauty. He had no standard of past depths from which he could view the glorious heights of God. The highlights of holiness were not enhanced against the black shadow of a guilty past. So he was lifted up in pride and wanted to usurp the very place of God. None of us will ever fall into that trap when we have passed out of this world into the light of Heaven. Though we shall be like our Lord Jesus Christ, we shall still know that we were sinners, that we are redeemed, and this minor chord, together with the major chords of His eternal victory, shall make up the eternal symphonies of Heaven.

A few years ago I heard of a man who had a gold-plated safety pin attached to one end of his watch chain. As he was frequently seen fingering it, someone asked him the meaning of the symbol. He told how he had run away from a fine home and had gone down to the dregs of sin. He had sold his overcoat for money to buy liquor, and on a cold winter night he had his coat pinned together with that safety pin. He walked into a mission to get warm, and there the Lord Jesus found him and saved him.

Life, after that, brought many successes and a wealthy material position. But the feel of that pin forever robbed him of any thoughts of pride. He knew that all of the merit was in the grace of Christ. He could remember the climax of what he had been able to do in his own strength, and he knew what the redemptive grace of Christ had done. He would not forget.

So, even in Heaven, we shall have the feel of redemption to remind us that we are what we are by the grace of the Lord Jesus Christ. In spite of the wonder of our high titles and position, we shall always know that we are washed . . . redeemed . . . And His will be *all* of the glory.

Can a Born-Again Man Apostatize?

Anyone who believes that one who has been truly born of God can get out of relationship with God and be finally lost is blind to great sections of truth in the Word of God. They look at some experiences in life instead of at the Word of God, and judge the Word by what they see in life, rather than judging life by what they see in the Word.

Martin Luther gave a very neat and beautiful answer to this question. Luther had a servant named Elizabeth, who, in a fit of displeasure, left without giving any notice. She subsequently became dangerously ill, and in her sickness she requested a visit from Luther. On taking his seat at her bedside, he said, "Well, Elizabeth, what is the matter?" "I have given away my soul to Satan," she replied. "Elizabeth, listen to me," rejoined the man of God. "Suppose that, while you lived in my house, you had sold and transferred all my children to a stranger. Would the sale and transfer have been lawful and binding?" "Oh, no, for I had no right to do that." "Very well, you had still less right to give your soul to the Arch-Enemy; it no more belongs to you than my children do. It is the exclusive property of the Lord Jesus Christ; He made it, and when lost He also redeemed it; it is His."

The one who has been made a partaker of the divine nature, having escaped the corruption that is in the world, has the very life of God. It is eternal life. By its very nature, there could be no other kind of divine life except eternal life. If we know anything about ourselves, we can say quite frankly that if God had not intended to keep us when He saved us in the first place, He might just as well not have wasted His time to begin with. But He has said Himself that we may be confident of this very thing that "He which hath begun a good work in you will perform it until the day of Jesus Christ" (Phil. 1:6). Truly we may believe in eternal security.

But it should be recognized that just as it is possible for an individual to stand up and preach and later apostatize, it is also possible for a man to deceive himself into thinking that he is saved. It is important that the Christian give diligence to make his calling and election sure. We do believe in eternal security, but we do not believe in eternal presumption. Let a man examine himself.

The Church

The Chief Function of the Church

It is a fairly well-known fact that a great majority of the criminals of this country are members of some church. There are certain publications which delight in the bravado of shocking the general public. Every so often they drag to the limelight the statistics on this subject, and draw conclusions uncomplimentary to the churches and to religion in general. An article in a much-read magazine presented this subject and concluded, "In brief, there is little evidence that the churches play any major part in the prevention of crime." As they had supported this charge with statistics, is there any possible comeback?

The church and the churches are not the same, though. The churches are organizations, and their members may or may not be Christians in the Biblical sense of the word. The church is the body of born-again believers in the Lord Jesus Christ. What is the chief function of the church? In the great definition of the church in Acts 15:14, we find that God has visited the Gentiles "to take out of them a people for his name." The church is a group called out for God's name. Its purpose is to bring glory to His name.

God's greatest glory is in His grace. Throughout eternity He will exhibit His grace in us, and for this purpose He has saved us, "that in the ages to come he might show the exceeding riches of his grace in his kindness toward us through Christ Jesus." God is not glorified by the moral life of an unsaved man. The church's business is not to try to keep unsaved people from wrongdoing, but to bring them to salvation in Christ.

God cannot be glorified by a sinful life. A more axiomatic statement could hardly be made. He is glorified by the yielded life of a Christian. "Being filled with the fruits of righteousness which are by

Jesus Christ, unto the glory and praise of God." The renewed heart has within it the desire to glorify God by presenting a moral life.

Membership in a church, observance of religious rites, and moral environment and admonitions will not prevent crime. The reason "the churches" do not "play any major part in the prevention of crime" is that they have confounded their chief function. They are presenting religion and morals instead of Christ. They are trying to keep unsaved men from wrongdoing instead of leading them to salvation through Christ. When a man has been born again, the moral results will follow. The process cannot be inverted.

If we could see the heart and know whether or not a man had been born again, we should be able to prove by statistics that the grace of God in Christ is effectual in preventing crime. But only God can see the heart. The statistics are in heaven. Our part is to preach the Gospel.

The Church and True Worship

Worship does not necessarily involve going to church. The word was originally "worth-ship," the quality of recognizing the worth of God. When we sing, "Oh, could I speak the matchless worth . . ." we are getting at the real meaning of the idea of worship.

In the Bible there are incidents which show that worship was carried out apart from any outward act of ritual or liturgy. "By faith, Jacob, when he was dying, blessed both the sons of Joseph and worshipped, strengthening himself with his staff" (Heb. 11:21). A careful study of the Old Testament passage to which the New Testament verse refers will reveal that the worship consisted in being firm to the end, in giving his sons a good example of faith in God, and following the commands given to Him by God.

A greatly misunderstood passage of Scripture is the reference to religion in the Book of James. "Pure religion and undefiled before God is this: To visit the fatherless and widows in their affliction, and to keep himself unspotted from the world" (James 1:27). Here, the word "religion" means "religious worship" or "religious exercise." The translation would then be understood as follows: "A pure and undefiled religious, worshipful exercise is to visit the fatherless . . ." There is certainly no intimation that social service work can replace the recognition of the worth of Jesus Christ. An unbeliever can never recognize the worth of the Savior, for no man calleth Jesus Lord except by the Holy Spirit (1 Cor. 12:3). But when a man is saved and has clearly recognized the love of Christ, he can then go about in the name of the Lord Jesus, doing deeds in His name, and the Lord will recognize those acts as being true worship.

A father might say that he is taking his boy out into the woods for a day of exercise. A Christian, starting off on a round of acts of kindness in the name of the Lord Jesus Christ, could say just as truly, I am going to worship. I am taking the Lord Jesus, who dwells in me, out for exercise. I am thereby recognizing His worth. The New Testament clearly reveals to us a church which was gathered around the Lord Jesus Christ. The acknowledgment of His worth and the worth of the triune Godhead was central to all gatherings of believers. When they were thus gathered in His name, He was in the midst.

As time went on error entered the church. The idea of priesthood came back from Judaism, and from paganism. The clergy became "priests" which means "sacrificers." The communion gave way to the "Mass"; now instead of a recognition of the worth of Christ there was a form and ceremony to take its place. Nature abhors a vacuum and spiritual nature abhors a spiritual vacuum. When the worship of Christ ceased to be the center of religious meetings, form and ceremony took its place and the word "liturgy" stopped meaning worship and began to take on its present meaning.

Scripture tells us that all things must be done "decently and in order" (1 Cor. 14:40). This does not mean, however, that the spontaneity of spiritual worship must give way to a priestly ritual which can occupy but never satisfy unregenerate hearts, and which will leave true children of God with a spirit of emptiness because form has taken the place of devotion to the Lord. "God is Spirit, and they that worship him must worship him in spirit and in truth" (John 4:24). To worship Him in spirit means that the Holy Spirit must be in our hearts; therefore, only redeemed people can worship Him in this manner. When the Holy Spirit guides, the service will be warm and alive, and Christ will be the center of it. Never will He be lost in the fog of ritual for the sake of the service.

The Church and Its Membership

Not everything that is aimed at is hit. This is true of more than guns and targets. I once listened to some Japanese Christians trying to sing a hymn in four parts. They can see from the printed music that one note is higher or lower than the one they have been singing, but just how much they are not sure, for the Japanese musical system is entirely different from ours. It is a matter of chance whether or not they hit the right interval. More often than not, they plunge in the general direction of the printed note with results that are fearful and wonderful to our western ears.

God looks upon the heart and is able to hear harmonics from the yielded spirit, though the voices may not follow any of the accepted rules of music. Those who teach others to sing can carry a tune and sing in harmony, but the road to the teaching of others is hard on the cars. The teachers must never drop the true standard of music for themselves or for their teaching. They must, however, have an infinite patience with those they teach, some of whom will never satisfy outward rules but will, nevertheless, make melody in their hearts to the Lord.

All of this is just as true for Bible teaching as it is for music training. Those of us who are engaged in Christian work must keep the clear sound of truth in our souls and before the minds of our hearers, but we must expect discords of truth among those who are growing in the truth. Not all believers can see truth quickly. Some remain babes in Christ for many years—in fact, through all of their earthly life span. This is why the churches are told that those who are weak in the faith are to be received into membership (Rom. 14:1). The Holy Spirit says that minor points are not to be erected as standards for church membership, and the questions on matters such as diet and the keeping of the Sabbath were eliminated by God as matters which must be settled by each individual. Some on both sides of these questions may think they have the mind of the Spirit, but their opinion is not to be forced on those who hold another honest, spiritual opinion. The Scripture is very definite on these matters.

There were no probation classes in the New Testament. Men who had never heard the Gospel before believed it, and were baptized within a few moments. Responsibility for individual growth rests squarely upon the individual.

The one thing about which Christians need be concerned is the confession of a true and saving faith in the Person and work of the Lord Jesus Christ. Of these matters there can be no compromise. When the serpent was lifted on the pole in the wilderness, those who looked from afar were healed the same as those who had a nearer and clearer view of the serpent lifted up. It was belief in God's Word, and acting upon the commandment to look which brought healing. It is precisely that which brings salvation—looking away from everything that is in self, and looking to the Lord Jesus Christ alone.

In other words, a reasonable belief that an individual has looked to Christ in personal faith is all that the church can demand of those who come seeking membership. This fact doubles the responsibility of the ministers and leaders of every church. The teaching must be definite, sound, and constructive if those who have become weak in the faith are to be strengthened. If this is not the case, the churches will be filled with those who have had the faraway look of true faith, but who have never found within the church that which will bring true growth in Christ.

The Church and Christian Growth

I once read an article by an English Baptist minister, Leslie Stokes. He wrote: "Once upon a time there was a tree. It was a lovely looking tree, shapely, strong, and stately. But appearances are not always to be trusted, and they were not in this case. For the tree knew inwardly that its massive strength was beginning to wane. When the wind was strong it had felt itself shaking ominously, and heard suspicious creaks. So, wisely, it took itself in hand. With much effort it grew another branch or two, and then looked stronger and safer than ever. But when the next gale blew, there was a terrific snapping of roots and, but for the support of a friendly neighbor, it would have been flat on the ground.

"When the tree had recovered from the shock, it looked at its neighbor curiously. 'Tell me,' it said, 'how is it that you have not only stood your ground, but are even able to help me too?' 'Oh,' replied the neighbor, 'that's easy. When you were busy growing new branches, I was strengthening my roots.' "

This is a parable, and a very good one. It represents the life both of churches and of individual Christians. One more paragraph from Mr. Stokes deserves application. "Many of us, when we begin to be concerned about our life and strength, grow new branches. We find it difficult to support the ones we already have—so we start new ones! New committees (how we love committees!), new movements, more societies, more meetings! Ought we not rather attend to the roots? To strengthen the meetings for prayer and Bible study, and to be more diligent about these things in private as well? Old-fashioned things these are, of course, but then, roots *are* old-fashioned. And no substitute has been found for them."

We are seeing great mass movements of evangelism, and we pray God's richest blessing upon them. Anything that can be done through Billy Graham and others who are having revival meetings with thousands of people in attendance is indeed a blessing. And while there will be many who will come to the knowledge of the truth and receive Jesus Christ as their personal Savior, it should be realized that *those who are already Christians are not going to grow spiritually through evangelistic meetings, nor through any activity in connection with them.* There is no possibility of spiritual growth apart from the prayerful study of the Word of God. Sanctification comes through the Word of truth (John 17:17). Growth comes by the Word of God (1 Peter 2:2). Faith comes by hearing the Word of God (Rom. 10:17).

Mr. Stokes ends his article with a neat phrase. "And—who knows?—perhaps some day you will be able to *afford* to have another branch or two!"

The Church and Ecumenism

Some people are constantly working for the fusion of various denominations. Ecumenism seems more important to them than anything else, but there is no Biblical background for their position. Christ spoke of sheep that were not of the Jewish fold, and said that He must bring them also, and continued, "There shall be one flock and one shepherd" (John 10:16). Note especially that we have used the Revised Version, for the Lord did *not* say what the King James Version records, that there shall be one *fold*. The Bible definitely teaches that there must be various branches of the church.

In the great passage that leads up to the doctrine of the Lord's Supper, Paul tells of the moral difficulties in the church and says, "I hear that there be divisions among you . . ." (1 Cor. 11:18). The word "divisions" in the original is *schismata,* an old word for cleft, or split, and was used in ancient times for "splinters of wood." These splinters were not yet shaped into separate organizations, but they would soon have to move in that direction, for the next verse says, "For there must be also factions among you . . ." (11:19). Why did God say that there must be denominations, divisions, sects? The answer is found in the preceding chapters. There was moral and ecclesiastical evil in the midst of the church; therefore, those who followed God's way had to take a firm and definite stand. This resulted in choosing, taking sides, holding views of one party, and that is what exists today. To get everyone in Christendom back in the same fold would mean smoothing over all the difficulties and differences that have arisen over the centuries. There are great and important differences, such as those which divide Romanism and historic Protestantism, which involve the sufficiency of Christ and His sacrifice; and there are minor differences concerning organization, bishops, ordination, baptisms, and so on, but these do not usually cause real separation. The true flock is divided into many folds, and there may be wolves inside the folds, but the sheep are all sheep and they know the Shepherd's voice.

The Church and Politics

What right has the church of Jesus Christ, as a church, to mix in politics? We hold that the separation of church and state is a fundamental principle of both civil and ecclesiastical polity. We remember that the Lord took the kingdom away from Saul and his dynasty because he had intruded into the priests' function; Uzziah was stricken with leprosy because he had offered incense in the temple. God will not entrust the office of civil leader and priest to any individual. The Lord Jesus Christ is the only one who can be Prophet, Priest, and King at the same time.

The individual Christian has every right to participate in politics; vote, run for office, be elected and serve, accept appointments—none of these is out of harmony with the Word of God. If the individual is seeking to be surrendered to the Lord every moment, he can witness to those with whom he comes in contact no matter where he is. But the church, as a church, will lose its power if it seeks to act as an individual. The idea of a church in politics can come only from that false postulate that the purpose of the church is to save the world.

I once found a booklet which made some rather extraordinary statements. Its author, in teaching that the purpose of the church was to save the nation, laid down the following proposition: "The position taken by a government with regard to morals and religion will in the long run, if unchecked, bring to its own likeness a majority of the people. Not all the people, but a majority will come to the position of the government."

Such lack of historical insight and spiritual comprehension would be difficult to parallel. Did the fact that the early legislators of the United States wrote into their laws full moral and religious principles bring the majority of the people to personal adoption of those ideals? But that is an example that might be open to debate or argument. Let us look instead at the priestly government of the children of Israel, which at the beginning took a position with regard to morals and religion that was never checked. Did these priestly laws bring a majority of the people to the position of the government? Of course not; but it is just as nonsensical to think that men can be legislated into being good in the twentieth century. When will we learn that man is a failure, whether it be a failure under the innocence in Eden, or under law from Moses?

The Bible is the story of "man's complete ruin in sin and God's perfect remedy in Christ." Men get into difficulties because they are not willing to admit that mankind's ruin was absolutely *complete*.

Christian Life and Growth

The Secret of a Healthy Christian Life

Professor Gordon W. Allport of Harvard University urges that more psychological studies be made of healthy people in order that we may learn what makes us tick. "Many psychological theories," he says, "are based on the behavior of sick and anxious people, or upon the antics of captive and desperate rats," and "few theories are derived from the study of healthy human beings, those who strive not so much to preserve life as to make it worth living." There have been many studies of criminals, he said, but few of law-abiders; many of fear, but few of courage; more studies of hostility than of effective living with fellow men.

Allport's comments are very applicable to Christians. We often think of the Christian life as a struggle against sin, instead of considering it as a record of the continuing triumphs of Christ. Many, many believers do not even approach the edges of what Christian life is to be. The experience of Christians is not necessarily Christian experience.

We are confronted early in our Christian life with the thought of the cross of Jesus Christ, and become accustomed to thinking of our salvation in terms of the death of the Savior. That death took place several thousand miles away and nineteen hundred years in the past, yet we early learn to annihilate the difference in time and space and think of the death of Christ as something that has immediate application to us. "Jesus, keep me near the cross," is entirely comprehensible. The cross is not at Jerusalem but wherever I am. The cross is not of the year A.D. 30 but as of this moment.

In exactly the same way we must look to the future and to the Lord seated in Heaven. Perhaps the most important verse in the Bible for Christian growth is that found in the second chapter of Ephesians where we read that He has "raised us up (not in the resurrection but in the *ascension*) and made us to sit with Him in the heavenly places in Christ." This is not a prophecy of our future but the available condition of our present sphere of life. This is the *normal,* this is the *healthy* Christian life. The throne of God is not to be distant but *here,* not future but *now.* Our life is to be lived on the earth, but God has made provision in Christ for us to go "in and out" (John 10:9), *in* to the throne and *out* to the earth; *in* to the source of power and *out* to the sphere of activity. No other life is spiritually normal.

The Christian's Personality

Many people today are seeking after various methods of improving their personalities. There are many books available on such topics as winning friends or influencing people, and one sees much advertising which features methods whereby dull people can become the life of the party, or wallflowers can win the hero of the neighborhood. These things would be more amusing were it not for the fact that many Christians follow this worldly lead and ape the earth-dwellers in their seeking for personality development.

There is a great Biblical doctrine, a doctrine which is right along this same line, which is often overlooked by many who should know better. That fact is that the Holy Spirit was given by God to take possession of the life and individuality of the believer, and to express His divine personality, or one small aspect of it, through the believer's life and personality. Let us approach this truth by the backdoor. The Bible tells of men who were possessed by demons whose lives expressed the identity of those demons. Anyone who approached these poor, stricken creatures could be immediately aware of the sinister personality controlling and dominating the stricken being. There are several descriptions found in the Gospels which show these personalities manifesting themselves in men: "exceeding fierce" (Matt. 8:28), "dumb" (Matt. 9:32), "lunatic" (Matt. 17:15), "unclean" (Mark 1:23), "crying" (Mark 5:5), "pining away" (Mark 9:18), a nudist (Luke 8:27), and other delineations of character which ceased with the departure of the demon.

If the presence of a demon in the life of a man could so alter his identity, covering the true human personality and exhibiting the demon personality, how much more shall the Holy Spirit's presence in the life of a believer dominate his personality by expressing the personality of God in the life of the yielded believer? Here is a clue to the inner meaning of the great verse: "The fruit of the Spirit is love, joy, peace, longsuffering, gentleness, goodness, faith, meekness, and self-control" (Gal. 5:22). You can't duplicate that by consulting a psychiatrist or by reading a book on self-expression. At times we meet people who, judged by the world's standards, are fearfully drab and colorless, lacking in what the world calls personality. Yet we note in many instances the definite marks of the presence of the Holy Spirit in that life. There is a warmth and tenderness towards life and its problems, a love and devotion not to be found in the selfish world, a color and life easily visible to the discerning eye. When we think of what these people would be without the presence of the Lord within them, we can glorify God in them. Let the Holy Spirit take hold of your personality.

Progress in the Christian Life

You may stop the hands of the clock, but time will go on just the same. True progress can never be permanently arrested. When Nicholas I became Tsar of Russia, he attempted to shut off his country from all intercourse with the outside world. A historian summarized the results of the Tsar's attitude: "Russians were forbidden to travel abroad. Nicholas referred to the Moscow University as a 'den of wolves,' and restricted the number of students to three hundred." Censors struck out of papers such phrases as "forces of nature" and "movements of minds." Nicholas himself was enraged at finding the word "progress" used in a report of one of his ministers and demanded its deletion from all future official documents. But progress could not thus be staved off.

There are people who wish to block spiritual progress in their own lives. There are many church members who act as if—and say so openly—they do not want to go any deeper into spiritual things than their present position. One might sometimes wonder if such people have really been born again. God has given definite statements concerning spiritual advance; there is no place in His program for standstill. We can at least say that those who do not go forward are not in the center of God's will and are thus out of fellowship with Him. The French have a well-known proverb, *Qui ne s'avance pas recule,* which means, "Whoever does not go forward goes backward." It is the same in the Father's dealings with His children.

Put these four verses together:

"He which hath begun a good work in you will perfect (ASV) it until the day of Jesus Christ" (Phil. 1:6).

"When I begin I will also make an end" (1 Sam. 3:12).

"My loving kindness will I not utterly take away from him, nor suffer my faithfulness to fail" (Ps. 89:33).

"The Lord will perfect that which concerneth me" (Ps. 138:8).

These promises, and others like them, are God's certain guarantee that He is not going to let us remain still for long. If we need it, He will chastise us to bring us to the place of true progress in Himself according to His good, agreeable, and perfect will. He has promised to supply all our needs, even the need of discipline, when He sees it to be necessary.

You cannot strike "progress" out of God's dealings with a soul.

Feelings and Feelings

There are certain words in the Scriptures which are used in opposite senses. The classic example is that of "works," which God curses and blesses. "Not of works lest any man should boast," is followed by "we are created in Christ Jesus unto good works" (Eph. 2:9, 10). Works upon which we are dependent for salvation must ever be cursed of God, but works which flower from the new creation of life in Christ Jesus, are not only blessed of God, but are also a part of the purpose of our new creation.

A word which is not found in the Bible on the same scale as the word "works," but which is capable of a double usage, is the word "feelings." When used in a non-Biblical sense, it has long been pilloried by those who would present the message of salvation in all its fullness. Salvation has never depended and could never depend upon the feelings of any individual. There are undoubtedly some who "feel" safe who are in reality lost souls because they have not trusted in Christ. There are others who do not "feel" saved, but who are no doubt true children of God.

There are feelings, however, which are perfectly legitimate. There are thousands of true believers who delight in the fact that they know they are saved not only because God says so, but because they also possess the quiet satisfaction of feeling that all is well. When David asked for the restoration of the joy of his salvation, he was asking for a feeling; for joy is most certainly to be classed with the emotions. There are many emotions which are quite proper in the Christian experience, and which should not be repressed. We love Him because He first loved us, and there is most certainly feeling, both in His love for us and our returning love. Wherever there is a conflict, though, between our feelings and the Word of God, we choose the Word of God. This choice flows from our very name of believer. We are those who believe the Word above all else.

Another common usage of the word "feeling" is that which expresses an absolute conviction of being in the Lord's will on the basis of the leading of the Holy Spirit. We say, for example, that we "feel led" of the Lord to do a certain thing. Is this an idle feeling, the mere equivalent of a human whim, the rising desire of the flesh? Not according to the Word of God. John gives us the basis of this feeling or conviction in his first Epistle. "For if our heart condemn us," that is, if we feel that we have offended the Lord, "God is greater than our hearts, and knoweth all things"; which is to say, God, who knows all things, will condemn us all the more. But then we read, "Beloved, if our heart condemn us not," that is, if we are in a course of action where we feel that we have the mind of the Lord as revealed by the indwelling Spirit, "then have we confidence toward God" (1 John

3:20, 21). Our confidence is a feeling; it is a firm assurance. We have sought the Lord's will by all the channels we know, and believe we have it and are yielded to it.

Sincerity

Words are more interesting than any puzzle. Sometimes the history of a word opens up a window on the habits and customs of a past generation. The common English word "butcher," for example, takes us back through the French "boucher," when "bouc" or goat meat was the chief meat on the diet.

Few words, however, have a more interesting lineage than the word "sincere." Among the theories advanced to explain this word is the one that sees its derivation from "sine"—without, and "cera"—wax. In the ancient Roman world a sculptor sometimes chipped off too large a piece from the marble. Rather than begin his work over again, he used wax to fasten the piece back onto the image. This would stand the temporary test and the sale would be made, but soon the fraud would show up. It became necessary, in drawing up contracts with sculptors, to insert the word "sinecera"—without wax.

The Greek word used in the classics and in the New Testament to express the idea of sincerity comes from the words meaning "sunlight" and to "unfold." When a product was examined in the clear light of the sun and found to be pure and unsullied, it was "sincere."

In the light of these meanings, what vigor is to be found in Paul's prayer for the Philippians. "That ye may approve things that are excellent, that ye may be *sincere* and without offence till the day of Jesus Christ"—that ye may be without fraud, unfolded in the sunlight.

The natural man loves darkness rather than light—loves his own opinions rather than God's revelation (John 3:19). David Nelson indicated, a century ago, that one small, cunningly-devised falsehood will influence the natural man more than one hundred plain and forcible arguments in favor of revelation. It is when a man is born again that he loves light and truth rather than darkness, and can live in a *sincere* way, that is, without fraud, and unfolded in God's sunlight.

Your Soul Is Showing

Girls are accustomed to being told that their slip is showing, if such is the case. One who is told too often may be considered a careless dresser. Worse than letting a slip show, though, is letting one's soul show. I quote from a letter which said, "There are some awful souls talking in Christian speech." Awful souls? I began to think about it. I knew what was meant, of course, but there was something here that needed clarification.

All souls are bad in the sight of God. Even when men of the world speak of some of the great and charitable as being "great-souled" they are not talking from God's perspective. They may fulfill certain human standards, and the vestigial remnants of the divine image that are in all men might be more dominant in such men. However, according to divine revelation, all the thoughts of man's heart are vanity. It is only when one has been born again that there is true life—divine life. If the Christian spirit is dominant in a Christian, it will be possible to see the presence and growth of the Lord. But if the soul is showing, it will always be the soul of Adam which can be seen.

The sad part of the phrase from the letter mentioned above is that which tells of the use of Christian speech by such souls. They are even glib at times with their use of Christian clichés. They can testify "Jesus saves and keeps and satisfies"—and can look around with a smirk and sit down in proud self-satisfaction.

There are professing Christians who get a completely carnal thrill out of revival meetings and other church services. One woman told me that she went forward in different meetings when the invitation was given because she "felt good" afterward. It was her soul that was showing. An outstanding minister of one of the largest churches on the Pacific Coast told me that he knew many people that came forward on an average of once a month for "decision." That can be an unconscious exhibitionism—the soul is showing.

Most commonly, though, the soul shows in the carnality of the Christian walk. The soul shows itself in prayerlessness or in failure to feed upon the Word of God. There is only one way to overcome this out-Jeering of the soul, and that is by having it put to death daily with Christ in His crucifixion. Then we shall be able to say truly, "It is no longer I (the soul) that lives, but Christ who liveth in me (the spirit)."

Help and Hindrance

The Christian life is presented to us in the Scriptures as a great warfare in which we are partakers. We have a great enemy, but we also have a great Ally. There is one, near at all times, who is the great hinderer and there is one, also near at all times, who is the great Helper.

The hinderer is Satan. Paul writes to the Thessalonians, "Wherefore we would have come unto you, even I, Paul, once and again; but Satan hindered us" (1 Thess. 2:18). The Helper is the Holy Spirit. Paul writes to the Romans, "Likewise the Spirit also helpeth our infirmities . . ." (Rom. 8:26). The two verbs are most interesting. Translated, "hinder" means to cut off, to strike in, and the noun in classical usage is used to describe a trench dug against a foe. "Help" means to lay hold with another, to give a lift, or to assist.

The one who is our Helper is the stronger of the two. It was Christ Himself who said, "Greater is he that is in you than he that is in the world" (1 John 4:4). It is this greater one who is our Helper and who helps at precisely the point where we most need help. For "the Spirit also helpeth our infirmities. . ." In other words, at the very point where we are weak the Spirit lays hold with us for our strengthening. It frequently happens in Christian experience that in the very points where a believer has been defeated he becomes strong because of the Spirit working through his own powers and faculties.

The spheres of the Spirit's help are threefold. It is through the Spirit that we are able to mortify the deeds of the body (Rom. 8:13), and it is in the body that the Spirit takes up His residence (1 Cor. 6:19). In the sphere of our souls, the seat of the emotions and the will, He comes to subdue and to fortify (Rom. 8:2–4). Lastly, He builds our whole spiritual life in its witness to others, in its prayer to God, and in its likeness to Jesus Christ.

Since we have this Helper, greater than any hinderer, why do we go along without recourse to His help? What sin to work and live in our own strength when He is within!

Fixed Purpose

It is necessary for us to have a fixed purpose if we are to do that which is well pleasing to our Lord and Master. There are too many Christians who seem to live and move by whim instead of by the will of the Lord. They are not steadfast to their tasks in life.

Let us draw an illustration from the nature of the Scotch shepherd dog. If he is left to guard his master's coat, for example, he will not leave it until the master returns. Nothing can draw him from the task to which he was appointed. A rabbit might run by, almost under his nose, but he will not move. A deer will break from a copse and go across the glen, so close to the quiet dog that it could easily have been brought down, but the dog will not move.

If the dog had the mind of some Christians he might reason, "Oh, my master was unaware that a rabbit would pass or a very valuable deer. Surely he expects me to use my intelligence and leave the thing to which I have been appointed and run after the game." Many Christians run away from the thing to which they have been appointed. The lure of the great or the showy draws them away from the steady devotion to the humble task to which they were appointed. For example, the will of God for a high school or college student is that he do his work well and get marks consistent with the degree of intelligence with which he has been endowed. No side work, *even Christian work,* should take the Christian student away from his task. He should maintain his soul with God in devotional study, give all the rest of the time required to his studies, and any remaining fraction should be spent on the active work.

No woman was ever called upon to neglect her home, even for child evangelism to other neglected children. If she does, she has left a coat to run after a rabbit. No man with a wife and children is called to enter the ministry if it means the neglect of the family, which must be his first consideration. If he does so, he is like the dog who has taken its eyes away from the coat.

We are not permitted to look for things which we think will be so outstanding that the Lord must commend us for doing them. "It is required in stewards, that a man be found faithful" (I Cor. 4:2). God's place for a country pastor may be a country parish. The dog knows the coat of its master by scent. The student, the mother, the father, the pastor, each will know the things of the Lord by an intimate living with Him in the Word. This is more well-pleasing to the Lord than great exploits.

Portable Strength

When Pope Gregory left the monastery to assume the Papacy, he lamented that he was "borne ever onward by the disturbance of those endless billows" and that he had almost lost sight of the port which he had left. There was much difference between the quiet of the monastery and the turbulence of the throne that dominated Europe.

Many Christians have expressed the regret that they could not carry the high moments of a convention or the spiritual grip of a communion service back into the life of school, office, store, shop, factory, or home. The difference between the daily round of life and the climax of a spiritual assembly comes from a profound truth that is revealed in the Word of God.

Our bodies are the temples of the Holy Spirit from the moment we are born again. Since the day God tore the veil in the temple there has been no building on earth that has been a true house of God. The finest church building in Christendom is empty of the presence of God when there is no human being within its portals; but let two or three children of God gather together in the name of the Lord Jesus, and in that moment He fulfills His promise—*there am I.* There is the added presence of the Lord in the midst of spiritual assembly, whether it be in a church building, a home, or on a ship at sea.

When we leave the spiritual assembly, the presence of the Godhead—Father, Son, and Holy Spirit—accompanies us in fulfillment of other promises. Though the high moment of the assembly may not continue, there is, nevertheless, a strength that goes with us. We need not complain, as Gregory did, that there is danger of losing sight of the port; the haven of strength is not a place of mystic contemplation away from the world, but in the active bustle of life. If we mean business with God we may be sure of the continued manifestations of His presence. This is not merely the ordinary indwelling presence of the Spirit, but the special power and presence that God grants to individual believers when they are ready to fulfill the conditions of surrender to His Lordship.

Every believer, whether in fellowship or out of fellowship, is sure of the indwelling presence of the Father (John 14:23), the Son (Col. 1:27), and the Holy Spirit (1 Cor. 6:19). When the Lordship of the indwelling Trinity is made secure by our yieldedness, His presence is in full control, and when we assemble with other believers there is an added dimension to His presence. Only one more step is possible. When He comes again we shall behold His visible presence and we will have no flesh life to detract from the completeness of the domination of that presence.

The Home of the Redeemed

Man has a great need for rest. The body will die without the proper rest in sleep; the mind will crack without proper relaxation; the spirit is forever dead until it comes to rest in God. In these days of restlessness and hurry it is very necessary that the Christian know where his resting place is, and that he flee there for quiet, rest, refreshment, and strength for his daily tasks.

The marvelous thing about our rest in God is that it accompanies us, though it is possible for the mind and heart to go forth from it, dwelling in the weaknesses of the resources of self, even when the strength of God gives us continuing life. The Psalmist had learned the lesson when he wrote, "He that dwelleth in the secret place of the most High shall abide under the shadow of the Almighty" (Ps. 91:1).

The secret place of the most High is the home of the redeemed. It is with us at all times if we will only enter its portals, refresh ourselves at its stream, rest ourselves in its shade, and feed at its table.

The difficulty with the human heart is that it is by nature a wanderer, and must learn the lesson of dwelling. Many years ago Blackstone, the great English jurist, was called upon to define "home." A British nobleman had died. He had inherited titles and castles from both English and Scottish forebears, but had lived most of his life abroad. If he were adjudged a Scot, his estate would be administered under Scottish law, but if English, under English law. Where was his home? The great interpreter of law was asked for a definition of "home." Blackstone wrote, "Home is that place from which when a man has departed, he is a wanderer until he has returned."

There is without doubt a spiritual application of this definition. Our home is in God. Augustine said, "O God, Thou hast formed us for Thyself, and our souls can know no rest until they rest in Thee." The tragedy of our Christian lives is that we so frequently live outside of the home that is God, the abiding place that we can enter at any moment. All of the problems of Christian life arise from the fact that men step over the threshold of God's presence and go out into a wandering journey in the lands of self. But if we abide . . . there lies our rest in Christ, our power in prayer, our strength to overcome. All is in Him.

The Heart

A story is told which is very gripping in its human interest. A young officer, blinded during the war, was rehabilitated in an Army hospital. During this time he met and later married one of the nurses who took care of him. He had a tremendous devotion to her and loved her dearly. One day his keen sense of hearing overheard someone in the distance speaking about himself and his wife. "It was lucky for her that he was blind, since he never would have married so homely a woman if he had had eyes." He rose to his feet and walked toward the voices, saying, "I overheard what you said, and I thank God from the depths of my heart for blindness of eyes which might have kept me from seeing the marvelous worth of the soul of this woman who is my wife. She is the most noble character I have ever known, and if the conformation of her features is such that it might have masked her inward beauty to my soul then I am the great gainer by having lost my sight."

The Bible says that God seeth not as man seeth, "for man looketh on the outward appearance, but the Lord looketh on the heart" (1 Sam. 16:7). The Bible also says that God prefers holiness to glamour (1 Peter 3:4). If someone possesses physical beauty he may be thankful for it, but he should realize what a temptation it can be, and he must ever surrender it to the Lord. If in any way there is an attempt to trade upon it, God must blast the spiritual life as a result.

A true understanding of these principles will not cause any Christian to despise any gift God has given him. We must not go to asceticism in denying the inward value of any outward grace. A Christian should always dress well; be neat and clean as becometh an ambassador for the Lord Jesus Christ. We must always seek to develop a yieldedness to His presence and power so that our inward character, renewed day by day, may show forth the life of the Lord Jesus Christ. The Lord Himself has put within us that which alone can please Him, and of this we may be glad.

Living

A person who really wishes to learn how to live life more successfully must first know whether he has life to live, or whether he possesses nothing more than mere existence. When a man knows that he has "life," he knows that it is not earthly life, but eternal life, and that it bears a divine quality which makes living something more than existence.

Living the Christian life becomes a daily process which may be likened to the water that flows from two different faucets, mixing together in one spout before it flows into the basin. The force of the life that flows from the fountain of the old nature is very great and terrible. It can be restrained only by our committing it to the hand of the Lord that He may keep its flow checked. Its washers are rusted out with sin, and its flow contaminates everything we are and do, unless it is kept in check by the momentary surrender to the life and power of the Lord that flows out of the new life which He has created within us. Paul, like us, knew that he lived *in the flesh,* but *by the faith of the Son of God* (Gal. 2:20).

The Christian must recognize that there are no degrees of right or wrong. Any wish or act in life comes from the flesh or from the Spirit. There is no other source of willingness or action. Satan and the world work through the flesh, and the latter is the source of all that is contrary to the Spirit.

The life that is lived by the Spirit is characterized by the fruit of the Spirit. This is "love, joy, peace, longsuffering, gentleness, goodness, faith, meekness, and self-control" (Gal. 5:22). When the source of true living is established and our relationship with our God becomes an integral part of us, then our living, as it affects those around us, takes on its true and holy pattern. We can never be critical of what we see in anyone else, for we remember the path along which our Lord has had to bring us. We become so grateful to our Lord for the blessings that He has showered upon us in the years of our spiritual immaturity that our hearts turn out for others who have not yet accepted the free-flowing life which He is so eager to give. We realize that we have a great distance to go ourselves and our motto becomes, "If any man think that he knoweth anything, he knoweth nothing yet as he ought to know" (1 Cor. 8:2). It is inconceivable to be other than kindly towards those who are on the same ladder that we have climbed and who may be a few rungs behind us. We can help them on, and in so doing climb together to His glory.

Members of the Body

The deep truth of our union with Christ, He the Head and we the body, has been a source of such blessing to believers that it is frequently studied. The other phase of that truth, though, that we individual believers are members one of another, is not so frequently stated.

The moment we are born again we are also baptized of the Holy Spirit into the body of Christ. By that act we receive from God gifts which are for the use of the whole church. These gifts are not confined to a few individuals; every believer is given some gift. No matter how humble, how ignorant, how unlettered a man may be when he is born again, God equips him supernaturally with some gifts which are more than the perfecting of the saints. This truth is presented in 1 Corinthians 12.

In another Epistle Paul points out (Eph. 3) that the gift received by the individual is given as a gift to the whole church. We belong, then, one to another. There is a place in the church for all. This does not mean, though, that there is a place for those who deny truth or who are not born again. The comprehensiveness of the church as taught by the modernists is not to be found in the Scripture. The inclusiveness of the true church is limited strictly to those who have been born again.

Some men may have more gifts than others, and it is possible to grow in gifts. We are directly told that we are to covet earnestly the best gifts (1 Cor. 12:31). They, like wisdom, are given to those who know their lack and who ask of God. Thus an evangelist will come into a church and do a great work in rousing the people. It is necessary that he should be followed by a Bible teacher. This man in turn may not have the gifts of the shepherd, and a pastor is needed to visit the flock, to bring comfort and encouragement.

I thought of this when I read a news item concerning two students in the Chicago-Kent College of Law. The high ranking scholar in the class was a young blind man named Overton. He insisted that half the credit for his honors should go to his companion, Kaspryzk. They had met in school when the armless Mr. Kaspryzk had guided Mr. Overton down a flight of stairs. The acquaintance ripened into friendship. The blind man carried the books which the armless one read aloud for their common study. Later they planned partnership.

Here is a true illustration of the way born-again believers should work together. We do not all have the same gifts, but those which we do have are for the common upbuilding of all believers. We should ask God to show us what gifts we have, and how they can be used and developed for Him. We must covet earnestly the best gifts; we must seek to grow in their knowledge. We must put at the disposal of other believers that which we possess. Only in this way can we be built up together until we come into the measure of the stature of the fulness of Christ (Eph. 4:13).

Practical Living

There is one part of Christianity which can never be confuted; that is the practical outworking of the doctrines which we hold as the revelation of God's will for us. An unbeliever may bring forth an argument against a doctrine, but he can never argue against a holy life, except to hate it and say that the one who is living it is missing the sinful joys which the world holds to be paramount.

In addition to the great doctrinal teachings concerning redemption which are found throughout the Word of God, there is the very practical teaching that there is no contradiction between human effort and humble dependence upon the help of God. This theme is supported by many parallels through the history of men of faith. It may be true, and the skeptics have not failed to bring it up, that our forefathers appointed a day of fasting and prayer in time of pestilence, while in our own day an immediate survey of the sanitary system is made. Any antithesis between the two methods of approach is a false one. It is true that the development of civilization gives us an increasing knowledge of such matters as the method of the spread of disease, but that in no wise lessens our utter dependence upon God.

The right arms of the Scottish soldiers were strengthened, not weakened for battle as they knelt in prayer on the field of Bannockburn. Oliver Cromwell spoke truly when he declared that his army did not become uniformly victorious until he had gathered into its ranks men of faith "who made a conscience of all they did." And who, in World War II, would dare to say that the ardent faith and daily prayers of General Montgomery had benumbed his energies or weakened his activity? The old gibe that Christianity is "dope" is notoriously untrue. To depend on God is far from paralyzing to the energies of man. It is instead the greatest possible incentive to activity, courage, and endurance.

There is not contradiction between the word, "Trust the Lord and keep your powder dry," and the Biblical word, "Some trust in chariots, and some in horses, but we will remember the name of the Lord our God" (Ps. 20:7). There may be many people who have more confidence in tanks and airplanes than they have in God, but the Christian knows that the Lord is the one who rules and overrules. Our trust is in Him.

Older Circles and Inner Circles

When a man becomes a Christian he not only gives assent to a new set of beliefs, but he also finds that he has a new life, a new stream of thought, and that he lives in an entirely different society. He is now a member of the body of Christ. He does not cease to be a member of his family, but he has a new relationship with that family. He does not cease to be a member of his work group, but he has a new relationship with that work group. He does not cease to be a citizen of his country, but he has a new relationship to his country. He will still live and move in the circles in which he has lived and moved before, but he will live and move in a different fashion. He will have added so much by becoming a Christian that he will draw all his resources from his new life and will therefore have a transformed attitude in all his older circles.

Mark tells us of the deaf man who lived in the Decapolis. He had a life in which there was the experience of sight, and of feeling, and of tasting, and of smelling but he had a life in which there was no sound. When the Lord Jesus opened his ears and loosed the string of his tongue (Mark 7:35), the man did not lose his sight and feeling and other senses, but his world was increased by the addition of the new dimension of sound. It is in this way that the Lord comes to those who put their trust in the Savior. A man doesn't change grandfathers, or lose his bank account, or live in a different circle of society by becoming a believer, but he keeps the old things and adds an immeasurably rich newness to life. It is true that the coming of the new sometimes will so transform the old that it will be altered beyond recognition. He may discover that he no longer wants to keep the same social relationships that he had before he was saved, but this is not relevant to our present subject.

The church of Jesus Christ is not a building where people come together for a religious service, but it is a gathering of people who come together in order to worship God and to build each other by mutual faith and strength. God even tells us that He puts people together in the church and gives each one something that all the others need. It is only as we come together in this manner that we can begin to understand the fellowship, the communion, that God has for us.

Therefore, if God has given you special spiritual blessings you are in special spiritual danger. The devil will never let you sit quietly in the midst of glorious blessings, but will come with the subtlest of schemes to turn you away from the triumph that God has for you.

There is no doubt that there are people in churches who know more about the Bible than others, but this knowledge should make them humble, not proud. There can be no doubt that there are people in churches who have been given much more spiritual discernment than others, and this will make them abstain from certain actions which others will practice; but this abstention should make them sweet and quiet and prayerful, not proud. Above all, there will never be the thought that they are in some inner circle, closer to God, or more blessed than others. It may simply be that they are in the place where some will arrive in ten years, and which others reached ten years ago. God has no inner circles. God has no favorite children. Those who are born again have become His through the Lord Jesus Christ, and their circle of fellowship must be the whole of the body of believers.

We may not draw lines of fellowship which are closer than that which the Lord has drawn. The prayerful consideration of that sentence should send shivers through the systems of those who want to limit the communion table to those who cross their t's and dot their i's in the same fashion. The line of fellowship must be made by the Holy Spirit. Are we going to be in Heaven forever in the body of Christ, redeemed by His blood? If we are, then in the name of God the Father, God the Son, and God the Holy Spirit, let us try to get together now and have fellowship here.

Any other attitude toward fellow believers is an attitude of carnality which the Holy Spirit must rebuke. If you are a wise old sheep and see a lamb which has mud on its fleece, don't push him in the mire; draw him out and tell him how to be cleansed. If the believers who are not taught deeply in the Word and of the Spirit sense an attitude of pride in you in something that God has given you, then you are carnal. Let the Holy Spirit make you Holy Spiritual; then you will be wholly spiritual.

Fellowship?

Yes, there is an interrogation point after this title, for we are interested in making you think about the word, and want you to ask yourself if you have any Christian fellowship. If you begin to think about the number of faithful Christians you know, and the good times you have had together, you have brought yourself to the place of vulnerability, and are wide open to the thrust we wish to make into your complacency.

A young Christian was talking about the parties, picnics, bowling contests, and other amusements that a group of splendid Christians have in common. He said, "All of them are born again. All of them have a witness. All of them are known in their secular circles of business as Christians. But I have noticed that what they call fellowship seems to be a group vacation from the Lord. If, in the midst of a conversation, the Lord is mentioned, there is a momentary pause, a hard moment, as though there is a conscious shifting of gears, and an adjustment has to be made." Yet most of the group would probably describe their encounter, whether they had been listening to records, swimming, or stopping at the soda fountain for some refreshments after a meeting, as good Christian fellowship.

Is it not true that such associations should be called, rather, the secular fellowship of Christians? It has its distinct place and is very important in the lives of young Christians, for the Lord has created our social nature as well as our spiritual nature. But there is danger of losing the spiritual fellowship by thinking that our social fellowship is the climax of all fellowship. It is possible for Christians to order their lives in such a way that the group association becomes the end instead of the by-product.

If there is an uneasiness at the sudden, natural, mention of the Lord after listening to a concert or between innings in a softball game,

there is something out of focus. There would be no uneasiness if someone said, "I ran across an interesting anecdote about Napoleon . . ."
Then why should there be if someone said, "I read a most interesting
verse this morning that I had never seen before. The Lord . . ."

Let us not lose the most wonderful fellowship of all, and the eternal blessing that accompanies the casual speaking and thinking of the
Lord.

Conscience

There are many people who believe that conscience is a safe
guide. There are those who refuse to accept Christ, as they claim to
find sufficient light in their own consciences.

The folly of such an attitude is apparent to those who know the
truth about the human conscience, and even more apparent to those
who know the Word of God. In the unregenerate man, conscience is
frequently twisted to be nothing more than a guardian of convention.
H. L. Mencken has said that conscience is an inner voice that warns us
when somebody is looking.

Many people have trained their consciences so that they will be-
have exactly as they wish them to. They are able to find a way to please
their own desires, while at the same time they are directly transgress-
ing that which they know to be true. Alexander Woollcott in his book,
While Rome Burns, tells of an experience in the great gambling casino
at Monte Carlo. He saw a "pallid old gentleman whose hands, as they
caressed his stack of counters, were conspicuously encased in braided
gloves of gray silk. It seems that in his youth he had been a wastrel, and
on her deathbed, his mother had squeezed from him a solemn promise
never to touch a card or chip again as long as he lived." He had lived
up to his promise, for his conscience had provided the gray silk gloves.

When man sinned, he learned the knowledge of good and evil.
This is conscience. For hundreds of years, from the Fall to the Flood,
it was demonstrated that this recently acquired knowledge could not
furnish the power to do the good and to avoid the evil. God's observa-
tion at the time of Noah was that "every imagination of the thoughts
of man's heart was only evil continually" (Gen. 6:5).

We may thank God that we do not have to live by conscience. Our Guide is the indwelling Holy Spirit who does not have to play upon the finer elements of the old nature, but provides a life that is not our own, and which ever points to the Word of God. This is infinitely safer than living by conscience.

The Demands of Holiness

Our God is a demanding God, an exigent God. His very nature demands of Him that He demand of us more than we can ever supply. The requirement of His righteousness is a righteousness equal to His own. He could never accept human righteousness as a compromising payment. Perfection demands perfection; that is why salvation must be by grace, and why works are not sufficient.

The glory of grace is that our God is not only a demanding God, He is a supplying God. Never has He required anything of us that He has not furnished us as a gift of His sovereign grace. His demand of righteousness has been fully met by that which was manifested for us in Christ.

In a devotional book the Canon of Winchester says, "The demands of holiness are so great that the resources to meet them are simply not to be found within the competence of our human nature." Who is sufficient, then, to meet the daily demands of God? Once more it must be seen that what God requires, He provides.

The Christian life comes on the installment buying plan. There is a down payment of righteousness and a daily installment of holiness, one required for the entrance into eternal life and the other for enjoying its fellowship and blessings. God will not accept human righteousness for salvation any more than an automobile salesman will accept counterfeit money as down payment on a new model car. Nor can He accept the average goodness of average Christians as the basis for showering us with the special, abundant blessings which He must reserve for those who bring Him that which His nature requires. Just as God has provided Christ as the down payment, so He has provided Christ as the continuing payment of holiness. The second must be appropriated by faith even as the first. "He is made unto us . . . righteousness, sanctification . . ." (1 Cor. 1:30). The Holy Spirit brings righteousness when He bears new life in us at the new birth, and He applies righteousness to us every hour of our life. The provision is fully made, and thus are the demands of holiness met.

Thus true likeness to Christ is no more dependent upon surrounding circumstances than the growth of a water lily is dependent upon the scene of beauty. That flower will often be found springing from the mud in quite ugly places. So it is with the likeness of Christ in the hearts of those who are yielded to Him.

One of the most holy men of the nineteenth century was Robert Murray M'Cheyne. His diary reveals that he maintained this holiness in the midst of a city where there was much godlessness, and at a time when there was ecclesiastical bickering. The true church was fighting for its very life, and many ministers were cold, if not dead; those who were channels of divine power were criticized for believing in the Lord's coming, for being young men, and for being fanatical. Furthermore, this personal holiness was maintained in the midst of great weakness which finally drew the spirit from the frail body at an age of only twenty-nine years.

Holiness is offered to every believer. If we are not living in Christ we should examine ourselves to see if we actually believe in the faith. The soul that lives in constant carnality has reason to pause to ask whether the planting has been the wheat of the Lord or the tares of Satan. God is so ready to maintain us in holiness!

Contented Discontent

There are many paradoxes in the Christian life. Paul speaks of being "unknown, and yet well known; as dying, and, behold, we live; as chastened, and not killed; as sorrowful, yet always rejoicing; as poor, yet making many rich; as having nothing, and yet possessing all things" (2 Cor. 6:9, 10).

In the same way there is such a thing as contented discontent. We are happy in our work, though we may wish that it were more fruitful; we are happy in our living, though we desire that our lives were more holy. We may be both dissatisfied and satisfied with our lot, our task, our circumstances.

In a conversation when a missionary friend was asked about his field of labor, he said that the Lord had given him a holy discontent in which he was properly contented. "But," he said, "when we were first looking toward the field, we asked the Lord most definitely to give us a very hard field. God both heard and abundantly answered that prayer, for He has given us one of the hardest fields in the world."

There are many lessons that can grow out of this line of thought. Like Paul, we can learn that in whatsoever state we are, therewith to be content. We can know how to be abased and how to abound (Phil. 4:11, 12). These things we can learn by the various places and circumstances in which the Lord is pleased to place us. For Paul says, "In all things I am *instructed* both to be full and to be hungry, both to abound and to suffer need." It would appear that the instructor, in this case, was none other than what we might call the vicissitudes of life—the ups and downs that go with living—the richer and poorer, the better and the worse, the sickness and the health, as long as we shall live. It is God that makes the circumstances in the life of the believer; nothing can ever touch us unless it has passed through His will. In the last analysis, it is the Lord Himself who is our instructor in these things, teaching us in fulness and in hunger, in bounty and in need.

While I was in the midst of writing this last paragraph, the typewriter remained still for more than an hour as I talked and prayed with a brother whose job was suddenly nonexistent because of the death of his employer and the liquidation of the jewelry business of which he had been a part for many years. Now, just past forty, he came, saying, "Pastor, I am in a fix." How happy I was to tell him that he was not in a "fix," but that he was in a path which had been ordered by the Heavenly Father, and that it was a part of the all things which work together for his good, since he truly loves the Lord and is one of the Lord's own. He had a right to be discontented that he was unemployed, for God requires us to be diligent and industrious, but he had the right to be perfectly serene in the contentment of his heart as he went about diligently and industriously seeking a new connection in life.

May we all learn to walk very close to the Father, and to seek every possible lesson that He would have us learn from Himself as an instructor using the object lessons of living.

The Quietness of God

The Christian has to learn to live in the world, but he must draw all his resources from outside of the world. The more he does for God, or rather the more he lets God do through him, the greater will be the need of renewing his strength in the presence of God.

A French writer, commenting on the accession of Edward VIII, spoke of the forces that had worked against him. Wherever he passed he was acclaimed, sought by journalists, photographers, and men and women who wished a nod, feeding on such recognition. To be sought after by the entire world is a sort of nightmare under which a Lindbergh, who was not prepared in advance, succumbed.

Howard Carter discovered the tomb of a king, and soon found that every tourist wanted to see the tomb and to see him. He was forced to refuse permission to those, even though highly recommended, who pushed themselves into his life. He said, "The worst of it is, that you are thirty and that I am only one, and that every day."

Thus the world will seek to press in on the Christian. The Christian must fight to be alone with God and to keep time for knowing God.

The disciples early saw the need of this aloneness. As the cares of the church increased, they demanded that deacons be appointed. It was not fit that they should leave the Word of God to become servants. Men who were filled with the Holy Spirit were to be chosen to take care of the details so that the disciples might give themselves "to prayer and the ministry of the Word." If the disciples had to fight against these inroads from without, how much more must we fight in this twentieth century of television and telephone, and of multiplication of meetings. God has answered all this with His definite command, "Study to be quiet" (1 Thess. 4:11). The quietness which we seek must not be mere rest and relaxation, but the quiet of the presence of God; the quietness which will enable us to hear the Word of God.

Such was the experience of King Saul's life. When Saul and his servant were about to depart from Samuel, the morning after they had lodged in the home of the great prophet, Samuel said to Saul: "Bid the servant pass on before us, . . . but stand thou still a while, that I may show thee the Word of God" (1 Sam. 9:27). God had a great purpose for Saul, though Saul did not know it, that he should be "a prince over His inheritance," a king for His own people. This was the first great critical hour of Saul's life. Though he did not know it, he was standing before an open door which would lead him out into greater opportunities than he had ever dreamed of. But before the great place of honor and usefulness could be given to him, Saul had to be quiet to hear the Word of God.

We are living in tremendous days, days when any morning we might suddenly find ourselves at a door with an opportunity before us greater than our prayers have ever asked for. In fact greater, perhaps, than we thought would ever be ours, involving greater burdens and necessitating greater strength than we have ever before known. We dare not undertake even what we know should be undertaken, and even that which we know God would have us to undertake, except with a deeper knowledge of His Word. And this means a deeper knowledge of God Himself, with new strength which can come from the Word of God alone, and with a new cleansing which only the Word of God can give us.

Saul did not know that God wanted to speak to him until Samuel told him so. Is not the Holy Spirit in the depths of your soul pleading with you right now to get alone for a day or two, or an hour every day for a week or two, that God might speak to you out of His marvelous Word? All He is waiting for is an opportunity to speak to you, when your soul is quiet before Him. What a blessing there would be in store for all of us if we could say with the Psalmist: "Surely I have stilled and quieted my soul!" (Ps. 131:2 ASV). "Be still before the Lord, and wait patiently for him" (Ps. 37:7 ASV margin).

Giving Up

The Christian does not have to give things up when he becomes a believer—things give him up. Unhappy is the man who spends time trying to give up things. He is seeking to perform a self-crucifixion which can never be complete. The only way to have an ordered life is to move to Christ, and He will make the changes as we move.

I had a remarkable illustration of this principle while driving through Texas. For about five days most of north and east Texas had been in the grip of its worst storm in years. Six to eight inches of snow blanketed much of the state, and all of the traffic in Fort Worth was slipping around on ice. Every automobile was undercoated with dirty ice, and icicles hung down from the fenders. As I started west from Fort Worth, I heard a grinding noise and thought that something was wrong with my car. In momentary anxiety, I put on the brake and the noise grew worse; then suddenly the noise disappeared entirely and the car seemed to jump forward a little. I wondered what had happened. Sometime later the same thing took place again. I stopped and saw that a large chunk of ice had fallen on the road. I soon realized that the warm weather was defrosting my car; moreover, I passed other large chunks of ice that had dropped from the cars of other drivers. The road was heavy with traffic, and we were following a path that was marked by chunks of dirty ice. The reason was that we were headed straight into much warmer weather.

If I had taken a chisel and started meticulously to deice my car in Fort Worth, I would have had a long, cold, thankless job. Moreover, the minute I started out on the road again, my wheels would have picked up new moisture and deposited it up on the car, and I would have had the job to do over.

Thus it is with giving up things. The best method is to drive as fast as we can toward Christ. The warmth of His presence and the glow of the new life will cause the old things to drop off. We will also be conscious of the fact that we are laying aside a weight and running more smoothly toward our goal.

Guest or Owner?

There is a great deal of difference between the position of a guest and that of the host. The guest necessarily enjoys his status only while he is a guest. The owner is owner wherever he is.

The Christian is far more than a guest with God. The Lord said to His disciples, "Henceforth I call you not servants; for the servant knoweth not what his lord doeth; but I have called you friends" (John 15:15). That is a wonderful position, an inestimable step above the position of a servant, but it did not stop there. It carried with it new privileges, and a new knowledge, since the verse continues, "for all things that I have heard of my Father I have made known unto you."

From this position of friend we have been exalted to the position of a son by the divine rebirth. "Of his own will begat he us with the word of truth that we should be a kind of firstfruits of his creatures" (James 1:18). And again, "Behold, what manner of love the Father hath bestowed upon us, that we should be called the sons of God" (1 John 3:1).

But the promotion still does not stop there. A son in a household often has fewer privileges than some of the servants, especially in his younger years. In fact, God says, "the heir, as long as he is a child, differeth nothing from a servant, though he be lord of all; but is under tutors and governors until the time appointed of the father" (Gal. 4:1, 2). Our Father has made the provision that we should be manifested as responsible heirs. We have been begotten as sons. The *adoptio* in Roman law was not akin to our practice of the adoption of another's child by foster parents, but rather the manifestation of a begotten son to the place of public responsibility in the affairs of the adopting father. The adopted son has the rights, privileges, and position of the owner. "All things are yours; whether Paul, or Apollos, or Cephas, or the world, or life, or death, or things present, or things to come; all are yours; and ye are Christ's; and Christ is God's" (1 Cor. 3:21–23).

The guest may have enjoyed a weekend on a beautiful estate, and in the following days, in the midst of the heat of the city, may wish for another invitation that he might enter once more into the pleasure of his position as guest. The owner may be in a distant city in the heat of a hotel room. His mind goes back to his pleasant acres, and in his imagination he breathes deeply of his memories of home, anticipating by right his return to their enjoyment. In Christ you are an owner, and may live in the enjoyment of your possession. All things are yours.

Knowing Christ as the Lord of Joy

If we do not read closely enough in the Bible we are inclined to get a distorted picture of Christ. We have heard so often that He was "a man of sorrows and acquainted with grief" (Isa. 53:3) that we overlook the fact that He must also be seen as a man of joy and acquainted with fellowship.

While He was on earth the contrast between Himself and His surroundings was so great that the suffering, sorrow, and grief seemed to be preeminent. The times when "he groaned within himself" (John 11:33) were numerous, and stand out because they are very visible to all, but the life and nature of Christ must be seen as men see the giant icebergs in the Arctic waters—only one-tenth above surface and nine-tenths in the depths below.

Twice we see the expression of His joy. "Who for the joy that was set before him endured the cross" (Heb. 12:2). "He shall see the travail of his soul and shall be satisfied" (Isa. 53:11). Joy and satisfaction! These are two of the marks of the Lord, and they are marks that carry across from earth to heaven and from time to eternity. No line in Scripture indicates any sorrow or grief in heaven. He was the man of sorrows, but He is now the man of joy.

If we look closely, we can see joy even during the time when He was here on earth. Children came to Him easily. Something about Him made it possible for Him to walk into a place where Jews of the lower class were congregating without making them feel uneasy. The Pharisees hated Him for this, and accused Him of associating with harlots and tax-gatherers. The people who felt uneasy in His presence were the hypocritical upper classes with their entrenched privilege and their false claim to religious power and leadership. To them He did not show the side of His joy, but only the face of His caustic judgment.

Today it is possible to know Him in His joy. There is a level of Christian living where, all sin confessed, forgiven, and forsaken, we are vividly aware of His presence, and live with Him in a carefree camaraderie. The familiarity and good will of a fellowship in which we yield ourselves to Him *and He yields Himself to us,* right in the midst of our most active experiences of living, is the height of Christian experience. He who has given us richly all things to enjoy becomes our joy, and that joy of the Lord is our strength. Thus, living in the resurrection, we know Him as we shall know Him in heaven, a man of joy and acquainted with fellowship.

Level Ground

In certain spots the contour of hills gives a tremendous illusion that the law of gravity is askew. Near Los Angeles there is a hill where thousands of motorists stop their cars, shut off the engines, release the brakes, and seemingly roll uphill. But if a plumb level is placed on the ground where the cars "roll up the hill," it can be seen immediately that the cars are actually rolling downhill. The eye can be deceived; the level cannot.

God has given us a similar apparatus—the Bible. When our situation in life is placed next to the Word of God, the Holy Spirit immediately establishes the true aspects of the situation and reveals whatever unevenness or distortion there is. It is not safe to form judgments on the basis of our senses or our emotions—we must prove and test all things (1 Thess. 5:21).

I thought of this as I read a heart-moving story of a garden which had been created for handicapped children. The donor had established a place where the crippled can play in surroundings of beauty, and even a bench of flowers for the blind that might be marked in Braille, "Please touch the flowers." It contains thornless cacti and a patch of herbs including several fragrant geraniums such as the lemon, rose, nutmeg, and mint varieties. The news report said that within hours of its dedication, the exhibit's leaves had been thoroughly pawed and many a blind child had pressed scented fingers to nostrils dilating with the joy of discovery.

Anyone with sensitivity cannot fail to be moved by such a story. Someone who heard the story wondered if the project was created by a Christian. A search soon revealed that the creator and donor was active in a religion that denied the Lord Jesus Christ. I remembered the passage in Romans where God condemns those who "rely on the law and pride yourselves in God and know his will and through education in the law have an idea of the essentials, and you believe yourself to be a guide to the blind, a light to those in darkness, a trainer of the simple, a teacher of the immature. . ." (2:17–20). Good and heartwarming as it is to let blind children touch flowers that are chosen for their fragrant and pungent qualities, such acts are not to be confused with spiritual actions that proceed from the presence of the Holy Spirit in the life of a believer.

Yes, many believers in Christ are so selfish, in spite of that which has been done for them, that they come out in second place in such social works as fragrant gardens for the blind, and ten thousand other similar works in the social realm. I wish that a believer in Christ had thought of this idea first, and had put it into effect. I wish that many such kindnesses could be thought up and performed in the name of the Lord Jesus Christ.

But let us avoid confusion in thinking that such actions are the guarantee of life in God and favor with Him. The level must be used in every situation in life. Then we will be able to say with the Psalmist, "My foot stands on level ground" (Ps. 26:12).

Meditation

There is a difference between prayer and meditation. In prayer we are talking to the Lord; in meditation we are thinking about Him.

A story is often told of the famed Dr. Thomas Chalmers of Edinburgh. The great preacher was walking down Princess Street with his head bowed deep in thought when a friend, watching him, finally walked beside him and touched his sleeve. Chalmers looked up, still deep in thought, and said, "That's a glorious verse—'My God shall supply all your need according to his riches in glory by Christ Jesus.' " He had been deep in meditation.

The Christian is not to spend all of his time in meditation. God has so ordered and arranged life that there are times when we must not think of Christ. The surgeon who is in the midst of an operation, the accountant who is adding up a column of figures, the driver who is speeding through crowded streets at the wheel of a car, the student who is engrossed in a lesson in some secular subject, should not turn his thought away from the task at hand. These tasks and occupations are provided for us by the Lord Himself, and He will best be served by our obeying His command to do with all our might what our hands find to do (Col. 3:23).

The Christian who knows the Lord and loves the Word of God will find that there are breathing spells, though, when it is possible to lift up the eyes from the surgery, or there will be a moment at the completion of the addition of the column, or there will be a traffic light where we pause for a moment and allow the Spirit to catch up with us. In these moments we may think again of the Savior and remember some of the wonders that are His glory.

That is what the apostle meant when he said that the life of the believer was to be "Casting down imaginations and every high thing that exalteth itself against the knowledge of God, and bringing into captivity every thought to the obedience of Christ" (2 Cor. 10:5). If you are able to cultivate this habit of occasional meditation, you will ennoble all your work. If you are a ditch digger, you will be a better ditch digger, and if you are a surgeon, you will be a better surgeon. "As the hart panteth after the water brooks, so panteth my soul after thee, O God" (Ps. 42:1).

Cat's Color

The French have a very famous proverb, "At night all cats are gray." The author of *The Three Musketeers* makes it the title of one of his chapters. The proverb expresses the idea that things must be looked at in their proper light if they are to be seen in their proper hues. It is a very important lesson, for we are living in the night of earth's time. The clear light of eternity has not yet blazed upon us except in the glimpses which have come through the work of the Lord Jesus Christ, the Word of His revelation to us.

In this night of the world many things are gray which will be seen in other colors when day dawns. One of the most important of Christian ideals is the discrimination of values. We must learn to see things in their right perspective against the background of eternity. An English writer once said that the ability to see things in perspective "is a characteristic so important as to be almost the test of complete sanity; for the word 'unbalanced,' used of those who have lost or never had the sense of the comparative values of things, carries with it the implication of a lack of complete mental health and poise."

The writer was thinking of schoolteachers, but how much more true it is in teaching any individual the method of living our daily life. The schoolteacher is taught that "the work of selection" is most important in teaching composition, for one of the most essential things is to know what may be left out and what must at all costs go in. If this is true with school English, how much more true of life. What are you going to leave out? What are you going to put in?

Some things which seem tremendously important to you today will be totally unimportant in just a short time. A nation pauses breathlessly to see which team will win the American League pennant, but ten years from now it will be a part of baseball statistics, practically meaningless to most men. It is a gray cat because it is earth's night.

Look closely at all things that swim into your ken. Let the radiance of the Word of God shine on them and then give them their places; let them stand in their true colors. It is the balancing of all things with eternity that counts in the true balance; anything else is unbalanced. What is done for Christ will last.

The Unused Bottle

I have a story that I have told for some years about an empty bottle. Now I have a new twist for it. A man bought a bottle of perfume in

Paris at a very good price and brought it home under his customs deduction. It was very expensive perfume in a very beautiful bottle. His wife was proud of it, and used the perfume until it was all gone. Even then she kept the bottle on her boudoir table so that her friends, in coming into her room, would say, "Oh, that was such-and-such perfume." There came a function for which she wished some of this expensive scent, but the bottle was empty, so she put a handkerchief into the bottle and closed it. After a day there was enough of the perfume on the handkerchief to give a faint fragrance, but after that it was all gone. There was still enough odor around the bottle so that someone could say, "Oh, that was such-and-such." Many people in our churches are like that. If you come near them and listen to their conversation you may be able to say, "Oh, grandfather was a Christian," but as far as they are concerned, the bottle is empty. They have no life and fragrance of Christ.

Once I told the story that way and at the close of the meeting was walking down the street to my hotel. I overtook three people who had evidently been at the church service, and one of them was saying, "I liked that story that he told about the perfume bottle because it reminded me of a very expensive perfume that Frank brought me from Paris. It is a beautiful bottle, but I have never broken the seal. It sits right there on my dresser and the light shines through it. It is a beautiful amber."

I broke into the conversation. They recognized me and laughed that I should have overheard them. "But," I said, "don't you see that the perfume was given to you for use? And what an illustration that is. There are so many Christians who have been given so much, but they keep it tightly sealed in themselves. No one passing near would know for a moment that they have the life of God in them, for not even the tiniest particle of the essence is allowed to come forth. And the wonderful thing about God's perfume is that as fast as we waft it forth He keeps filling the bottle and it would seem that its fragrance changes and grows and is more glorious every time we send it forth. That is God's way." "Now thanks be to God, which always causeth us to triumph in Christ, and maketh manifest the perfume of his knowledge by us in every place" (2 Cor. 2:14).

Bushel Basket

It is a terrible thing not to live up to one's capacities. When we face the fact of that sentence, we admit immediately that not one of us does live up to his or her capacities. We bury our talents in the field, we hide our light under the bushel basket.

I once had occasion to enter into conversation with a man of seeming rough appearance who was called "foolish" and "eccentric" by people of his acquaintance. His manner was brusque, his air uncouth, his speech abrupt. I had had some contact with him over a long period of time and had, little by little, accepted that general verdict concerning his nature and capacity.

An occasion arose which changed the concept completely. It was a discussion on economic theory. I had read several books on economics and gave out my conclusion drawn from one of the outstanding writers on economy in our country. The man in question broke out violently that this well-known economist was "crazy," "wild," and "foolish" to say some of the things he had put forth in his book. I would have dismissed this outburst as a diatribe from a pretentious ignoramus were it not for the fact that suddenly, almost with the air of a sop thrown to a dog, the man tossed out one or two sentences which were sparkling in clarity and which threw much light on the subject under discussion. I asked a question and suddenly, with an air which seemed to be one of condescension, the man began to speak on economic theory. I interjected a question from time to time and kept the man going for nearly three hours. It was immediately plain that here was a man eminently qualified to handle the subject and undertake discussions with the best of the experts in the field. As I later studied the man and talked about him with certain of my acquaintances, I became convinced that he had a mind so keen that he was living on a mountain peak by himself and had become adamant in his intolerance of lesser minds. He had, thereby, bitter enemies, and had failed to progress in life since he had failed in his relationships with men.

There is a spiritual analogy of great importance. The Christian by the new birth has been made a "partaker of the divine nature" (2 Peter

1:4). Christ has been "made" to us "wisdom" (1 Cor. 1:30), and "we have the mind of Christ" (1 Cor. 2:16). There is, therefore, the temptation to sit in our high position, aloof and content, and to fail in our witness to others, hiding the light of our eternal life from those around us through contempt for the failure of the unsaved to see truth as we see it.

Poor unsaved man does not know any better. "If our gospel is hid it is hid to them that are lost; in whom the God of this world hath blinded the minds of them which believe not, lest the light of the glorious gospel of Christ, who is the image of God, should shine unto them" (2 Cor. 4:3, 4). "The preaching of the cross is to them that perish foolishness" (1 Cor. 1:18). We must at every point recognize this fact and proceed with a tact which can only come from a complete surrender to the Holy Spirit. I had told this man, in a kindly way, that the reason his ideas were not accepted among men was because he had failed to be tactful, for most men will receive error with politeness but few men receive truth without it.

Let us be willing to cast aside everything which will keep the light of the Lord Jesus Christ from shining into the hearts of men. Our attitude must not be that of Jove, alone among the clouds, nor of one condescending toward unfortunates, but rather let it be that of those who have no pride in seeing their own opinions vindicated in an argument, but only a desire that the truth of God should go through to take root and produce fruit unto life eternal.

Educated Man

I once ran across a typed statement under the glass top of the desk of a student, which bore the title "Marks of an Educated Man." I copied them in order to dissent from them.

"1) He cultivates an open mind; 2) He always listens to the one who knows; 3) He never laughs at new ideas; 4) He knows the secret of getting along with people; 5) He cultivates the habit of success; 6) He links himself with a just cause; 7) He knows it is never too late to learn; 8) You can't sell him magic."

Obviously there are some points in the list that are good, but that the list summarizes an educated man is questionable. There probably are many men who could be described by these eight phrases who are, nevertheless, not educated. For example, it would be possible for a homespun sage to have all of these but be uneducated because he had never had the opportunity of being associated with the world of books. It would also be possible for a man to go to college, work in a library, and still be an ignoramus.

There are some divine statements that are pertinent. 1) "The fear of the Lord is the beginning of wisdom" (Ps. 111:10). This, of course, does not mean the fright of the Lord, but the godly desire to please Him and be submitted to Him. Such a man will have the breadth of the Word of God without having the shallowness which so often goes with the broad and open-minded men of the world.

2) "If any man lack wisdom, let him ask of God who giveth to all men liberally" (James 1:5). The important part of this inspired statement is not merely that we must pray for wisdom but that we do lack it, so that we will be willing to pray for it. 3) "Prove all things; hold fast that which is good" (1 Thess. 5:21). The frame of reference is the Word of God.

4) "A man who would have friends must show himself friendly" (Prov. 18:24). The Christian, with the love of Christ within him, will naturally love his fellowmen. 5) Cultivate the habit of surrender to the truth. "If ye continue in my word, then are ye my disciples indeed; and ye shall know the truth, and the truth shall make you free" (John 8:31, 32). 6) The believer is linked to the Lord, which is more than being linked to a cause. 7) The path of the just is as the shining light that shineth more and more unto the perfect day (Prov. 4:18). We shall learn through all eternity (John 17:3). 8) Spiritual discernment from God will keep us from accepting the counterfeits which Satan and men try to pass on us.

You can see that we have revised the eight concepts stated above. It is the leading forth of the soul and spirit as well as the intellect which constitutes true education. Men may make their definitions and call themselves educated, but in the wisdom of God, the world by wisdom knows not God (1 Cor. 1:21). And can any man be considered really educated when he does not have any knowledge of omniscience?

Dependence on God

Crowds can be very dangerous. I am not speaking of riots, or accidents of stampeding crowds, but of common ordinary crowds, moving lazily or briskly along the sidewalks, occupied with business, shopping, or pleasure. The very existence of a crowd has a tendency to dull the sense of our dependence upon God. It is somewhat like the little girl in an old story.

A father asked one of his three little girls who had just gone to bed if she had said her prayers. She said that she had not. He asked her if she were not afraid to go to sleep without having prayed. She answered, "Not tonight, for it is my turn to sleep in the middle."

When telling that story a generation ago, Dr. John Robertson of Scotland said, "Before God, I know that feeling. When I was in the multitude I did not have to lean upon God. A great kirk I had about me, great ecclesiastical authorities about me, and I was an ecclesiastically big man myself. I was moderator of the Metropolitan Presbytery of the city of Edinburgh, and I did not feel a great need to lean upon God. I felt that I could do somehow without the prayer, for I was in the middle. But now I need to cry to God, for I am no longer in the middle. I need to wait upon Him. I can't do without the Lord Jesus."

The Bible is filled with stories about God's methods for making men lonely that they may learn to lean upon Him. Abraham had to go alone into the hill country when Lot had chosen the plain. Then Abraham, with the relatives and crowds of the city far away, learned to lean upon God. Elijah had to flee the city to his place of meeting with God under the juniper tree. David was a fugitive before he learned to sing hymns in the darkness. Daniel knew the loneliness of a strange land and the companionship of lions. The list is long and can be extended beyond the pages of the Word in all of men's experiences with God throughout the history of the church.

Perhaps in this principle we have the philosophy of the old saying of William Cowper, "God made the country and man made the town." And certainly we have the spiritual reason why God so often cuts the props from beneath us in life. Our readiness for Heaven is Christ, but after we have received Him as Savior, the Father works at the task of making us lonely in order that we may find satisfaction in Christ alone.

Playing God

One of the most dangerous things within the bounds of Christendom is the tendency to play God for others. I pass over the organized efforts to be God and guide for all people, such as is found in Romanism, to concentrate on the tendency found among many fundamental Christians.

Examine yourself. Do you ever have the thought that someone is not quite as good a Christian as yourself because he does not share your opinions on such matters as amusements or cultural practices?

Once while dining with an official of an outstanding Bible institute I learned of some of the criticisms that are received by their contributions office. One woman wrote a letter to the institute, noting that a photograph of some of the students showed that some of the girls had "short" hair, and asking the institute to justify this procedure before receiving any further contributions. Another contributor noted in the student news that there had been a "class play," and was going to withdraw his support because of this. When he was told that it was not exactly a play but a "dramatic skit," he wrote thanking them for the explanation, and continued his gift.

The psychology that is behind such incidents lies in the fact that the old Adamic nature has exalted itself, so that a man (or a woman) is thinking of himself more highly than he ought. If we were ready to obey the Word of God and esteem others better than ourselves, this whole frame of mind would be altered.

Some claim that their position does not come from any motive of self-exaltation, but from a great desire to see that no one lets down the bars on Christian living. I answer without hesitation that God did not put us in charge of the bars for anyone except ourselves. See that you do not let the bars down for your own standards, but also see that you commit all other Christians to God, who is their Judge. "Judge nothing before the time," said Paul, and he goes on to say (1 Cor. 4:5) that when the Lord comes, He will bring to light the things now hidden in darkness and will disclose the purposes of the heart. He then concludes: "I have applied all this to myself and Apollos for your benefit, brethren, that you may learn by us to live according to scripture, that none of you may be puffed up in favor of one against another" (RSV). May God teach us not to judge, that is, not to play God for others.

God's Second-Chance Men

The Word of God has a great deal to say about second chances. This does not mean that any man is to have a second chance of salvation, after death has removed him from earth's scene. The Bible distinctly says in John 8, "If ye die in your sins, whither I go ye cannot come, and if ye believe not that I am he, ye shall die in your sin." This shows us that the issues of eternity are settled in this life.

But there is a glorious sense in which there is a second chance for men, or rather we should say, for believers. Abraham, who lied and was willing to hide behind the honor of his wife, was graciously brought back to a place of usefulness and blessing. Jacob, the swindler, became a prince with God. Aaron, who officiated at the worship of the golden calf, was anointed as God's high priest, a type of Christ. Moses, the murderer, was met by God at the burning bush, and was used to display the power of God before Egypt, and to lead the chosen people to Canaan. Jonah, who ran away from God, was overtaken and brought safely to the field of his ministry to be an instrument of the power and grace of God. David, the murderer and adulterer, became the author of the Psalms which speak more often of the coming Messiah than any other portion of the Old Testament.

The same blessing of a second chance is to be found in the New Testament. Peter denied Christ, but was chosen to preach at Pentecost and in the house of Cornelius. Paul, in great willfulness, went up to Jerusalem and was arrested at the temple just before he was about to offer a blasphemous sacrifice, but later was made the channel for the glorious prison Epistles.

All these examples show us that God's Word spoken through the prophet, "I will restore to you the years that the locust hath eaten the cankerworm, and the caterpillar, and the palmerworm" (Joel 2:25), is true. No person who reads these lines need fear that God will not receive him. Our Lord has said (John 6:37), "Him that cometh unto me, I will in no wise cast out." We may be certain that He will receive us at the moment that we come, for all His workings with us are on the principle of grace. He knows our old nature and has said that it is incurably sick (Jer. 17:9). Therefore, while providing the way of fellowship in grace, He writes to us "that ye sin not." Nevertheless, He has provided a way whereby fellowship might be constantly maintained through our risen Advocate, the Lord Jesus Christ, who knows our frame and remembers that we are dust.

True Ambition

Paul wrote to the Corinthians, "Wherefore we labor, that whether present or absent, we may be accepted of him" (2 Cor. 5:9). Brookes translated it, "Wherefore we make it our aim, whether at home or absent, to be well-pleasing to him." Rotherham translates it, "Wherefore also, we are ambitious, whether at home or away from home, to be well-pleasing to him." The emphatic Diaglot renders it, "Therefore we are very ambitious, whether being at home or away from home, to be acceptable to him."

What did a man like Paul care for the opinions of other men about himself? He had one great longing, one consuming ambition, which was to be well-pleasing to Christ. If someone thought ill of him it made no difference, for if he had the smile of Christ he did not need to worry about the frowns of men. And, on the contrary, if he had the frown of Christ all the human smiles in the world could never compensate for the loss.

Of all the ambitions that men may have, this is the most important. The next verse shows that Paul was very conscious that all his life and work would be reviewed at the judgment seat of Christ, and his great longing was to be approved there. "For we must all appear before the judgment seat of Christ; that every one may receive the things done in his body, according to that which he has done, whether it be good or bad" (2 Cor. 5:10).

The Lord Jesus, after His resurrection, said to the disciples, "As my Father has sent me, so send I you" (John 20:21). It is a very intimate phrase, for the pronoun "my" is not found in the original. Literally it is, "As Father has sent me, so send I you." The most important word in the verse is *so*. "*So* send I you."

How did the Father send Christ? He sent Him as flesh to dwell among us (John 1:14). "He took on him the seed of Abraham; wherefore in all things it behoved him to be made like unto his brethren" (Heb. 2:16, 17). If we are to be sent in the same way, it means that we must become like those whom we would win to Christ. The reason there are so many unsaved people in the slums is that too many people live in fine houses in the suburbs and simply go to visit the missions in the slums. How many people are willing to live in a house with cracked plaster and faulty plumbing in order to lead their neighbors to Christ? Now don't misunderstand me. If you are *sure* that God has called you to live on the Main Line, or the North Shore, or wherever the wealthy and fortunate live near your city, then do so, for you should be very ambitious to please Him in all things. But if He has called you to witness to men of low degree, then live among them. Let us stir up our thinking, appraise our situation, find out just what the will of God is for us, and then be sure that we are very ambitious to do that will.

The King's Business

The King's business often requires slowness. That may be the opposite of what you have been taught by the tradition of men, but that is what the Word of God teaches. If you rub your eyes at this statement and say that your memory surely serves you well that "the king's business requires haste" is a Bible quotation, you are in error.

True, the phrase about haste and the business of the king is in the Bible, but the words were spoken under such circumstances that a study of the context reveals that it was a lie. Saul was furious against

David to the point of hurling a javelin against his own son, Jonathan, who interceded in David's behalf. David was forced to flee, and arrived at the house of Abimelech without his weapons. He lied to Abimelech, saying that he was on a secret mission for Saul. He needed arms and said to his host, "Is there not here under thine hand spear or sword, for I have neither brought sword nor my weapons with me, because the king's business required haste" (1 Sam. 21:8). It was a lie on top of a lie.

This lie has been quoted numerous times by people who wanted to do God's business with speed, but the teaching of the Word of God is that we should wait on the Lord. There are more than a dozen Hebrew words translated by the one English word "wait." They include waiting in silence, waiting in hope, waiting while standing still, waiting with expectation, waiting attentively, and waiting in observance. There are half a dozen more Greek words translated "wait." They include the ideas of waiting patiently, waiting perseveringly, and waiting for a long time.

In addition to all the verses which tell the Christian to wait, there are others which tell us to sit still, stand still, or be still. Then there are the definite statements against haste: "He that hasteth with his feet sinneth" (Prov. 19:2); and "He that believeth shall not make haste" (Isa. 28:16).

In our way of living we often put everything into high gear, but it is time that we slow down to God's pace for Christian living. Too many people are too occupied with many things, and not enough occupied with Him. The beginning of the business of the King requires that we spend time with the King. Then we shall carry on His business as He desires and not in the fleshly speed of our own willfulness.

Triumph

The possibilities of triumph in Christ are unlimited. The position to which He has called us is as high as heaven (Eph. 2:6). The power that He has provided for us is the power of omnipotence (Matt. 28:18; Acts 1:3). The wisdom He has in store for us is the wisdom of omniscience

(1 Cor. 1:30). The peace He has made for us is the quiet calm of eternity (Col. 1:20). The love which He has toward us is His own infinite being (1 John 4:16). The blessings with which He has blessed us are guaranteed in the heavenly places (Eph. 1:3). The resources which He has deposited to our account are presently and readily available (Phil. 4:13). The battles which we must fight have already been won for us by the triumph of Christ upon the cross (1 Cor. 10:13; Col. 2:15).

It is well for us to go over these assets, not as a miser counting gold, but as a philanthropist balancing his accounts so that he can distribute to the need around him and live plentifully while he blesses others.

In a watchnight meeting at the end of the year, a young woman who has suffered for her witness for the Lord gave a testimony of triumph that was a blessing to all who heard it. She quoted the verse of a hymn which, when I heard it, I knew immediately I must procure from her and pass on to others. I have not yet located its source, but the lines breathe the triumph that has been provided for us by our Savior.

> I hear the accuser roar
> Of sins that I have done.
> I know them all and thousands more;
> Jehovah findeth none.
> For though the angry foe accuses
> Sins recounting like a flood.
> Every charge my God refuses,
> Jesus answers with His blood.

Here is the ground of our faith, the basis of our full assurance, the source of our power, and the comfort of our hope. Here we see ourselves accepted in the Beloved and know that our God, "who spared not his own Son but delivered him up for us all, will also, with him, freely give us all things" (Rom. 8:32). We must never forget that we have eternal life and that it is our privilege to live that life of eternity even in our own world of time. The more we enter into it, the more the things of earth will grow dim and we shall know a life that is a surging triumph.

Forgiveness

What Is Forgiveness?

This question of forgiveness arose in the lives of some Christians that I know, one of whom did a very grievous wrong to some other children of God. There was deep sin involved, including a definite transgression of at least three of the Ten Commandments. There were several friends involved who sided with the transgressor. One of these bystanders talked on the telephone with the Christians who had been sinned against, and in the course of the conversation the latter said, "Of course, we are ready to forgive . . . we must forgive . . ."

Later, the friends were amazed that this forgiveness did not include the condoning of the sin which had been committed. "But you said that you forgave him . . . How can you proceed in this manner when you definitely said that you were ready to forgive?" And so on.

There was no spiritual comprehension of the nature of forgiveness, and the fact that forgiveness may be proffered without being accepted. Even accepted forgiveness demands the righting of wrongs where it is possible, no matter what the cost.

When did the father forgive his prodigal son? The answer is that he forgave him the moment he went to the door to look for his return. That did not mean that the father was to follow him to the far country and feed on husks with him; the forgiveness could not be applied until the son had had enough of his sin and returned to the father. The forgiveness caused the father to look down the road and to run to meet his son. The son rehearsed a longer speech than he got a chance to recite, for his father listened to just enough of the confession, and then forgiveness stopped him with a kiss and would let him say no more. But there could never have been fellowship without the prodigal's mental change and his trip back home.

True forgiveness will not ask for the pound of flesh; it will act in holiness. That which overlooks or condones sin is a mawkish sentimentalism that the world may pass for forgiveness, but it has no kinship to the forgiveness which is from above. The father did not follow the prodigal down the road with offers of rings and fatted calves, but when the heart of the son started home, the heart of the father was all the way down the road to meet him. This is forgiveness in holiness. Nothing else is worth the name.

Forgiving and Forgetting

When we forget, it is an indication of weakness, but when God forgets, it is a sign of power. Men have to use all sorts of devices to help them remember. Notebooks, daily reminders, records, all are a necessary part of our equipment. Without them our minds would not hold the things which we must remember.

God is not like man. His knowledge is perfect and not for a moment does. He forget the tiniest detail of His vast creation. His Word gives us beautiful teachings about His love and His creation, for He does not only remember the laws of the universe or the provision for His creatures, but in an even deeper way He remembers those who are His children. The great cry of love found in Isaiah 49:15 belongs primarily to the Jews. God has promised not to forget them, for they are His chosen people, graven upon the palms of His hands, His forever by covenant relationship. But the verse belongs to us too, for we are His because we have been bought with the blood of Christ. We can take this reassuring message to our hearts, "Can a woman forget her sucking child, that she should not have compassion on the son of her womb? Yes, they may forget, yet will I not forget thee." There is our confidence. God remembers us with infinite love.

But just as truly, God has the power to forget. We cannot forget at will; that which has been marked upon our minds with the indelible pencil of circumstance cannot be erased merely because we wish it to be erased. But God can forget. He says, speaking of those who have come to the Lord for forgiveness of sins, "And their sins and iniquities will I remember no more." In heaven, the only reminder of our sins will be the scars in the hands and feet of the Lord Jesus Christ.

We cannot praise God enough for His infinite goodness to us, but we can bring joy to Him by trusting Him completely. We can also ask Him to teach us how to forgive and *forget,* in obedience to His Word.

Imagine my amazement and horror when I heard of the following incident.

An elderly woman, Mrs. X, had a daughter, Miss X, whose close friend was Miss Y. The latter two were mature Christian women. It seems that many years ago, perhaps fifteen or twenty, Miss Y made an indiscreet statement about Mrs. X in a letter to Miss X. The letter was read by the mother, who from that time on never permitted Miss Y to come into her home. The home was also the home of Miss X, who provided the major support for it but who, out of deference to the mother, respected her wish. The two Christian friends, therefore, always met outside of the home.

I spoke to Mrs. X, pointing out the necessity of Christian forgiveness, and suggested that she show real Christian spirit and invite Miss Y to her home for dinner. I repeat that I was horrified when I heard the reply, "Oh, I have forgiven her but she can stay in her own place."

Our Lord said, "When ye pray, say . . . we also forgive every one that is indebted to us" (Luke 11:2–4). Forgiving without forgetting is like a vulture feeding on a dead carcass, until even the breath of prayer smells of the putrid thing.

The Lord said, "If ye forgive not men their trespasses, neither will your Father forgive your trespasses" (Matt. 6:15). This does not mean that sin will remain in the account of that believer, but it does mean that the terrible sin of unforgiveness is a blight upon our Christian life that can rob us of the joy of the Lord. It can block the free flow of communion with our Lord and can embitter all of the relationships of life.

You will find that a double blessing of God comes to you when you ask that He bless those who have truly offended you. Never forget that "the Lord turned the captivity of Job, when he prayed for his friends; also the Lord gave Job twice as much as he had before" (Job 42:10).

An Ounce of Plutonium and a Ton of Sin

On November 20, 1959, a small amount of solvent exploded and blew open the door of a processing cell at the Atomic Energy Commission Oak Ridge laboratory. About one-fiftieth of an ounce of plutonium was scattered into the air. The AEC later reported on what it took to clean up this minor atomic mishap.

All those who were within a four-acre area of the explosion turned in their laboratory-issued clothes to be decontaminated. Their urine was checked to insure that they had not inhaled or ingested any plutonium. The processing plant and a nearby research reactor were shut down. The buildings were washed with detergents, and the buildings' roofs were resurfaced. The surrounding lawn was dug up and the sod carted to a deep burial place. The surface was chiseled off one hundred yards of a nearby asphalt road. To anchor any speck of plutonium that might have survived, the buildings were completely repainted. Final cost, including resodding, repaving, and reroofing: approximately $350,000.

The AEC will go to all that trouble for a fraction of an ounce of plutonium, yet there are some light-thinking Christians who believe that all that has to be done when sin has touched the life is to pray, "I'm sorry. Please forgive me. In Jesus' name, Amen." In many circles the attitude regarding sin is outright flippancy.

Every night before we sleep we should make a careful analysis of the day, its deeds and its thoughts. We must acknowledge the exceeding sinfulness of self. We must have a deep desire for the Holy Spirit to expose any surface that has been contaminated by sin, and if there has been some willful sin, it must be the work of God to remedy it.

Yes, we may be sure that the Heavenly Father forgives us because of the death of Jesus Christ, but in addition to forgiveness there must be a cleansing of the contaminated area. What caused the Adamic nature to break out in fleshly act or thought? What unguarded avenue did we leave open to the rise of the flesh or the entrance of the world? What device of Satan did we ignore? Did we fail to have our whole being insulated by the power of the Holy Spirit? Did we fail to feed our spirits with the Word of God?

We are told that "godly sorrow worketh repentance" (2 Cor. 7:10), but how much do we know of such sorrow and repentance? When Paul wrote to the Corinthians these hard words about their laxity, there was an immediate effort at complete decontamination. We read, "I rejoice . . . because you were grieved unto repenting; for you felt a godly grief, so that you suffered no loss through us (through the firmness of his reproof). For godly grief produces a repentance that leads to salvation and brings no regret, but worldly grief produces death. See what earnestness this godly grief has produced in you, what eagerness to clear yourselves, what indignation, what alarm, what longing, what zeal, what punishment!" (2 Cor. 7:9–11).

Surely a comparison of the methods used by the Atomic Energy Commission over a mere one-fiftieth of an ounce of plutonium and that of most Christians over a slight attack—say a ton—of sin reveals a light and frivolous attitude on the part of the believer towards something which can contaminate all of life. May God teach us the nature of godly sorrow that leads to no regrets.

The Soft Answer

"I," "ego," "self," always wants to defend itself. The most "natural" thing in the world is for our human nature to rise against the slightest attack made upon us. Self always wishes to take care of its own interests, its own reputation, and its own rightness. We frequently see the attempts of men to justify errors, simply because they themselves have originally committed them. To admit wrong is to wound ego.

Culture and education, and the good manners produced thereby, have formed certain patterns by which the most proud and selfish can go through life protecting ego at all vulnerable points, yielding only where politeness demands. The Christian learns that the Holy Spirit is at war with his ego, and that in order to be saved, ego has to admit that self is on its way to a Christless eternity. This is the essential reason why not many noble, not many wise are chosen (1 Cor. 1:26). The Christian learns that ego has to be crucified with Christ.

A friend told me something which happened several months before in one of our great cities. The friend lives in a very beautiful home
in a lovely suburb, and when someone bought the next-door lot, a
house was built very close to the property line. The new neighbors
seemed arrogant and were definitely not Christians. Months passed by
and the Christians, two women living alone, hardly saw their new
neighbors who kept very much to themselves and their coterie of
friends. Matters came to a crisis when the non-Christian neighbors sent
a message through their butler to the ladies' gardener, informing them
that their hymn singing and the barking of their watch dog was very
annoying.

Here was a good occasion for ego to rise and defend itself, for the
old nature stands upon its rights. Some people would have redoubled
their noise, built spite fences, and carried on neighborhood warfare in
defense of the wounded ego. The Christian described how the crisis
was actually met. A letter, somewhat as follows, was written.

"Dear Neighbor: I am sorry that my dog has annoyed you, but we
are two ladies who live here alone, and we have found it necessary to
keep a dog since prowlers have recently been seen in the garden.

"When your dog barks we are glad that you have a good watch
dog that is protecting you. When your little girl cries, and it sounds as
if it is right outside our windows, we realize that every normal child
cries, and we are glad that you have a precious little child in your home.
When we are wakened early in the morning by the water running into
your pool, we think what lovely times you will have in that pool, and
we are glad. When we hear your beautiful music we are glad that you
have such a medium of self-expression. When your guests' cars start
under our bedroom windows at all hours of the night, we are glad that
you have so many friends and can enjoy their fellowship. When your
tennis balls fly onto our lawn we will continue to toss them back into
your court, as we have done. But please never again ask us to stop our
singing. We have had sorrow in this home deeper than most people
could realize, and it takes the courage of song for us to continue."

The note was handed through the gardener to the butler and to
the neighbors. It was a Christian answer which not only turned away

wrath but caused non-Christians to more than respect the rights of others. It was only the spirit of the Lord Jesus Christ that could have made such an answer; the incident was praise to Him and a mouthful of dust to the enemy of our souls.

Forgiving Oneself

A correspondent wrote to ask me a question and said, as so many do, that it was a question which could not be asked of his own pastor.

Whenever I see that statement in a letter, I am tempted to think that the correspondent does not want the personal humiliation of making some sin or difficulty known to his pastor. The flesh often does not want to meet and talk year after year with a pastor who knows the innermost secrets of the soul. There is, of course, the possibility that the pastor is not faithful to the Word of God, and that therefore his counsel is not trusted. In this case it is perfectly legitimate to write to someone else, and it is in this sense that the correspondent has been answered.

The letter contained this paragraph: "I wish I could ask you *how to forgive* oneself? I believe that God has forgiven *me* but that does not give peace, although I believe all of the Bible, that it is the Word of God. One has to simply believe, accept, and surrender. I have done this and wonder why I cannot have peace of mind."

There is no information whatever as to the matter involved, but for the sake of a definite answer we shall say that it is some sin, a grievous one, which has touched the heart of this writer. The Biblical steps have been followed, the sin has been confessed and forsaken. On the authority of I John 1:9 we know that God has forgiven, cleansed, and restored to fellowship. On the grounds of Romans 5:1 we know that justification brings peace with God. Paul tells us in Philippians 4:6, 7 that a life of prayer and trust brings the peace of God. We must conclude therefore, that the writer of the letter is not living a life of prayer and trust.

What is peace? When we know that we have been born again we know that God can never again hold us liable for our sins. The burden of sin is thus dissipated. We can sing, "My sin, O the bliss of this glorious thought; my sin, not in part but the whole, is nailed to His cross and I bear it no more. Praise the Lord, praise the Lord, O my soul."

When we have confessed sin, we must take the attitude of St. Paul, "forgetting those things which are behind, I press toward the mark for the prize of the high calling of God in Christ Jesus" (Phil. 3:13, 14).

When we know that we have been justified, when we know that we have surrendered everything to the Lord, when we believe His Word about what He has done with our sin, when we are feeding upon the Word of God, when we are obeying Him and forgetting the things which are behind, peace *must* follow. When it does not, we have every right to ask God to rebuke Satan, who is seeking to destroy our peace by casting doubt upon God's Word about it all.

Now as to forgiving oneself, that simply is not to be done. Self is to be dealt with by crucifixion, not forgiveness. We must realize that the sin came out of a carnal mind which is enmity against God. We must realize that we can never deal with it ourselves, never seek to forgive it. Yielding it to a death by crucifixion is the only way the problem can be handled.

No Offense

"Great peace have they that love thy law; and nothing shall offend them" (Ps. 119:165). Some people are hard to get along with because they take offense easily, and others are very easy to get along with because they do not take offense easily. A person who has the life of God through faith in Jesus Christ should be governed by the truth which is expressed in this great verse. *Nothing shall offend them.* How may we live so that we never take offense? The answer is found in the nature of those things which could give offense to anyone.

It is possible to hurt the feelings of an individual by saying something about him that is true or something that is false. Suppose that a true Christian finds that someone has discovered something about him which is true, and is telling it to others. What should be the attitude of the Christian toward the incident? He should be driven into the presence of God with a prayer of sorrow that something which he has done should cause the testimony of the Christian to be lessened. It should be: "O God my Father! My old nature broke out and they have discovered it and are telling it. It will lessen my witness for You, and I am sorry. Forgive me for being a stumbling block, and so work in my life that I shall not dishonor You again." If taxed personally with the fault, the Christian should say: "Yes, I am sorry to say that the rumor is true; and by the grace of God I have confessed it, forsaken it, and am trusting the Lord for cleansing and strengthening, that it may not happen again. I am not offended that this has come out, but I am grieved for my Lord's sake. I am sorry."

But suppose that someone lies about the Christian? It occurs more frequently than it should in Christian circles, that plain lies are told about Christians, sometimes by fellow Christians. When such a lie comes to the ears of the one against whom it is being circulated, what should he do? The answer is in the Scripture. "Blessed are ye when men shall revile you, and persecute you, and shall say all manner of evil against you falsely, for my sake. Rejoice, and be exceeding glad; for great is your reward in heaven; for so persecuted they the prophets which were before you" (Matt. 5:11, 12). So when a Christian learns that a lie is being circulated against him he should look up to heaven and say: "Thank You, Lord! You have told me to rejoice about this, and I will obey You. This lie is the equivalent to the decoration of the Purple Heart, or the Distinguished Service Cross, or the Medal of Honor. You have counted me worthy to suffer for Your name's sake. Most certainly I should not be offended because of this."

And the Christian will remember that the best defense of all history was that of the Man who answered not a word. When He was reviled, He did not speak back. When we act in the same manner we follow His steps. "Great peace have they that love Thy law; and *nothing* shall offend them."

Witnessing

Effective Witnessing

Every believer should be a witness. In fact, every believer is a witness whether he wants to be or not. An impression goes out from every one of us concerning what we believe. Those in closest contact with us will know how much our beliefs really count in our lives.

Paul desired that his converts should be effectual in their witness, and wrote to Philemon expressing the secret of fruitful living. His prayer for the younger Christian was "that the communication of thy faith may become effectual by the acknowledging of every good thing which is in you in Christ Jesus" (Philemon, v. 6). The implications of this verse are stupendous. When the truth of this verse was brought home to me by the Spirit, it was almost as though a new verse had been written in the Bible. I had been over this verse many times before, but had not seen all that is involved in it.

You have faith in the Lord Jesus Christ? Then you are a child of God, and your body is the temple of the Holy Spirit. The Lord is dwelling within you, and you are commanded to witness the truth of Jesus Christ. This witness is the communication of your faith, which may be effectual or ineffectual. If that communication is to be effectual it must be done in the way that God has provided. You must acknowledge every good thing that is in you in Christ Jesus, and to acknowledge something is to believe it and act upon that belief.

Recall from the Word of God the promises that are ours in Christ. It is not that I live but that "Christ liveth in me: and the life which I now live in the flesh I live by the faith of the Son of God, who loved me, and gave himself for me" (Gal. 2:20). That fact must be acknowledged. This means that we must deliver ourselves over to the Lord for the crucifixion death of the old nature daily (1 Cor. 15:31). We must look at ourselves as being dead unto sin and alive unto God (Rom. 6:11). If we are alive unto God, risen with Christ, we must be seeking those things which are above (Col. 3:1). We must be freed from the law, and standing in the liberty and grace of our position as sons of God (Gal. 5:1; Rom. 5:1).

It would be possible to go on and on through the Epistles, pointing out our glorious position in Christ. Every detail is ours because we are "in" Christ and the effectiveness of life is that He is "in" us, the hope of glory and the power of daily living (Col. 1:20; Rom. 8:10).

The more we enter into the acknowledgment of His presence, the more the communication of our faith will be effectual. Just as our Lord tells us that we have not because we ask not (James 4:2), so He tells us that we *are* not because we believe not. If we really wish to be something for the Lord Jesus, the secret of that power is readily available.

Love of Witness

At the Battle of the Nile, one of the British ships, the *Culloden,* was driven ashore just before the fight, and Captain Trowbridge and his men were unable to take part in the battle. "The merits of that ship and her gallant captain," wrote Lord Nelson to the Admiralty, "are too well known to benefit by anything I could say. Her misfortune was great in getting aground, while her more fortunate companions were in the full tide of happiness." This is a notable expression, for it was to be "in the full tide of happiness" that Nelson destroyed five thousand, five hundred twenty-five of his fellow creatures and had his own scalp torn open by a piece of shot. This was life and happiness to him. In another battle, Aboukir, the same great admiral, flew six colors on his ship so that even if five were shot away it should not be imagined that he had struck color and surrendered.

Even greater than all this is the desire of the true believer to be at work, making Christ known. Greater than Nelson was Paul when he spoke of his "earnest expectation and hope, that in nothing I shall be ashamed, but that with all boldness, as always, so now also Christ shall be magnified in my body, whether it be by life, or by death" (Phil. 1:20).

Greater than the joy which mother and father have in holding their firstborn is the joy of seeing a soul pass out of death and into life. In the widest variety of sensation and experience, nothing can be found to equal this. Correspondingly, there is no pity greater than that which we feel for the Christian who allows something to interfere with his witness. More than the naval hero could ever feel for the coward who would flee fight through fear of his own skin, we feel sorrow for Christians who fritter away their opportunities.

It is God Himself who says, "He that winneth souls is wise" (Prov. 11:30), and when Nelson's statue in Trafalgar is worn away to dust, "They that be wise shall shine as the brightness of the firmament; and they that turn many to righteousness as the stars forever and ever" (Dan. 12:3). Since whatever God says is true, then He will fulfill His promises, and so full is His Word with promises that His Word shall outlast the heavens and the earth.

But there is one rich promise which God entrenches with double certainty. It would be wonderful if we could read "He that goeth forth and weepeth, bearing precious seed, shall come again with rejoicing, bringing his sheaves" (Ps. 126:6). Read it closely, however. Such a promise is certain, but God adds that the one who thus goes forth "shall *doubtless* come again with rejoicing, bringing his sheaves."

This is a word for those who are witnessing for God; the only condition is that we go weeping. Here, however, is the touchstone of defeat or victory in Christian work. The witness is told in the New Testament in categorical terms "thou shalt both save thyself, and them that hear thee" (1 Tim. 4:16). Here is another one of God's certainties. Some people have said that duties are ours and results are God's. While in one sense this is true, there is another sense in which the faithful witness *must* see the fruit of his labor. The condition in the New Testament promise is like the need for weeping in the Old. "Take heed to thyself." This will be a divine calling of personal holiness; tears will flow for the failure we are; tears will flow for the wonder of redemptive grace; tears will flow for the desperate need of those to whom we witness. Take heed to thyself. Go forth weeping. Thou shalt save them that hear thee. Thou shalt *doubtless* come again with sheaves.

"Therefore, my beloved brethren, be ye steadfast, unmovable, always abounding in the work of the Lord, forasmuch as ye know that your labor is not in vain in the Lord" (1 Cor. 15:58). Who is sufficient for these things? The *therefore* which begins this passage points to the answer in the previous verse, "But thanks be to God, which giveth us the victory through our Lord Jesus Christ."

Love of Souls

There is a Jewish legend which says that the phylacteries of the great Baal Shem Tov, the cabalist, were miraculous. At prayers, when he fastened them to his forehead, the world unrolled before him like a scroll and he saw the doings of men, good and evil. It is told how one morning he left them on his bench in the synagogue and a simple merchant hurried in from the marketplace. His mind filled with his trading, and starting a hasty, perfunctory prayer, he picked up the Baal Shem's phylacteries and put them on. And behold, all the world of men moved before his astonished eyes, and he saw all the evil on the earth; in a distant place he saw men bent on destroying one another; he saw oppression, and murder, and torture.

He cried out in horror and anguish at what he saw; "Stop them! I cannot bear this," and turned to find the Baal Shem at his elbow. "If you cannot bear the sight," said the Baal Shem gently, "you have only to take off the phylacteries."

Jesus Christ, when He left this earth, directed that the Holy Spirit should come to dwell within the heart of the believer. He gave His Word to be our guide, and to be the revelation of Himself. There are many believers who look through the Word, and who are guided by the Spirit. They see, therefore, the great need of the world. They see the horror of life and know that only the Gospel can reach the need. That is why they are obedient to the command to "preach the word, be instant, in season and out of season . . ."

There are thousands of Christians who have found the vision too exacting and who have torn the Word out of its rightful place in their lives. The result is that they are carnal, sleepy Christians, being carried to the skies on flowery beds of ease. God says (Amos 6) that He hates such case.

There are also those who look at the world through the Word of God. *The burden of lost souls is, therefore, upon them.* These will ever be the ones who cry, "Woe is me if I preach not the gospel!" These will be the ones who, if they are led of the Lord to stay at home, will be the prayer partners of those who carry the message of salvation to the uttermost parts of the earth. These will be the ones for whom no sacrifice is too great, if only the Word can be spread a little farther abroad.

Such Christians are so few in number because very few believers have a real love for souls. In fact, probably not more than four or five out of each thousand church members ever ask unsaved people to come to hear the preaching of the Gospel. Probably not more than the same number really give sacrificially to the extension of the rule of God over the hearts of men. How many who read this could honestly repeat to God the words of David? "Rivers of waters run down mine eyes, because they keep not thy law" (Ps. 119:136).

Two men in the Bible went much further than this. Moses and Paul told the Lord that they would be willing to go to hell providing unsaved people could be brought to salvation. Here is true love for souls. It is something that cannot be pumped up out of the emotions. It is something that should never be spoken of to men, but we should ask the Lord to search our hearts to reveal to us where we are lacking.

Moses saw the terrible sin of the people and realized that they should be punished. In his prayer to God for grace he could not even finish the sentence. It is perhaps the one unfinished sentence in the Bible. It is a sigh, a groan, a cry. "Oh, this people have sinned a great sin, and have made them gods of gold. Yet now if Thou wilt forgive their sin . . ." The grace of God cannot be turned by logic. It is sovereign. But Moses continues, in a new sentence: "and if not, blot me, I pray thee, out of thy book which thou hast written" (Exod. 32:30–32). It was a prayer to be sent to hell. To be blotted out of the book of God would mean to be a lost soul. Moses wasn't putting on an act; his heart was bare before God. He loved souls.

Paul was inspired by the Holy Spirit to give a true account of his love for Israel when he wrote, "I could wish that myself were accursed from Christ for my brethren, my kinsmen according to the flesh" (Rom. 9:3). To be accursed from Christ would also mean being a lost soul. Paul wasn't saying pretty words for a sermon illustration. His heart was bare before God. He loved souls.

Christ said, "No man taketh my life from me, but I lay it down of myself" (John 10:18). In laying down His life He showed His love for souls. It was impossible for God to blot Moses out of His book, or to count Paul accursed, but Christ drank the cup of the second death (Matt. 26:39; Heb. 5:7) and became a curse for us (2 Cor. 5:21; Gal. 3:13). He did this because of the joy that was set before Him (Heb. 12:2). He loved men.

There is only one way to develop a true love for souls. If we study the Word of God and surrender to the life of Christ within, we shall be more like Christ. His life within us can then do its work of loving souls and bringing them to Himself. We can never do it by ourselves.

Shepherd of Souls

Whenever we put the actions and the character of the disciples into contrast with the action and character of the Lord, we have a sharp distinction which shows only the wonderful glory of the Lord. The disciples were selfish, but "Christ pleased not himself" (Rom. 15:3).

One evening when the disciples were walking with the Lord, a great crowd followed Him. He, with His shepherd heart, was concerned with the need of the crowd. He was moved with compassion toward them because they were as sheep not having a shepherd; and He began to teach them many things. At the same time the disciples drew off by themselves and began to consider how the presence of the crowd might inconvenience them. But lost souls were never an inconvenience to Jesus Christ. Upon this evening occasion the disciples looked at the crowd and said to one another that they were in a desert place, and that there were no provisions. So with their wise folly they came to the Lord with the advice, "Send them away . . ." (Mark 6:36). Let them shift for themselves.

What are we doing for the souls in need round about us? Are we disturbed because we think that they might interfere with our plans? Is it not true that there are some who are more occupied with the organization of religion than they are with the souls around them? There are many people who feel that they are "disturbing" the minister by bringing their problems to him. How far from the truth if the man is a real minister, a real shepherd.

The object of Christian work is not the preparation of a sermon or the quiet, meditative and contemplative life. I once saw a little sign on the door of a Christian worker which read, "At prayer—do not disturb." I thought immediately of the many times the Lord was disturbed, but that He was always ready to meet the souls and their need. Prayer was important, vitally important, and He had to depart into the wilderness in order to seek it; He had to rise well before day in order to be left alone by the crowd. But when people were present, they were preeminent in His thought. They needed shepherding and He was the shepherd.

In a small city of Europe I saw a statue of an old man, and read beneath the figure that the monument had been raised by the grateful hearts of the people in memory of a parish priest who had loved his people for more than forty years. The inscription stated that there was no problem too small for his love nor too great for his care. I thought immediately of the Lord Jesus. This priest had made his parishioners feel the way all people should feel toward the disciples of Christ. It is only when we doubt His power to feed and supply the need of the crowd that we shall ever give way to the desire of asking Him to send them away. Rather let us pray, "Lord, send me a soul to disturb my little plans, and work through me the miracle of salvation and blessing for sorrowing hearts." Then shall we rejoice to the full.

Value of a Soul

A columnist in a San Francisco paper wrote concerning the callous unconcern of the general public to those who are in real need. He had interviewed a man who had notified bridge police that a woman was attempting to climb over the railing of the Golden Gate Bridge.

The police had been totally unconcerned and a little while later the woman had succeeded in plunging to her death. Her life could have been saved. The columnist went on to tell a story of a destitute woman who lay unattended on a pallet, ill with pneumonia, in a nearly unfurnished apartment. The furniture had been repossessed by an installment store. A man from the water company had entered the apartment to turn off the water and was moved to indignation by the woman's enforced suffering. Later, after she had died and there was a great outcry in the press, he expressed his indignation. But he had turned off the water. It was the same with the rent collector who had thought it was such a terrible thing and something should have been done about it, and then acquiesced to the janitor's turning off the heat in the apartment "as a matter of policy." The neighbor across the hall didn't like the dead woman because she had once given gay, noisy parties. Everybody, in this as in the bridge story, was busy minding his own business.

If life ended with death we would need have no concern about the going out of one more personality, but the soul lives on forever and Christians must show concern for those around them who are on their way to a Christless eternity. The Psalmist cries out, "No man cared for my soul" (Ps. 142:4b). It is quite understandable that the world in general should mind its own business, especially in teeming cities where life can be made very complicated for someone who is a witness or who helps a victim who may later die. Perhaps Christian unconcern comes from contact with this general attitude which is to be found in the world. It may also come from the fact that many Christians do not really believe that all souls around them are eternally lost, and that we have been ordered to witness to them of the saving power of Jesus Christ.

Perhaps a reader will say, "How can I increase my concern for the souls of men around me?" There is only one answer. Never can love for souls be induced by any other method than contemplating the price God paid to redeem them. As we look at the cross of Calvary and realize what the Lord Jesus Christ did for men, we shall little by little be willing to obey Him and to go out and tell others. Probably the callousness of the average church member toward the souls of the multitudes around him comes from a failure to contemplate the cross of Jesus Christ. True zeal with knowledge comes only from the realization of God's valuation of a soul.

Words Fitly Spoken

"A word fitly spoken is like apples of gold in pictures of silver" (Prov. 25:11), or perhaps a little closer to the Hebrew, "like apples of gold sculptured against a background of silver." The idea is that an arrow which hits the target is better than a dozen arrows which fall short.

One of the happiest things that a minister of the Gospel can hear is that a word he has spoken in his sermon, when totally unconscious of the need of an individual, has been the exact word needed for an individual.

Some time ago in Schenectady, N.Y., before an audience which included many young engineers from General Electric, I spoke of feeding upon Christ, pointing out that the physical action of today was the result of last week's food, and that the spiritual action in any life is the result of previous feeding upon Christ. I said, "For example, a young man trained as an engineer, with bright prospects before him, hears the call of God to go out to Africa as a missionary, leaves his position, and faces the Dark Continent. He has been feeding on Christ."

I had no more than pronounced the benediction than a young man came up to me and asked, "Why did you say what you did about an engineer going to Africa?" I answered that, as I was preaching, the Holy Spirit had led me. And the young man replied, "I am an engineer and God is calling me to Africa, and I must leave my career and go there as a missionary." It was a "word fitly spoken" which reached his particular case.

I once received a letter from the pastor of a Baptist church in suburban Philadelphia who wrote of having attended my church on a Sunday night. His letter contained this paragraph. "Last August I buried my three-year-old nephew and the following Sunday his parents attended your evening service with us. You preached from 1 Peter 5:10, and probably without knowing the reason you said, 'God had a purpose in taking your three-year-old son . . .' and that 'God would strengthen, establish, and settle the sorrowing heart.' Those parents are born again but your message brought increased faith and strength."

I did not have the remotest idea that anyone was in the audience who had lost a three-year-old child. But the Holy Spirit knew and gave the fit word for that particular need. It is possible for a believer to be so in the will of God that as he unconsciously lives and speaks, the words which fall from his lips shall be of the Spirit and shall reach the needs of those around us. Thus we become a believer out of whose innermost being flows the river of living water. The Lord is the source, and the Lord is the supply. His is the glory.

The Fallacy of the Sanhedrin

The power and boldness of those who witness for Christ do not come from any spiritual experience of the past, but from present, active contact with the risen Lord. The first experience is not to be discounted, but in no wise can it be made to account for the present strength of believers.

As children, many of us learned a hymn that told of the days when Jesus was on earth, and suggested that it would have been nice to have been living at that time. Would any Christian who knows Biblical truth really say for a moment that he would prefer the days of Christ's earthly ministry to those in which we live? Would the touch of His hands upon our heads or the look of His eyes be comparable to the indwelling presence of the Holy Spirit who reveals the things of Christ to our hearts?

In the early days of the church, the Sanhedrin attributed the power of the apostles to the fact that they had been the disciples of Christ during the three years of His earthly ministry. This was the judgment of unsaved men. "When they saw the boldness of Peter and John, and perceived that they were unlearned and ignorant men, they marveled; and they took knowledge of them, that they had been with Jesus" (Acts 4:13). The psychology of the Sanhedrin was that three years of contact with Jesus was sufficient to give these men a fanatical frame of mind and a boldness that goes with fanaticism. This, however, is not the case, and the explanation, as seen in the light of the previous action of these men, is totally inadequate. Peter had denied the Lord with oaths and cursings, and even John had forsaken Him in the hour of crisis.

The explanation was not that they had been with Jesus in the past, but that they were filled with the Holy Spirit for the present need. They had been born of the Spirit through faith in Christ on the day of Pentecost; they had been baptized by the Spirit into the Body of Christ, and sealed with the Spirit unto the day of redemption. Even this would not have accounted for their power and boldness had they not been filled with the Holy Spirit for the need of each moment. So we read a few verses before the conclusion of the Sanhedrin that "Peter, filled with the Holy Spirit" spoke unto them.

Attitude

The world neither expects nor understands devotion to God. Non-Christians are actuated entirely by motives that are of and for self. When the unbeliever sees a believer looking to the Lord he turns his gaze heavenward, and seeing nothing but clouds, he thinks that there is something slightly wrong with the believer.

This fact was called to my attention by two incidents that revealed the incomprehension of the unsaved. I entered the dining car of my train and ordered breakfast. The waiter brought a half grapefruit and set it in front of me. I bowed my head to thank the Lord for it and was immediately interrupted by the waiter: "What's the matter with it? Isn't it all right?" I looked up at him and said, "It looks perfect to me." He replied, "But I saw you looking at it." "No," I answered. "I was merely thanking my heavenly Father that He had been so kind and loving as to create such things as grapefruit. Suppose that He had created us so that we were like donkeys, to have nothing but oats and hay, hay and oats." The waiter nodded and repeated, "I knew you had found something wrong with the grapefruit."

The night before this incident, just before I had gotten on the train, the man who had charge of my meeting schedule had handed me some expense money which had been taken out of the offering just as the people had given it. Included in the sum were two or three dollars in nickels and dimes. When I left the train in the morning I checked in at my hotel and went to the cashier's window to give up my pocketful of change for some currency. The girl looked at me with a broad grin and said, "Ah! The winner. Was it stud or draw?" I looked at the girl and replied, "As a matter of fact, I was not playing poker at all. This comes from a church offering and represents the love and sacrifice of people who put those very coins into the offering as a gift of thanksgiving to the Lord Jesus Christ for having saved their souls, and for having provided all their daily needs." She looked at the pile of coins in front of her with strange eyes, her hands suspended above it as though she were afraid to touch it.

Peter tells us that the unsaved "think it strange that you run not with them to the same excess of riot" (1 Peter 4:4). I was able to witness to the waiter and the cashier of the saving grace of God, and I thanked God for the grapefruit and the coins which had been the means of exalting His name. Christ was able to lead a soul to Himself by asking the woman of Samaria for a drink of water. Grapefruit, coins, water—and everything else in life—can be the means of glorifying our Lord.

Terror

There is terror in the Bible as well as comfort. Some time ago a woman asked a Christian friend what warrant there was for saying that there would be some people who would not be in heaven. Why would not everyone be saved? The Christian gave an astonishing answer, but one which is perfectly valid. She replied that John 3:16 was the greatest proof that there were people who would be lost.

The inquirer was amazed and answered that she had learned John 3:16 when she was a little girl and had always thought of it as *the* great gospel verse. The Christian replied that it did have magnificent glories in its depths, but that it also had in it the most terrible word in the English language—perish. "God so loved the world that he gave his only Son that whosoever believes in him should not perish . . ." Then there are those who will perish; there is a terror that lies before some souls. The Lord Jesus was given by the Father in order to save men from perishing.

In the hot sands of Egypt archaeologists have discovered thousands of documents that have come down to us from the times of the New Testament. These papyri give us great insight into the meaning of the New Testament vocabulary of the original language. One interesting find was a nursery rhyme that was composed of lines each beginning with a succeeding letter of the alphabet. The whole rhyme concerns the story of the loss of a garment. In the middle of the poem is the Greek word that is used in John 3:16 for "perish."

> leon ho aras
> moros apolesas

"a lion he was who took it, a fool who lost it."

We know that the Lion of the tribe of Judah brought salvation to us by dying on the cross. Whosoever believes in Him shall not be lost— and surely He was right when He called the rich man a fool for thinking of new barns for bigger crops instead of thinking of his eternal state. He was a fool indeed, and he perished because of it.

It is hard to write this without weeping. Why is it that men will persist in folly when it will take from them everything that they desire? How senseless is the course that leads a man to perdition. If you are a believer in Christ you are responsible to warn those who are on this course—but oh! Do it in love.

Neighbors

Neighborliness is disappearing, according to a writer in a contemporary magazine. What was formerly meant in that word is now combined in corner store, newspaper, telephone, and television. One does not need to borrow a pound of sugar from a neighbor if there is a chain store across the street. Newspapers and television give the news, and telephones unite friends who live across the city but who are not close neighbors.

There is a neighborliness, however, that is necessary and which can be used of God in witnessing. The article mentioned above told of an accident that occurred in a farm community. When the news came to one family, the father and mother immediately set out to help. While the father went to help the man who had been injured, the mother sat down beside the wife, who reached over and took the visitor's hand. The neighbor put her arm around the upset woman, but said nothing. Soon the grieving one put her head on the neighbor's shoulder. Some months later, she came to visit the neighbor who had been of such comfort and said, "As long as I live, I will never forget the way you came and sat down by me. When you were with me, it seemed as if I were getting hold again." "There wasn't anything I could do," replied the neighbor miserably. "You didn't need to do anything," the other woman said, "I just wanted somebody there—somebody that cared."

The Christian who takes time to be friendly, to be neighborly, often without an accompaniment of preaching, will find that when there is a spiritual need, his influence will be doubly acceptable. I know of one instance where a woman spoke to a neighbor about the Lord and had her witness rejected. For five years she continued being friendly and neighborly without ever speaking about the Lord. One day the one in need came to the Christian and said, "For five years I have remembered what you said about God. I have never been able to get away from it and I want you to tell me how I may become a Christian. I am tired of living as I am living now."

One summer on a transatlantic steamer we met a young woman who had just graduated from one of America's foremost universities. She had come to the church service on the boat and had afterwards opened a conversation that made it possible for me to witness to her. She asked if, practically, people were really profiting in their personal lives by the faith we were teaching. I happened to know a strong Christian who had graduated in the same class from the same school, so I mentioned her name. I was immediately answered by a frank admission that I was right. "There was not anything she was unwilling to do for the other girls." The neighborliness had been an effective witness for the Lord Jesus Christ.

Givers or Receivers?

Too many Christians have the attitude that they should be recipients instead of givers. They think that they are to go to church, sit in the pews, and receive teaching. Then by paying the salary of some "full-time" Christians they can hire the visiting of the sick, hire the work of missions, and hire the spreading of their faith.

This idea is alien to true Christianity. The Christian must get up and move out into the world. I once talked with members of a certain church which had planned a special "revival" to reach the unsaved. Dates were set, special music was prepared, a preacher was secured, advertising was written, and then, suddenly, a terrible light shone upon them. The Christian said to me, "We realized, all at once, that none of us had any unsaved friends. We had lived to ourselves. We had drifted into a Christian fellowship which had alienated us from the world. We had become inbred to the point that we were absolutely sterile."

A false idea of separation is behind this situation. Some have taught separation from the world to such an extent that they have tried to take believers to heaven before God is ready for them. He left us here on earth to be witnesses. The early church thrived in the prison, the army, the slavemarket, and even in the halls of the courtesan. Thais was a slave who had no ownership of herself, but whose beauty brought great wealth to her master. Her witness for Christ was so great to the high Roman officers to whom she was rented that at least one of them was saved. The matter became known when he refused to throw incense on the altar of the gods, and he, with Thais, was martyred in the Forum.

Paul told the Corinthians that they could accept invitations to dinner in the homes of unbelievers. There was no stricture on the matter other than their personal desire for the contact. They were to eat what was set before them and were to ask no questions for conscience sake (1 Cor. 10:25). That is, if they suspected that their host had been to the butcher shop in the temple of Venus and had procured meat which had been offered in sacrifice to the demons, they were to eat it and say nothing. Only if the host boasted about it were they to abstain; otherwise, they were to fit into the social life of the unbelieving household.

The pertinent question that you must ask yourself is this: *Do you know any unbelievers well enough to have them invite you to dinner?* If you don't you are a poor witness.

An Olympic Example

One of the most tragic incidents to the participants of the 1936 Olympic games was the loss of the women's four hundred meter relay race. The Germans were far in the lead when the third runner passed the baton to the last runner. With a clear five-yard lead and the race as good as won, she dropped the baton. Pictures showed the despair on the face of the last runner when she realized what had happened.

Shortly after the games I was looking at an illustrated magazine with pictures of the Olympics. The magazine happened to have texts under the pictures in three languages. The English said, "They muffed the baton," and the French said they dropped "le temoin." This is the ordinary French word for *witness*. The idea was that the runner who reached the tape had to have the baton as a "witness" that the full distance had been covered by each of the runners.

This is a great spiritual lesson. If the witness is lost, the race is lost. Here is the true meaning of the famous passage in Paul's first letter to the Corinthians. "Know ye not that they which run in a race run all, but one receiveth the prize? So run, that ye may obtain (it) . . . I therefore so run, not as uncertainly; . . . But I keep under my body, and bring it into subjection; lest that by any means, when I have preached to others, I myself should be a castaway" (1 Cor. 9:24–27).

This is a true Olympic picture. The German girls had made the Olympic team and had the honors attendant upon their prowess. They were eligible to run the race. They lost the prize, however, by losing the witness. They were castaways from the medals.

So it is in the Christian life. All who are born again are eligible to run the race, and no one can run the race until he is made eligible through saving faith. All who are received into salvation in Christ will be in heaven, but not all will receive the prize in addition to salvation. Some have lost the witness, like the church in Ephesus to whom the Spirit of God said, "Thou hast left thy first love. Remember therefore from whence thou art fallen, and repent, and do the first works; or else I will come unto thee quickly, and will remove thy candlestick out of his place, except thou repent" (Rev. 2:4, 5). The context shows that these people were saved. They were in the race, but they had dropped the witness. There was just time, though, for them to pick it up and go on to win. Paul would never have said he was going to win the race and the prize, no matter how far out in front he found himself. He said, "I count not myself to have apprehended: but this one thing I do, forgetting those things which are behind, and reaching forth unto those things which are before, I press toward the mark for the prize of the high calling of God in Christ Jesus" (Phil. 3:13, 14).

The concern that Paul had shown over his Christian standing was with him until the end, and then God let him see that the prize was his. "I have fought a good fight, I have finished my course, I have kept the faith: Henceforth there is laid up for me a crown of righteousness" (2 Tim. 4:7, 8).

The girls who lost the witness in the Olympic relay will regret their carelessness until the end of their lives. The 110,000 people in the great stadium saw them drop the witness. "Wherefore seeing we also are compassed about with so great a cloud of witnesses, let us lay aside every weight, and the sin which doth so easily beset us, and let us run with patience the race that is set before us, looking unto Jesus the author and finisher of our faith; who for the joy that was set before him endured the cross, despising the shame, and is set down at the right hand of the throne of God" (Heb. 12:1, 2).

Thanksgiving

Thanksgiving

I was once invited to a luncheon where thirty or forty Christians—ministers and laymen—were gathered together for discussion of a certain problem of Christian work.

A well-known layman was asked to return thanks before the meal. I have heard the blessing asked hundreds of times, but suddenly my attention was aroused. The man who was praying said, "We thank Thee for all these gifts, for our food, for our water . . ."

I do not know what else was said in the prayer, but that thought gripped me. Thank God for the water . . . I have asked the blessing before thousands of meals, but that day for the first time, I thanked the Lord in spirit and in truth for common ordinary water, and for the Living Water. I then began to think of other common things for which we never thank God, and began thanking Him.

What are you really thankful for? Do you realize that God tells us we are to be thankful for *everything?* Have you thanked God for inflation, for the loss in buying power of the dollar, for the difficulties through which the world is passing? Some will say that these things work misery and hardship to many people and that they are not a subject for thanksgiving, and others will say that if we are to be thankful for them we should desire them to continue.

Both of these conclusions are false. If the difficulties reach us personally, we should take the attitude which the Spirit taught Paul when he said, "Most gladly therefore will I rather glory in my infirmities, that the power of Christ may rest upon me" (2 Cor. 12:9). Since *we know* that all things work together for the good of those who love the Lord (Rom. 8:28), we must take the attitude of thankfulness for anything that the Lord sends to us, even though, through our tears, we are forced to say to the Lord, "No chastening for the present seemeth to be joyous, but grievous" (Heb. 12:11).

If we see the world in the midst of misery, but the difficulties do not reach us personally, we can be thankful nevertheless, for we know that the world is entering surely and swiftly into the vortex of wrath which has been so plainly written in advance in the Word of God. We can be thankful as we see it, since we know that the tempest of judgment is to be followed by the eternal calm of the triumph of the plan of God.

On the other hand, we should not be thankful for the miseries of the world with that cynical hardness that sometimes characterizes Christian thought. There must be compassion and tenderness toward those who are suffering, as there must be strong effort to alleviate the ills that we see around us and effort to mitigate their pressure upon the unfortunate.

Thanksgiving Day dates back to the day when the Pilgrim fathers were filled with joy as they saw their barns well filled and their larders stocked against the approaching winter. Yet Thanksgiving Day for the true Christian is something far deeper and far wider than the joy of autumn harvest blessings. Thanksgiving Day for the Christian is an entrance into the deepest thoughts of God, so that we may say "Yes, Father, I am learning to be thankful for *everything*."

Is Thanksgiving Always Possible?

The Word of God commands us to give thanks in everything (1 Thess. 5:18). This is not just a casual remark, for added to it is the reminder that "this is the will of God in Christ Jesus concerning you." This addition to the commandment of thanksgiving gives it an importance surpassing mere exhortations of the Word. God's definite will for the believer is that he shall be a fountain of praise and that his life shall be in thanksgiving to God at all times and in all circumstances.

The Lord God, who is the Author of all our blessings, appreciates, desires, and even seeks our praise and thanksgiving. "The Father seeketh such to worship him," the Lord told the woman at the well

(John 4:23). "Whoso offereth praise glorifieth me" (Ps. 50:23). And the Psalmist also said, "Every day will I bless thee, and I will praise thy name for ever and ever" (Ps. 145:2).

These verses show that thanksgiving has no relationship to circumstances. We are to thank God in all things; the Lord knows what is best for us, and He is ordering the course of our life, bringing the details to pass in the time and manner of His desire. He has never made a mistake, and what He allows to come into the life of His child is for the good of that child and for the glory of God. Any chastisement that ever reaches us comes for our profit, that we might be partakers of His holiness (Heb. 12:10).

One of the great preachers of the past, the saintly Rutherford, went through persecutions beyond the lot of most men. Yet at the end of his life he could write:

> Deep waters crossed life's pathway,
> The hedge of thorns was sharp;
> Now these all lie behind me,
> Oh, for a well-tuned harp!

It is wonderful that a man who has been through sufferings akin to those of Job should cry out in desire for a heart to praise the Lord. Such desire is proof of confidence and trust in the Father, for it is the acknowledgment that He does all things well. Thanksgiving in all things, this is the will of God.

Ingratitude

Sometimes it is worthwhile to have a special Thanksgiving Day all to ourselves, months away from November. There will be no Presidential proclamation, no special services, no glutton's dinner, but there can be real thanks to God the Father from the heart of an appreciative child.

Failure to thank God is recorded in the Scriptures as one of the great steps away from God. Man is able to look up and see the glories of the universe. This should turn his heart toward God, for the Heavens declare His power and Godhead, thus taking every excuse away from man. There is sufficient condemnation in the beauty of the stars and the reddening of the sunset sky to send a sinner away from God forever if he is not melted by the sight and turned to thoughts of repentance.

"When they knew God, they glorified him not as God, neither were thankful" (Rom. 1:21). Does not this indictment put man below the level of the beast? The dog knows the hand that feeds him; the sow will come at the call of the one who brings her food. Man alone, of all the creatures of earth, fails to acknowledge the hand that feeds and governs. The vast majority of mankind never gives a thought of gratitude towards God for all His care and blessings.

This lack of thanksgiving was the second step in the terrible march to barbarism in which so much of humanity still remains. They did not worship; they were not thankful; they became vain; their minds were clouded; they became idolaters; God finally gave them up to uncleanness. There is the chain. There is no missing link in God's plan of evolution.

A visitor in an insane asylum was accosted by one of the inmates. This patient had full possession of his faculties but was subject to fits of insanity that made it unsafe for him to be at liberty. The visitor, who had come to preach to those who could comprehend, was startled to have this man come to him with a direct question, "Sir, have you ever thanked God for your reason?" The preacher had never done so, but he vowed that he would be unthankful no longer.

There are thousands of things besides your reason for which you might well bow your head right now and give a heartfelt prayer of thanksgiving to the Father.

The Christian Paradox

"As sorrowful, yet always rejoicing" (2 Cor. 6:10). Life is replete with paradoxes. Whichever path we tread, sooner or later we understand the poet who sang,

> Oh, my love for thee, Mavourneen,
> Is a bitter pain . . .

And if the narrow passes of life teach us the lessons of the mountain way, it is even more true with the experiences of the Christian life.

"As unknown and yet well known; as dying, and, behold, we live; as chastened, and not killed; as sorrowful, yet always rejoicing; as poor, yet making many rich; as having nothing, and yet possessing all things." The close walk with God will ever lead the Christian in these paths, for so it was with our Lord. He was sorrowful as He beheld the world and its godless ways, yet His legacy to the apostles contained not only the gift of "in this world ye shall have tribulation," but also "My peace give I unto you." What word characterizes Him more than the word "peaceful"? How can it be otherwise with us? The one who has the Spirit of the Lord Jesus Christ cannot help but partake of the sorrow of that man of sorrows. Paul speaks of being "sorrowful, yet always rejoicing," for the joy can never be absent either. Sorrowful as we see the misery around us, as we see men loving darkness rather than light, as we see them deliberately treading under foot the Son of God, counting the blood of the covenant an unholy thing, and despising the Spirit of grace. Sorrowful as we behold the fact that often the bitterest foes to the progress of the Gospel are to be found in the heart of the church organization. Sorrowful as we note the selfishness of so many of those who call themselves by His name. Sorrowful as we behold ourselves and see how far we fall short of a "worthy" walk.

Rejoicing, though, as we see our place in Christ; rejoicing as we realize that it is of us that God speaks when He says, "Who shall lay anything to the charge of God's elect? God has justified us. Who can condemn? Christ has died." Rejoicing as we wait for His coming, looking for the one who is altogether lovely. Rejoicing as we realize that God is never surprised by anything, but that His plan takes full account of everything, and rejoicing that we have a God who has never made a mistake and can never do so.

So we go on our pilgrim way. We forget the things that are behind; we press forward always. Sorrow may be ours, but He is coming back for us.

Rejoicing Heart

The Christian is the only person in the world with a right to rejoice. The Psalmist sang, "Our heart shall rejoice in him" (Ps. 33:21). This is true for the Christian in any circumstance whatsoever. The believer can rejoice even in the midst of the deepest distresses. Calamities, like a tidal wave, carry off the unsuspecting, but having swept away the debris which we believers have accumulated about us, leave us standing on the rock. Our shore is swept clean and we have a new glimpse of the ocean of God's grace. The air is fresh washed by the storm and our lungs are filled with new vigor as we breathe it.

The unbeliever often breaks before calamity, or takes the dull, depressing attitude of the stoic, that one must make the best of a bad job. A stoic may be more admirable than a whiner but he is no whit happier. The roots of Christian calm go deep into the very heart of God.

When we understand this, there is a sense in which we can reverse one of the great thoughts of the New Testament. Paul tells us that the Lord's Spirit beareth witness with our spirit (Rom. 8:16). That is a motion which begins with God and comes down to us. There is also a sense in which our spirits bear witness with His Spirit. The yielded Christian has an uprising of the Spirit which constantly moves towards God. This is one of the marks of the twice-born man; we reach out towards God. Some of the words used by men in the Book are "yearning . . . panting . . . waiting . . . looking . . . longing . . . watching . . . desiring. . . ."

We reach up into the being of God and find that our all in all is there in Him, and our heart comes back rejoicing. In fact, the only people who really are happy are among those who have been redeemed. The world has gaiety, but no happiness; forgetfulness, but no peace. The world counterfeits every Christian grace, but never is able to produce a coin with the right ring. It is popular to say that "the man worthwhile is the man who will smile when everything goes dead wrong," but even then the weight of unforgiven sin hangs over the heart, and the despair of the old nature has not been removed. Underneath the surface the unsaved are "like the troubled sea, when it cannot rest, whose waters cast up mire and dirt." They are without peace.

The Christian possesses the joy of the Lord. It is his strength. The basis for this joy is obvious. "Rejoice in the Lord." How can there be reality in joy that has no foundation outside this changing world? All passes; Christ remains. Fix your joy in Him and it will be steadfast. As Paul suggests in the wonderful Epistle to the Philippians, we who are in Christ are honest with God and ourselves. Our worship is in the Spirit, our rejoicing is in Christ Jesus, and we have no confidence in the flesh. This, of course, is the exact opposite of the world's joy which is fixed in self alone and does not look to Christ. "Rejoice in the Lord always, and again I say, rejoice."

Singing for Holiness

Robert Murray M'Cheyne, the great Scottish preacher, was a very gifted man in many ways. He had no inconsiderable knowledge of music and his voice was frequently heard in praise to God. Those who lived with him were frequently awakened early in the morning as he began the day with a Psalm of praise.

In his diary, which is one of the outstanding documents of its kind in Christian literature, we see the growth of this great soul as he so earnestly sought after God's own holiness. He finished theological seminary when he was only twenty-one, and was licensed as an assistant pastor a full year before his ordination. Lines from his diary show his constant grief over the presence of his sinful nature. One day he sought to prepare his heart for the next day of preaching. He wrote "Is it the desire of my heart to be made altogether holy? Is there any sin I wish to retain? Is sin a grief to me, the sudden risings and overcoming thereof especially? Lord, Thou knowest all things. Thou knowest that I hate all sin and desire to be made altogether *like Thee* . . . Felt much deadness, and much grief that I cannot grieve for this deadness. Towards evening revived. Got a calm spirit through Psalmody and prayer."

Here is the experience of a heavy heart singing its way to peace. David said, "What time I am afraid, I will trust in thee" (Ps. 56:3). Of M'Cheyne it could be said that when he was spiritually cold he sang the praises of God until his heart was warm. The oil of joy was his instead of mourning; a garment of praise displaced the spirit of heaviness. He knew himself to be a "righteous tree planted by the Lord" (Isa. 61:3). The Christian needs to realize the power of praise as a weapon to defeat the enemy. Israel, out of the will of God, wept by the rivers of Babylon, and harps were hung in the willows instead of being used to glorify the Lord. Praise would have been the shortest road to power.

Christ, in the midst of His people, was always praising the Father. It is said in the Old Testament and quoted in the New that our Lord is the one who leads the singing of His saints. "I will declare the name unto my brethren, in the midst of the church will I sing praise unto thee" (Ps. 22:22; Heb. 2:12).

If you are despondent or discouraged, speak now to the Lord who dwells within your heart. Say to Him that you know you have been redeemed, and acknowledge His presence and His character as being more than worthy of praise. Ask Him to kindle the song. Have it on your lips even if you do not feel it in your heart. Ask him to give you a realization of the truth of your singing, for then praise will go to your heart as you yield your song of praise to the Lord.

Southern Exposure

In the Book of Ezekiel there is a wonderful prophecy of the Kingdom age and the glories of that time. There is a description of the temple of God and its surroundings. In the midst of the description there is a beautiful phrase about the apartments of the singers: "Without the inner gate were the chambers of the singers . . . and their prospect was toward the south" (Ezek. 40:44). Southern exposure! Their life was the life of song, and their chambers were filled with the sunshine of God. When they looked out their windows they could see the landscape, drenched with beauty, and praised God.

In the early chapters of First Chronicles there is a beautiful passage concerning the singers in the temple of God. The Revised Version translates it: "And these are the singers, heads of fathers' houses of the Levites, who dwell in the chambers and were free from other service;

for they were employed in their work day and night. These were heads of fathers' houses of the Levites, throughout their generations, chief men: these dwelt at Jerusalem" (1 Chron. 9:33, 34). These are men who have finished the course of their active life. They are the old men; the men who have reached the age of being heads of the various divisions of the Levites. They were now retired and God gave them a pleasant place to live. They were always in Jerusalem, the city of God. Their apartments were joined to the sanctuary, and judging from the passage in Ezekiel, it is more than probable that they had the southern exposure also. They had the sunshine of God, they dwelt near His house, and their service was the ministry of song, day and night.

There is something precious in thinking of these elderly men, serving God in their declining years. God does not hear music as we hear it. Some may have thought that the days of their robust song were ended, and that these old men's voices, slightly querulous, and cracking before the difficulties of some of the music, was hardly a praise to the Creator. But their song was precious to God, and He let them live next to His house. Youth may do better, but youth lacks experience. The older men had long walked in the ways of God and their voices were the true voices of experience. They knew the meaning of true praise, and glorified God. Here was thanksgiving indeed.

In prison Paul and Silas "prayed and sang praises unto God, and the prisoners heard them" (Acts 16:25). There was southern exposure at midnight; there was a jail filled with the sunshine of God's blessings. Their backs were lacerated with the scourge and they were in circumstances that called for weeping, as far as the world is concerned. They were not even facing toward the frigid north; they were in the darkness of the world's midnight. But the darkness and the light are both alike to our God (Ps. 139:12). Happy are the men who learn this truth and bring the sunlight of God into the chambers of their dwelling, always looking out over the southern prospect which God has given them.

The Home

How to Choose a Wife

Solomon had many blessings from God. These came originally because of the covenant which the Lord swore unto David, his father, and were confirmed to Solomon because the latter set his heart to walk in the Lord's way. As Solomon grew older he made the choice of wisdom rather than riches, and obeyed the plan of God to build the house of the Lord which his father, David, had had the desire to build. But when the house of the Lord was finished Solomon settled back and began to indulge himself. In the parlance of our modern young people, he began to get ideas.

We discover that Solomon took the daughter of Pharaoh as a wife. This, of course, was contrary to the will of the Lord and was one of the first steps in the degradation of the great king. There is one phrase about the marriage which is very interesting and revealing, for it shows us that Solomon still had a sense of the fitness of things. In 2 Chronicles 8:11 we read, "And Solomon brought up the daughter of Pharaoh out of the city of David into the house that he had built for her; for he said, my wife shall not dwell in the house of David, king of Israel, because the places whereunto the ark of the Lord hath come are holy."

In other words, Solomon said to himself, I recognize that this woman doesn't fit in with the faith in which my father brought me up. Her ways of life and thinking are not in keeping with the holiness of God. I can't take her to a house where I am reminded of all the things of God. Since my conscience accuses me, I will build another house for her and I will dwell with her there, and I shall not be troubled by the association of ideas which shall remind me that I am out of the will of the Lord.

When a young man or a young woman marries it is possible to marry with the old nature or the new nature. It is often said that no one can truly understand a man until we see what kind of a wife he chooses. Some men seem spiritual until you get a good look at their wives; then you comprehend, immediately, that they have married with the choice and desire of the natural man, and not with the choice and desire of the spiritual.

But, says the young man, I looked into her eyes, my heart thrilled and I realized that I loved her, so what was I to do? We answer, Ridiculous. That excuse is no more valid than that of the automobile thief who would say, I looked at the car, and I thought, How wonderful it would be to drive this car, so I got in and drove away. The flutter of the natural heart may occur many times and is what underlies the evil of divorce. It cannot constitute grounds for disobeying the Word of God. The love of the Spirit is a supernatural thing which is a gift of God. "Be ye not unequally yoked together with unbelievers; for what fellowship hath righteousness with unrighteousness . . ." (2 Cor. 6:14). No young person should choose a spouse who cannot be brought into the house of David where the ark of the Lord has rested, and where there is an association with holy things.

Winning Unsaved Husbands

A score of times each year I hear women asking for prayer for the salvation of their husbands. The Bible furnishes a definite technique or procedure for the Christian wife to follow in order to lead her husband to a knowledge of Jesus Christ.

First, though, let us understand that the mixed marriages of which the Bible speaks became mixed after the marriage and not before! In other words, the predicament of the Christian women with unsaved husbands did not come from their sinful disobedience in marrying unsaved men. The picture is clearly that of a pagan society where the Gospel has entered a pagan home and saved one of the unbelieving pair. The problem that then arises concerns the conduct of the soul-winning campaign on the part of the believer to draw the unsaved partner to the Lord.

We must, therefore, begin with a definite understanding of the problem. If someone finds himself married to an unbeliever, there must be a definite confession. Did I as a Christian, enter into this marriage in disobedience to the command of the Word of God, "Be not unequally yoked together with unbelievers" (2 Cor. 6:14)? There have been Christians, married to unbelievers, who were startled when told that they had to get down before God and confess that their marriage was a positive sin against the will of God. Frequently such confession clears the way for entry into a new fellowship with God, which soon brings the conversion of the unsaved partner.

Where this problem is settled, or where the believer has been saved after marriage, the procedure must be a spiritual one. Peter tells us how a wife is to act in order to lead her husband to Christ, even if he will not listen to the Gospel. The saved woman is to be in subjection to the unsaved husband (1 Peter 3:1) so that, "if any obey not the word, they also may without the word be won by the manner of life of the wives." How significant is that phrase "without the word." Peter realized the hatred that these unsaved people would have towards the written or spoken Word. "Don't nag me with your Gospel" is a phrase that is as old as the Bible. "Without the word" the husbands may be won by the life of the wives. God says so. And the verses which follow give the procedure which every woman should study with care. Even those women whose husbands are saved may read it with profit, for the passage describes the dress, habits, and life of the soul-winner.

The Wife with Two Heads

When we speak about the wife with two heads we are not talking about unsaved wives, but about women who are professing Christians. So often their husbands are not interested in the things of God, so the family drifts along without any spiritual cohesion. Perhaps they all go to church together on Sunday morning, and the wife goes to all the activities of the week, but the husband seems uninterested. Why?

Perhaps the wife has two heads.

"But I want you to understand," God tells us, "that the head of every man is Christ, the head of a woman is her husband, and the head of Christ is God" (1 Cor. 11:3). I can hear the outraged cry that goes up from many a woman, "But if I didn't use my head, where would we be?" There are two ways in which a Christian woman can use her head. She can use it to think independently and for her own interests, or she can use it to think in the spiritual terms which God has laid down. With delight she learns the joy of knowing it is her husband's house, his home; the children are his; she is his wife. When a woman realizes and acknowledges this, the life of her husband will be transformed, and the entire home will be changed.

Nothing is better calculated to smooth the rough corners of a man's life than the realization that his wife loves him and that she loves him in the way God intended a woman to love a man. When a man sees his wife centering her whole life in him, he realizes that this is more than mere human love; there is a divinity in the daily round of chores and the provision for his comfort. When he understands what God has said, that the man was not created for the woman but the woman for the man (1 Cor. 11:9), the husband will soon learn that in the Lord he is not independent of his wife (11:11).

And the woman who follows this spiritual direction will more than likely find that she is getting what she wants without having to take it. A woman is never happy with what she takes, only with what is given her in love. By losing her selfish head she is no longer a monstrosity but becomes what the Lord meant her to be. Therein she will find all joy.

The Word of God and Marital Problems

Man is constantly trying to better the conditions of this world, but is leaving out the one thing that would enable him to make real progress. We know from the Word of God that the failure of man will continue, and that it will be the Lord who will establish righteousness upon the earth.

We are often reminded of man's incompetence by legal decisions that are so contrary to absolute truth as it is revealed in God's Word, that the contrast can be seen without any difficulty.

In England a doctor enticed a grocer's wife and was sued by her husband for alienation of affections. The noted judge, Sir Henry Alfred McCardic, handed down a decision against the grocer. He said, "I must tell you that a woman's body does not belong to her husband. It is her own property not his . . . She can leave her husband by her own will . . . and can decide whether and when to bear children. . . . She is a citizen, not a serf."

Throughout the world men and women are in turmoil because of marital difficulties. States make laws and judges hand down decisions, but the Word of God still stands. The greatest degree of happiness between man and woman will be achieved only when the principles of the Word are taken as the basic foundation of the marriage relationship. This means, of course, that both parties must be born again in Jesus Christ. Only then can these principles become operative. Contrast the judge's decision with this statement in the Word of God. "The wife hath not power of her own body, but the husband: and likewise also the husband hath not power of his own body, but the wife . . ." (1 Cor. 7:4).

There is no place of privilege given to either the man or the woman. The union between them is such that each is the master of the other. Thus comes true happiness. The world laughs when it thinks of "the old bachelor, Paul" speaking about marriage. The world reads, "Wives, submit yourselves unto your own husbands . . . As the church is subject to Christ, so let the wives be to their own husbands in everything" (Eph. 5:22, 24). This is all the world sees, but with one more verse the picture changes. For though it is true that the woman is given as her standard of love the highest type of human love, that of the church for Christ, the man is given an even higher standard. To the man is written, "Husbands, love your wives, even as Christ also loved the church and gave himself for it." No woman will have any difficulty in submitting to a man who would be willing to be crucified for her.

Children and Home Training

In 1898 a schoolteacher polled 1,440 children, aged twelve to fourteen, to find out what sort of heroes and heroines the children had. In

that era 90% of the children picked their heroes from history and letters. Washington and Lincoln led the list, followed by Whittier, Clara
Barton, Julius Caesar, and Christopher Columbus. Very few of them
gave first place to living notables, even such national characters as
champion skater John S. Johnson or heavyweight boxer James J.
Corbett.

Midway during the twentieth century a professor in the Massachusetts State Teachers College took a similar poll and discovered a
great change in modern youth. Only 33% picked their heroes and
heroines from history. Franklin Roosevelt had passed Washington and
Lincoln, though Clara Barton still led among girls. Thirty-seven percent of the votes went to the contemporary stars of screen, sports, radio,
and the comics.

"It is a rather significant commentary," concluded the professor,
"that four times as many boys chose Gene Autry as chose Jesus Christ;
that as many chose Jack Benny as chose priests, ministers, and missionaries combined . . . and that, among the girls, twice as many wished to be
like movie actresses as wished to be like all religious figures combined."

The real importance of this survey was that these young people
would be the fathers and mothers of the next generation. Some may
point out that, after all, the previous generation became the parents of
the fathers and mothers of this generation. The answer is that the im-
pact of modern inventions, the movies, television, radio, and comics,
caused a disintegration. These things were allowed priorities in the
home and the young people were not carefully trained. The next generation will have even less discipline.

Christians should seek in every way to place their children under
the finest spiritual influence at all times, to impress upon them the necessity of holy living, and they must seek to exert every effort to evan-
gelize the children of parents who are lax. Ministers and Sunday
School teachers must realize that anything other than solid presentation of the great evangelical truths can ultimately do nothing for the
child. It is the Gospel that is the power of God unto salvation.

A pastor of a church in a small town once gave me a graphic illustration of this truth. At the close of a meeting the pastor introduced

his two daughters who were about twelve and fourteen. I asked if they were saved, though the spiritual beauty of their faces gave the answer before the girls gave their testimonies. The father joined with joy in the testimony of his daughters, adding, "I led them to Christ myself. How ashamed I would have been if anyone else had led my children to Christ."

There is real beauty in that sentence, for it presents a great spiritual principle. The born-again parents should lead their children, who are children of the covenant, to the knowledge of Christ as personal Savior. If the child is trained in the way he should go, he will never depart from it in later life (Prov. 22:6). If a child grows to the age of reason and is yet unsaved, it is a sad testimony to the quality of the home life. No parent should allow the child to grow without bending over it every day in prayer, teaching and training the infant lips to repeat the words of salvation which become a very part of the being.

There is a vast difference between this spiritual testimony of parents to the children and merely forcing the children to attend formal religious services. Truly spiritual parents will discern the difference and will find joy in their testimony. For parents to see a child grow up without Christ is a far greater dereliction of duty than for parents to have children who grow up without learning how to read or write. The State, in most cases, prevents the latter, but there is nothing to enforce the former. That is why there are so many spiritual illiterates. The parents of these children will be more than ashamed at the Lord's coming.

Love and Juvenile Delinquency

The human being is built by God in such a way that he must have love. If there is a gross deprivation of love, the individual may flame out into the wildest delinquency. That phrase "gross deprivation of love" is taken from a report by Dr. Laurette Bender, senior psychiatrist at Manhattan's Bellevue Hospital, on the causes of delinquency. Speaking before a law school forum at New York University, Dr. Bender challenged the idea that there is a growth in juvenile delinquency in the United States. She reported that a careful study of history and statistics reveals that there was just as much juvenile trouble at the turn of the century as there is today, if the matter is considered proportionately. "Half a century ago the communities had to cope with exactly the same types of crime as we have today, and proportionately as often. And that was in a day of no mechanization, no easy communication and transportation, no radio, no television, no movies, no comics, no sight method of teaching reading, no world wars."

The study of eight thousand of the worst cases of delinquency at Believue shows that the problem always has several causes. The commonest of these are "gross deprivation of love, severe punishment and brutality at home, enforced submissiveness and isolation, learning difficulties and organic disorders—especially of the central nervous system. It takes a combination of several of these," said Dr. Bender, "to push a child along the road to delinquency."

How can we give children the love that they need? There should be little problem in our own homes, though it is common to see parents so involved in activities that they neglect to give their own children the love and care that they need.

A little five-year-old boy in a fine Christian home was travelling with his mother and said, "Mummie, isn't it wonderful that the Lord Jesus loves us and that He is all around us like a fence, and that Satan cannot get through to hurt us unless God lets him." The mother told this anecdote to the child's Sunday School teacher, who reacted by saying, "Oh, don't ever teach such horrible things to a child. They scare me to death; what must they do to a child?" The mother, of course, had taught her son well and the other woman should not have been teaching a Sunday School class. If a child can be made to feel the love of the Lord Jesus, and to know and feel the love of God for him through the Savior, there will never be a sense of gross deprivation of love, and the child will be on the way to real maturity.

The child learns very quickly the attitude which he sees in his own parents. If they rest quietly in the power, love, and care of God, the love will come through to the child.

Obedience

When my four children were young I demanded instant obedience. Whenever possible, I explained why the child should obey, but when necessary the child was to obey without explanation. There was severe punishment for any delinquency in this field.

An item in the news illustrates the need for absolute, unquestioning obedience. A small child squeezed past the metal railing that keeps spectators six feet from the lion cages at the Washington Zoo. When her grandfather ordered her to come out, she backed away teasingly. The waiting lion grabbed her, clawed her into the cage, and with his mate mangled her to death. A child must be taught instant obedience. Such obedience may save the child's life, but even more important, it will teach the child to obey God's Word without hesitation. A child who is allowed to back teasingly away from a grandfather will grow up to also back teasingly away from God.

God has given us commandments and principles that are for our good; God never gives us a commandment because He is arbitrary, or because He doesn't want us to have fun. God says, "Thou shalt have no other gods before me," not because He is jealous of His own position and prerogatives, but because He knows that if we put anything, *anything* before Him, it will hurt us.

If we understand the principle behind this fact, we can also understand why God chastens us. "Whom the Lord loves, he chastens" (Heb. 12:6). He doesn't want us to back into a lion, for there is a lion, the devil, seeking whom he may devour.

Our obedient attitude should be that of the Psalmist who said, *"Cause me to hear . . . cause me to know . . . teach me to do . . ."* (Ps. 143:8, 10).

Loneliness

Loneliness is undoubtedly one of the most grievous emotions of man. Human beings are naturally gregarious, so many people fling themselves to the world because they have not learned how to live alone with God.

The thronging city masses move on their way, and multitudes are longing for a companionship which they never find. I received an anonymous letter from a man who was just learning the first lessons of turning to Christ. In this letter was a phrase which laid bare the soul; the writer spoke of "the despairing need of an infinite capacity, which fate has sentenced to longing."

One of the glories of the Christian message is that Jesus Christ can fully satisfy the human heart: the young heart, the old heart, the ignorant heart, the learned heart, the heart of the man with the knowledge of great capacities, and the heart of the man who has accepted the fact that he will never leave the ranks of mediocrity. All needs are satisfied in Christ. The farm wife who looks at the cars passing on the distant highway, the small boy who sees the trains carrying busy passengers somewhere and back again, the drifter in the Wall Street crowds at noon or along Broadway at night—all of these needs are fully met in Christ Jesus if we are willing to submit ourselves to Him.

Moses was lonely in the court of Pharaoh, but was satisfied in the desert. Jesus Christ, utterly aware of His superiority and with the knowledge that no human being could meet with Him in a way that would satisfy the longing of His soul, nevertheless found satisfaction in the perfect oneness with the Father. So He went about doing good and bringing satisfaction to others. It was with forethought that He put His hand on the head of the leper. He could have healed him with a simple word, but the leper needed a human touch. There are so many around us whom "fate has sentenced to longing" instead of fulfillment of deep capacities, that we must be willing to fill some of that great need. We have received His comfort which He desires us to pass on, for He gives Himself to us "that we may be able to comfort them which are in any trouble, by the comfort wherewith we ourselves are comforted of God" (2 Cor. 1:4).

The Senior Citizen

I once received a letter asking me to write about the plight of Christian old folks. The correspondent thought that young Christians should call on elderly folk and perhaps offer to dust the room or just straighten up the house a bit. She wrote, "An old lady of means, but alone and arthritic like me, called on the phone and said, 'Mrs. X, I'm going to starve to death in my own home because I'm unable to stand at the stove and prepare a decent meal.' I told her, 'I'm in the same fix.' I can't stand pity, but I would like Christian understanding. I can still read the best of books, although my eyes are getting bad cataracts. When folks can walk and all, I wonder if they are thankful. A preacher's wife wrote me a note some time ago and said she would send some of their young folks to sing to me. I wrote back that I have a radio for singing, what I need is a good book and people who can just talk about things in general...I need company who will not talk to me as though I were senile."

God has told us in James 1:27, "Pure religion and undefiled before God and the Father is this, to visit the fatherless and widows in their affliction..." All the available statistics point to a tremendous increase in the elderly population of this country. The life span is being prolonged. Millions of people over seventy will be living in our country in the course of the next few years. It is the Christian duty of the churches to organize social activities for those over sixty, and above all, it is the Christian duty of individuals to seek out old folks and to talk to and care about them. A member of my congregation who is a woman past seventy, broke down and cried to me because of her loneliness. She lived in a single room in central Philadelphia, and was so lonely that she bought her groceries one item at a time so that she might hear the voice of the clerk speaking to her in a moment of conversation.

I was once in the home of an old man who also wept because of his loneliness. He told of going out to the cemetery where his last loved one lay buried, and of crying in loneliness at the tomb. He told of putting the key into the front door of his house, knowing that the loneliness of his heart was as great as the emptiness of the house where no one lived but himself.

I pointed out to this believer that Christ was able to meet his need, though I did make a mental reservation to tell his friends to speak to him a little oftener, to call on him a little more frequently, and to include him in their plans from time to time. The gift of companionship which we may give to others is at once the most inexpensive and the most costly gift we can bestow. It is inexpensive for it costs us nothing financially, but it is costly for it takes our very selves.

Those of us who live normal family lives and who are in constant contact with people cannot understand the fantastic loneliness of the lonely. You should get into the habit of giving one hour a month to visiting some elderly person who is alone. Don't go merely to read the Bible to them, for they have probably read it over and over again. You may move in that direction, but be ready to follow their lead and talk about the weather, the football game, the new book, the magazine article, clothes, fishing, or whatever the interests of that old person are. Above all give them plenty of chance to talk. It may bore you, but it will be a psychological release for them that will be better than a week in the Florida sun. And don't forget that God Almighty has said that this is "pure religion."

Index of Illustrations